Identity and Form in Contemporary Literature

This ambitious and wide-ranging essay collection analyses how identity and form intersect in twentieth and twenty-first century literature. It revises and deconstructs the binary oppositions identity-form, content-form and body-mind through discussions of the role of the author in the interpretation of literary texts, the ways in which writers bypass or embrace identity politics and the function of identity and the body in form. Essays tackle these issues from a number of positions, including identity categories such as (dis)ability, gender, race and sexuality, as well as questioning these categories themselves. Essayists look at both identity as form and form as identity.

Although identity and form are both staples of current research on contemporary literature, they rarely meet in the way this collection allows. Authors studied include Beryl Bainbridge, Samuel Beckett, Brigid Brophy, Angela Carter, Inga Clendinnen, J.M. Coetzee, Anne Enright, Jonathan Safran Foer, Mark Haddon, Ted Hughes, Kazuo Ishiguro, B.S. Johnson, A.L. Kennedy, Jonathan Lethem, Andrea Levy, Toby Litt, Hilary Mantel, Robert Lowell, Ian McEwan, Alice Oswald, Sylvia Plath, Jeremy Reed, Anne Sexton, Bapsi Sidhwa, Jeanette Winterson and Virginia Woolf.

The book engages with key theoretical approaches to twentieth- and twenty-first century literature of the last twenty years while at the same time advancing new frameworks that enable readers to reconsider the identity and form conundrum. In both its choice of texts and diverse approaches, it will be of interest to those working on English and American Literatures, gender studies, queer studies, disability studies, postcolonial literature, and literature and philosophy.

Ana María Sánchez-Arce is Senior Lecturer in English at Sheffield Hallam University, UK

Routledge Studies in Contemporary Literature

Identity and Form in Contemporary Literature

Edited by Ana María Sánchez-Arce

Routledge
Taylor & Francis Group

LONDON AND NEW YORK

First published 2014 by Routledge

2 Park Square, Milton Park, Abingdon, Oxfordshire OX14 4RN
711 Third Avenue, New York, NY 10017

*Routledge is an imprint of the Taylor & Francis Group,
an informa business*

First issued in paperback 2018

Library of Congress Cataloging-in-Publication Data
    Identity and form in contemporary literature / edited by Ana María
Sánchez-Arce.
        pages cm. — (Routledge studies in contemporary literature ; 11)
    Includes bibliographical references and index.
    1. English literature—20th century—History and criticism.   2. Identity
(Psychology) in literature.   3. Other (Philosophy) in literature.   4. Self
in literature.   I. Sánchez-Arce, Ana María, 1974– editor of compilation.
    PR478.I44I44 2013
    820.9'009—dc23
    2013010947

ISBN13: 978-0-415-82161-2 (hbk)
ISBN13: 978-1-138-54797-1 (pbk)

Typeset in Sabon
by IBT Global.

Contents

PART III
Physical Forms, Formal Identities

Acknowledgments

I have accumulated many debts as I have worked on this book. I am particularly indebted to all the contributors without whose work and infinite patience this volume would not have been possible. They believed in the project and my ability to see it through to publication, even after unavoidable delays due to pregnancy complications followed by having to care for an ill baby. For your faith and unwavering trust I thank you deeply. The book has followed closely the life of my child, from conception in 2009 as I organised a conference on Identity and Form at Sheffield Hallam University through to wellness and publication. Without the conference there would not be a collection today, so I am grateful to all those who helped me organise it, most of all to my co-organiser, Rebecca Mallett, and colleagues in English who were enthusiastic and offered support, including Alice Bell, Annaliese Connolly, Claire Drewery, Steve Earnshaw and Harriet Tarlo, as well as Samm Wharam at the research office who worked tirelessly and found resources in the most unexpected places and Nick Hodge who helped Rebecca and I apply for funding. Gemma Tissington (neé Bradshaw) from Yorkshire South (Sheffield Convention Bureau) offered invaluable logistic support. The Humanities Research Institute and its head, Chris Hopkins, have been behind the project from the beginning, providing financial assistance as well as research leave to complete it. Chris Hopkins not only helped, he also mentored me and provided endless optimism when I needed it most. I am also grateful to the staff at Routledge. Successive Editors for Routledge Research, Liz Levine and Emily Ross, believed in the project from the start and saw it to completion. Andrew Weckenmann and Michael Watters have patiently answered all my queries throughout the process. The anonymous readers of the manuscript offered invaluable advice to improve the collection.

Thomas Docherty's essay for the volume draws on material from a previously published chapter. Many thanks to Bloomsbury Academic for authorising the republication of material from the chapter "Official Identity and Clandestine Experience" in Docherty's *Confessions: The Philosophy of Transparency* (2012, The WISH List series). Thanks are also due to Liverpool University Press for permission to reprint Stuart Murray's article "From Virginia's Sister to Friday's Silence: Presence, Metaphor and the

Persistence of Disability in Contemporary Writing", originally published in the *Journal of Literary & Cultural Disability Studies* 6.3, 2012. I am incredibly grateful to The Estate of Beryl Bainbridge and Ed Wilson of Johnson & Alcock Ltd. for generously granting permission to quote unpublished material from the Beryl Bainbridge archives at the British Library.

Heartfelt thanks go to Professor Mike Smith, former Pro Vice-Chancellor for Research and Knowledge Transfer at Sheffield Hallam University, who not only supported the original conference but made this book possible by introducing me to Professor Mary Renfrew (University of York), who diagnosed my son and gave me my life (and sleep!) back. And, as always, I owe most to my fellow sufferer and teammate at home, Jonathan Ellis, proof-reader, cheerleader, provider of intellectual stimulation and silly relief from it. Whoever thought it was a good idea for both of us to have the same deadline for edited books? For devoting time to helping when you most needed it for yourself, thank you.

Identity and Form in Contemporary Literature
An Introduction

Ana María Sánchez-Arce

The idea for this volume originated many years ago as I was finishing my PhD thesis on authenticity and authenticism in contemporary British literature. Then, as now, I was fascinated by how identity in its many forms has become a touchtone for literary criticism and how that relates to canonicity and value. Coming from a feminist and postcolonial background, I am particularly interested in ethnicity, gender, and nationality. In 2007, I joined Sheffield Hallam University, where one of my colleagues, Rebecca Mallett, was thinking along similar lines in relation to disability. In what became a fruitful collaboration, we organised a conference on "Identity and Form in Twentieth- and Twenty-First-Century Literature" in 2009. Some of the chapters in this collection developed from papers delivered at that conference, whereas others have been especially commissioned for it.

One of the things that Rebecca Mallett and I discussed was the need to place identity-centred discourses in an historical context, not necessarily as the "new kid on the block" anymore (although disability studies is a developing field of study and, as Stuart Murray's chapter for this volume argues, the representation of disability in literature and the study of it have a long way to go) but as approaches that have already been around for decades and have become part of the establishment for literary criticism and other humanities subjects. Narratives about the development of literary theory and critical approaches to literature often place traditional criticism, formalism, and New Criticism as the establishment and identity-centred criticism as the challenger to this establishment. But is this still the case? The development of identity-centred approaches since the 1960s and their current strong presence in literary criticism unravels this once justified perception. One could say that from the 1960s forward, to use Robert Frost's famous phrase, literary criticism took the road less travelled, that of thinking about things first, formal matters second. This road has become very busy over the past fifty years. Can we still think of it as less travelled, or has it become another well-trodden path?

Unfortunately, the process of establishing identity-centred criticism in the 1970s resulted in an unproductive dichotomy being set up between those critics concerned with identity and those who focused on form, just as politics is still frequently found in opposition to form or aesthetics, or the ethical to the literary. A famous example of this division being used is Harold Bloom's labelling of identity-centred approaches as "the School of Resentment" in 1994 (4, 7, 20–29). Although these stereotypes are not representative of the rich and diverse critical practices in contemporary literature, they are still in play. Dismissing analyses based on identity politics as non-literary is as easy as labelling calls to consider form conservative or reactionary. It is difficult to work on both identity *and* form. One is prone—as Salman Rushdie once said in relation to Indian writers in exile—to "fall between two stools" (15), or to feel like one is trying to take two roads going in opposite directions. This is an odd state of affairs because, to borrow Thomas Docherty's words, "the question of the relation of literature to politics" is a serious issue: "How might literature relate to the production of autonomous human individuals, subjects, citizens?" (135). Furthermore, what part does the interpretation of literature play in the production of individuals and to what extent are they autonomous or subjects? Although individual chapters in this volume do not provide easy answers to these questions, they will prompt readers to ponder them. Ultimately, the aim is to engage with both form *and* identity in a variety of ways to enable readers to create and follow their own roads not travelled.

Whereas contributors may reach different conclusions or speak at times from conflicting perspectives, they all share the view that considering identity and form together may provide a space to reconsider their meaning and function and help develop new ways of thinking about literature and the study of it. For this reason, chapters in this collection can be read as individual analyses of specific authors, texts, and approaches, but also used to rethink the binary oppositions identity-form, content-form and body-mind through discussions of the role of the author in the interpretation of literary texts (including the ways writers bypass or embrace the constraints created by readings based on identity politics) and the function of the body and materiality in form. The collection is divided into three parts: Part I, "Beyond Identity and Form"; Part II, "Formal Prescriptions and Identity Politics"; and Part III, "Physical Forms, Formal Identities." The chapters in Part I open up theoretical questions surrounding the relationship between identity and form, followed by Part II, which focuses on the role of the author in interpretation, reception, and identity politics. Part III has the body at its centre, considering its relation to identity and form. Nearly all the chapters step back from their immediate critical task to reflect upon the terms and presuppositions of analysis. For this reason, the volume not only provides exposure to contemporary literature, but more importantly, it responds to that literature to query our reading protocols.

The binaries of identity-form, content-form, and body-mind are revised and dealt with differently in the chapters. For example, Thomas Docherty and Ana María Sánchez-Arce consider identity *as* form, whereas Karen Zouaoui sees form *as* identity. Amy Prodromou and Ulrike Tancke explore the role of the body in the construction and destabilisation of narratives of the self. Whereas Prodromou, through a study of autobiographical narratives of illness, concludes that the body destabilises the self, Tancke argues that the body and materiality are inescapable in identity formation. The body is thus both content and form. Goran Stanivukovic explores the AIDS-ridden body as providing a new way of imagining the past through queer eroticism and deconstructing gendered and sexual identities as well as forms such as biography and historiographic representation. Murray looks at the role of the body in form, in his case through a discussion of the dichotomy able-disabled and an attack on established ways of thinking about disability as a metaphor in literary studies. Indeed, all the chapters in the collection refer to one or more of these binary oppositions. Kym Martindale, for example, analyses Alice Oswald's constitution of the self through "listening" rather than the more conventional process in "identity-based writing and criticism, which cries out against that which has silenced or ignored it" and "is anxious to establish itself, to voice *its own* story, which is then fenced off and carefully policed." The chapter shows how Oswald attempts to excise the poet from the poetry, discussing her strategies in relation to form, including her revision of the traditional body-soul dialogue.

Nearly all of the chapters tackle the role of the author and authorial persona because the perceived identity of the author, despite Roland Barthes' injunction not to privilege the author, has become an important component to many critical approaches and to the marketing of literature in the contemporary period. Chapters discuss how the author's identity has been (ab)used in the reception of literature, reflecting on how authors bypass or embrace the constraints created by pegging their work to identity. In most cases, this leads to a critique of identity-centred criticism that fosters the use of ready-made identities to interpret literature and polices the boundaries of these identities in its criticism of writers' works.

Identity and form are keywords in the study of literature and other cultural artefacts nowadays. This has not always been the case. Formal study of literature achieved prominence in the early twentieth century and "has in recent years come back into fashion" (Leighton 23), whereas identity became a staple of literary criticism and the way we think about the world in the late twentieth century. The change in status of identity as a keyword is reflected in its omission from Raymond Williams's seminal book, *Keywords: A Vocabulary of Culture and Society* in 1976, and inclusion in Tony Bennett, Lawrence Grossberg, and Meaghan Morris's revised 2005 edition (cf. Robbins). Williams and his followers concern themselves with the "*social* etymology of words, their function over historical time." They see language as "causative," which means "that the active meanings and values expressed in language exert a formative social force" (Patterson 67). In short, language shapes how we think about the world and ourselves. It is therefore significant that in thirty years "identity" has gone from not featuring in the original *Keywords* to being given a three-and-a-half page entry in the revised edition including views on it as "natural" and socially constructed (cf. Robins).

Whereas Williams and his followers reflect on the "*social* etymology of words," Michel Foucault approaches language and knowledge not as something that changes with society, but as active agents of social and subject construction. Identity from a Foucauldian point of view is not a product of individual freedom, but is tied to sociohistorically available identity categories. In effect, identity categories contain and shape how we and others identify ourselves as X, Y, or Z, even if our identity is figured out as–X,–Y, or–Z, or any possible combination of these. Foucault's insights into identity as something constructed are backed up by current research in neuroscience. Susan Greenfield, for example, argues that identity is different from mind and consciousness (but needs both of these to exist) and that it is "realised" in "the final cohesion of brain connectivity into a single framework of temporal and complex cause-effect, action-reaction description" (108):

> [I]t seemed plausible that identity developed in parallel with the development of the individual brain: since the genes and brain regions are already in place in the infant, the only level of operations with the requisite dynamism and flexibility—mediating between single cells and whole brain regions—consists of the complex and dynamic networks that [. . .] are the physical arena for the neuroplasticity of the brain. The conclusion was that 'a real understanding of identity involves subjective accounts', namely personal views on the world, indeed beliefs. So can we actually describe beliefs in the terminology of neuronal networks, above and beyond plasticity itself? It seems that we can. (99–100)

Greenfield draws on research about beliefs published in 2002 by psychologists Bohner and Wänke that described how beliefs are used as structures to organise complex information:

> This structure is assembled on accessible information, both chronic and temporary. In turn the accessibility of such information will depend on its organisation in memory, namely how many associations it triggers, along with the frequency and recency of its activation. Perhaps not surprisingly, attitudes based more on chronologically accessible information will be more stable across contexts than attitudes primarily made up of temporarily accessible information. However, even attitudes primarily based on temporarily accessible information may reflect stability over time if the context remains stable. In any event, beliefs or attitudes will be determined by the associations they trigger within a 'semantic network', a scheme that could be related directly to neurophysiological parameters. (100–101)

"Semantic networks" seem to be crucial to beliefs and identity. Greenfield argues that the more frequent and recent the connections, the stronger they become, but these are also affected by when the connections were formed, whether there are other associations that may weaken these, and so on (102). Greenfield's theories support Williams's beliefs that language is "causative" and Foucault's views that we are subjected to pre-existing discourses.

Identity—or, to be more precise, identities—is produced within the brain as a result of interaction with the external world, with society. Identities may be unique to every individual because the neurological connections (assemblies) are unique, but also follow pre-established patterns in that assemblies are triggered by exposure to specific experiences that form beliefs and, more importantly, ways of thinking about the world (what Foucault calls discourses). It could therefore be argued that identities are not just content (what we and/or other people think we are) but form (how we and/or other people shape our views about ourselves and the discourses that our thoughts follow). These forms, despite Western emphasis on individual freedom and autonomy, may change over generations, but are not as flexible as one may think. Thomas Docherty's opening chapter for this volume deconstructs the identity-form dichotomy to argue that all identity is in itself form, as we are all made to fit ready-made, "official" identities and that "identity can be described properly as *conformity to a rule.*" Docherty claims that identity-based criticism authenticates identity rather than aiming to understand it, and exhorts readers and critics to abandon searching for official identities and open up to "clandestine experience," an experience that, he suggests, "has no form."

As Steph Lawler states, "[i]f the social world is always storied, it puts constraints on the stories we produce, since our own narratives of identity would simply not make sense if they did not accord with broader 'intelligibility norms'" (20). Following Foucault, Lawler describes how "[t]hrough subjectivation, people become tied to specific identities: they become subjects. But also they become subject-ed to the rules and norms engendered by a set of knowledges about these identities" (62). Subjectivation involves self-address or self-identification as well as other people addressing/identifying us because, as Greenfield comments, "unlike the mind, identity is dependent on the context and interaction with others" (80). Identity is thus conceived at the edge of social interaction, in the playful and sometimes painful space where "I" is defined by "you." Literature and form support this way of seeing identity in many ways. Literature, for instance, has been used as a powerful instrument to create identification and develop empathy and feelings in subjects, which in turn aids subjectivation.

Form, like identity, has also been described as the result of "edging one thing against another":

> The question 'what is outside or what is inside a form?' perfectly captures the way that form is both a container and a deflector. Imagined

> visually, it looks two ways: to the shape it keeps in and the shape it keeps out. It is a wall or line between two objects, or between two blocks of space, and thus offers a choice: there are apples, or there is an apple-shaped 'weight of space'. Form, then, is the distribution of space caused by edging one thing against another, so that each calls attention to the other. It is not so much a dispensable holder of content, as a line, perhaps a very fine line between two alternatives which are actually two ways of looking at a work: now-you-see (apples) and-now-you-don't. Apples, as such, are not important. [. . .] To learn to cross from one dimension to the other is part of the dynamics of form itself. [. . .] Form, by this account, is not a fixed shape to be seen, but the shape of a choice to be made. (Leighton 16)

In discussing Picasso's insightful comments on the work of Cézanne, Leighton makes the leap from the dynamics of form in the visual to the literary which, she explains, is three dimensional: aural, visual, and material. Form is seen as a boundary between diverse ways of perceiving, "a very fine line" that acts as a hinge, so to speak, between the viewer or reader's choice to see the inside or the outside, the apples or the apple-like shape. This is an inspiring account of what form may achieve, although perhaps it goes too far in its dismissal of the "something" being "brought to mind." Leighton's central thesis is that form "looks two ways," and this potential to send viewers or readers in different directions is what makes it an exciting and creative force. For me, seeing form as "a line," even a "very fine" one, without qualification is too definitive, too exact in its division of the two worlds on offer. Even my earlier image, a hinge, is not good enough to describe the porosity of form and its agency as a binder of multiple perceptions. If we return to the line, we may perhaps be able to visualise its potential. Modern mathematics sees the line as an undefined object that varies according to what type of geometry is being described. The line in painting has been found to be not necessarily continuous and impenetrable, but discontinuous and porous, allowing the "inside" and "outside" of form to mingle. Cézanne himself frequently obliterated lines with brushstrokes, although at times he left lines that were nevertheless cross-cut with brushstrokes. This less forbidding and permeable view of the line might allow us to think of form not as "the shape of a choice to be made" but the shape of a choice not made.

Similarly, identity is at its most productive when it reveals the weakness of monolithic ways of thinking about it. Indeed, it is not by chance that identity has become central to literary studies just as its unity and continuity have been scrutinised as never before and that the most studied examples of identities are those that subvert or are at the edges of well-known identity categories. The appeal of these identities lies in a position that may enable the subject to "look two ways," although this may not be easy. Seeing from multiple perspectives or holding opposing views can be frightening as well as exhilarating. Multiplicity in identity and perception is something that has caused terror and been maligned throughout history as in, for example, the biblical figure of Legion, the possessed man.[1] What better reminder of the sublime in the Romantic period and beyond?

Iain Boyd Whyte explains that Kant believed that "the sublime exists not in an object that has tangible form, contours, and dimension" (4), but "only in our own perceptions, when our inability to estimate the magnitude of things makes us aware of a supersensible faculty within us. This is the paradox of the sublime. The gap between tangible, empirical objects, on one hand, and the world of the supersensible, on the other, is absolute and unbridgeable" (5). Kant distinguished between the form of an object, its boundary, and the formless object which can only be grasped through intellectual perception:

> In other words, we can know the ocean through our senses and dip our toes into the briny, but the vastness of the ocean is an idea that cannot be an object of sense experience, because it lacks contours and boundaries. Rather than in the thing of nature, the sublime is to be found only in our own perceptions, when our inability to estimate the magnitude of things makes us aware of a supersensible faculty within us. (Whyte 5)

Unity and multiplicity coexist in the sublime as in the awe-inspiring yet frightening possessed man. Both form and identity partake of this interplay of boundaries and boundlessness, both can be seen as open and closed systems, both are paradoxically shaped or bound and vast, undefinable, uncontainable.

Edging against each other, these supposed contradictions are also at play in the ancient dichotomy: body and mind or self. Traditionally, the body has been seen as the "tangible form" and the mind as part of the "world of the supersensible." The body can be seen as the poor relative of the mind, the "something brought to mind," as opposed to the sublimation that selfhood represents. And yet, particularly in light of the brain's involvement in the production of mind and identity and the extent to which cultural meanings attached to physical characteristics play a part in most of the major identity categories,[2] the body seems also to be the source of and pretext for identity. In this collection, Amy Prodromou and Ulrike Tancke consider bodies and materiality alongside the postmodern tenet that narratives produce the self. Prodromou's chapter argues that autobiographical writing in relation to illness both proves and problematizes ideas that the autobiographical self is whole, stable, and continuous. Showing "the interplay between multiple identities and whole selves" in Hilary Mantel and Inga Clendinnen's autopathographies, Prodromou sees illness as destabilising the self but cautions that writing about illness is not always a way to heal or re-form the self. Tancke also discusses the role of the material, the body, and narrative in identity formation and advances the theory that the body is the basis of the self and materiality is inseparable from identity. Through an analysis of Anne Enright's *The Gathering* as a trauma narrative, her argument moves beyond the distinction between body and mind to highlight how the contemporary fascination with trauma and concern with storytelling reflect our ambiguity towards the body and narrative: "we tend to approach the material with disgust and rejection and seek to transcend it, although we are aware of the futility of such endeavour. And yet it is also the material that provides a firm grounding and a reliable core of selfhood. A similar ambiguity accrues to narrative."

Abjection, specifically "specular abjection" in relation to sexual orientation, is also at the heart of Goran Stanivukovic's contribution to this volume. Stanivukovic analyses Jeremy Reed's *The Grid* as an "anti-historical novel," a text that plunges us into a dystopian world where queer identities are forged as the past merges with the future, "pushing the boundaries of the historical novel in a new direction of erotographic temporality, that is, the kind of erotic writing which is not bound by different moments of historical time." The nightmarish world of *The Grid* "urges readers to think about tradition"—including biography, history, and historical fiction—"differently." Narrative form and the homosexual subject are explored as both expressing repression and undermining conventional literary representation. Stanivukovic ultimately argues that *The Grid* "plays an important role as cultural critique because it is a work that disavows the slowness of modern writing to free itself from the chains of historical context which often determines and limits, rather than challenges and liberates, our thinking about the past." As such, it challenges established scholarship and biographies of Shakespeare and recent calls to move beyond sex in queer studies. Stanivukovic's answer is emphatic: "As the last line of Reed's novel shows, the two national poets fixed in a sexual embrace against the apocalypse of London state symbolically that after sex, comes sex." *The Grid* ends not only with a sexual act that brings bodies to the fore, but also with an attack on London that recalls the attack on the Twin Towers in 2001, an attack that, according to Whyte, has sparked a rethinking of the sublime "and has already generated new studies in the aesthetics of terror" (15). The ending of *The Grid* may be trying to harness some of the energy released by the incomprehensibility of the 9/11 attacks to emphasize the momentousness of the sexual act across the ages. Anecdotally, Christopher Marlowe's murder, which is the main event at the heart of *The Grid*, is also present in another of the texts discussed in this volume, B. S. Johnson's *Albert Angelo* (which is analysed by Karen Zouaoui in Chapter 2). In both texts, the murder is used at the level of form and content, and perforates (in *Albert Angelo*, literally) the comfortable boundaries between historical periods, identities, and narratives.

Whereas Tancke's and Stanivukovic's analyses of abjection are grounded in the material, in the actual body, Marsha Bryant tackles it in a discussion of "the confessional other," a figure with origins in the Romantic period (De Quincey's *Confessions of an English Opium-Eater* in particular) that "shadows the *I*" in confessional poetry "underwriting the writer's signature style. For at the most heightened, unstable, and distinctive parts of the text, we find that the confessional writer is never truly alone." Bryant focuses on the black confessional other of white confessional poetry, concentrating on the work of Robert Lowell, Sylvia Plath, and Ted Hughes, but also looks to Sylvia Plath's appearance as an "exotic white ghost of postwar domesticity" in Elizabeth Alexander's poetry. For Bryant, the confessional other problematizes the continuing cult of personality in confessional writing by "dislodging the *I*," appearing during breakdowns of identity and form in texts. Bryant ultimately suggests that the "confessional other" haunts both content (the writer's fictional identity) and form when readers expect writers to be most autobiographical. The "confessional other" can be seen as both an *alter ego* and a formal device that shows how permeable the line between identity and form can be. As Leighton says: "Far from being cut off from purpose and affect, authorial or readerly interests, form brings them all energetically into play. From the hard-edged, untouchable scuptures of modernism we have moved into a de Quincean world, where form is imagined as the uncontrollable, promiscuous 'animism' of a dream, or of nightmare" (17). The confessional other is seen by Bryant as a "generative" force behind constructions of self, family, and nation and, simultaneously, as an aporia that helps deconstruct confessional poetry. Note here how the porousness and deadlock coexist in a figure that acts both to usher in change and disrupt the narrative of the confessional *I*.

Samantrai's chapter also discusses a potential generative force—Black Britishness—that could in this case have altered the discourse of the nation, namely Englishness. She tackles the narrative of the nation in relation to the inclusion of a Black British Identity, analysing Stuart Hall's seminal essay, "Ethnicity," and Andrea Levy's *Small Island* to argue that whereas the social identity of Black Britishness had the potential to oppose and revise the idea of the nation as homogeneous, it has been assimilated by it. "The nation," Samantrai argues, "survives as the still privileged form of history" and Black Britishness "provide[s] an alibi for [its] continuing validity" at the "level of form."

If identities are created together with the formation of the neuronal networks that help narrativise experiences and beliefs (whether these have been directly experienced or not), insights into literary form may be useful in exploring the workings of identity as form, rather than content. Karen Zouaoui's chapter achieves this. By analysing the work of Brigid Brophy and B. S. Johnson, she argues that these experimental writers do not, as commonly thought, write solipsistic texts. On the contrary, she states, these so-called "narcissistic narratives" aim to change society and the way we read and write by breaking the objective correlative. Experimentation with identity and form go hand in hand in what Zouaoui calls "desperate attempts to give the subject a voice" and "a dramatic quest for truth" in the face of the "avant-garde idea that the society we live in is inherently fictional." Zouaoui's chapter shows how identity and form feed each other in narratives that highlight crises in both. Crises of representation and identity are ultimately the same because, as Paul Ricoeur points out, "the self does not know itself immediately, but only indirectly by the detour of the cultural signs of all sorts which are articulated on the symbolic mediations which always already articulate action, and among them, the narratives of everyday life" (198). Ricoeur inextricably links identity and narrative and goes as far as saying that "we equate life with the story or stories that we can tell about it" (194) and "the crisis of character is correlative to the crisis in the identity of plot" (195). Retelling stories activates the information accessible in the neurological networks, which in turn reinforces these associations within what Greenfield calls a "semantic network" and may be central to our sense of having a continuous identity. Metanarratives thus expose the unity and cohesiveness of identity and form, although these technical devices can be and have been incorporated into the formal definitions of identity and of form.

Ideas about the origins and classifications of genre such as those of Tzvetan Todorov and Jacques Derrida may also open up different ways to conceive identity. In disagreeing with those who think that genre is exhausted as a way of categorising literature, Todorov argues that all texts, even those that may appear not to belong to any genre, display generic elements that can also be found in ordinary language: "Where do genres come from? Quite simply from other genres. A new genre is always the transformation of an earlier one, or of several: by inversion, by displacement, by combination" (15). He concludes that "literary genres originate, quite simply, in human discourse" (26). Derrida, on the other hand, suggests that genre boundaries do not belong to the genre they supposedly demarcate, thus making all genres inherently impure: "Every text *participates* in one or several genres, there is no genreless text, there is always a genre and genres, yet such participation never amounts to belonging" (230). Chris Hopkins explains that Derrida sees "genre as an inherently necessary but unstable system, a system with a systematic flaw. It is no wonder, if this is so, that generic descriptions and the continuity of features across members of a genre are complex: both are attempts to describe something which does not have a clear existence" (243). Huw Marsh addresses the thorny issue of genre in relation to Beryl Bainbridge's claims that her work is not feminist. Drawing on archive material, Marsh argues that Bainbridge's comic tone and her mimicry of traditional male genres such as lad-lit have obscured the fact that this very mimicry enables Bainbridge to rewrite the male tradition in a way similar to what Teresa de Lauretis has called "feminist rewriting." Marsh analyses Bainbridge's work, in particular *Sweet William*, as a revision of the assumptions about masculinity upon which novels such as Kingsley Amis's *Lucky Jim*, Bill Naughton's *Alfie*, and Keith Waterhouse's *Billy Liar* are predicated, as well as a critique of the failure of the sexual revolution in the 1960s. Ultimately, Marsh exhorts readers and critics to look closely at the genre of texts, even if this means ignoring the author's own definition.

Todorov and Derrida's ideas about genre are useful in thinking about the position of identity as a boundary and a category in itself, as well as the complex perception of identity as both sameness, self-sameness, and individuality. Genre comes from the French for kind, sort, or people—*genre*—a word that is related to the Latin *genus*, race, kind, and also grammatical gender, a term that is still used in science including biology. All things belonging to a genus (and a genre) share at least one characteristic that makes them distinctive as a group whilst at the same time differentiating them from other genuses (and genres). Genuses and genres, like people, are not just identified by what they have in common, but how they are different from others not belonging to the genus, genre, or type of person. Besides this, it is possible to see how individual items differ within the genus or genre. Genres and genuses are used to classify, contextualise, and distinguish types of things (e.g., writing, animals, etc.) from each other. Identity works similarly. As Lawler states:

> The notion of identity hinges on an apparently paradoxical combination of sameness and difference. The root of the word identity is the Latin idem (same) from which we also get 'identical'. One important meaning of the term, then, rests on the idea that not only are we identical with ourselves (that is, the same being from birth to death) but we are identical with others. That is, we share common identities—as humans, say, but also, within this, as 'women', 'men', 'British, 'American', 'white', 'black', etc. at the same time, however, there is another aspect of identity, which suggests people's uniqueness, their difference from others. Western notions of identity rely on these two modes of understanding, so that people are understood as being simultaneously the same and different. [. . .] But within this overarching and apparently capacious category of 'the human', there are various forms of identity with which people identify. (2)

The etymology of identity points to self-sameness and sameness within specific groups, although it is easy to think of examples that would contradict this, and much late twentieth-century criticism and sociological research point to the fallacy of conceiving identities as uniform, hence the pointed use of plural forms for "identities," "feminisms," "women," and so on. Paradoxically, individual identities are seen as being "simultaneously the same [part of group identities] and different." Identity as sameness and self-sameness has nevertheless been undermined from many theoretical angles, not just in literary studies, but also sociology and neuroscience.

Despite this, identity is still predominant in the way we make sense of the world, including literature. Could this be, to return to Foucault and

Greenfield, a result of how existing discourses about the self shape our brains as "semantic networks" develop in the growing child and adult? Patsy Stoneman, for example, charts her changing response to literature in "Thirty Years of Feminist Teaching." Having been educated in a formalist tradition, Stoneman was "astonished to learn that [*To the Lighthouse*], which I had read as an exercise in aesthetic experimentation, was about a Victorian family, about stereotypes of masculinity and femininity, about the effort of an emancipated woman to break free from the expectations of marriage and procreation" (115). What Stoneman clearly describes is not just the rise of feminist approaches to literature in the 1970s, but also what Stanley Fish might characterise as an "interpretive community" (171). This is a reminder that what is commonplace today was not so forty years ago.

The emergence of identity-driven interpretive communities was a watershed in literary studies. These interpretive communities are still being developed today as identities are reshaped and new ones emerge. Stuart Murray's chapter for this volume illustrates this; Murray's wide-ranging analysis of disability is not only a major contribution to the field of disability studies but also an exhortation to all scholars working on literary studies to review their use and interpretation of disability. This work would not be possible without the recent rearticulation of identity based on the challenge to the able-disabled dichotomy. Identity-driven interpretive communities carry out important work that in many cases offers a critique of our subjection to preexisting discourses. In the light of theories that see language as "causative" and our "semantic networks" as developing through exposure to triggers, Docherty's question about "how literature relate[s] to the production of autonomous human individuals, subjects, citizens?" is prescient. Every analysis that uses identity categories may nevertheless be reinforcing their presence in our mind. Literature and its interpretation may relate both to the production of individuals and of subjects and citizens. Current sociological research on "psy knowledges" by Valeria Walkerdine may even end up dismantling the current Western conception of the individual as autonomous (cf. Lawler 75–6).

In 1995, Kwame Anthony Appiah and Henry Louis Gates, Jr. warned that "'race,' 'class,' and 'gender' threaten to become the regnant clichés of our critical discourse" (1). Their use of "cliché" is telling. A cliché is a stereotyped or commonplace expression in everyday use, but its origins are in "the French for a stereotyped block, applied esp. to a metal stereotype of a wood-engraving used to print form" ("Cliché"). Identity as cliché is identity as manufacturing, as a mould, an identikit method of interpretation. In effect, the danger was and still is that identity categories will be used unproductively, as a means to interpret texts by rote rather than engagement. This is a concern of many contributors to this collection (Farkas, Marsh, Martindale, Prodgers, Ryan-Sautour, Sánchez-Arce, Stanivukovic), particularly in Zita Farkas and Ana María Sánchez-Arce's chapters. Farkas explores contemporary tendencies to use the figure of the author both to interpret literature and to justify aesthetic readings not based on identity politics. The reception of Jeanette Winterson's work is analysed at length, paying particular attention to how Winterson's sexual identity has played a major role in the marketing and criticism of her novels. Farkas reflects on how the author's own words are used to justify universalist and postmodern or poststructuralist interpretations, suggesting that the author "should be released from the constraints of his/her identity." Ultimately, she gestures towards a new articulation of what is "lesbian fiction" by suggesting that "the lesbianism of any author is not determined by the sexuality of the writer but it is primarily determined by the text: its queer aesthetics and lesbian topics." By separating the writer from the text, Farkas is countering the impulse to see form and content as an expression of the author's identity in feminist, lesbian, or queer readings, much like Bryant revises confessional writing as the expression of the writer's identity by locating a formal and thematic figure that undermines those interpretations.

Sánchez-Arce also discusses critical reception, this time focussing on Kazuo Ishiguro. She argues that contemporary identity-driven interpretations of texts are often prescriptive and have become forms in themselves, much in the way suggested by Appiah and Gates. Writers who do not conform to certain approved subjects according to their implied identities can be accused of being traitors or lying to themselves, their work made to fit specific interpretive angles or found at fault if it does not. The chapter suggests that Ishiguro's mock-realist style and experimentation resist identity-driven interpretations, ultimately calling for a rethinking of the relationship of critical labels based on identity to writers and writing because these have in effect become formalised ways of thinking about identity. Like Samantrai, Sánchez-Arce analyses how national identity (Englishness and Britishness in particular) deals with writers who do not fit its imaginary boundaries, but whereas Samantrai concludes that the narrative of the nation has absorbed Black Britishness, Sánchez-Arce concludes that there is still much to do until writers like Ishiguro are given "full status as English writers."

The struggle of some writers not to be identified or bound to a perceived identity, as in the cases of Winterson and Ishiguro, is further analysed by Michelle Ryan-Sautour in a chapter that explores the contradiction between many readers' impulse to look for a feminist ideology in Angela Carter's writings and Carter's own disorienting techniques, which resist any one reading. Ryan-Sautour sees Carter's authorial persona as performative. She studies critical commentaries surrounding Carter's oeuvre to illustrate how Carter constructs a metamorphic authorial self through polyvocality that is as fictional as her other works. By liberating the author from the shackles of social determination, Carter also frees the reader from the authority of "the author."

Finally, Lucy Prodgers develops the theories of Gilles Deleuze and Félix Guattari to encourage readers to move away from "representational readings which rely on reasserting pre-existing formulae." At the same time, she cautions against taking Deleuze as an ur-text to "apply" to literature and discusses the singularity of A.L. Kennedy's short stories and Toby Litt's novels in a comparative chapter that looks at how they complement (rather than replicate or illustrate) Deleuzian thought. In so doing, Prodgers looks in the direction of a new literary-critical aesthetics.

This collection aims to be exploratory and encourages off-roading, but it is not a manual that offers a definitive or final account of how form and identity ultimately fit together in the contemporary period. Even if the chapters sometimes offer conflicting perspectives, the questions they raise are worth consideration. Such questions, many of which have been outlined in this introduction, go to the foundational concepts of the discipline. Both the roads of identity and form are now well travelled. But perhaps, by trying to "look two ways," by smudging the already porous line between identity and form, we may just about see the outline of a choice not made, the options edging against each other. And, like the speaker of Frost's poem, who ultimately takes both roads (after all, he is remembering "The Road Not Taken"), we may well travel on both.

NOTES

1. For an analysis of Legion in relation to European identity, immigration, and postcoloniality, see Sánchez-Arce. This essay tentatively links multiplicity in identity and intertextuality.
2. Here I am drawing on and expanding Stuart Hall's argument about race as a "floating signifier."

REFERENCES

Appiah, Kwame Anthony, and Henry Louis Gates, Jr. "Editors' Introduction: Multiplying Identities." *Identities*. Chicago: University of Chicago Press, 1995. 1–6. Print.

Bloom, Harold. *The Western Canon: The Books and School of the Ages*. London: Macmillan, 1995. Print.

"Cliché." *Oxford English Dictionary*. Web. Accessed 4 December 2012.

Derrida, Jacques. "The Law of Genre." *Acts of Literature*. Ed. Dereck Attridge. London: Routledge, 1991. 221–52. Print.

Docherty, Thomas. "The Question Concerning Literature." *The Question of Literature: The Place of the Literary in Contemporary Theory*. Ed. Elizabeth Beaumont Bissell. Manchester: Manchester University Press, 2002. 126–41. Print.

Fish, Stanley. *Is There A Text in This Class? The Authority of Interpretive Communities*. Cambridge, MA: Harvard University Press, 1982. Print.

Greenfield, Susan. *You and Me: The Neuroscience of Identity*. London: Notting Hill Editions, 2011. Print.

Hall, Stuart. *Race: The Floating Signifier*. Media Education Foundation, 1997. DVD.

Hopkins, Chris. *Thinking about Texts: An Introduction to English Studies*. 2nd ed. Houndmills: Palgrave Macmillan, 2009. Print.

Lawler, Steph. *Identity: Sociological Perspectives*. London: Polity, 2008. Print.

Leighton, Angela. *On Form: Poetry, Aestheticism, and the Legacy of a Word*. 2nd ed. Oxford: Oxford University Press, 2009. Print.

Patterson, Annabel. "Keywords: Raymond Williams and Others." *English Studies in Canada* 30.4 (December 2004): 66–80. Web. Through Literature Online. Accessed 4 November 2012.

Ricoeur, Paul. "Narrative Identity." *On Paul Ricoeur. Narrative and Interpretation*. Ed. David Wood. London: Routledge, 1991. 188–99. Print.

Robbins, Kevin. "Identity." *New Keywords: A Revised Vocabulary of Culture and Society*. Eds. Tony Bennett, Lawrence Grossberg, and Meaghan Morris. Malden, MA: Blackwell, 2005. 172–75. Print.

Rushdie, Salman. "Imaginary Homelands." *Imaginary Homelands: Essays and Criticism 1981–1991*. London: Granta, 1992. 9–21. Print.

Sánchez-Arce, Ana María. "'My Name Is Legion': An Exploration of Immigration and Postcoloniality in Intertextual Studies." *European Intertexts: Women's Writing in English in a European Context*. Oxford: Peter Lang, 2005. 41–58. Print.

Stoneman, Patsy. "Thirty Years of Feminist Teaching." *Diacrítica. Ciências da Literatura*. 22.3 (2008): 115–25. Print.

Todorov, Tzvetan. "The Origins of Genres." *Genres in Discourse*. Trans. Catherine Porter. Cambridge: Cambridge University Press, 1990. 13–26. Print.

Williams, Raymond. *Keywords: A Vocabulary of Culture and Society*. Originally published by Fontana, 1976. London: Harper Collins, 1988. Print.

Whyte, Iain Boyd. "The Sublime: An Introduction." *Beyond the Finite: The Sublime in Art and Science*. Ed. by Roald Hoffmann and Iain Boyd Whyte. Oxford: Oxford University Press, 2011. 3–20. Print.

Part I

Beyond Identity and Form

1 Official Identity and Clandestine Experience

Thomas Docherty

When Vincent Descombes ponders what it means to be a historical agent, he states pithily that "To act in history is to work at *not being* what one is;" and this—acting in the world of *history*—is unlike the world of *nature*, where, as he puts it, "being signifies identity" (37). In the opposition of worlds of history and of nature here, we see the remnants of a Romantic sensibility. Descombes pits a stable world of exteriority (the world as "given," where being signifies identity in the form of immutable self-sameness, self-coincidence) against a world of interior consciousness characterised by *imagination*, by thinking oneself as other than one is. In his formulation, acting in history involves establishing conditions where the world of imagination impinges on the world of exterior nature; and the desired result is a change that must, of necessity, be at best a change in the *relation* between interiority and exteriority, and a change, therefore, in the self or subject (working at "not being" what we are).

The two realms are distinguished by this power of simultaneously seeing things "as they are" and also "as they might otherwise be." Exteriority here is immune to consciousness. Consequently, any change is fundamentally a change in consciousness itself: a change or difference that now constitutes, paradoxically, the subject's identity. It is the "I" of consciousness, and not the world of which the "I" is conscious, that is the locus of change. We usually call this "reflecting on the world," or "thinking about one's place in history." This neo-Romantic structure, however, is not straightforward, and it essentially gives us the predicament of our "modernity," as I shall show.

In Descombes' logic, "The historical protagonist *is* insofar as he acts, and he acts insofar as he is always *being different*" (37). Consequently, we have a counterintuitive understanding of identity, as sameness predicated on difference, or as difference camouflaged under the sign of self-coinciding. Behind this is a contradiction within the very concept of identity. On one hand, identity is precisely "self-sameness," the coinciding of two (or more) instantiations of "I"; on the other hand, the mere fact that there *are* two (or more) such instantiations indicates that the "I" exists in time.

Identity, considered then as a *temporal* "I"—a historical, secular subject—*must* acknowledge that such coincidence is simply impossible: by definition, the "I" in history, the "I" as a material "somewhat," enters into the realm of self-differing. "Self-sameness" in the secular realm is impossible. The prevailing neo-Romantic sensibility revealed by Descombes construes the relation of self to history in *spatial* terms (interiority of self, exteriority of world); but what is primarily at stake here is the *temporality* of identity. It is temporality that causes the problem.

Here is our conundrum, as expressed by Descombes:

> there is identity not only, as formal logic would have it, between identity and identity, but between difference and difference; there is a certain *being* in *not-being*. Now, is there the slightest difference between the identity of identity with identity, and the identity of difference with difference? Certainly not. For there is no more *identity* between identity and identity than there is between difference and difference. And there is no more *difference* between difference and difference than there is between identity and identity. And yet identity and difference are clearly different types of relation. Yes, certainly. So the *identity* between, on the one hand, the identity of identity and identity, and on the other, the identity of difference and difference, is the very factor of *difference* between identity and difference. (38)

This linguistic wrestling is the attempt to grapple with identity as a historical and temporally mutable concept. Yet it implies much more. If identity has some relation to the narrative of a life, then, of logical necessity, one has to consider the intimate relation of identity to *autonomy*, to the human as historical agent, and neither simply a product, nor merely an effect of that history. There is a dialectical relation between consciousness and exteriority. Against this, we usually consider that it is precisely a preexisting identity of consciousness that grounds the specific action that an agent undertakes in bringing about the state of affairs constitutive of exteriority at any given time: the imagination working on nature. I act as I do, we say, because of who I am; and I am as and who I am because of the very actions that define me. The issue is fundamental to any theory that sees identity as being related to the social: it is the question of the possibility of *change*. Is change possible; and if so, how is it effected?

My argument is that, in our prevailing modes of criticism, our identities, far from being autonomously determined, are, in fact, typically *given* to us. Further, they are given to us as a means of officially delimiting and regulating our possible behaviours. Our identity is "official," an office limiting our possibilities precisely to the circumscriptions delineated by that office. Consequently, any genuinely historical act that we would commit is necessarily clandestine, a breaking with or a nonconformity with our office. We are denied the possibility of acting as autonomous historical agents by being ascribed an "official identity," an identity precluding the possibility of our narrating a life, precisely at the moment when our alleged identity is being confirmed by our actions.

The tongue-twisting formulation of Descombes shows that, in our prevailing modes of thought—caught up in the modernity that has its roots in a certain Romantic sensibility—identity is itself identified as a form of self-sameness, or that identity can be described properly as *conformity to a rule*. This is so even if one identifies oneself as difference, or as constantly self-differentiating: constant self-differing itself becomes the very rule to which the self conforms. The important thing is the *rule*: identity is a matter for *regulation*.

There is a "law of identity," and identity is first and foremost a legal matter. The demand for identity is a demand for one's papers, and these *formal* and *official* papers have both enormous power and an authority that is abstract and determining. One's papers become more important than the historical individual carrying them, at least in terms of the *verification* and authentication of identity; and entitlement to an identity is always something to be authenticated rather than something to be understood. I'll return to this relative importance of verification in relation to authenticity later. The passport—the abstract and "official" identity—as it were, *is* the identity, even when the passage of time and experience means that one no longer looks like the face pictured on it. Official identity operates at a remove from actuality, from an experience that is now relegated to the realm of the clandestine.

This present argument is determinedly on the side of the *sans-papiers*, those who are "not entitled" or who have no identity, no passport or papers. To put this in terms directly related to literary or aesthetic criticism, my argument is *for* literary *experience*.[1] First, I explore the relation between identity and experience to show that, actually, identity *is* form, and that *formal* identities have little time for any specific actual *content*. To gain access to such content, secondly, I argue that we must find ways of describing the priority of our "becoming" over our "being." Consequently, I contend that the expression of an identity—our making it available as a public and social entity—depends upon a fundamental act of confession. In this, identity becomes something constituted by change. The identity of the self is necessarily predicated not just on self-criticism but upon a form of confession that is intrinsically tied to a conversion. Finally, I explore the politics of this, especially for any form of literary or cultural criticism that is based upon identity politics.

EXPERIENCE

In "De l'expérience," Montaigne suggests that "There is no desire more natural than the desire for knowledge." When reason fails to give us such knowledge, we turn to empirical evidence, or experience, "which is a feebler and less worthy means" of gaining knowledge. Following classical rhetorical procedure, he reaches for an example, which he finds in his contemporary French legal process. France has more laws than the rest of the world put together; yet, no matter how many laws we have, we can never encapsulate the infinite variety of possible legal cases.

In every new case, the judge will have to exercise a judgement which, at least in some particulars, must be made without recourse to previous laws. This brings a predicament regarding judgement and justice; and he turns to cases of miscarriages of justice. He writes:

> Certain men are condemned to death for a murder; their sentence, being agreed upon and determined, though not pronounced. At this point the judges are informed by the officers of an inferior court in the neighbourhood that they are holding some prisoners who openly confess to this murder, and throw unquestionable light upon the whole affair. And yet these judges deliberate whether they ought to interrupt or defer the execution of the sentence passed upon the first prisoners. They discuss the unusualness of the case, and the precedent it may set up for the reversal of judgements; for the sentence being juridically correct, the judges have no reason to change their minds. In short, these poor devils are sacrificed to the forms of justice. (Montaigne, *Essays* 351)[2]

The particularity—the historical, material *actuality*—of individual humans is ignored in order to preserve the *form* of justice, not its content. In this judgement, what is at stake is not the identity of a murderer but the identity of the law: the identity of the law with the law. When experience, as material history, calls the judgement into question by providing the *content* of a countervailing or critical experience, then that experience must be discounted in the interests of conformity to a rule: in this case, preserving the *office* of the law, and, more importantly, that of the *officer of the law*.

This is my first example of an "official identity": the identity of an officer of the law. It is an identity established by the silencing of experience, by relegating experience to a clandestine place underground: invisible or illegitimate. The identity of the judge triumphs over the facts of experience (or of history, truth, reality). How can this identity be "true," "real," or materially historical? How can it be a *substantive* identity, an identity based upon the material facts of historical agency or existence?

By extension, I contend that the same thing happens in literary and cultural criticism: the identity of Montaigne's judge maps directly onto the identity of the contemporary critic (my second example: the official identity of the critic). This is what we have learned to call a cultural criticism determined by identity politics, and it helps explain the triumph of what Philippe Lejeune called an "autobiographical pact" in criticism. The consequence of this pact is that criticism becomes an act of signing one's name.[3] Such critique is a matter of style, of the reduction of the self as a location of experience to the pure emptiness of style, or to my "office" as "Irish," "working class," "specifically sexed" and so on. In these, I am no longer simply Irish, but am instead "an Irishman"; nor am I sexed in terms of my behaviour in life, but rather I become the sign that represents "the gay" or "the straight"; nor am I an electrician, but rather a representative of working-class interests in general. Not even my proper autobiography is told in this, for I become not an individual but the *sign* of an individual, a generalised representative of an office. Putting matters bluntly, we are all bureaucrats now, in this form of criticism.⁴ The prioritisation of identity politics reduces experience to what I can now call my "official" identity: an identity focused on the priority of being over becoming, and an identity devoid of historical substance.

In the middle of the last century, Leslie A. Fiedler pondered something similar in relation to abstract art. In "Archetype and Signature," he argued that: "The abstract painter, for instance, does not, as he sometimes claims really 'paint paint,' but signs his name. So-called abstract art is the ultimate expression of personality" (263).

Fiedler was perplexed by contemporary visual art, and especially by abstract expressionist painting. His point was that the artist, by endlessly repeating the same configurations on the canvas, was essentially making herself or himself "recognisable" immediately. Ovals between perpendicular lines *are* "Robert Motherwell"; rectangles of colour present "Rothko"; parallel lines successively moving towards the centre of the canvas but always following the shape of the canvas mean "Frank Stella."

For Fiedler, these painters paint a signature, and we approach "Warhol" as a kind of "normative" art or art-value. It is, then, less surprising that a critical attitude in the years after this—broadly during the 1960s—witnesses essays charting the alleged "death" of the author: if the prevailing mood is one seeing art as the celebration of the very being of an author, in the expressing of her or his name and identity, then it is not surprising that criticism—especially a criticism that sees itself as "oppositional"—will want to call that identity—or more precisely that *being*—into question.

Fiedler's argument can be applied to any art that lends itself to repetition and thus to parody. In all cases, what is at stake is the triumph of a style over a substance (and we will consider such "substance" more fully later). For this argument, what is at stake is the triumph of form over content to the extent that the content can be evacuated of primary significance. It is the *form* of the work that gives it its identity, and that even *constitutes* identity for its author and its reader. This last point is important: the allegedly stable identity of an author, standing over her or his stylised text or signature, also serves the function of imputing to the reader an ostensibly stable identity as well. The reader, receiving the autograph of the writer, knows where she or he stands in relation to the writer, takes her or his bearings from that stability, and finds her or his own name—and critical office—thereby.

Such a view narrows and delimits the artist's possibilities. Her or his biography can no longer recognize other and disparate experiences that would result in different types of work. A biography is thus reduced to a persona or personality. This explains the single most dominant form in contemporary popular culture: identity given in the form of "celebrity" where an *ethos* or disposition, with all its mutable content and responsibility for decision making or judgement, is reduced to the merest identity-image. Such identity is entirely consistent with a capitalist ethos that thrives on "branding," the marking of ownership and servitude on one's skin. I will address the politics of this in my final section.

One way of describing this prevailing state of affairs—the condition of criticism in which identity and identity politics becomes a grounding for value, truth or significance—is to say that, in a modernity that has favoured abstraction over experience as a means of verifying truth, the *forms* of the law of identity are more important than the *content* of that law. Habermas characterised this as a legitimation crisis: a condition in which "the belief in legitimacy shrinks to a belief in legality; the appeal to the legal manner in which a decision comes about suffices" (98).

In such modernity, legitimacy shrinks to mere legalism, the proper and decorous observation of the offices. We witness the triumph of that form of bureaucracy that sees identity as something to be *managed* rather than to be represented or lived. By working within the rules like this, we lose our *ethos* and, with that, we also lose any ethical prerogative that might shape the possibilities of our being together or recognising each other's identities in a commonality of experience: the public sphere.

If identity is a matter of conformity, and if that conformity is (as the word suggests) not only conformity to a rule but also conformity to a formal practice (especially to a formal *legal* practice), then we can conclude that there is indeed an intimate relationship between form and identity. Identity, in short, is a formal matter: identity *is* form; or, alternatively put, form is that which gives identity its specifics. Identity, as currently construed—that is, as a neo-Romantic negotiation of the exteriority of a material world by the interiority of consciousness—is intrinsically *unethical*. Identitarianism is inimical to any ethical position or philosophy. This is true especially when we confound ethics with morality.

Individual particularity—the very stuff that should be constitutive of identity—disappears as a consequence of this. One's identity is reduced to an abstract mythic being, doomed forever to repeat the "same" aspects of existence. In short, one is denied historical existence, never allowed to "become" anything, and reduced to the status of "merely" being. Specificity, as that which would counter mythology, is erased. Yet more precisely, the specific material and historical *events of experience* are occluded in this. Experience is reduced to nothing, evacuated of substantive content.

BECOMING

Against all this, we might begin with a simple observation: the identity of an entity that acts in history is complex, and requires an unusual ontology.

Fundamentally, the attempt to grasp an identity-in-history—the identity of a living individual—is conditioned by the fact that such an identity is necessarily elusive. It is never a *being*, always a *becoming*; and, accordingly, if we are to grasp it, we need some understanding of an ontology that is grounded in becoming rather than in being. Deploying a Deleuzian philosophy, I can now argue for a criticism that takes seriously the issue of becoming, considered in terms of material or historical *force*.

Reviewing Jean Rosset's *Forme et signification* in 1963, Derrida realised that the great strength of structuralism was that it dealt expertly with matters of form. In his review, "Force et signification," Derrida did not oppose form to content, but rather set form against force. He contended that "*Form* fascinates when one no longer has the force to understand force from within itself. That is, to create. This is why literary criticism is structuralist in every age, in its essence and destiny" (4–5). Put succinctly, structuralism (and we can now say all forms of identitarian critique, critique that prioritises form-as-identity) triumphs when one reduces force to significations of force, to stable representations or signs of force. "Force" is Derrida's term for what I have been calling the material contents of history or of experience.

Deleuze was also interested in force. Deleuze saw history and material realities precisely as the play of forces, forces that, as in physics, lead to *arrangements* of *events*: *des agencements* that are constitutive of *les événements*. This "event" is central to his ontology of becoming, and to any ontology that is aware of the actual facts of material history, the grounding *conditions* or even *pre-conditions* and thus determinants of the possibilities of our being.

We need precision here, on two counts. First, we might say that "becoming precedes being," so to speak: it is not the case that we *are* something and only then become something else; rather, the change that we call "becoming" is the very condition of the possibility of our being at all. Secondly, the event in Deleuze is not a definite something that is occasioned or brought about in a world of supposed "exteriority" by an "interiority" of consciousness that can determine material conditions in the world. The world of an alleged exteriority "as such" does not in fact exist; or it exists only as an aspect of the arrangement or *agencement* of forces that are episodic and radically singular.

This requires further clarification. Deleuze learns much from Bergson and Spinoza. From Bergson, he derives the importance of *time* and of *movement*. He does not simply rehearse the Bergsonian notion of *durée*, duration, but prefers to give it a specific inflection. Duration, he says, "is a becoming that endures, a change that is substance itself" (*Bergsonism* 37). This is already a major step. He then takes from Spinoza a very particular sense of *difference* and of *singularity*. The "scandal" of Spinoza is the scandal of dismissing any idea of the world as a duality at all, especially and above all a duality between a world of interiority and one of exteriority. "According to the *Ethics* [. . .] what is an action in the mind is necessarily an action in the body as well, and what is a passion in the body is necessarily a passion in the mind. There is no primacy of one series over the other" (Deleuze, *Spinoza* 18). Deleuze's ontology is entirely an ontology of becoming rather than of being.

At the start of his *Ethics*, Spinoza is especially engaged by the question of the substantiality of God. This is where Deleuze finds an absolute or primary difference: not difference that defines itself in opposition to something else, something "self-same" or self-identical; rather, difference is an absolute condition of the very possibility of identity. Spinoza's case, at the opening of his *Ethics*, is that God is at once infinite (and thus containing an infinity of possible attributes) while at the same time unique (and thus not amenable to re-presentation). As Michael Hardt puts it: "God is both unique and absolute" (61). For Deleuze, this offers a consistency with his reading of time and movement in Bergson, for it offers a version of substance that is *intrinsically different*: not "different *from*" something else, for there *is no* something else (God is infinite), and not differing from itself in time (God is one thing). Rather, this is pure difference as constitutive of the substance of being.

The result, once theological issues are removed from the equation, is that one is never in a state of being (a being that would allow me to give an account of "my identity"), but only becoming (in which "I" never quite coincide with myself, since my temporal condition precludes any such possibility, and since the "I" is a product of the movement or arrangement of forces). "Being" would equate with death, and is negative; "becoming" is equivalent to living and is affirmative, joyful. Moreover, becoming is thus also the matter of material history itself: living.

Consequently, all things are necessarily always in flux. In fact, yet more radically, anything that we might want to identify as a specific "somewhat" (or some "thing") is nothing more than a pure instantiation of a play of forces that makes the somewhat *as it "is"* an interruption in the otherwise continuous flow of becomings. Further still, the perceiver of this "somewhat" is herself or himself but an accident of the play of forces that phenomenologically brings the perception into line, however momentarily, with the perceived. To perceive is momentarily to arrest the flow of becomings, the play of forces that constitutes history, as it were. Within this, therefore, any "event"—like the event of perception—is a kind of "accidental condition" of history.

There is, thus, no "I" other than the play of forces that allows me, at whatever moment, to pretend to arrest the flows of becoming. This substantially affects human agency, and, beyond that, freedom. This is a way of describing how Deleuze thinks of "events." At one level, events constitute history; yet we must be careful to distinguish events from spectacle. The event takes place in what Deleuze calls *"le temps mort"*:

> the event is inseparable from dead time. It's not even that there is dead time before and after the event, rather that dead time is in the event, for

example the instant of the most brutal accident confounds itself with the immensity of empty time in which you see it arriving, as a spectator of that which has not yet happened, in a long suspense. [. . .] Groethuysen said that every event was, as it were, in the time when nothing happens. (*Pourparlers* 218; my translation)[5]

The event is not something determined or even predetermined by a consciousness; rather, the emergence of the consciousness is that which comes about precisely as a result of the encounter that *is* the event itself, the play of forces that constitutes this "dead time," a time that is taken out of formal narrative but that allows for the constitution of a subject.

In many other philosophies or social theories, especially those based either upon forms of psychoanalysis or upon forms of "identity politics," the subject is often typically characterised and described by her or his desire. For Deleuze, desire is not a matter of exerting a will upon exteriority, much less a matter of "choice," either consumerist or existentialist: desire does not "bring something about." Rather, desire is that which is produced through the encounter that, in the first place, is constitutive of both subject and object, and constitutive of them *as* subject and object. What Deleuze is trying to do is to find a way of addressing movement as the fundamental form of ontology, but ontology considered as the conditions of our becoming rather than as being.

The result is the production of *accidental conditions* of consciousness or of desire. We are not here talking of desire as a set of "wants" or "choices" based on lack or need or wish. Rather, desire describes the production of force. The play or arrangement of forces that constitutes becomings-in-time is something that is itself in constant flux; and it thus produces desire simply as the condition of producing yet more arrangements, more becoming. Desire becomes pure "affirmation," the affirming of positive becoming; and the significance of this is that it flies directly in the face of most radical "critical" thinking that derives from Hegel or from any notion of criticism-as-negation. Desire, here, is what philosophy—and, by extension, radical social theory—should be about: it is about the production of more becoming, more *concepts*.

Insofar as this desire is the very production of an affirmation that constitutes the momentary instantiation of a subject, we can name it more conventionally as a mode of "confession" or revelation. The confession in question, though, is not the revelation of something that was occluded prior to its being narrated; rather, the confessing is the very elaboration of forces that constitute that subjectivity in the first place. Augustine famously asks "*cur confiteor?*"—why do I confess?—why indeed, given that God, by definition, already knows the contents of my consciousness and the history of my deeds. The Deleuzian reply might be something along the lines of *Confiteor ergo sumus*, meaning that I confess (or "am confessed") as a very condition of the possibility of my being at all, and any such being is always already situated in relation to other potential subjects, a public sphere of "confessors." It is to this that we can now turn more explicitly.

CONFESSIONS

In some at least minimal fashion, the literary text is essentially an act of confession, founded in a confession or revelation or "expressing" of identity. Put more dramatically, we might say that every literary act is an act of nomination. That is where Montaigne starts in his advice "au lecteur" at the start of the *Essais*:

> I want my portrait here to be drawn after how I actually am, simple, natural and ordinary, without research or artifice: for it is I that I am painting. My faults will be clearly discernible, as will my unvarnished form, or at least to the extent that public reverence can accept these things. ("Au lecteur" 35; my translation)

It is also where Rousseau starts in his great text of self-identification, the *Confessions*:

> I have resolved on an enterprise which has no precedent, and which, once complete, will have no imitator. My purpose is to display to my kind a portrait in every way true to nature, and the man I shall portray will be myself. (17)

Long before these, Augustine had delineated the predicament. Augustine's *Confessions* begin with a philosophical meditation on experience, considered in terms of an inner and outer space of the self. In Book I, Chapter 2, he tries to establish the proper relation between himself and God, conceiving it in spatial terms:

> How shall I call upon my God for aid, when the call I make is for my Lord and my God to come into myself? What place is there in me to which my God can come, what place that can receive the God who made heaven and earth? Does this then mean, O Lord my God, that there is in me something fit to contain you?. . . . Or is it rather that I should not exist, unless I existed in you? For *all things find in you their origin, their impulse, the centre of their being.* This, Lord, is the true answer to my question. But if I exist in you, how can I call upon you to come to me? (22)

In passing, we might see here the perfect illustration of what Marx will eventually call "alienation," that process whereby the human individual creates something within herself or himself, and then expresses it as a really existing power outside of the self, and a power that now has to be obeyed. This is that "modern" framework whereby the question of identity is construed as a spatial relation of interiority to exteriority, asking how we regulate the competing claims to power and supremacy of each. For my own purposes, we also see the question of how the self is always alien to itself, always governed through alterity.

Fundamentally, Augustine's question is whether God exists within Augustine, or whether Augustine exists within God: is God within or outside the self; and is the self outside of God or somehow held within God? Clearly, this affects Augustine's identity. The *Confessions* is at once an exercise in distinguishing Augustine from God while at the same time identifying Augustine with God. It is for this reason that it *has* to be a "*conversion*" text, charting the distance from distinction to intimacy; and it is for this reason, further, that it is the original *Bildungsroman*. It is a conversion text because it must chart the movement in Augustine from a position of being distanced from God to one where, changed, he is intimate with God; and it is a *Bildungsroman* because it sees the narrative of this movement as a process of learning or development, coming towards truth from falsehood or deception.

It therefore must delineate a self fundamentally shaped by two things: (a) experience within the self; and (b) the expression—the putting outside of the self—of a version of that experience. It is structured around the necessity of confession as revelation of an obscured interiority; and it helps start the process, in one reading, whereby that interiority is characterised as selfhood.

I suggested earlier that every literary act is in some minimal sense an act of nomination. An act of nomination essentially requires a scene of recognition, in which there are at least two subject positions or two positions that have the potential for subjectivity, for pronouncing the deictic "I." This is essentially a confessional scene: a scene in which an "I" presents or reveals itself before some other "I": "Call me Ishmael," perhaps, would be the fundamental American version of this, as in Melville (11).[6] In this, "I" present myself *as if* something interior is "ex-pressing" itself to an exteriority. However, we have already argued that such a spatialised version of this state of affairs is essentially limited and circumscribed by a "modern" mentality, a mentality that leads to a construction of selfhood in which identity is set up in a contest between the human consciousness and a world of nature.

We can now see that a better way of thinking about it is to see that the "I" in question is always already in a scene of recognition, but one where it is recognising *itself*, and doing so *in time* and as a substantive differing, as Deleuze would have it. The I recognizes itself as a name, as an identity, if and only if it constructs a *narrative* scene in which recognition (and misrecognition of itself) is possible. The self is that which confesses itself to itself; and this is why, in Augustine, the question of who is inside whom (God within Augustine or vice versa) is resolved eventually as it is, as a question of *time* and not of space.

Early in the text, Augustine ponders his infancy: "My infancy is long since dead," as he puts it, "yet I am still alive" (26; Book I, Chapter 6). These two things can only be reconciled in the odd temporality of God:

> you are infinite and never change. In you "today" never comes to an end; and yet our "today" does come to an end in you, because time, as well as everything else, exists in you. If it did not, it would have no means of passing. And since your years never come to an end, for you they are simply "today." The countless days of our lives and of our forefathers' lives have passed by within your "today." From it they have received their due measure of duration and their very existence. And so it will be with all the other days which are still to come. But you yourself are eternally the same. In your "today" you will make all that is to exist tomorrow and thereafter, and in your "today" you have made all that existed yesterday and for ever before. (Augustine 27; Book I, Chapter 6)

That is how Augustine initially phrases things. However, the entire point of the text of the *Confessions* is to find an intimacy with God, to come to a position not where God knows Augustine (since God knows everything, he already knows Augustine entirely), but rather to a position where Augustine knows and can name God, and, in so naming, find and name himself.

Augustine's final recognition scene arrives at the end of the text. Much remains mysterious about the relation between himself and God, but in the very final paragraph, he presents himself as a man knocking at God's door: "Only then shall we receive what we ask and find what we seek; only then will the door be opened to us" (347; Book XIII, Chapter 38). The final meeting is presaged at the end, but presaged as a narrative possibility in and through which the I finds itself as a subject in time; but also as a subject of a conversion, a change. By this stage in the text, a significant change has taken place in Augustine. At the start, he had pondered the question of whether he was in God or God in him. Now, at the end, he sees things differently. Instead of there being a dialectic between interiority and exteriority, Augustine sees the relation of himself to the world as one that is essentially *mediated* by the odd temporality of God's existence.

In Book XIII, Chapter 38, he writes that "We see the things which you have made, because they exist. But they only exist because you see them." So who is actually seeing these things? The answer comes: "Outside ourselves we see that they exist, and in our inner selves we see that they are good. But when you saw that it was right that they should be made, in the same act you saw them made" (346). Here, an important distinction is being made. On one hand, there is God, for whom there is an intimacy between *logos* and *ergon*, such that the thinking of something *immediately* brings it about. Such an intimacy is identified with God for whom all time is eternally present: God has no *Bildung*, as it were: by definition, this intimacy, constitutive of the being of God, is itself a state of "truth": God's word cannot lie, its "confession" or expression *is* the creation of the real ("You are Goodness itself," Augustine writes in this same chapter). On the other hand, there is the human "being" (actually now a human becoming), for whom there remains a distinction between the realm of value ("we see that they are good") and the realm of fact ("we see that they exist"). Crucially, in explanation, Augustine explains that "It was only *after a lapse of time* that we were impelled to do good" (emphasis added). This temporality, our condition of *becoming* on the way to *being*, is the story of a confessing, the story of how Augustine comes to take his stand, an "I" before the door of God (346; 347).

POLITICS

In his "Foreword" to the English translation of Jean-Luc Nancy's *The Experience of Freedom*, Peter Fenves makes an extremely interesting series of observations on the relation between ideas of experience and facts of freedom. "Empiricism, as a doctrine of experience," he writes, "and civil liberties, as the political content of freedom, are united [in Anglo-American thought] in their effort to remove unjustified authorities" (xiii). For Nancy, freedom is in some moments a matter of surprise: it is related to the concept of the event, or that which cannot be pre-programmed, that which opens us up precisely to the temporality of history whose opposite is Augustine's God. Augustine's God, being beyond history, being beyond becoming, is, of necessity, the eschewing of politics as such; and thus, this God is also the site where freedom is denied, replaced by an idea—a tragic Hegelian-Marxian idea—of history-as-necessity, *Ananke*.

Can experience be tied at all to political freedom; and can these have a bearing on the philosophy and practices of literary and cultural criticism? As critics influenced in recent times by various strands within Continental philosophy, we have in general been schooled to mistrust experience as a category, identifying it all-too-readily with ideology. Giorgio Agamben writes: "It is the character of the present time that all authority is founded on what cannot be experienced, and nobody would be inclined to accept the validity of an authority whose sole claim to legitimation was experience" (*Infancy* 14). We mistrust experience initially because we see it as subjective, and therefore not only not scientific or based in objective truth but also because, as a matter of subjective life, it is prone to ideological distortion. Experience, in fact, is almost aligned with ideology purely and simply. Yet, what is history if not the summation of actual undergone experiences? Without this, we are in the realms of the absolutes and abstractions of theology (as in Augustine's God); or, at the least, we open ourselves to the dangerous possibility of the reduction of history to myth or abstraction and of identity to "office," to the formal and official "being" that constitutes my function in an organisation or whole. It might even constitute my "function" or office as, say, proletarian or revolutionary in literary criticism.

Behind this lies the question of the relation of form and identity to questions of autonomy: how does a subject distinguish and identify itself in relation to the authority of tradition? In other terms, how does the I make a difference or "emerge" from a weight of history that yields the I as an already-given identity?

Arendt is helpful here. In her essay "On Violence," she considers how we can intervene historically in the world, writing that "What makes man a political being is his faculty of action." Further, more suggestively still, she argues that "To act and to begin are not the same, but they are closely interrelated" (179). This is her version of "events," which, for her, "are occurrences that interrupt routine processes and routine procedures" (109). She argues that we have a tendency to ignore events, especially events whose *actual* happening threatens the sanctity of our reasoned theory or prediction of what the theory says *should* take place in any given situation. The parallel, for my own argument, is with formal and official identity: we ignore any act of actual becoming that has the potential to contradict the sanctity of our office, our being, our "identity." The price we pay for such ignoring, according to Arendt, is that we remove the theory "further and further from reality" ("On Violence" 110). Likewise, our formal identity is what removes us from the possibilities of reality or of experience: identity such as this—identity politics in criticism—paradoxically is the very thing that *distances* us from history.

Like Agamben much later, Arendt also saw a problem concerning authority, and especially the formal authority of what we are calling tradition, the weight and burden of the past that seems to condition our present. In a prefiguring of Agamben's actual phrasing, she writes that:

> authority has vanished from the modern world. Since we can no longer fall back upon authentic and undisputable experiences common to all, the very term has become clouded by controversy and confusion [. . .] a constant, ever-widening and deepening crisis of authority has accompanied the development of the modern world in our [twentieth] century . . . ("What Is Authority?" 91)

The thing about authority, here—the authority that we have been systematically losing—is that it is akin both to religious thought and also to an ontology of being:

> Authority, resting on a foundation in the past as its unshaken cornerstone, gave the world the permanence and durability which human beings need precisely because they are mortals [. . .] Its loss is tantamount to the loss of the groundwork of the world, which indeed

since then has begun to shift, to change and transform itself with ever-increasing rapidity from one shape into another, as though we were living and struggling with a Protean universe where everything at any moment can become almost anything else. (Arendt, "What Is Authority?" 95)

This is the crux: does our identity conform to that which we are given by the authority of another (the past); or do we adopt the troubling condition of Protean instability which, for all its vexations to us, nonetheless offers the possibility of change, of events, of action (and thus of political life)? Arendt herself is relatively clear here:

> the loss of worldly permanence and reliability—which politically is identical with the loss of authority—does not entail, at least not necessarily, the loss of the human capacity for building, preserving, and caring for a world that can survive us and remain a place fit to live in for those who come after us. ("What Is Authority?" 95)

It follows that, if we are to have a political living at all, then we need to accept the vexing problems of instability—and above all, of instability in what we call our own identity. Like Proteus, we are historical beings only to the extent that we change, becoming other than we are. All else belongs, as in Augustine, to God and to other forms of absolute—and essentially therefore mythic, nonhistorical—form, or office.

In that mode of absolutist thinking—the thinking of official identity—we open ourselves to the dangerous possibility that large terms like "Holocaust," in the wrong hands, are presented not just as myth but also as lie. My tendentious claim is that "the wrong hands" are the hands of those who consider that we need to "verify" or validate an identity in relation to such events. What we are saying of course, is not that we should avoid the term "Holocaust," but rather that we should realize that the Holocaust is not one simple or single identifiable thing: it is many experiences (between six and nine million at least). It is Primo Levi, it is Elie Wiesel, it is all the many stories of Claude Lanzmann's *Shoah*, it is Christian Boltanski's *Dead Swiss*. In short, it has no identity—and to give it an identity is to reduce it to form, to evacuate it of content, to hand it over to the right wing for reduction to myth.

We have a modern example of a fictional character who is caught in the Augustinian trap, pondering the location of a selfhood in terms of the relation of interiority and external history: Beckett's Unnamable. Consider this self-identification:

> [. . .] perhaps that's what I feel, an outside and an inside and me in the middle, perhaps that's what I am, the thing that divides the world in two, on the one side the outside, on the other the inside, that can

be as thin as foil, I'm neither one side nor the other, I'm in the middle, I'm the partition, I've two surfaces and no thickness, perhaps that's what I feel, myself vibrating, I'm the tympanum, on the one hand the mind, on the other the world, I don't belong to either, it's not to me they're talking, it's not of me they're talking, no, that's not it, I feel nothing of all that, try something else, herd of shites, say something else [. . .] (Beckett 386)

The identity here becomes unnamable, "improper." The self is reduced to Agamben's "bare life;" but in Beckett this is formulated as if the Unnamable's self is pure skin, the site of a feeling or of a visceral experience: "I don't know what I feel, tell me what I feel and I'll tell you who I am [. . .]." However, his skin is, in Beckett, the site of a writing or of a representation; and we can see the terrifying logic here, as the formally identifiable body becomes the site of a tattoo, and thus also for a taboo[7]. The body here is a site on which a number, say, can be tattooed. This is an effect of the prioritisation of official identity, of identity politics.

In more precise political thinking, this in turn is fully shaped by the aporia of Auschwitz. Here is Agamben from the preface to *Remnants of Auschwitz*: "Some want to understand too much and too quickly; they have explanations for everything. Others refuse to understand; they offer only cheap mystifications. The only way forward lies in the space between these two options [. . .]" (13).

This matters because Agamben sees "the aporia of Auschwitz" as something profoundly philosophical. Auschwitz is characterised by a situation where its survivors are witness to "the only true thing" and, at the same time, this truth is "irreducible to the real elements that constitute it," and so we face "a reality that necessarily exceeds its factual elements." And so, as he puts it "The aporia of Auschwitz is, indeed, the very aporia of historical knowledge: a noncoincidence between facts and truth, between verification and comprehension" (*Remnants* 12). Fact need not be truth, in this. There is a noncoincidence between fact and truth; and this would be important if we are to counter Augustine's conception of God, for whom fact and value are one, unified or identified with each other through the power of God's word-as-deed, word-made-flesh, as John has it in his Revelations or "confessional" Gospel.

Now, however, let us place Agamben's insight in the context of Montaigne's "legalism." The result is that we have, in criticism, actually prioritised verification over comprehension by our prioritising of identity and its forms. We thus understand or comprehend nothing. To comprehend, in this case, will mean to explore that space between the options of explanation and mystification of which Agamben writes as he tries to find a new ethics of criticism.

In these terms, formal identity is that which effaces historical experience, which must now become clandestine if it is to exist at all. Formal or official identity—and identitarian politics with its preference for verification over comprehension—is that which operates and becomes valued when our society has become fully "bureaucratised." Identity politics in criticism might present itself as radical and critical; yet, as the foregoing shows, it is entirely complicit with the very conservatism of the social formation that it pretends to oppose. Bureaucracy in governance and bureaucratic government exist in order to manage behaviour in predictable fashion, and thus to preclude the very possibility of there ever being an action or an event at all. As Arendt argued, "It is the function [. . .] of all action, as distinct from mere behaviour, to interrupt what otherwise would have proceeded automatically and predictably" ("On Violence" 132–3). Official identity— and a criticism based on "who I am" rather than on "how we change"—is anathema to historical materialism, and to the necessary "witnessing" of literature that calls us into becoming and into political activity.

To be a "witness" to literature will mean opening ourselves to the fact of the clandestine experience, the experience that can have no formal presentation because it cannot be verified. And yet, at the same time, an experience that is not itself constitutive of identity. Yes, we can experience, we must acknowledge experience; but we can now do so only in a clandestine fashion. Our experience cannot be officially acknowledged; for we live in a critical age of official identity, bureaucratic identity. This is what has shaped the criticism based on identity politics which, while assuming itself to be radical, is in fact entirely in conformity with the law of the bureaucracy that demands one's papers. The more radical move—indeed, the move that is more radical precisely because it acknowledges limitations and strives for comprehension—is the move that abandons the ID card and steps firmly onto the side of the *sans papiers*.

NOTES

1. See my essays "For A New Empiricism" and "Aesthetics and The Demise of Experience." For other essays on "New Aestheticism," see Joughin and Malpas.
2. For the original, see Montaigne, *Essais: 3*, 281.
3. See Veeser and also Lejeune.
4. I explore this in Docherty *The English Question* where I consider what has happened to the discipline of English studies in a politics governed by audit culture, bureaucracy, the administrative priorities of a society that has seen the rise and triumph of the managerialist class.
5. The reference is to Bernard Groethuysen, (who studied under Dilthey), a philosopher better known in France than in the anglophone world.
6. I am indebted to Geoffrey Hartman for the speculation here about the status of nomination. In private conversation, July 1983, he suggested that "all acts of narrative are, in the end, finally acts of nomination." I am extending this here beyond the scope of narrative; and am relating it to the status of confession.
7. I am indebted to Jim Byatt for a number of conversations through which this link of Beckettian skin to taboo, and to this specific taboo, came to

be developed. Behind these formulations, I think we can hear the ghost of that archetypal first modern man, Hamlet, pondering his own potential for action or agency, pondering his identity and whether to bring it to an end or to a definite conclusion in his famed soliloquy: "to be or not to be." One reason why this is a *question* for Hamlet, and one that might yield a resolution, is that he thinks in terms of being itself, and not in terms of how he might *become* other than he is. In Shakespeare, typically, it is the *female* character who is cast in terms of becoming: 'I do beguile the thing I am by seeming otherwise', says Desdemona. Shakespeare's day, of course, called this "mutability," ascribed it to femininity, and devalued it. However, it is perhaps better regarded as the emergence, into modernity, of the pressure of an entire philosophy of difference, an ontology of becoming.

REFERENCES

Agamben, Giorgio. *Infancy and History*. Trans. Liz Heron. London: Verso, 1993. Print.
———. *Remnants of Auschwitz*. Trans. Daniel Heller-Roazen. New York: Zone Books, 2002. Print.
Arendt, Hannah. "On Violence." Rpt. in *Crises of the Republic: Lying in Politics; Civil Disobedience; On Violence; Thoughts on Politics and Revolution*. New York: Harcourt Brace & Co, 1972: 103–84. Print.
———. "What Is Authority?" *Between Past and Future: Eight Exercises in Political Thought*. Harmondsworth: Penguin, 1977: 91–141. Print.
Beckett, Samuel. *Molloy, Malone Dies, The Unnamable*. London: John Calder, 1959. Print.
Deleuze, Gilles. *Bergsonism*. Trans. Hugh Tomlinson and Barbara Habberjam. New York: Zone Books, 1988. Print.
———. *Pourparlers*. Paris: Minuit, 1990. Print.
———. *Spinoza*. Trans. Robert Hurley. San Francisco: City Lights Books, 1988. Print.
Derrida, Jacques. "Force and Signification." *Writing and Difference*. Trans. Alan Bass. London: Routledge, 1978. 3–30. Print.
Descombes, Vincent. *Modern French Philosophy*. Trans. L. Scott-Fox and J.M. Harding. Cambridge: Cambridge University Press, 1980. Print.
Docherty, Thomas. "Aesthetic Education and the Demise of Experience." *Aesthetic Democracy*. Stanford: Stanford University Press, 2006. 61–77. Print.
———. "For A New Empiricism." *Parallax* 5.2 (1999): 51–64. Print.
———. *The English Question; or, Academic Freedoms*. Brighton: Sussex Academic, 2008. Print.
Fenves, Peter. "Foreword: From Empiricism to the Experience of Freedom." *The Experience of Freedom*. By Jean-Luc Nancy. Trans. Bridget McDonald. Stanford: Stanford University Press, 1993. xiii–xxxi. Print.
Fiedler, Leslie A. "Archetype and Signature: A Study of the Relationship between Biography and Poetry." *Sewanee Review* 60 (1952): 253–73. Print.
Habermas, Jürgen. *Legitimation Crisis*. Trans. Thomas McCarthy. London: Heinemann, 1976. Print.
Hardt, Michael. *Gilles Deleuze*. Minneapolis, MN: University of Minnesota Press, 1993. Print.
Joughin, John, and Simon Malpas, eds. *The New Aestheticism*. Manchester: Manchester UP, 2003. Print.
Lejeune, Philippe. *Le pacte autobiographique*. Paris: Seuil, 1975. Print.

Melville, Herman. *Moby Dick*. Ed. Charles Child Walcutt. New York: Bantam Books, 1981. Print.

Montaigne, Michel de. "Au lecteur." *Essais: 1*. Paris: Garnier-Flammarion, 1969. 35. Print.

———. *Essais: 3*. Paris: Garnier-Flammarion, 1969. Print.

———. *Essays*. Trans. J.M.Cohen. Harmondsworth: Penguin, 1958. Print.

Rousseau, Jean-Jacques. *Confessions*. Trans. J.M. Cohen. Harmondsworth: Penguin, 1953. Print.

Saint Augustine. *Confessions*. Trans. R.S. Pine-Coffin. Harmondsworth: Penguin, 1961. Print.

Veeser, H. Aram, ed. *The Confessions of the Critics*. London: Routledge, 1996. Print.

2 "To be engulfed by you"

The Pull of Alienation in Narcissistic Narratives of the Sixties[1]

Karen Zouaoui

In *The Novelist at the Crossroads*, David Lodge notes that "[t]he situation of the novelist [at the turn of the 1970s] may be compared to a man standing at a crossroads" (18). Following Scholes and Kellog (1966), he says that branching out of the main, realistic road are the paths of nonfiction and "fabulation" (19) and then adds:

> To the novel, the non-fiction novel, and the fabulation, we must add a fourth category: the novel which exploits more than one of these modes without fully committing itself to any, the novel-about-itself, the trick-novel, the game-novel, the puzzle-novel, the novel that leads the reader (who wishes, naïvely, only to be told what to believe) through a fair-ground of illusions and deceptions, distorting mirrors and trap-doors that open disconcertingly under his feet, leaving him ultimately not with any simple or reassuring message or meaning but with a paradox about the relation of art to life. (22)

Lodge comments here upon works which emulated the playfulness of Laurence Sterne's *Tristram Shandy* (1760) and which became paramount in the 1960s. He quotes, as "a case in point," B. S. Johnson's *Albert Angelo* (1964) and notes that this type of literature points to a distressed quest for truth and a deep distrust of authority (9). Such distrust leads to a radical challenging of the genre of the novel, as if the chaos experienced by the characters and narrators had to be mirrored by the text. In *Albert Angelo*, as the anti-hero is revealed to be a construct and a reflection of the implied author, the creative process and its artificiality become the main focal point. Similarly, Brigid Brophy's *In Transit* (1969) tackles the very concept of identity through a narrator who fails to remember what sex he or she is, thus questioning along the way our tendency to take the world and society for granted.

B. S. Johnson's *Albert Angelo* and Brigid Brophy's *In Transit* tackle the typically avant-garde idea that the society we live in is inherently fictional. Society, just like a novel, is a pure construct that can, and should, be exposed for what it is. Yet readers should not lose their subjectivity in the process. On the contrary, it is through the exercise of interpretation and through the form of the novel that a subject can come to terms with their inherent "vulnerability" and play with it. The novel in the 1960s has indeed become the *locus* of epistemological and cognitive questioning thus giving the much-used Derridean statement "There is nothing outside the text" (227) its full meaning. The aim is not so much to reveal that there is *nothing* behind those structures as to show that those same structures are *everything*, everywhere and omnipresent. Narcissistic narratives as such do not represent a dead end, a loss of meaning and significance in solipsism, but rather send a message that this very same society can be *re-formed*, if only the main protagonist of all texts, the reader, will play their role.

The equation between text and identity upon which these experimental texts rely seems natural in a poststructuralist age. Continental structuralism was indeed very strong in some literary circles in the Great Britain of the 1960s. As a matter of fact, experimental fiction entirely relies on a sense that life as we experience it is the result of a congregation of structures. The latter was made evident by Ferdinand de Saussure's *Course in General Linguistics* (1916) first, and was later more widely applied and adopted by the ethnologist Claude Lévi-Strauss, namely through *Tristes Tropiques* (1955). In addition, the publication of Jean Piaget's *Structuralism* in 1968 witnesses a general recognition of its input in sundry disciplines, literature being no exception. Some ten years later, when Lucien Dällenbach puts forward the "specularity" of the text, that is to say, its ability to mirror its devices, he, in fact, describes the practical effects of structuralist theory on literature. What is more, Patricia Waugh explains that from the 1960s onwards, literature develops steadily in a way which "draws attention to the fact that life, as well as novels, is constructed through frames, and that it is finally impossible to know where one frame ends and another begins" (*Harvest* 29–30). This self-conscious literature is what is more commonly called metafiction.[2] In the 1960s, authors like John Fowles, Christine Brook-Rose, Ann Quin, J.G. Ballard, and John Berger all capitalised on a reflection of, and on, their own devices—mainly through a mirroring of the implied author's consciousness. The trend was to be carried out through to the postmodern literature of the 1980s, 1990s, and 2000s. The influence the trend has had on British literature is exemplified by Salman Rushdie's *Midnight's Children* (1981), Jeanette Winterson's *The Passion* (1987), and Ali Smith's *The Accidental* (2005), to quote but a few acclaimed works.[3] All these contemporary works explore the limits of storytelling and take the reader "through a fair-ground of illusions and deceptions, distorting mirrors and trap-doors" indeed.

The playfulness with which postmodernism is so often equated, and which started being prominent in the literary avant-garde of the 1960s, should not be read as a distraction from reality, no matter how averse to it their "tricks" might seem. What transpires from these manipulations of reader expectations and narrative logic, going against the traditional tripartite structure with a beginning, a middle, and an end, is a will to make readers see *through* the narrative in which they themselves play a part in their everyday lives. The literary avant-garde of the 1960s stands out from mainstream literature by not relating directly to reality, through straightforward *mimesis*, but by questioning the very notion of reality. Patricia Waugh captures the spirit of the time in a few lines:

> Metafiction pursues such questions through its formal self-exploration, drawing on the traditional metaphor of the world as book, but often recasting it in the terms of contemporary philosophical, linguistic or literary theory. If, as individuals, we now occupy 'roles' rather than 'selves', then the study of characters in novels may provide a useful model for understanding the construction of subjectivity in the world outside novels. If our knowledge of this world is now seen to be mediated through language, then literary fiction (words constructed entirely of language) becomes a useful model for learning about the construction of 'reality' itself. (*Metafiction* 3)

In other words, metafiction, through an "auto-consciousness" of its codes and structures, provides an incentive and tools to question our perception of "reality." Note that the terms, albeit synonymous, are not interchangeable (Chanady 144). Auto-consciousness is a specific subjectivising device that aims at revealing the organic dimension of the text. Metafiction, as a submode within the mode of fiction, tends to rely heavily on such heightened consciousness in order to reach out to the reader. One paradox of this practice, however, is that while those texts implicitly criticise what we take for granted in society, they are often deemed too solipsistic and deconstructive to lead to any stable representation—so much so that Linda Hutcheon calls these, "narcissistic narratives" (16).

The term "narcissistic narratives" is necessarily ambivalent. Hutcheon's main line of thought is that of the paradoxical relationship "nonfiction" entertains with the realist novel, being both an "outgrowth" and a direct challenger of the traditional nineteenth-century novel (16). One aspect which is secondary in Hutcheon's analysis and which I will stress here is the paradox posed by works which, while discarding any claim to authority, constantly draw attention to the authoring process. For while metafictional texts constantly reassert the presence of the author, they also tend to undermine his/her role by always enhancing the relativity of points of view. The figure of the author indeed appears to be in a double bind, torn between the wish to play a role in the text and in society at large, and the wish to repudiate taking responsibility for the creation of meaning. What seems of greater importance is not so much *mimesis* as the showing of a creative process. B. S. Johnson himself admits to having been attracted to his own reflection in his work, he recalls in his memoirs: "I really discovered what I should be doing with *Albert Angelo* (1964) where I broke through the English disease of the objective correlative to speak through directly if solipsistically in the novel form, and heard my own small voice" (*Aren't You* 22). For Johnson, then, looking at himself in the mirror his text provides, coincides with a moment of epiphany; Johnson is telling us that he could not *be* (a writer) until he was able to *see* (himself) as such, by "hear[ing] [his] own small voice." The Cartesian correlation Johnson establishes between *seeing* and *being* becomes all the more powerful when one thinks of his tragic death by suicide. Could it be that Johnson was a literary Narcissus who lost himself in the reflection of his text? That the life, work, and death of B. S. Johnson lend themselves to romanticising is in my opinion a consequence of the use of metafiction which tends to confer consciousness not just to texts, but to authors too. I will argue here that this "added subjectivity" has more to do with a formal device that B. S. Johnson's *Albert Angelo* and Brigid Brophy's *In Transit* bring into play to create new textual identities, whether they be generic (aimed at reforming the genre of the novel) or subjective (intended to give a fuller sense selfhood to writer and reader alike) than with an actual transference of "real" experiences.

The emphasis laid on subjectivity and perception begs a number of questions. Why should the act of seeing and its different manifestations matter so much to the reader? How much do Johnson's hermeneutics and Brophy's questioning of authority and authorship owe to the "structure of feeling" (Williams 64–88) of the 1960s? What "reality" exactly, does metafiction purport to affect through its quest for new ways of signifying? While the idea itself is not novel in literary criticism, there has been next to no detailed demonstration of how this "dissident reading" (Sinfield x) is conveyed in the text. I argue here that these authors' ethics pertain to a certain existential phenomenology that often equates seeing and acting (and necessarily reading) with being, as we will see first with B. S. Johnson's quest for authenticity, and secondly with Bridig Brophy's constant reminder of the relativity of our perception of ourselves and of reality.

"FUCK ALL THIS LYING" (*ALBERT ANGELO* 167) B. S. JOHNSON'S DESPERATE QUEST FOR AUTHENTICITY

The creation of textual identities in B. S. Johnson's fiction is fraught with contradictions and confusion. The implied author's relentless quest for authenticity employs metafictional devices such as *mise en abyme*, a term coined by the French writer André Gide, to refer to the process of adding internal references—which mirror the main themes of the work itself—to a main work. While *mise en abyme* is generally used to draw a multidimensional picture of a motif, Johnson uses the device to baffle his reader. The plot itself is quite straightforward. *Albert Angelo* portrays an eponymous character who strives to cope with a sense of failure. His job as a supply teacher in London typifies all his failures. At work, he experiences a deep sense of irrelevance, not only because he was trained to be an architect and failed to make a living of it, but also because he is quite disconnected from an environment he has no interest in. Most of the time, Albert bitterly reflects on his lost love, Jenny, whom he tries to join in his daydreams. The narrative technique in *Albert Angelo* is meant to emphasise the mimetic potential of the book by allowing for concomitant trains of thought to be shown in the form of columns that stand for internal and external speech.

Johnson carefully selects the typography of his pages to physically reflect the isolation of internal thoughts and to peg them against external utterances. The device allows for some comical passages as when Albert threatens his pupils, who are concealing from him the stone he passed round for pedagogical purposes, to "report this affair to the Headmaster" whilst commenting to himself *a la* Lucky Jim: "Who will do fuck-all about it" (90). The use of columns is one of the examples of the *mise en abyme* to which Johnson resorts. They provide a reflection of, and an expansion on, the unfolding event of a lesson taught by Albert, to bring in more subjectivity. The device creates the effect of a theatrical aside, helping the reader feel closer to Albert's experience. It is as though the author had tried to encourage moments of sympathy, to make the reader "feel" what the main character experiences. It is no coincidence, for example, that the reader gets access to Albert's daydreams in one of these columns, and that these stand out from the external utterances of Albert's pupils poking fun at him in the left-hand side column. While it might be tempting to assign to this typographical trick a form of value judgment, the actual content of these utterances prevents us from reaching such clear-cut conclusions about them as they are both tinted with irony. The treatment of Albert's deep-felt thoughts about his romantic past, for example, of which his pupils make fun, suggests that not one utterance, or by extension, not one discourse can ever have precedence over another.

By making the limits of the discourses appear so permeable, these columns reflect what Emmanuel Lévinas calls in *Humanism of the Other* "the vulnerability of the self" (124). For Lévinas indeed subjectivity and vulnerability cannot be separated. In Johnson's fiction, subjectivity is capitalised upon, whether it be through the figure of the author, or through the extreme sensitivity of its characters in order to make the Other, and its vulnerability, visible to the reader. Johnson's juxtaposed monologues or semi-dialogues create just such an absence of realisation of what the Other might feel. Hence the fluctuating narrative modes of *Albert Angelo*. The novel opens, for instance, with a third-person narrative, showing us Albert talking with his friends, to be then followed by a first-person narrative, until the viewpoint changes again and it is his pupils who talk about him. For instance, the prologue reads:

Luke said:	You an [sic] artist, then?
Albert said:	Well, sort of. I'm an architect—that is, I'm a teacher really, but I want to be an architect. No, that's the wrong way

	round, I'm an architect but I have to earn my living by teaching.
Joseph said:	What, do you do drawings of buildings and things?
Albert said:	Yes.
Luke said:	What buildings have you done, then?
Albert said:	Ones that have actually been built?
Luke said:	Yes.
Albert said:	None. I just design them. (12–13)

In the "Exposition" chapter, it is a flamboyantly confident "I" which carries on the narrative: "I think I shall visit my parents every Saturday, as a rule, as a habit. Occasionally Sundays: instead, though, not as well. But usually Saturdays, as a rule, as a habit almost. Yes" (19). Yet, it soon becomes clear, from the end of that first paragraph, that this apparently confident "I" may be a means of masking the character's vulnerability. Asserting his choices indeed seems like a difficult enterprise at this stage for the character, but the triviality of the subject matter says something of the character's deeper concerns. Very rapidly, the shift from a first-person narrative to a third-person narrative appears to be a powerful means to reflect the interpenetration of the characters' idiosyncrasies and how these must remain unfathomable to each other. When the reader reaches the chapter entitled "Development" and the passage where Albert is giving a lesson to school children, the fragmentation of discourse in columns emphasises the difficulty of saying "I" in this novel. The columns reveal an unstable universe where *being*, which takes time and space to grow, is constantly hindered by the Other or, if being is made possible, then it comes at the expense of the Other (Lévinas *Autrement* 127). This can be seen, for instance, when Albert's soliloquies silence the whole classroom. Danger, for Albert's sense of being, and for his "actual" life in the novel, arises when his pupils find their own voice. As a matter of fact, this coming to being of the pupils through the writing of essays where they are allowed to say what they think of their teacher Albert will climax with their teacher's murder.

The emergence of the pupils' forays is foreshadowed by the holes which appear two-thirds into the novel. These are physical holes that at first appear to be a gimmick meant to whet our curiosity about the development of the plot; the holes let through a fragment of the narrative a few pages later where a murder takes place and reads thus: "struggled [*sic*] to take back his knife, and inflicted on him a mortal wound above his right eye (the blade penetrating to a depth of two inches) from which he died instantly" (149). However, the holes are also a formal device that provides an insight into Albert's gruesome future, for the text we are made to see through the slashes tells the story of Albert's murder. The slashes made to the pages of the book thus physically foreshadow the violence the character will endure, as he will be thrown into the Thames by some of his aggressive pupils. In addition, the device is interesting because it shows how the experimental novel seeks to increase its mimetic potential by foreshadowing the plot and by physically conveying a sense that its characters are endangered, while at the same time being misleading. The effect is indeed to delay the moment of realisation of what crime has taken place. Indeed the hole created by the slashes comes after the description of a skirmish in which Christopher Marlowe would have famously lost his life. The immediate link that is made by the reader peeping through that hole *seems* to be the actual death of Marlowe. Because Marlowe's death itself constitutes some sort of literary myth readers will be acquainted with, the murder itself that is recounted in that gap may not shock them quite as much. In that regard, the formal device is misleading as it defers, while announcing, a shocking denouement to the narrative we are reading. In a way, this device is not too dissimilar from Hitchcock's in *Psycho* (1960) where the director famously pieced together some fifty shots of the murder scene in the shower, thus creating momentum and delay at the same time. In the span of time created by the extra space of these cuts, Johnson allows for a moment of reflection for the reader. Not only is the reader compelled to reconsider his or her reading habits but he or she must confront the close relation between the body of the text and the organicity of the fictional body of the character. In the last resort indeed, the reading lesson that is bestowed by the playful device of the holes tends to construe an image of the subject as being eminently contingent to the larger text in which it is inscribed, thus demonstrating that the self should never be taken for granted.

The porousness of the self thus construed through the manipulation of discourses is highly reminiscent of James Joyce's *Finnegans Wake* (1939) with the difference that while Joyce points at interchangeability between characters, to a "process" (Beitchman 12), Johnson points to the threat made to a character's sense of being. This distinction undermines any thought that Johnson may be a poststructuralist. For, although some of Johnson's practice seems to align him with poststructuralists, his practice reveals he is far too anxious about what happens to the subject in society to do away with it completely in fiction. If anything, his narcissistic forays into the novel are desperate attempts at giving the subject a voice. Thus, when the narrator's auto-destructive drive exposes the "deceit" of the novel with a diatribe on fiction it is first and foremost the "I" that is trying to speak:

> —fuck all this lying look what im [*sic*] really trying to write about is writing not all this stuff about architecture trying to say something about writing about my writing im [*sic*] my hero though what a useless appellation my first character then im [*sic*] trying to say something about me through him albert [*sic*] an architect when whats [*sic*] the point in covering up covering up covering over pretending pretending [*sic*] i can say anything through him that is anything that I would be interested in saying. (167)

Johnson echoes here the epigraph to the novel from Samuel Beckett's *The Unnamable* (1953): "There is nothing else, let us be lucid for once, nothing else but what happens to me." Johnson's creed is indeed to go against a would-be traditional approach of the novel in which authors would "lie" to their readers by giving them fiction to read when the self of the writer is omnipresent. Thus, in his introduction to the collection of short stories, *Aren't You Rather Young To Be Writing Your Memoirs?* (1973), Johnson claims that he wants to break "the English disease of the objective correlative" (22) in order to set the "I" free. In this paragraph, the absence of punctuation and the repetitions show that the "I" is rebelling against necessarily frustrating writing conventions. In another passage, the figure of the author explains: "—look, I'm trying to tell you something of what I feel about being a poet in a world where only poets care anything real about poetry, through the objective correlative of an architect who has to earn his living as a teacher" (*Albert Angelo* 168). Very small at first and as if atrophied ("i", "im"), the "I" that comes to life on page 167 must stutter when faced with a frame that does not satisfy its aesthetic and ethical needs. Johnson takes this wish for authenticity to the subject and the text literally, by forcing his narrator to confess what "really" happened when he goes back on some trivial information:

> —A few instances of the lies. It was Jim Wales not Wells kept [*sic*] the greyhounds; my parents used to live in Hammersmith but now live in Barnes; [. . .] and my parents have two cats, not one dog, who eat nourishing Fidomeat, not Felixmeat, which I made up, yes, I'm guilty [. . .]; and . . . I could go on and on, through each page, page after page, pointing out the lies, but it would be so tedious, so tedious. (172–3)

From then on, the figure of the author and the narrator seemingly combine to speak with one dissident voice against "lying." And yet, this last comment on the "tedious[ness]" of these endeavours cannot but undermine them to the reader and himself. Indeed, this last repetition of "tedious" can be read as a comment on the first occurrence of "tedious." One may see in its repetition an inkling of the fact that this very same condemnatory discourse is "thickened" or "doubled-up" by its metafictional other. This is just one example of how the text constantly refuses to be defined, precisely by making the reader aware of the artificiality of the structures that organise our experience. We cannot even trust the very same authorial voice that so desperately calls for attention. Similarly, when the author claims that "[t]elling stories is telling lies" (*Albert Angelo* 172–3), the reader cannot but see a major contradiction in the creation of this narrative and its dismissal.

The same tension happens in more contemporary novels like Winterson's *The Passion* but the difference here is that the real author, B. S. Johnson, is well known for having tried to push forward a theory of the novel as distinct from fiction. In *Aren't You Rather Young To Be Writing Your Memoirs?* Johnson explains how, precisely because his work tells the truth, it cannot be called fiction:

> The two terms *novel* and *fiction* are not [. . .] synonymous, as many seem to suppose in the way they use them interchangeably. The publisher of *Trawl* wished to classify it as autobiography, not as a novel. It is a novel, I insisted and could prove; what it is not is fiction. The novel is a form in the same sense that the sonnet is a form; within that form, one may write truth or fiction. I choose to write truth in the form of a novel. (14)

Johnson's distinction between the novel *form* and the fictional *content* shows how literally his own axiom "telling stories is telling lies" affected his work. Such a sharp and hardly tenable distinction can only create more confusion in the readers' mind as to the ethical ends of the whole text they are reading. This is also perhaps the reason why B. S. Johnson's work is more strictly speaking avant-garde than Rushdie's, Winterson's, or Smith's fiction have been, because a whole new vocabulary is required to make sense of the artistic construct and what its purpose is (Josipovici 3). The fulcrum of this intricacy in Johnson's, as in Brophy's work, is the construction of an "I" which is always incredibly complex to reach. The passage where *Albert Angelo*'s narrator tries to redeem his lies reveals the complexity of the use of the pronoun "I" in alleging there is a truer, more authentic, "I" than the one we have been given to read in the narrative so far. Yet, posing a truer "I" inevitably makes readers question the validity of this "I" who claims to be telling the truth. Indeed, if the "I" of the narrative was nothing but a simulacrum for the implied author, it is not at all evident that readers will consider this new, emerging "I" any more worthy of their trust. Metafiction thus makes it impossible to create a stable point of reference, still less a stable identity of the text or of the authorial figure. This in itself is daring insofar as not only does the author run the risk of exposing his vulnerable position to his readers, but he also runs the risk of rejection from them. Patricia Waugh talks about "frame breaking" as "the laying bare [of] the function of literary conventions" (*Metafiction* 87–8). One might want to add that metafiction is perhaps first and foremost the laying bare of authority which marks a relinquishing of authorship. When Johnson decided to stage *Albert Angelo* as a failing fiction, the author was appealing to the readers' ability to take control of the construct that reading is. Eventually, by questioning and repositioning themselves constantly in the face of the novel's contradictions, the readers are expected to create their own texts. For what Johnson's "narcissistic narrative" achieves in the end is to prompt a more critical approach to texts in general and a certain awareness that their ultimate interpretation is in the readers' hands.

BRIGID BROPHY: THE FICTITIOUS AUTHOR
TALKING TO FICTITIOUS READERS

Like Johnson, Brigid Brophy also stages a dramatic quest for truth in *In Transit* where the main character loses his/her identity. The androgynous quality of the narrator recalls Virginia Woolf's *Orlando* (1928) with the difference that the narrator in *In Transit* does not settle into a clearly female or male body. The narrator recalls the event off-handedly in an anecdote a third of the way into the novel: "It was during the scudding of the back of the spoon across the opaque liquid that I realised I could no longer remember which sex I was" (69). Failing to find answers to his/her questions in his/her direct environment, the character sets out in a surrealist tale to find out by himself/herself what gender he or she belongs to. However, while the character seems anxious to find out his/her sexual identity, everything concurs to make the usual signs, such as dress codes, irrelevant. The narrator comments on the fact that the androgynous fashion of the 1960s meant that haircuts and clothes were hardly clues of somebody's sex, as men wore long hair and women wore trousers. This dislodging of identity in a modern society is furthermore illustrated by the metaphor of the airport where the character decides to remain "in transit." The symbolic force of the place lies in the fact that it stands for the condition of man in the second half of the twentieth century:

> Perhaps our whole century is in transit—a century whose suctions and pressures seek to dislodge you, its inhabitant, from it, a wind-tunnel of a century, on whose sides we sit insecure, scarcely able to snatch breath for the vacuum-force gale sucking us towards the sci-fi-futuristensce [*sic*] and the gritty, soiled, brickdusty, industrial-Zephyr sand-blasting us back to the Glasweg-Edwardian [*sic*] rose-red soot-gothi-stone [*sic*] tenements which our own architecture can't/hasn't-time-to think up a replacement for. (*In Transit*, 23)

These challenges confronting the individual in a modern society take the form of dislocations which are here well conveyed by the alliterations in [s] that are jostled against plosives in this description. Brophy also renders this general disappropriation of a sense of identity through a manifestation of what the narrator calls "linguistic leprosy" (11) opening the novel with: "Ce qui m'étonnait c'était qu'it was my French that disintegrated first" ("What surprised me was that it was my French that disintegrated first" 11). The simultaneity of the two processes of, on the one hand, the contamination of language and, on the other, the dislocation of the body, suggests that the two are structurally akin. This notion of a subject coming to existence through language is a leitmotif of the then emerging discourses of the philosophy and psychology of language which paid particular attention to the interaction between words and actions. J. L. Austin's *How to Do*

Things with Words (1962) paved the way for a theory of action in language, thus broadening the imagination of all. Similarly, though less well known, Robert F. Terwilliger's *Meaning and Mind, A Study in the Psychology of Language* (1968) exemplifies a scientific interest in the relation between action, perception, and language. Interestingly, the observations that are made in *Meaning and Mind* on "Language Disturbances" (224–57) seem to account for a majority of the dissolution and breaking up of language in Brophy's novel.

Not only does the narrator of *In Transit* lose control of language but he/she engages in a great number of slippages and neologisms. The novel is fraught with so many slippages, assimilations, and misuses of words that they "often seem to come out all mixed up together" (Terwilliger 227). Commenting on a pornographic book available at the airport's bookshop, for instance, the narrator pinpoints in a humorous tone the decadence of the book, itself a *mise en abyme* of the novel we are reading: "The management trussts [*sic*] the clientele has by now observed that at least one of the hero(in)es immolated throughout these pages is language" (219). Earlier on, the narrator engages in a Joycean purple patch:

> We Irish had the right word on the tip of our tongue, but the imperialist got at that. What should trip off if we trip over. Our slips are enlarged into tumbles of petticoats and camiknicks. We pick ourselves up out of their foam, high-camikicking. What begins as endemic lapsus linguae we peddle as precious lapis, with which we illuminate our Book of Sells (an early Book of Ours). We are never knowingly underbold. We are in the grip of compunsion. Youlysses have fore-suffered all. Before the Jew wandered, jew did. Is that another of your dog-headed Irish slips? (Pardon me, ma'am, your mollibloomers is shewin'.) Cynoscephalae, ladies, sigh no tom-moore. (We lost Thermopylae, the double pompom Bloom.) (35–6)

It would be easy to read those neologisms and "slips" as a playful reference to Joyce's *Ulysses* (1922) if it was not for the narrator's revelation that their choice to remain "in transit" must have originated in the loss of their parents in a plane crash at the age of three (*In Transit*, 6). It is therefore tempting to read these "language disturbances" as what the psychology of language would call "functional" disturbances. Terwilliger explains that these "are 'psychological' in nature. That is, they are learned or in some sense a product of the individual's life experience" (224), as opposed to "organic disturbances [which] are presumably due to some wound or injury to the central nervous system itself" (224). Terwilliger puts forward a "Freudian hypothesis" according to which "neurosis often stems from some emotionally traumatic experience" (227), a traumatic experience on which Brophy's narrative indeed capitalises. Furthermore, reading Terwilliger's notes on functional disturbances, one realises that the crisis experienced by the main character could be read as a schizophrenic one—in which case, the playfulness bestowed would be a lot more problematic. "Schizophrenia," he explains, "is a mental disturbance which commonly produces extreme functional language disturbances" (225). Terwilliger indeed reminds his readers that, "[i]t is not suprising that a person as withdrawn from social contact as is the schizophrenic would show disturbances in his use of language; for language is, after all, a social behavior by definition" (226). The psychologising of the narrator's experience that is hinted at by the text reveals an alienated subject who, precisely because they are excluded from society, can have a negative discourse on it. In other words, the alienated subject is an excellent trope to highlight all that is odd, and that yet the others take for granted, in society. At a time when social theorists like Raymond Williams (19–56) cannot stress the importance of communication in society enough, this playful experiment with the limits of language and meaning is indeed a radical gesture to draw attention to a vital process.

Brophy playfully draws our attention to these numerous thought processes in the chapter entitled "Interludibrium"—a pun on interlude and *ludibrium*, which is Latin for "mockery"—thus suggesting the *ludi*crous aspect of writing. The narrator explains:

> [y]ou might conclude I'm playing games, like a painter who includes in his picture a mirror in which he shews [*sic*] himself standing outside the picture painting it. An alienation effect may be a fiction within fiction, purporting to thrust the spectator back into the real world outside the frame but in practice drawing him deeper into the fictitious perspective. (69)

The passage, which is highly reminiscent of Velázquez's "Las Meninas" (1656), shows mirrors and frames being held indefinitely against each other. Ironically, this exposure of the artificiality of narratives also reveals the deceit of metafiction. Metafiction, as a secondary discourse, is indeed supposed to *enlighten* readers and not to *alienate* them.[4] As the psychologist S. I. Hayakawa states: "any ambiguity in word meaning is a possible source of conflict" and "[a]t the very least, it can render the act of communication suspect" (qtd. Terwilliger 230). Yet the uncertainty and mistrust introduced by the secondary discourse of metafiction is eminently didactic. For, effectively, what it achieves is to make the very concept of identity relative to perception:

> Suppose for the sake of the argument that I am a fictitious character or at least one who appears so to you. I have invited from you a certain temporary identification. I am prepared to be taken over, possessed, by you. In your own eyes, I don't doubt you, you are a very real part of the real world. But please remember that, to me it is you who are fictitious—the, indeed, entirely notional—character. (*In Transit*, 70)

Luigi Pirandello's *Six Characters in Search of an Author* (1921) seems to have set the blueprint for the fictional scenario in which the narrator operates. Given how scandalous the play was at the time, one can see how Brophy is deliberately seeking to further mystification. This is daring for an author insofar as this confusion the narrator generates can "in turn sugges[t] that the entire basis of social interaction is ambiguous and that there is no real contact or communication between people" (Terwilliger 230). By portraying a "sick" character and by provoking the reader, Brophy seeks to trigger a reaction in her reader. Raymond Williams even suggests that the representation of alienation in a work of art should not be feared as he explains that "[w]e respond to disturbance not only by remaking [ourselves], but, if we can, by changing the environment" (43). If our perception and our imagination are to have any significant impact on society, the experimental novel must be able to convey that what we hold to be real is always relative, and that, as historical subjects, we need to be able to *see* those structures and institutions that make us who we are.

Making us doubt our existence, making us question and challenge the texts society provide and demand we take for granted, such is the task of what Lamarque and Olsen identify as "notional fictions" (175). According to them, amid the five categories of fiction that address the question of truth and authenticity (these are "logical fictions," "epistemological fictions," "notional objects," "fictions of convenience" and "non-entities") the notional theory of fiction insists on the fact that "notional worlds are relative to individual subjects" (175). Lamarque and Olsen explain that this trend actually derives from the philosophy of phenomenology and Brentano's concept of intentionality (cf. Jacquette) of which the reader can indeed find traces in Brophy's novel. To paraphrase Lamarque's and Olsen's description of notional fictions, the beliefs in Brophy's novel must be "characterised *de dicto* not *de re*," that is to say, in the event of reading and writing (179). Effectively, Brophy reverses the polarities of power by demonstrating that the reader must play an active part in this construction if the novel is to work properly: "To be engulfed by you into an identification must be like being nibbled at, ticklingly, by a void. I have to summon my weightiest resources of gravity to take you seriously. I don't even know, for example, what sex you are" (71). The clever twist of this breaking of frames is that the mirror held to the text, then to the author, is ultimately held to the reader to reflect—nothing! It is common sense that the reader must remain unknown to the author, but here the author must conjure up her reader for the completion of her aesthetic and ethical project. Indeed, not only does it suggest that self-reflexivity is endless, but it also suggests that it can grant the reader power through language. In the previous quotation, the narrator underlined the relativity of the experience that validates or invalidates reality: "*In your eyes*, I don't doubt you, you are a very real part of the real world . . ." In effect, what the narrator does here is not only to defer authority but also to draw attention to where the nexus of truth lies, namely in the concomitant acts of writing and reading.

Reading *Albert Angelo* and *In Transit* together has the double advantage of putting into perspective their practices but also of encouraging a more refined understanding of the concept of narcissism in literature. Two types of narcissism emerge from this close reading: narcissism as a form of *mise en abyme* and narcissism as a manifestation of solipsism. The two types of narcissism can obviously not be exclusive of each other; if only because narcissism will always play a metafictional role. What I suggest is to take into account the prevalence of one over the other. *Albert Angelo* reflects the author's solipsism while making points about our reading habits that are just as entertaining and enlightening as Laurence Sterne's were in *Tristram Shandy* (1767). Conversely, the narcissism in *In Transit* more clearly bears on the metafictional device of the *mise en abyme* and serves the purpose of embedding a series of narratives while highlighting the absurdity on which they rely. What is interesting is to see how "narcissistic narratives" have in the end more to do with the figure of the author than with the creation of original formal devices. Johnson's authorial figure is desperately seeking attention and acknowledgement from his readers, while Brophy's is more adventurous and perhaps more inclined to draw a critical picture of the human condition in the twentieth century, and *a fortiori* today. Yet both tell a story of re-subjectivisation through the authoring process. Their identity as authors must be reinvented through their practice if they want to become alert subjects who can themselves encourage a sense of agency in their readers.

NOTES

1. The term "narcissistic narratives" comes from Linda Hutcheon's *Narcissistic Narrative: The Metafictional Paradox* (16).
2. This term was coined by William H. Gass in 1970 (cf. Waugh, *Metafiction* 2).
3. For an overview of the development of experimental fiction since the 1960s, see Onega and Ganteau. Authors discussed are John Fowles, Brigid Brophy, B. S. Johnson, Peter Ackroyd, Angela Carter, A. S. Byatt, Martin Amis, Zadie Smith, Will Self, Ian McEwan, and Julian Barnes.
4. David Lodge argues: "The function of the avant-garde is to win new freedom, new expressive possibilities, for the arts. But these things have to be won, have to be fought for; and the struggle is not merely with external canons of taste, but within the artist himself. To bend the existing conventions without breaking them—this is strenuous and heroic calling of the experimental artist. To break them is too easy" (170).

REFERENCES

Austin, J. L. *How To Do Things With Words*. Oxford: Clarendon, 1962. Print.

Beckett, Samuel. *The Unnamable*. London: Calder and Boyars,1975. Print.

Beitchman, Philip. *I Am a Process with No Subject*. Gainesville, FL: University Press of Florida, 1988. Print.

Brophy, Brigid. *In Transit*. London: Penguin, 1971. Print.

Chanady, Amaryll. "Une métacritique de la métalittérature: Quelques considérations théoriques." *Études françaises* 23.3 (winter 1987): 135–45. Print.

Dällenbach, Lucien. *Le récit spéculaire, Essai sur la mise en abyme*. (Trans. *The Mirror in the Text*). Paris: Seuil, 1977. Print.

Derrida, Jacques. *De la grammatologie*. (Trans. *Of Grammatology*) Paris: Editions de Minuit, 1967. Print.

Hutcheon, Linda. *Narcissistic Narrative: The Metafictional Paradox*. Ontario, Canada: Wilfrid Laurier University Press, 1980. Print.

Jacquette, Dale, ed. *The Cambridge Companion to Brentano*. Cambridge: Cambridge University Press, 2004. Print.

Johnson, B. S. *Albert Angelo. B. S. Johnson Omnibus*. London: Picador, 2004.

———. *Aren't You Rather Young to be Writing Your Memoirs?* London: Hutchinson, 1973. Print.

Josipovici, Gabriel. *What Ever Happened to Modernism?* New Haven, CT: Yale University Press, 2010. Print.

Joyce, James. *Ulysses*. London: Penguin Classics, 1992. Print.

Lamarque, Peter, and Stein Haugom Olsen. *Truth, Fiction and Literature*. Oxford: Clarendon, 1996. Print.

Lévinas, Emmanuel. *Autrement qu'être ou Au-delà de l'essence*. (Trans. *Otherwise than Being or Beyond Essence*) Paris: Le livre de poche, 2004. Print.

———. *Humanisme de l'autre homme*. (Trans. *Humanism of the Other*) Paris: LGF Poche, 1987. Print.

Lévi-Strauss, Claude. *Tristes Tropiques*. Paris: Union générale d'éditions, 1962. Print.

Lodge, David. *The Novelist at the Crossroads*. London: Routledge & Kegan Paul, 1971. Print.

Onega, Susana, and Jean-Michel Ganteau, eds. (2007) *The Ethical Component in Experimental British Fiction since the 1960s*. Newcastle: Cambridge Scholars Publishing, 2007. Print.

Pirandello, Luigi. *Six Characters in Search of an Author*. London: Penguin Classics, 1985. Print.

Rushdie, Salman. *Midnight's Children*. London: Cape, 1981. Print.

Saussure, Ferdinand de. *Course in General Linguistics*, Trans. of *Cours de linguistique générale*. Wiesbaden: O. Harrassowitz, 1967. Print.

Scholes, Robert E. and Kellogg, Robert. *The Nature of Narrative*. New York: Oxford UP, 1966. Print.

Sinfield, Alan. *Faultlines: Cultural Materialism and the Politics of Dissident Reading*. Oxford: Clarendon, 1992. Print.

Smith, Ali. *The Accidental*. London: Hamish Hamilton, 2005. Print.

Sterne, Laurence. *Tristram Shandy*. New York: W. W. Norton & Co., 1979. Print.

Terwilliger, Robert F. *Meaning and Mind, a Study in the Psychology of Language*. New York: Oxford University Press, 1968. Print.

Waugh, Patricia. *Harvest of the Sixties, English Literature and its Background 1960 to 1990*, Oxford: Oxford University Press, 1995. Print.

———. *Metafiction, Theory and Practice of Conscious Fiction*. London: Routledge, 1990. Print.

Williams, Raymond. "The Creative Mind." *The Long Revolution*. Harmondsworth: Pelican Books, 1981: 19–56. Print.

Winterson, Jeanette. *The Passion*. London: Bloomsbury, 1987.

Woolf, Virginia. *Orlando: A Biography*. Oxford: Oxford World's Classics, 2008. Print.

3 Literature in Process
Deleuzian Dynamics in the Fiction of A. L. Kennedy and Toby Litt

Lucy Prodgers

The philosophy of Gilles Deleuze, in part a reaction to structuralism and Freudian psychoanalysis, is primarily concerned with becoming rather than being. Interested in the flows and fluctuations of all—not just human—life, Deleuze's work moves away from stable singularities, such as the idea of a static human identity with an established and definable point of origin, towards a flux of multiplicities, ongoing processes to which there is no ground or foundation: a human being is a moment of relative stability in the continual flux of becoming. Deleuzian thought promulgates no standard meanings or rigid, hierarchical structures, but instead promotes the conception of blurred boundaries in which identities flow and interconnect without ever settling into definitive or stable formulae.

Central to Deleuze's philosophy is his interest in literature, as explored in his books *Kafka: Toward a Minor Literature*, cowritten with the psychoanalyst Felix Guattari, and *Essays Critical and Clinical*. His approach focuses on the question of what literature *does* over and above the more orthodox question of what it *means*. Moving away from representational readings which rely on reasserting preexisting formulae to explain a story's theme, characterisation, or plot, Deleuze contemplates how the very fabric of a story—its rhythms, language, tone, and style—can open up new potential spaces within which to think and question existence:

> A work of art always entails the creation of new spaces and times (it is not a question of recounting a story in a well-determined space and time; rather, it is the rhythms, the lighting, and the space-times themselves that must become the characters). A work should bring forth the problems and questions that concern us rather than provide answers. (Bontizer et al. 370)

For Deleuze, the point is not what literature can resolutely tell readers by re-presenting what is already given, but how it can provoke innovative thought, allowing us to sense, feel, and experience that which we have never sensed, felt, and experienced before. As such, a "minor" literature is one that is radically productive; unlike "majoritarian" or "major" literature which works to signify something that already exists, the force of minor literature resides in its power to create new experiences, going beyond what already "is" and producing future potentials for life. Part of minor literature's power lies in its ability to generate becomings. Becoming, according to Deleuze, is a nonfixed state, a continuous process of flux that is poles apart from being. An intense movement and an undoing of form, becoming is not a reproduction of some state of being or an imitation of some other life form, but a freeing of consciousness beyond binary and static identities typical of Western psychoanalytic thought.

Traditional interpretative readings of literature and identities, then, are discordant with Deleuze's approach in which the text is read in terms of its potential, rather than in terms of what it signifies. Minor literature generates affects, singular experiences that are freed from any individual subject or organising principle: they are sounds, sensations, and images which are not located within a certain character or subject, but are created through the language, rhythms, and tones of a text. As such, the interest is not in preexisting identity formations or categories, but in identity as a *dynamic*, a multiplicity of infinite flows and sensations which never actually come to rest in a single, stable form. This does not mean to say, of course, that all literature is open to a Deleuzian reading or, indeed, that we would even *want* to read all texts from a Deleuzian perspective. To simply apply the theory to literature would be in and of itself "anti-Deleuzian." There is not a simple or straightforward way in which a text can be read through Deleuze, there is no apparatus which can be applied and reapplied as such an apparatus would solidify the very becomings that the texts create.

Despite increasing academic interest in Deleuze's work over recent years, the impact has been mainly in the fields of film and philosophy. Of the work that has been produced on literature, most notably Ian Buchanan and John Marks's collection of essays, *Deleuze and Literature*, focus is divided between explorations into and analysis of Deleuze's own encounters with texts, on the one hand, and how texts can be read in a Deleuzian way, on the other. The latter use literature as "a way in and a way out of Deleuze" (5)—that is, the texts become a means by which one can enhance their understanding of Deleuzian philosophy or open up new areas of interest in his work. Timothy S. Murphy's "Only Intensities Subsist: Samuel Beckett's *Nohow on*," for example, extends Deleuze's original reading of Beckett to develop a better understanding of his concept of intensity: "Deleuze's thought stages or dramatises (rather than reads or explicates) Beckett's prose [and] Beckett's prose stages Deleuze's thought" (229). According to Murphy, then, Beckett's writing is not simply an example of Deleuzian "intensity" but is itself engaged in a philosophical activity of its own. Ultimately, however, the literature acts first and foremost as a guide to Deleuze's existing philosophies by offering new insights into his work.

In a departure from this focus, I will look at how the fiction of two contemporary authors, A. L. Kennedy and Toby Litt, not only offers insights into Deleuze's thinking but generates entirely new "Deleuzian" dynamics of its own to complement, rather than replicate, existing philosophy. Here it is the very dynamic of writing that becomes, unleashing entirely new subversive and deconstructive flows. The aim is not to shed light on or return to Deleuze's original writings on literature, then, but to foster the spirit in which these writings were conceived in a literary-critical aesthetics of my own. In the case of A. L. Kennedy, it is her short fiction, over and above her novels, which fully embraces this dynamic. The language of the stories refuses to be pinned down as traditional methods of interpretation are evaded and characters refuse to take coherent form. This is most interesting in the case of relationships and gender, as masculinities and femininities move from majoritarian structures to radical minoritarian lines of potential, which manifest productively in the powerful, emancipatory dynamic of what I term the "unwife." In the case of Toby Litt, the entire body of his work refuses categorisation as he moves from one genre to the next to create webs of connectivity with no clear sense of direction or intention. This becomes most apparent in his novel, *deadkidsongs*, which unleashes what I term an "apocryphising dynamic" of narration. Taken from the term apocryphal, which is normally used to describe biblical texts of doubtful authenticity, this apocryphising dynamic connects with Deleuze's concept of the rhizome. It has no main root or central point of organisation; rather, it consists of a complex interweaving of multiple paths, images, and ideas. Each moment of apocryphisation occurs as the novel reveals a further layer of potential, thus problematising the idea of a "true" version of events, of a linear trajectory or of stable character identities.

It would not be helpful to think in terms of either/or, here. Although the work of both authors could be read using orthodox interpretations of identity in its various forms, the texts themselves appear to repel such a reading. "Characters" continuously evolve and shapeshift as part of the very process of their being written. Rather than revert to fully rounded characters with psychological depths, the writing generates intense pulses of affectivity as what one may consider to be representations of "real life" suddenly shift to become blended with hitherto unforeseen strange, surreal, and dream-like potentials. To adopt conventional, identity-based readings of these texts would be unsatisfactory, then, as the work actively drives against orthodox interpretation.

In A. L. Kennedy's short stories, narrative patterns, characters, themes and motifs recur in a compulsive dynamic, as reality becomes entwined with complex imageries of shapes and lights which echo both within and across her four collections, *Night Geometry and the Garscadden Trains*, *Now That You're Back*, *Original Bliss*, and *Indelible Acts*.[1] According to Moira Burgess, "a typical Kennedy story opens in a wandering, casual mode. Hard to see what, if anything, is ever going to relate to anything else" (Burgess 100). To compound matters, the greatest challenge for Kennedy's characters is to "contemplate what it might mean to be 'one hundred per-cent me'" (Norquay 144). Indefatigably, they struggle for a kind of completeness that must ultimately remain unattainable. As dialogue becomes increasingly disjointed, consisting of "almost entirely guttural exchanges" (Tew 130), Kennedy's characters press on with their search for meaning, yet no matter what emotional intensity they find, their "lives are denied a density or profundity outside of the habitual" (124). The stories and the characters that inhabit them—desperate for "some proof, while I'm here, that I exist" (Kennedy, *Night Geometry* 34)—fail to locate meaningful reference points that might help them construct viable identities. As Helen Stoddart suggests, Kennedy's writing tends to "snag against the very thing it describes" (137), militating against its own *telos*.

Unlike in her novels, the events and characters that unfold in Kennedy's short stories never result in finalised accounts, or complete and coherent people, but instead dismantle established models of characterisation and emplotment. Whereas the novel demands psychological depth and consistency of character within the context of elaborate plot trajectories, the short story enjoys a greater freedom to experiment, capturing momentary impulses and providing snapshots of lives which come into being only for a fleeting moment of intratextual configuration. In their reading of Kafka's fiction, Deleuze and Guattari suggest that it is the novel which is most open to a becoming-minoritarian due to the short story's alleged tendency to "close up" (*Kafka* 38). Such a reading overlooks the subversive potential of the form, however. As Nicole Ward Jouve explains, in the short story collection "there is no risk of totalisation [. . .] the drive to homogenise experience by making what is diverse and specific into a unified whole, which is the overwhelming temptation of the [novel]" (37). This certainly seems the case in Kennedy's work. Several of her novels show her experimentalism, yet they do not go as far as the short fiction. *So I Am Glad* embraces the fantastical in the figure of Savinien Cyrano de Bergerac who returns from beyond the grave to modern-day Glasgow and the home of Jennifer Wilson, a sexual sadist who has lost the capacity to feel, for example. Yet although the novel is highly unconventional, it forms one coherent unit geared towards resolution: Jennifer's sadism is linked to her abusive childhood and eventually cured by her love for Savinien. The narrative comes full circle as Jennifer's discontent is replaced by a growing sense of satisfaction: "I will miss this and I will miss Savinien and I will be glad" (280).

In the short stories, such unity of plot and characterisation is never attempted. In "Breaking Sugar" (Kennedy, *Original Bliss* 109–23) the fantastical returns in Mr Haskard, "a quiet household god" (111), who lodges at the home of Nick and his wife. Although the story appears similar to *So I Am Glad*—it is uncertain whether Mr Haskard is real or a figment of the couple's imagination while his magical presence improves their waning love life—it becomes increasingly fissured by Kennedy's nonrepresentational techniques. Eccentric actions are never fully explained; no logical reason is given for why Mr Haskard and the wife take all of the couple's furniture outside one day, or indeed why, as the title suggests, Mr Haskard breaks sugar in the dark to create "unexpected light" (*Original Bliss* 123). The psychology of the characters dissolves in a convergence of sensations and affects, and the story seems desultory, refracting like the shards of light that Mr Haskard sends erupting into the air. The traditional story format is burst open, eschewing consistency in favour of a mobile textuality.

Just as the stories never coagulate into unities, the collections as a whole resist any definitive constructedness. Their individual ingredients freely interconnect and interpenetrate, at times clustering harmoniously while always maintaining their singular separateness. Although the stories return to familiar themes, characters, images, and even turns of phrase, each recurrence is strikingly distinct. The stories and collections thus become what I term "amorphic refrains," Deleuzian processes of limitless repetition and transformation that create a web of intimate connections within and across individual texts. These taut networks of connectivity remain in constant motion, refusing to settle into anything fixed or wholly recognisable. The short story genre thus offers Kennedy what the novel cannot: rather than "close up" as Deleuze and Guattari would suggest, it is experimental by definition, subversive, and able to rupture ruling narratives. The full potential of her stories can therefore only be revealed by moving away from purely representational readings towards a nonrepresentational understanding of how the writing disrupts and resists formalisation.

Kennedy's characters never evolve into rounded personages in any traditional sense, but constitute mere clusters of distinct, mutually corresponding sensations, affects, movements, and images. Rather than being fixed representations of certain types of people, her characters never individuate: they constantly shapeshift and vibrate, deconsolidating any stable subjectivity and thereby facilitating a flow of diverse singularities that touch each other and intersect in an evolution of ongoing emergence. In "Christine" (*Now That You're Back* 13–28) the eponymous figure appears as a chaotic, seemingly desultory flow of actions, images, and feelings. Rather than merely described as accident-prone, shy, or vague, the character *is* a clumsy walk that manifests as a fall in the playground and momentarily takes shape as the blood from an injury. Equally, both her personality and life history— her "identity"—manifest as a blushing face, a martyrdom, a pain, a "light kind of whoop," a mere impact upon the ground (14). Lacking psychological fibre in the traditional sense, her actions seem at once flawless and unmotivated; there are no biographical reference points that might explain her "nature." "Christine" does not form a stable character. She is not a representation at all, let alone that of a unified person, but an almost arbitrary convergence of multifarious intensities and affects. This unusual, expressly nonrepresentational process of characterisation pervades both individual stories and whole collections: Mr Haskard in "Breaking Sugar" becomes flashes of violet light in the darkness of a kitchen and a "minute shudder through the air," while Amanda in "Spared" (*Indelible Acts* 3–23) is the sweat in the curve of a knee, the ink of a phone number on Greg's wrist and the "flavour of her *maybe* and her *yes*" (4). These clusterings grow into modes of forever emergent *expression*, articulating emotions and themes by evocation alone instead of embodying them as absolute constituents of psychologically consistent, unequivocally intelligible beings.

This handling of identity continues in Kennedy's treatment of gender. A large number of the stories explore masculine attempts at dominance over the feminine, and abuse—sexual, emotional, or otherwise—at the hands of male or masculine characters is a regular occurrence. Her collections throb with variants of an ominous masculinity marking an adamant refusal to facilitate, let alone embrace, the liberatory potential of Deleuzian becoming. According to Deleuze and Guattari, all becomings must move through a "becoming-woman" due to woman's "special situation" (*Thousand Plateaus* 321). As "man" is the standard for humanity, the foundation upon which all other human identities (sexual, gendered, racial) are based, he is the "majoritarian par excellence" (322); his image perpetuates the idea that individuals are concrete beings with coherent psychologies and structures of identification. As a result, there can be no becoming-man, only a man-as-being: within the established model of "man," humanity is confined within ostensibly preordained structures rather than realising its potentialities out of and beyond such a restrictive organisation. There is no such standard or norm of "woman"—within majoritarian binary logic she is the indistinct, unknowable "other" of "man"—and she therefore possesses a greater potential to open up to desire as well as becoming due to the very obscurity which places her outside masculinist structuring and conceptualisation.[2]

Deleuze and Guattari's use of gender here is clearly problematic and has been treated with suspicion by feminists due to its seemingly phallocentric appropriation of woman. As Elizabeth Grosz suggests, becoming-woman "has very real effects, not in the valorization of femininity, but, on the contrary, in its neutralization or neuterization" (188). Although the implications of this cannot be avoided, for the purposes of brevity it is important here to consider the positive potentials that Deleuze and Guattari's becoming-woman can offer. As Grosz goes on to explain: "Becoming-woman involves a series of processes and movements outside of or beyond the fixity of subjectivity and the structure of stable unities. It is an escape from the systems of binary polarization that privilege men at the expense of women" (207). As such, although problematic, becoming-woman's championing of the molecular over the molar can provide useful ways of thinking beyond systems that stabilise and fix identities into traditional binary, homeostatic divisions,[3] as Kennedy's fiction clearly demonstrates.

The flows of Kennedy's ominous masculinities slow into near-coagulation, giving the molar illusion of fixed and static personages. In "Christine," the narrator's sensory capabilities appear jammed up within an opaque and dense masculinity. Remaining nameless, he does not communicate intimately with anyone as he does not "have that kind of nature" (*Now That You're Back* 23). His is a dark, inflexible masculinity, all the more troubling for its inarticulacy and secrecy; we learn that he harbours "ungentle things" (14). These disturbingly sinister aspects of his masculinity fix him within a man-as-being structure, his attempts to "disappear" only effecting a replication of pre-given identifications. He *pretends* to be from different regions of the country rather than *becoming* them through genuine emotional engagement. Despite his assertions to the contrary, such a mode of self-enactment must ultimately remain unsatisfactory. His urge to feign a fixed spectrum of identifications "makes all situations alike for me—I am consistently slightly out of place, but never uncomfortably so" (15). His attempt to create new identities ultimately fails as his impersonations create only further molar identifications. He finds himself unable to move towards a liberatory becoming-imperceptible—the ultimate becoming, a fluid state of consciousness where potential new planes can be perceived, where all is saturated and, through this saturation, becomes transparent—and instead is burdened with an alienating, majoritarian predictability.

Rather than assuming any absolute shape, Kennedy's masculine meshings undergo infinite and indefinite transformations throughout the collections, uncovering potentialities beyond the merely oppressive and destructive. The radically deterritorialising dynamic adopted by Kennedy means that "masculinity" no longer designates a fixed gender construct; nor is it confined exclusively to male characters. As characters fracture, both masculinities and femininities come to roam Kennedy's texts as free, vibrant forces, shattering attempts at monolithic or strictly cohesive gender identification as well as the illusion of a fixed gender order.

The ultimate exemplification of this comes in "Original Bliss" (*Original Bliss* 151–311) with the unleashing of what I term the "unwife" dynamic. The central figure of the story is Mrs Brindle, who appears the epitome of patriarchal wifeliness, tightly encapsulated in a stultifying routine of marital domesticity, "stumbl[ing] through tea-making and toast [. . .] even if you're crying tired" (*Original Bliss* 206). Yet from the outset she also displays a marked unconventionality: she first appears lying not in the marital bed, but alone on the living room floor unable to sleep (154), and for the first twenty-nine pages, even her role as wife remains vague, alluded to only by her conjugal title. Only gradually does her husband's presence become more pronounced and Mrs Brindle takes shape as an extreme binarist response to the unified structural stance of her husband's man-as-being. Her life with him turns out to be one of oppressive fixity as their marriage has lapsed into a vicious circle of domestic violence. Her daily routine is enforced upon her, the threat of violence hanging over her every action: "she'd tried to bring him a coffee in the sitting-room and dropped the cup [. . .] Mr Brindle [. . .] stepped forward and slapped her. 'Cunt.'" (290). Cowed by her husband's aggression and in direct response to his expectations, Mrs Brindle hardens into a wife-shape, assuming the form of woman that his masculinity demands. She embodies perfect passivity when with him, internalising his pulses of admonishment that connect with her own sensations to create unwholesome vortices of self-reproach and low self-esteem. She is "nothing but wrong ideas" (223) and she fears she does not work "correctly" (183) as her guilt thickens to cement her wifeliness.

The text traces the gradual dismantling of this wifely "shape" as Mrs Brindle reaches out to connect with the new masculine force of Edward, a professor of cybernetics. As affective clusterings, Edward and Helen appear at once strikingly different and strangely alike. Helen's fear of the masculine is a crucial constituent of her permanently guilt-ridden and self-punitive disposition: she panics when her husband tries to touch her, though she admits, "I don't mind that [. . .] fear seems to be good for me" (183). Her apprehensiveness resonates sharply, and shockingly, with the images of hardcore pornography to which Edward has become addicted: "The girl in this picture [. . .] I want to know how she feels right up inside, when I'm up to my balls in her" (219). The two initially seem entirely incommensurable. Just as Helen's experience has become arrested by her husband's virulent masculinity, Edward's original vibrancy is thwarted by hardcore pornography's sexually exploitative male gaze. Both afflictions result in difficulties with intimacy: Helen believes relationships are not her "strong point" (228) whereas Edward is "not good at touching" (249). In combination, however, these two contrasting masculine and feminine clusters turn out to be mutually remedial and begin to create a new potential for closeness and intimacy that ever more expressively reinvigorates the text. Each becomes a new dynamising rhythm in the other's life. Their intimacy unravels their assumed fixities and unmoors them. In Edward's presence, Helen becomes "networks. And webs. [. . .] Woven. Spun out of need and hope and, um, love" (261). Similarly, Helen's presence transforms Edward into "a leap of faith [. . .] a constant singularity—a perpetual process of massive change" (214). Their intimacy fuels their becomings as their companionship demolishes the oppressive majoritarian relationship structures that previously weighed them down so deleteriously. They become-together, the masculine and feminine rhythms of their clusterings harmonising to create a beautiful textual impulse of love.

Helen thus unleashes the dynamic of the "unwife," an anarchic, emancipatory becoming which ruptures the majoritarian constructions of wife and marriage. She vibrates like an epiphany onto herself, frighteningly powerful in her accomplished newness. Compelled by the expressive forces that she has come to experience, she resolves to show her naked form to her husband. Turning the guilt of her adultery into a pure, if potentially apocalyptic force, she pushes herself towards an incandescent moment of near-ruinous self-revelation: "You are aware of a lightness in your hands and limbs [. . .] the press of black air against your flesh, your cleaned and uncovered self [. . .] Mr Brindle is sitting up in bed [. . .] he lifts his head [. . .] sees what you need him to see [. . .] He is finding out what Edward has done to you and what you wanted Edward to do to you" (292). The scene is both terrifying and intensely liberating. The impending horror of Mr Brindle's violence, which Helen's attempt at apotheosis is sure to unleash, is to some extent assuaged by the joy incorporated in Helen's powerful demonstration of unwifely love and self-possession. Waking up badly hurt in hospital, she becomes a vision of liberation (she was "cut loose and floated for a time" [295]) and even the details of her beating become tinged with a sense of magic: "Helen watched and watched a sort of dance where Mr Brindle twirled her body so that it banged and cracked and splashes of light appeared with colours in time to his beat" (296). Her abuse takes on the quality of dance, its twirling rhythms resembling the intensive movements of a new femininity. It brings about an explosion of light and colours, releasing new lines of light while breaking out from the dark masculinity of her husband in a moment of passionate, at once intensely physical and disembodied, enlightenment. As Helen and Edward set out to make love for the first time at the end of the novella, their combined textual embodiment pours forth like liquid in gentle, sensual movements, affirming the redemptive strength of their connection: "they cover each other up [. . .] and begin the gentle, strenuous fight to cling and be still and kiss and move and touch every place when there are acres of places [. . .] wanting to be touched" (308). Touching, once forbidden, reveals itself as original bliss as the lovers' intimacy stimulates their integration one into the other, their pulses of masculinity and femininity harmonising for the first time to create pure and intensive flows of affect.

The Deleuzian affects at work in Toby Litt's fiction develop in an entirely different, albeit just as fascinating, way. On being asked why the titles of his books follow an alphabetical order, Litt states: "I would like people to read all my books, to read them in order, and to read them in relation to one another. They are to be thought of as a series, although not in the most obvious of senses. Each book reacts to the previous one and prepares the way for the next" (Litt, *Hospital* 101). At least superficially, then, Litt's production of texts appears highly structured, their alphabetical sequence producing a linear trajectory as the books build one upon the other in the creation of what one might want to term the "Littian" oeuvre. Yet on taking a closer look, it becomes clear that this structuring is not as straightforward as it seems. Litt is determined not to be pigeonholed as a writer who practises a specific style; rather, his work covers a range of genres. For example, the aptly titled *Ghost Story* is Litt's take on the haunted house tale, *deadkidsongs* is a *Lord of the Flies*-esque story about the violent extremes of boyhood, and *Finding Myself* is a tongue-in-cheek foray into "chick lit." There is no such thing as a typical Litt book, as each novel or short story collection develops its own distinct voice and direction.

The resistance to categorisation of Litt's texts and the seemingly anarchic manner in which they evolve frustrate conventional readings and this is particularly the case in his third novel, *deadkidsongs*. Deleuze's concept of the rhizome offers a way into this complex and often paradoxical text. In *A Thousand Plateaus* Deleuze and Guattari distinguish between arborescent systems, which have a pre-given hierarchical structure and destination, and rhizomatic machines which, with no actual beginning or end, are made up of diverse lines that can break, transform, and connect with any other points within that rhizome, regardless of how similar or disparate they appear to be. As such, multiple entryways are created: there is no unique "starting point" or path that has already been traced and which moves towards a specific end point; rather, there exists a perpetually transformative network of lines, or a matrix in motion (13–14). Whereas the "arbour" or tree incurs a trace relating each subsequent point back to an original point of departure, the rhizome unfolds as a productively erratic map, ceaselessly burgeoning new lines and connections which do not refer back to any one particular, central point, but constitute in and by themselves a new relational dimension. Although the initial appearance of Litt's texts as an alphabetically organised sequence must therefore strike us as arborescent, his books create an anti-order by virtue of their generic ambivalence, creating a marked alinearity which veers into unforeseen paths, even if read in linear order.

Familiar characters and settings appear throughout Litt's texts to create webs of connectivity. For example, Sheila Burrows, the reporter from *The Mirror* who hounds Conrad in *Corpsing*, returns in *Finding Myself*; the fictional town of Amplewick, Midfordshire, is the setting for both *deadkidsongs* and the short story "Of the Third Kind" (*Exhibitionism* 105–117); and hospital visits appear in all of the novels apart from *Beatniks*. Substantial links between the novels and short stories fail to manifest, however. Instead of producing any palpable intertextual structure, Litt's texts work rhizomatically to create new entry points into the corpus without any apparent logic. Motifs recur, yet in an abstract and seemingly unconnected way. This is most striking in the case of the image of the hare.

In the prologue to the novel *Ghost Story*, a hare bounds among trees that have grown out of library desks as Litt reveals that "for some little while now I have been chasing a hare" (xi). This hare is "a rapid-moving summat up ahead—a horizontal streak, appearing in front of and disappearing behind the vertical rhythm of the treetrunks; a real rubato, a pulse" (xvi–xvii). On Litt's website, this "chase" continues, so that, by following the clues left in an online blog story and on Litt's MySpace page, readers can find further writings and musings on the hare and its influence on his work. By clicking on images of the creature, a small piece of prose entitled "The hilltop" is revealed. It begins: "I am haunted by an image: oak trees on a hilltop against a sky full of thunderclouds [. . .] We chase the hare down the hillside, with no expectation of catching it. The hare of Identity" (*Hilltop*). Litt describes how this image of the hare and the trees has become a nostalgic reflection on his childhood embellished by a plethora of personal and cultural images and experiences:

> The hilltop trees are a nostalgic image, from my childhood. But they are a false, agglomerated image bodged together from at least a thousand different times and places, films and photographs, album covers and videos. I recognise this, and am haunted by how much this, the image I have chosen of my deepest Identity, no longer belongs to me. (Litt, *Hilltop*)

Litt is disturbed by the realisation that the very image in which he has invested as a foundation for his identity is, in fact, not a stable bedrock, but a process that is constantly in motion. The nostalgic trees turn from a reliable image into a map that undergoes perpetual transformation as new connections—with films, places, times—are made. As such, his "identity" cannot be captured as it is "already out of sight" (*Hilltop*). There is no singular or centred "me," no "belonging" to a particular version (or vision) of oneself; instead, there is a world of multiple potentials for life, which intersect and cross one another in a network of transverse flows.

The hare becomes an entryway for Litt into the rhizome of his own work, opening both his identity and his creativity up to the powers of Deleuzian becoming. It disrupts the imagined security and rigidity of the tree image—a marker of an arborescent system of representation and identification, or the centred "I"—and thus fractures it, taking flight down the hilltop and resisting capture. The hare cannot be caught as its identity refuses to be constrained into one specific, predetermined type, version, or image of being: its potential is open and it is endless. Rather, the hare constantly changes shape, morphing to reappear in another form elsewhere, both in the books as well as in life: "The hare in one place becomes another hare in another place. Spooky" (Litt, *Slice*). "I" is no longer singular, but multiple, no longer logically sequenced, but chaotic, no longer a traceable image, but a dynamic map, creating unforeseen lines of experience. By virtue of this intensive trait of the hare, the trees too become rhizomorphous, transforming from arborescent root-structures into rhizomatic flows (Deleuze and Guattari, *Thousand Plateaus* 17): the rhizomatic chase is on and it is virtually endless.

At first sight, Litt's novel *deadkidsongs* seems to be the haunting tale of boyhood masculinity gone awry. Set in the 1970s, the novel follows the adventures of four young boys—Andrew, Matthew, Paul, and Peter—over the course of one fateful year. Warfare and military games colour the boys' friendship; together they are "Gang." Not only do they have a "command structure" (10) and secret base camps set up around their village, but they also each have a rank: Andrew is Sergeant, Matthew a Sub-Lieutenant, while Paul and Peter are Corporals. Underlying the seemingly innocent child's play, a more sinister drama unfolds. The boys aspire to a violent and patriarchal ideal of masculinity. To appear weak by crying or breaking rank is to fail as a "proper" man. The members of Gang, led by Andrew, embark on increasingly dangerous and disturbing missions. Thus, after being grounded by his father, Paul is trapped by the other boys in an underground pit and subjected to an intensive and terrifying interrogation before being allowed re-entry into Gang (73). With similar relentlessness, Paul's father's cat is killed, and later the animal's decomposed body is found hanging from the family's washing line (321–2). Finally, the boys conspire to exterminate Matthew's grandparents. When Matthew dies very suddenly from meningitis and the boys learn that their friend's illness had initially been overlooked as something less serious by the elderly couple, they determine to exact revenge for their lost comrade. "The Dinosaurs," as the couple are now known to Gang, "must be extinct before Christmas" (206).

As this startling threat begins to play itself out and a battle for dominance between Andrew and Paul ensues, chaos reigns in the novel. Just as the boys' behaviour spirals out of control and their acts of revenge become increasingly more vindictive and disturbing, so the text and its coherency begin to unravel. There are constant shifts in narrative mode. Divided into four sections, the narrative of the main text changes from first-person plural, to first-person singular, to third-person limited, before reverting back to the first-person singular. There is a double ending: "Chapter Thirteen" is followed by "Chapter Thirteen, Also," in which totally different events take place, and there are stutters in pagination as page numbers in the second Chapter Thirteen revert back to follow Chapter Twelve and, at another point, disappear altogether. Within the individual chapters, each named after and supposedly recounted from the point of view of one of the boys, the tone and temporal context of the narrative changes. Narratives which once reported events as they happened and in a childish tone, switch to narratives which reflect back on events in a more distanced and adult manner, and vice versa.

Far from being the conventional novel one may have expected, the narrative becomes ever more disjointed and fragmented as a confusing and often contradictory welter of events unfolds. There is no definite or reliable notion of what has taken place, let alone of the final outcome or resolution, as narratives break down, stutter, and overlap. As more and more mutually incompatible accounts of significant events occur, multiple realisations of the friends are created so that ultimately the boys begin to merge: one boy's acts in one section are attributed to another boy in a preceding section and so on, until in the final chapter the ambiguous title "Peter (Paul)" creates a further sense of disorientation. One feels compelled to ask just who is narrating and what is the authorial motivation behind the creation of these multifarious narrative perspectives.

By virtue of the constant shifts in narration, then, each chapter produces a new version of the boys, which does not merely fix a different interpretation or "view" of them, but remains productively inchoate as a tentative actualisation of their virtual potentials. According to Deleuze, there are both virtual and actual characterisations of the real; a virtual image is just as real as an actual image, even though it is immaterial. The actual-real consists of everything that exists independently of our perceptions of it, such as bodies and objects, whereas the virtual-real is the realm of transcendental conditions of experience, such as ideas and intensities. Each actuality is surrounded by a "cloud of virtual images [. . .] composed of a series of more or less extensive coexisting circuits, along which the virtual images are distributed, and around which they run" (*Dialogues* 148). Unlike the oppositions true/false and real/unreal, then, Deleuze's distinction of the actual/virtual is not polar, as the two terms are not diametrically opposed; rather, an actual image is always surrounded by a "cloud" of virtual images and, similarly, virtual images react to, blur into, and overlap with actual ones. Since the reality of an actual being must always spring from some virtual idea or image, every perception and experience must move through a dynamic virtual plane to be actualised. An object therefore exists not only in its actual material state, but also in virtual form, in the ideas we hold about it.

When *deadkidsongs* unfurls different Deleuzian becomings of the boys, what takes place is not a question of real and unreal, true and false: every becoming is distinct and equally real. Instead, what we come to witness is a process of actualisation whereby virtual ideas and newly imagined realisations of the boys are actualised through the very process of writing and reading. There is not one "proper" version, but instead an almost limitless, unforeseen quasi-random proliferation of virtual and potential boy-becomings, some of which actualise through the process of narration, whilst others remain mere potentialities. The novel therefore creates a world in which the reader cannot comfortably rely on one rational realm of experience, but must open themselves up to the potential of diverse experiential flows.

To add to these complex narrative layers and becomings, *deadkidsongs* is surrounded by multiple frames, or, what Gerard Genette terms the "paratext" (1–2). The paratext encompasses devices both inherent within the text, such as the title page, dedication and preface, as well as those extraneous to it, such as its advertising campaign and critical reception. It acts as a hermeneutic key, manipulating the reader's expectations and providing clues about the "type" of text they are about to read. Rather than reliably guide the reader towards what is to come, the multiple paratextual layers of *deadkidsongs* work to dislocate and productively alienate expectation by compounding the mystery of "what actually happens." For example, on what can only be described as the contents page, the sequencing of "SUMMER–AUTUMN–WINTER–SPRING" suggests that the text will trace some kind of strictly chronological progression. But spring never arrives in the novel, and against expectation, the fourth section of the book is titled "WINTER, ALSO." As a result, the text seems cut short, prompting the question whether the work deliberately withholds information, or whether indeed it is finished.

By far the most obtrusive paratextual layer in *deadkidsongs* is provided by Litt's move to furnish each chapter with an epigraph, introducing a snippet of verse from Gustav Mahler's song-cycle version of Friedrich Rückert's *Kindertotenlieder (Songs on the Death of Children)*. Providing the basis for the novel's title—and thus demonstrating their significance to the text—the poems were originally written by Rückert in response to the tragic deaths of two of his children over a period of just sixteen days. In sharp contrast to the boys in *deadkidsongs*, the children in *Kindertotenlieder* are represented as angelic, blessed, and idealised creatures. Far removed from the harbingers of death and violence at the centre of *deadkidsongs*, the children in *Kindertotenlieder* are paragons of innocence. Accentuating by virtue of their dissimilarity the powerful extremism of the boys' behaviour, the epigraphs become a crucial part of the novel's Deleuzian dynamic.

Litt admits that his translations of the poems are fairly improvised and "quite distorted" (qtd. in McCrum, n.pag.) and, as a result, both their authenticity and authority are dubious. At times the translations oscillate between the bizarre and the totally corrupt. By the final chapter, the verses have changed virtually beyond all recognition. For example, what in Emily Ezust's translation details the children resting as if at their maternal home, unafraid of any storm and "covered by the hand of God" (Rückert n.pag.), transmogrifies in Litt's version into, "They rest, as after Matricide,/Not Storm-terrified,/By Godhead sanctified,/They rest, as after Patricide,/They rest, as after Fratricide" (373b).[4] Hence, rather than helping to amalgamate the novel's vision, Litt's epigraphs create further disruption. Stability and coherency are eschewed in favour of an errant, quite deliberately deviant form of storytelling. Instead of elucidating and "containing" the novel, as one would expect, the paratextual frames work only to obfuscate, disperse, and unravel.

It is this layering of subversive paratext together with the frequent shifts in narrative mode, time, and voice that unleashes what I designate as an "apocryphising dynamic" of narration, which, through an obfuscation of the text, ultimately unleashes endless virtual potentials for life. As such, the pulsing rubato of Litt's creative hare is let loose: it reverberates with a plethora of virtual and actual images to open up multiple potentialities and narrative "versions" which can fork, split, and jump to create further new zones of narrational experience. Each new fork stutters the preceding version to destabilise its authenticity and the idea of a singular "truth" or "fact." If one is to attempt a traditional, or what Deleuze might term an arborescent, reading of *deadkidsongs* by querying its underlying meaning, the "true" and chronological sequence of events and the "real" psychologies and personalities of its characters, one is ultimately thwarted by the narrative's insistence on apocryphisation. The apocryphising dynamic synthesises the text's disparate versions into a Deleuzian matrix of multitudinous potentialities which incessantly vibrate and echo to produce a ripple of new textual affects. As *deadkidsongs* progresses, the authenticity of what we at first assume to be a reliable text narrated from the perspectives of the four boys comes into doubt. There is no clear indication as to which one constitutes the text's authoritative version as the very dynamic that informs and propels the narrative works simultaneously to unmoor, rupture, and undermine its integrity.

In *deadkidsongs*, as multiple and disparate narrational potentials unfold and the paratext unravels apocryphally, the reader's suspension of disbelief is frustrated. We are reminded that what we are reading *is* a fiction, and the parallel world into which we attempt to immerse ourselves buckles to burgeon a myriad of new shoots and directions of growth. Manifold worlds are created as endless versions of characters, situations, and plots are unleashed within a kinetic Deleuzian matrix. The traditional, arborescent text that the novel could have been—a straightforward rewrite of Golding's *Lord of the Flies*, for example—begins to resound with apocryphal potentiality. Textual echoes ripple outwards in eccentric waves, so that as the end of the novel is reached, the anticipated arrival of "Spring" becomes "Winter, Also," we are faced with not only two distinct actualisations of winter, but all the virtual potentials of the seasons that have not yet been actualised. Within each of those versions, further layers radiate: Paul's parenthetical echo of Peter in "Chapter Thirteen, Also" creates another double layer, for example. The reader must relinquish their suspension of disbelief as Litt's authorial control has yielded to the very dynamics of the narrative which he writes: his hare is on the run in a vibrant matrix of storytelling. It seems Litt can no longer even attempt to coherently structure the disparate resonances of narration that actualise themselves in his writing. Ironically, then, it is only through its obscurity that the novel's virtual potentiality fully reveals itself.

Despite clear stylistic and thematic differences, the fiction of both Kennedy and Litt frustrates traditional literary critical approaches which search for meanings or identities within preexisting social and cultural frameworks. The texts discussed traverse and elude conventional categories and molar structures on a hare-like chase which never settles or slows for long enough for characters to simply "be." Unthinkable and unimaginable paths unfold, intersect, and connect to create multitudinous matrices of potential for life. Like Litt's hare, identities do not form and settle on the page, but evolve and disperse within complex narrative dynamics that have no apparent direction and no end point: the texts produce no answers, only more questions. Though it would not be possible to read all texts in this way—much fiction is not open to the becomings that Litt and Kennedy's work continuously unleash—and the attempt to establish a specific Deleuzian method of interpretation would seem beside the point, a freer and more liberatory approach to both reading and writing could offer both authors and academics alike a new way to conceive and interact with literature and philosophy. Such an approach would not merely assert new models of thought but engage in recurrent processes of transformatory becoming which see beyond the static and the concrete and look instead towards the unknown and the potential.

NOTES

1. Kennedy has since published a fifth collection of short fiction, *What Becomes.*
2. Importantly, Deleuze and Guattari assert that ultimately—irrespective of their biological sex—all human beings can become-woman as it "necessarily affects men as much as women. In a way, the subject in a becoming is always 'man', but only when he enters a becoming-minoritarian that rends him from his major identity" (*Thousand Plateaus* 321).
3. Ian Buchanan and Clare Colebrook's *Deleuze and Feminist Theory* provides an excellent way into this debate, whilst also considering how Deleuze's work may be of use to feminism.
4. To prevent confusion, the pagination of quotations from the second Chapter Thirteen will be referred to as "b."

REFERENCES

Bonitzer, Pascal, et al. "The Brain is the Screen. An Interview with Gilles Deleuze." *The Brain is the Screen: Deleuze and the Philosophy of Cinema.* Ed. Gregory Flaxman. Trans. Marie T. Guirgis. Minneapolis: University of Minnesota Press, 2000. 365–73. Print.
Buchanan, Ian, and John Marks, eds. *Deleuze and Literature.* Edinburgh: Edinburgh University Press, 2000. Print.
Buchanan, Ian, and Clare Colebrook, eds. *Deleuze and Feminist Theory.* Edinburgh: Edinburgh University Press, 2000. Print.
Burgess, Marie. "Disturbing words: Rose, Galloway and Kennedy." *Calemadonnas: Women and Scotland.* Ed. Helen Kidd. Dundee: Gairfish, 1994. 92–103. Print.
Deleuze, Gilles. *Essays Critical and Clinical.* Trans. Michael A. Greco and Daniel W. Smith. London: Verso, 1998. Print.
Deleuze, Gilles, and Felix Guattari. *Kafka: Toward a Minor Literature.* Trans. Dana Polan. Minneapolis, MN: University of Minnesota Press, 1986. Print.
———. *A Thousand Plateaus: Capitalism and Schizophrenia.* Trans. Brian Massumi. London: Continuum, 2004. Print.
Deleuze, Gilles, and Claire Parnet. *Dialogues II.* Trans. Barbara Habberjam and Hugh Tomlinson. London: Continuum, 2002. Print.
Genette, Gérard. *Paratext: Thresholds of Interpretation.* Trans. Jane E. Lewin. Cambridge: Cambridge University Press, 1997. Print.
Grosz, Elizabeth. "A Thousand Tiny Sexes: Feminism and Rhizomatics." *Gilles Deleuze and the Theater of Philosophy.* Ed. Constantin V. Boundas and Dorothea Olkowski. New York: Routledge, 1994. 187–212. Print.
Jouve, Nicole Ward. "Too Short for a Book?" *Re-reading the Short Story.* Ed. Clare Hanson. London: Macmillan, 1989. 34–44. Print.
Kennedy, Alison L. *Indelible Acts.* London: Vintage, 2003. Print.
———. *Night Geometry and the Garscadden Trains.* London: Vintage, 2004. Print.
———. *Now That You're Back.* London: Vintage, 1995. Print.
———. *Original Bliss.* London: Jonathan Cape, 1998. Print.
———. *So I Am Glad.* London: Vintage, 1996. Print.
———. *What Becomes.* London: Jonathan Cape, 2009. Print.
Litt, Toby. *Beatniks.* London: Penguin, 2004. Print.
———. *Corpsing.* London: Penguin, 2000. Print.
———. *deadkidsongs.* London: Penguin, 2001. Print.

———. *Exhibitionism.* London: Penguin, 2002. Print.

———. *Finding Myself.* London: Penguin, 2004. Print.

———. *Ghost Story.* London: Penguin, 2005. Print.

———. "The hilltop." *Toby Litt.* N.p., n.d. Web. 7 Apr. 2008. <http://www.toby-litt.com/thechaseproper.html>.

———. "Hospital 101, 13th March 2007." *Toby Litt.* My Space, 2007. Web. 7 April 2008.

———. "Slice: Unfiction, 29th April 2008." *Toby Litt.* My Space, 2007. Web. 29 October 2008.

McCrum, Robert. "It's a boy book." *The Observer* 11 Februray 2001. Web. 24 April 2008.

Murphy, Timothy S. "Only Intensities Subsist: Samuel Beckett's *Nohow On.*" *Deleuze and Literature.* Ed. Ian Buchanan and John Marks. Edinburgh: Edinburgh University Press, 2000. 229–250. Print.

Norquay, Glenda. "'Partial to Intensity': The Novels of A. L. Kennedy." *The Contemporary British Novel.* Ed. James Acheson and Sarah C. E. Ross. Edinburgh: Edinburgh University Press, 2005. 142–53. Print.

Rückert, Friedrich. "Kindertotenlieder." *The Lied, Art Song, and Choral Texts Archive.* Trans. Emily Ezust. Rec Music Foundation, n.d. Web. 1 December 2008.

Stoddart, Helen. "'Tongues of Bone': A. L. Kennedy and the problems of articulation." *British Fiction of the 1990s.* Ed. Nick Bentley. London: Routledge, 2005. 135–49. Print.

Tew, Philip. "The Fiction of A. L. Kennedy: The Baffled, the Void and the (In)visible. *Contemporary British Fiction.* Ed. Richard J. Lane, Rod Mengham and Philip Tew. Cambridge: Polity, 2003. 120–39. Print.

4 History's Subjects

Forming the Nation in Andrea Levy's *Small Island*

Ranu Samantrai

With the concept of a Black British identity firmly established in the national imagination, it is difficult to remember that scarcely a generation ago the notion was contested and, for many, outlandish.[1] For its apologists, the moniker rejected the demand for assimilation into a normative white Britishness and altered the presumptive racial terms of national belonging. By contesting the racial closure of the nation, Black Britishness promised to destabilize the foundational assumptions of romantic nationalism. It would do so by replacing biological essentialism with political contingency, such that the nation imagined as a small, enclosed community of kin would give way to a fluid collective of disparate peoples brought together by their joint history.

But the discourse of nationalism has proven surprisingly resilient. Rather than fatally unravelling an exclusionary enclosure, Black Britishness itself has become assimilated and nationalised, ironically through the very device of a shared history. In this chapter, I will argue that even as we break with biological or cultural essentialism as the foundation of the nation, history can step in to suture symbolic borders. In fact, threats to ideological closure—the role attributed to the black presence in the national formation—provide necessary drama for the teleological story that posits the past as the deep history of the present. I will look to two examples of historical narratives, one theoretical and the other fictional, that trace a linear causality from past to present. Both Stuart Hall and Andrea Levy use the past to authorize the postcolonial black presence in Britain. In so doing they position the Black British as the avatars of a good, because diverse, society. Formal analysis proves particularly useful for examining how the impact of the Black British is contained and domesticated to serve the telos of the nation, which retains its primacy as the true subject of history.

THE BANANA BOAT ARMADA

In the midst of delineating vast global and epistemological shifts in his oft-quoted essay on "Ethnicity," Stuart Hall enacts a little drama between England and its postcolonial settlers. Much of the essay is devoted to explicating the untethering of the modern self from its moorings in what Hall identifies as the "great stable collectives of class, race, gender and nation" (12). The nation serves as prime example of a collective under attack from above and below, within and without. "[Besieged] from on top by the interdependence of the planet," it is simultaneously fragmenting as "Peoples and groups and tribes who were previously harnessed together in the entities called the nation-states begin to rediscover identities that they had forgotten" (13).

At least two responses are possible to such challenging conditions. For Hall, one tack is exemplified by Margaret Thatcher, the prime minister who promised to make Britain great again. Thatcher's promise amounted to a determination to revivify an imperial Britain, to restore an almost lost ideal that is capable of providing a secure tether in a world of flux. And, indeed, with victory over Argentina regarding the Falklands/Malvinas, she was able to declare "the re-discovery of ourselves": "[We] rejoice that Britain has rekindled that spirit which has fired her for generations past and which today has begun to burn as brightly as before. Britain has found herself again in the South Atlantic and will not look back from the victory she has won" (Thatcher). This tactical retreat to a better past, or rather, this determination to prolong a narrative from the past regardless of its obsolescence, is for Hall the essence of Thatcherism:

> Thatcherism is *in defense* of a certain definition of Englishness. England didn't go to the Falklands War inadvertently. It went because there was something there about the connection of the great imperial past, of the empire, of the lion whose tail cannot be tweaked, of the little country that stood up to the great dictator. It's a way of mythically living all the great moments of the English past again. (17)

But, as Hall tells the story, Thatcher's ambition to consolidate an identity at home by imposing a presence overseas was checked by "some *other* British folks"—the great wave of postwar migration from South Asia and the Caribbean. With gleeful flourish Hall declares: "Just in the very moment when they decided they could do without us, we all took the banana boat and came right back home" (17).

In Hall's account, two armies—or rather, navies, since both are aquatic expeditionary forces—face off. But the stage for this drama is history itself; on that battleground the two forces are not equal. The first force, the English armada, redoubles on itself. Having pushed outward, it returns to its true mission at home: the rediscovery of its past self. Its victory is the efflorescence of the past, its journey home a return to that past. All the activity of this force accomplishes a nearly closed loop. Having nowhere to remain and nothing much to do in the Falklands/Malvinas, the English armada comes about in the middle of the Atlantic and returns home. It thus draws its line back to itself and is left finally floating alone, self-enclosed, anchored to nothing but its own deep past.

The second force, the advancing wave of migrants and settlers, is uni-directional. It does not turn back. Unlike English battleships, this armada of banana boats has landed successfully. "We now stand," declares Hall, bringing the expeditionary force to shore (17). And this stealth force adapts quickly to its new home and forges its own path to the future:

> Every time they walk out on the street some of us—some of the Oth-er—are there. There we are, *inside* the culture, going to their schools, speaking their language, playing their music, walking down their streets, looking like we own a part of the turf, looking like we belong. Some third generation Blacks are starting to say 'We are Black British.' (18)

This is a victory speech, dipping over into triumphalism as its repetitions emphasize the scope of the surprise conquest. But the conquest, although proceeding through the repeated confrontation of "we" and "their," has a twist, for in victory the conquerors are transformed. In the space of two sentences, settlers morph from outsiders and newcomers to part owners (not a complete takeover, notably), to belongers, to an entirely new being, one specific to this place. At the end of the paragraph, "they" have dropped away and only "we" remain.

The contrast is dramatic: whereas the English appear to have no option other than hoping for time to stop and for the past to continue without end, their former slaves and servants own the future. Moreover, the failure of the English strategy is inevitable, for even should past selves struggle on, they will find their safe home, their place of retreat, transformed from the inside. They cannot avoid obsolescence, in sharp opposition to the beings that can adapt, thrive, and so shape the future. If the English are not to be cast adrift in a future in which they have no secure place, their only hope is to share the turf—the ground where, as Hall has already declared, the Black British now stand, and where, presumably, all old selves must give way to new.

Victory and defeat, then, are not straightforward, for both lead to a new settlement forged by transformation and sharing. In the same manner, past and future are interestingly nuanced. The Black British are harbingers of the future for Hall because this identity does not stake its legitimacy on an essence—be it the biological essence of racialism or the folk essence of romantic nationalism. Instead it is situational and experiential, evolv-ing in response to the conditions of its existence. This is the great lesson of the notion of Black Britishness: rather than clinging to obsolete collec-tive structures that are everywhere in disarray, Black Britishness offers a usable model of a mobile identity. Especially as we move from modernity to postmodernity, its way of doing identity evidences the vanguard status of the Black British. But, again, past and future are not allowed to remain in mutually exclusive opposition. Just as he appears to be sounding the death knell for Thatcher's appeal to the past, Hall adds, "the past is not only a position from which to speak, but it is also an absolutely necessary resource in what one has to say" (18–9). There is much to honor in "hidden histories," much to value in "traditions and inheritances of cultural expression and creativity" (18).

Hall resolves the opposing pulls of continuity and change by advocating a nonessential relation to the past, an attitude that acknowledges that we construe the past in part in response to the present: "We tell ourselves the stories of the parts of our roots in order to come into contact, creatively, with it. So this new kind of ethnicity—the emergent ethnicities—has a relationship to the past, but it is a relationship that is partly through memory, partly through narrative, one that has to be recovered" (19). Here again the Black British play a privileged role, as do the settlers who preceded them. Already the banana boat armada enacted a paradoxical journey. Imagining himself at the scene Hall turns the metaphors of imperialism on their head: "We turned up saying 'You said this was the mother country. Well, I just came home'" (17). Of course, for many who made that voyage the arrival was not a return and not to a home, except in the metaphorical sense—that is, in the sense that turns the narratives of the past into resources for the present, the very process at work in Hall's rhetoric. When he declares, "We now stand as a permanent reminder of that forgotten, suppressed history" (17–8), Hall proffers a model of a creative construction of the past. In his brief account we see enacted the creative relation that puts the past and present into productive contact in such a way that the narrative of the past serves the needs of the present.

These passages from Hall are an object lesson for history writing, particularly for those who look to the past as a resource for creating usable narratives for the present. The first principle we can derive concerns the persistence of the past, with attempts to jettison it met by an unexpected haunting and a return of the repressed in the heart of the protected present. But, second, haunting also suggests that rather than existing as a fully recoverable experience, pace Thatcher, the past can be discerned only in its unexpected impact upon the present. We are not mired in the past; nor is its meaning fixed. On the contrary, its implications have to be interpreted within the terms provided by the present. Third, such creative construction, exemplified by the haunting of a former colonial power by its formerly colonised, has enormous consequences for the present. In the turn of the dialectic it is the dispossessed that are best able to take advantage of the conditions of the present. Prepared by previous losses of their experiential worlds and already adept at reinventing themselves, migrants become avatars in the global transition from modernity to postmodernity. And, finally, these newly privileged figures are also the hope of the nation's rescue: the nation can find a better future if it is willing to learn from those it would disavow and acknowledge itself as a shared space co-created by settlers old and new.

But in every strategy there are dangers. Hall is able to make enormous claims for the historical value and political efficacy of the Black British, but at a cost. Examining the scene of meaning making we see not only that positive narrative outcome, but also the meanings that are foreclosed as the past is made productive for the present. Here a slippage is particularly revealing: initially Hall asserts triumph for a collective comprised of "Jamaica, Pakistan, Bangladesh, India" (17)—of course already a representative sampling of the former colonies, but a gesture toward heterogeneity nonetheless. That representative gesture gives way as Jamaicans come to stand in for all others, as when Hall says, "We're not Jamaicans any more" (18). The story being told is of how the many became one, how the disparate peoples of the empire became the Black British. The story itself is the process writ small: in order to serve its narrative function, the new collective coheres into "We" by progressively shedding its original multiplicity, strategically preferring the rule of the same to the messiness of its past. Hall confirms as much with the story of how he learned to think of himself as an immigrant and Black, rather than as Jamaican (15).

My purpose in this counter-reading is not to scold against the trap of identity formation with its inevitable homogenisation of difference. Indeed, Hall uses his arrival story to caution against that premature closure and advocate in its stead a nonfoundational identification that recognizes negotiation with difference as the condition of its possibility. And perhaps the process of generalisation, homogenisation, and substitution is necessary to construct a portable narrative that allows multiple pasts to lead up to this present. All linear historical accounts posit a causal relation between past and present; the nation is hardly alone in excluding other possible meanings of the past, other possible relations between past and present. Rather than simply berating that gesture, I'm interested in thinking through its consequences. In this instance, the story of the Black British sutures the nation's past to its future. Besieged by the twinned forces of globalisation and localisation, and with its imperial pilings crumbling, the nation requires another source of stability, authority, and relevance. It finds renewal as the location where the dialectic of history makes its next move, where the disenfranchised emerge into prominence and become the agents of history itself. And the nation survives as the still privileged form of history. The Black British may instigate certain adjustments in content, but at the level of form they provide the alibi for the continuing validity of the nation.

We can read Hall's account along the grain of his intentions as the rescue of a weakened nation, or against the grain as the success of a wily one. My objective is not to unveil a true meaning; more interesting is the slipperiness of meaning itself, evidenced in the multivalence of Hall's rhetoric and in the resourcefulness of a discourse as compelling as nationalism. Here we see how the claim of a shared history, intended to disrupt the logic of romantic nationalism with the introduction of contingency, can become the device that contains the threat of the Black British. By linking the imperial past to the postimperial present and on to the multiracial/cultural future, this account of the Black British bridges over potentially disruptive fissures in the national story. Its protagonists might play the role of rescuing hero, but in Hall's linear history the nation competes, perhaps successfully, for the role of telos. It eclipses the Black British because it is the ground of their existence in the present; its present makes sense of their past; and it holds out the promise of a utopian future when it will be the site of the finally good, because diverse, society.

AN ETHIC OF EXCHANGEABILITY

What are the consequences of the inclusion/conscripting of blacks in the national story? For Andrea Levy, the consequences are both personal and social. She explains, "My need to explore my own heritage and to bring that heritage into the mainstream of British thought or British understanding is powerful" (Interview 330). Her own father came to England from Jamaica in 1948 upon the now iconic Empire Windrush. By incorporating that family history into her fiction Levy resists the "collective forgetting" that would discard certain pasts as "not even worthy of history [. . .] not even worthy of being remembered"—a forgetting she regards as "horror" (Lima 74). Joined to that personal or familial quest is the problem of a nation that, as the protagonist of *Fruit of the Lemon* puts it, is "unaware of our shared past" (326; qtd. Lima 56). To counteract that ignorance Levy emphasizes the importance of bringing her parents' story "and their parents' story and their parents' parents' story into the mainstream of British culture" (Interview 329). That is to say, she does not regard these stories as marginal or the experiences therein as characterising a minority. On the contrary, these historical experiences warrant recognition as forming the heart of a shared culture.

In *Small Island*, Levy sets out to secure that recognition by way of the story the nation tells itself about itself. The novel's four protagonists, two black and two white, are brought together in the London of 1948 as the nation emerges from the war victorious but nearly devastated, with its grip on its empire beginning to loosen, and on the cusp of a new chapter in its history. Hortense and Gilbert, arriving from Jamaica, take lodgings in a once grand, now decrepit house owned by Bernard and maintained in his absence by Queenie. At the end of the novel, the four converge around a biracial baby, child of Queenie and another Jamaican serviceman. The baby, a literal manifestation of co-creation, is given by Queenie to Hortense and Gilbert. The narrative closes with the two new settlers assuming responsibility for this small citizen of the tired nation as they leave to begin rehabilitating another decrepit, though salvageable old house.

Unusually, the novel, which has no epigraph, provides that authorial commentary at the end of the narrative with the oft-quoted words of Winston Churchill: "Never in the field of human conflict has so much been owed by so many to so few" (439). Intended by Churchill to honor the Royal Air

Force during the Battle of Britain in 1940, here the words acknowledge the many warriors and many battles represented by Levy's characters. Indeed Levy finds the quotation "wonderfully apt for the Jamaicans, the guys off the Windrush (of which my Dad was one), coming into this country and having to forge their identity and make this life for people like me" (Interview 337). She muses, "I just thought, I wonder if Churchill were alive, could I persuade him to say that this could be apt as well for the immigrant population?" Answering her own question, "I doubt it," she nevertheless redirects Churchill's gesture of honor. Normally reserved for combatants, Levy harnesses its affective value for the less glamorous stories of women and men, black and white, who maintained and revitalised a decrepit, though potentially salvageable country.

The affective valence of Churchill's words augment the intensity of the narrative climax as a child is relinquished by a grieving mother and hesitantly accepted by a hopeful new family. With a powerful plea to the emotions the novel aims not only to persuade readers to accept a revised historical narrative but to feel for black precursors as deeply as for white as fully members of the national family. The form of the domestic melodrama casts an enveloping arm around black and white protagonists alike, drawing them into the familial circle as all participants in the drama that initiates the child's future. Levy thus aims to transform that intangible yet determinative quality of everyday, collective life that Raymond Williams tried to capture as "structures of feeling" (Williams 129). If the reader accepts her account and responds affectively as directed, the novel contributes to the experience of "conviviality"—Paul Gilroy's term for the "processes of cohabitation and interaction that have made multiculture an ordinary feature of social life in Britain's urban areas and in postcolonial cities elsewhere" (xv). Indeed, Gilroy's optimism regarding Britain's structure of feeling provides an apt description for Levy's endeavor:

> Even after that low ebb [the reaction to the events in the U.S. of 11 September 2011], half the country's yearning to be a different kind of place seemed worth noting, pausing over, and thinking with. A new set of issues had emerged to prompt the remaking of the nation's relationship with its imperial past and to feed the hope that its buried and disavowed colonial history might become useful at last as a guide to the evasive, multicultural future prefigured everywhere in the ordinary experiences of contact, cooperation, and conflict across the supposedly impermeable boundaries of race, culture, identity, and ethnicity. (xii)

My reading thus far understands *Small Island* as an allegory of the nation. Indeed, the novel not only invites but insists upon allegorical reading. The nation is figured as a house, owned by but not cared for by the Bligh men. The Bligh surname is shortened from Blight, a multivalent echo that locates in the patriarchal tradition the substance of old Blighty while also identifying that tradition as the nation's blight. In Bernard's absence during the war, the house is maintained by his wife, Queenie, whose name is actually Victoria (yes, like the queen), and under whose rule it draws in people from the far reaches of the world. Such allegorical reading can go on ad infinitum.[2]

But the novel also contains obstacles to allegorical reading. The decrepit urban house, for instance, departs from the pastoral convention of the country house as nation. And the characters are individuated in ways that hamper their representative status. Queenie's double name signifies not her proximity to but her distance from the white women who benefit from the privileges of empire, as signaled by her desperation to rise to the middle class.[3] Bernard is a failure as a patriarch, in love with a man and unable even to engender his physical lineage. His father, Arthur, although in the position of father/patriarch/king, has been emasculated by the demands of his nation. Equally, on the other side of the racial divide characters are unable to stand for a seamless blackness. Gilbert, the dark-skinned man who most identifies as black, is the son of a European Jew. Hortense, also fathered by a white man and thus what we might call the bastard child of empire, is most emphatically not a rebel and has no intention of playing the subversive return of the repressed.

Such point-by-point refutation of ideals and types orients us towards idiosyncrasies and details, suggesting the messiness of truth hidden by the too-neat myth. The novel thus makes a mimetic claim to the real, and offers representation as the means for authenticating the black presence in England. Its claim of verisimilitude is substantiated by Levy's historical research, acknowledged via citation in the novel (440–1) and emphasised by the author in interviews and public appearances (Interview 337, Lima 78–9). And it is buttressed by Levy's references to her parents and parents-in-law as models for her characters and source of her stories (Interview 330–1).

What should we make of the contradictory pulls of this novel that at once demands and resists allegorical reading? Let us consider Levy's repeated reference to her father's arrival on the Windrush. On her personal website the author's biography begins: "In 1948 Andrea Levy's father sailed from Jamaica to England on the Empire Windrush ship and her mother joined him soon after" ("Biography"). That this sentence precedes even her date of birth indicates the priority and weight invested in her father's story as an authorising gesture. Levy can point not only to a metaphorical truth but to a person who went through a historically verifiable experience. But her father is also one of the 492, the number of men who travelled on the Windrush to arrive at Tilbury on 22 June 1948. The Empire Windrush itself is no ordinary ship; with the passage of time it has become the flag-ship of the banana boat armada. It has lent its name to a generation, an era, a story, a foundation, a jubilee, a city square, a garden, and numerous books.[4] There is even a movement afoot to establish a public holiday on June 22nd to be known as Windrush Day (Vernon). The ship and its cargo, as Matthew Mead puts it, have become "metonymic of the post-war boom in immigration into Britain" (137). Mead argues that although all manner of "facts" about the Windrush arrival are in dispute, including the number 492, their repetition has the effect of "cumulative sedimentation" until a collective account renders "the 492 migrants into something monumental" (139): "The iteration of the *Windrush* as a cultural symbol, and in particular of the figure '492', marks a transformation of the event from a collection of individual histories into a composite, symbolic, imagined and monadic moment of arrival" (140).[5]

Inserted into the "curiously empty" (140) container of "the 492," Mr. Levy's story becomes an instance of a grander narrative. Its details are swept up by the ceremonial reverence conferred upon the symbol of "Windrush" by utterances of memorialisation. At the same time, even as he turns into a meaningful figure in a historical landscape, he does not lose his status as a discrete historical personage. He is simultaneously individual and typical, at once subject of a specific biography and representative of many biographies. Kenneth and Winston Levy, the author's father and uncle, travelled together. Mead notes "that their names are borrowed in *Small Island* for the tenants of Queenie Bligh's ground floor room" (144). On the one hand, this borrowing lends credence to the documentary quality of the novel. On the other, it suggests a substitution that aims for a higher, more abstract verisimilitude than that of documentary realism. Kenneth and Winston Levy can become characters in novel a precisely because they fill a narrative space. Their specificity can be evacuated, or it can take the place of other specificities that are as a result evacuated, eclipsed by a more urgent similitude that refers us away from the individual and toward the greater truth of "the 492," "the Windrush generation," "the Windrush pioneers," and other such sedimented, consecrated symbols.

This gesture of generalisation and substitution is repeated over and again in the novel as the relation between individuality and typology is revealed to be fundamental to each character arc. In myriad small formal gestures the narrative instructs the reader to move from singular to representative. For instance, Queenie's brother defends his generosity toward his impoverished classmates, saying, "But he were hungry, Queenie, he were hungry" (201). He is echoed by Queenie's mother who says of those who come to her back door looking for scraps, "They're hungry, Queenie, they're hungry" (203). The repetition of syntax as well as of words lifts the utterances out of the discrete and transforms them into iterations of an incantation. Queenie's memories are no longer of unique incidents but of a type of experience, the whole raised to the level of epic by the accompanying chorus—the fate of her mother and brother in her heroic narrative of separation.

Moreover, the novel relies on this gesture of generalisation, homogenisation, and substitution to develop an ethic of racial harmony, primarily by emphasising cross-racial similarities. Characters that admit the possibility that they occupy a position that is equally occupied by others, especially others of a different race, are granted epiphanies and rewarded with agency that extends into the future. Those that do not suffer the silencing of obsolescence.

The ethic of exchangeability is articulated by Gilbert in the novel's climax as he appeals to Bernard to recognize their experiential and qualitative similarity, against the enormity of which skin colour does not signify. "'You know what your trouble is, man'" he challenges Bernard:

> 'Your white skin. You think it makes you better than me. You think it give you the right to lord it over a black man. But you know what it make you? You wan' know what your white skin make you, man? It make you white. That is all, man. White. No better, no worse than me—just white. [. . .] We both just finish fighting a war—a bloody war—for the better world we wan' see. And on the same side—you and me. We both look on other men to see enemy. You and me, fighting for empire, fighting for peace. But still, after all that we suffer together, you wan' tell me I am worthless and you are not. Am I to be the servant and you are the master for all time? No. Stop this, man. Stop it now. We can work together.' (435)

Gilbert's repetition of "we" and "you and me" emphasizes a shared history; in a neat parallel his appeal ends with a potentially shared future. The narrative backs Gilbert's epiphany with demonstrations of the many similarities between the two men. Both join the RAF during the war dreaming of the glory of flying, but neither gets the glamorous job he desires. Both spend their war on the ground, performing the tasks that allow others to soar. Nevertheless, both are moved by the deadly beauty of the war machine–surprisingly, they share an aesthetic sensibility that appreciates that display of dangerous power (111, 342). They share, too, a masculinity that recoils at the sight of a wife on her knees before men—present in flesh or in memory—of another race (263, 432). These parallels prepare the way to Gilbert's invocation of "you and me," two figures in a landscape that could, in a pinch, stand in for each other.

But Bernard does not assent to Gilbert's plea. At the other end of the spectrum in this cautionary tale, Bernard's "we" contracts over time until, like the incredible shrinking man, he disappears. He recognizes only one collective to which he might belong—the white English. Unfortunately, that identificatory ideal shrinks away from him. It is never a large collective, at the start only the three other men with whom he socializes in his pub (283). It momentarily expands to white soldiers in India (281), but there begins to contract, losing first the army (290), then enlisted men with leftist sympathies (311), and then senior officers in the RAF (327). The gesture of distancing and refusing recognition of similarity is Bernard's core reflex. Accordingly, he is progressively isolated until there is no one else whom he recognizes as like him. First he is the lone Englishman in a prison cell filled with Indians whom he does not acknowledge as in any way sharing his experience, and then in England he isolates himself, believing himself to be suffering from syphilis. From this solitude he never recovers. At home at last he finds that his pub mates have been dispersed by the war, as the neighbor who shares his racial phenotype and fears escapes to the suburbs.

Bernard refuses the knowledge made available to him by his war experiences and his encounters with the wider world. Consequently, the narrative grants him no epiphany or future. His final words, spoken in response to Gilbert's powerful plea, are "'I just can't understand a single word that you're saying'" (434). And with that admission of obdurate nonunderstanding he vanishes. The other characters continue to speak and act. Even Queenie remains a textual presence to the very end, communicating through the objects she leaves with her child and through the twitch of the curtain that is her final interaction with Hortense (438–9). But all trace of Bernard ceases. Having refused the novel's moral, his punishment is erasure from the text and from the future it proffers. The England he represents at the allegorical level of the novel—the England of patriarchal succession, racial homogeneity, and comfortable imperialism—simply cannot continue.

In between the poles defined by Gilbert and Bernard are Hortense and Queenie, and with the two women the potential of substitution is realised. Again the path toward the moment of successful exchange is laid with evidence, available to the reader, that the characters uncannily echo each other despite the racial divide. Each woman is of a class lower than she would like, and each struggles to rise to the level she believes she deserves. For that rise, each has to modify her speech, to make it less the speech of the provinces and more the received pronunciation that passes for generic English (274, 372). Although both women begin as snobs who lack empathy, they are able to learn through hardship to recognize themselves in others. For Queenie, that moment comes when a bomb reduces her to "population," although even then she needs an additional prompt to accept that she is now one of those who need help rather than one of the helpers (251). Similarly, Hortense holds knowledge of her lack of distinctiveness at bay long past the Fanonian moment of interpellation that makes it plain to the reader (Fanon 276). Not until all that she offers to the mother country has been rejected does she acknowledge to an old, dirty, smelly, poorly dressed black man—the return of her nightmarish repressed—a shared experience of England's cold (386). Finally, both women desire the same man and together are able to mother his child. Whereas mutual recognition between men is blocked, a literal substitution takes place between women. An initial description of the final scene of exchange would see the women exchange the baby and the baby as the object of exchange. But the scene can also be described thus: the women exchange positions relative to the baby; the women are the exchangeable objects. Queenie is the mother who gives birth to the child; Hortense, midwife at the birth, becomes the adoptive mother who will rear him. Both are generalisable as Mother.

I am not suggesting that *Small Island* jettisons race in favor of a universalism that makes deracination the fundamental human condition and assimilation the condition of national membership. On the contrary, Levy privileges experience—historical as well ahistorical—as the generator of similarities and differences within and across racial boundaries. Race figures as a primary shaper of experience in the England of 1948, but the novel reaches for a beloved community in which recognition of mutuality is possible along and across lines of race, gender, class, and even aesthetic sensibility. We are all alike in having "private conflicts," Bernard reflects, unknowingly naming the paradoxical commonality of distinctiveness at the heart of the ethic of exchange (350). Unfortunately, the lesson Bernard takes from this gain in understanding is that solitude is absolute and each of us is trapped in our "own pitiful story." His bleakness is contradicted by the novel itself, the thing of beauty made from stories brought together (350). Characters are simultaneously idiosyncratic and representative so that they can encounter each other in their difference and their similarity. Race matters because it signifies a boundary between similarity and difference, but also because it cannot guarantee complete similarity or absolute difference.

Put another way, race remains significant precisely because it is the boundary that must repeatedly be crossed. Refusing its offer of order through segregation carries the ethical charge of Levy's story, for individuals and for the nation. In the biracial baby—jointly produced by representatives of black and white, colonizer and colonised, male and female—Levy creates an emblem of the hoped-for national community that finds its legitimation not in an atavistic homogeneity but in the experience of heterogeneity. Queenie, née Victoria, channeling Penelope, knits and unravels and knits again the same skein of wool until it becomes the knitted pouch that contains her legacy for the baby she relinquishes to Hortense (437–8). Then we know that the hero whose return she awaited was not Bernard, for she began knitting before he left for war; nor was it her lover, Michael, for she continued knitting after his departure. Her Odysseus, the hero who will save the nation, was the baby all along. And if the baby is the embodiment of a shared past and denizen of the future, the novel valorizes the nation's black citizens as its proper guardians. Crucially, these black citizens already contain whiteness within them. As in Hall, the nation is fortunate to have these already experienced guides as it faces a future of unavoidable heterogeneity. Far from being erased or assimilated, the Black British again play the role of rescuers, their very presence creating the opportunity for the nation to redeem its troubled past by embracing its multiracial nature. As individuals Hortense and Gilbert act heroically in *Small Island*; as representatives they are invested with the hero's task of bearing the nation's hope.

EMPTY TIME

"The past," writes Elizabeth Ermath, "however diffuse or hard to specify, is always seen in hindsight from a future vantage point which discovers a past that is by definition embedded in a controlled pattern of significance" (25). The pattern, in the case of *Small Island*, becomes apparent as five lives converge in one room. It becomes important when the exchange of the baby becomes the moment of the present—the brief, still point where the past meets the future. History is shaped here like an hourglass: the array of stories represented by the adults in the room pours into that scene, are bound together by the baby in a slim moment, and together meld into "the past." Immediately after that compression the adults disperse into the multiple possibilities of the future. But this future will be different from the past in one significant aspect: as it was being lived the meaning of the past was not known, its pattern not apparent; the future, on the other hand, can be anticipated as the future of the baby, the new thing that organizes all that precedes and initiates all that follows this moment. Perhaps instead of hourglass we should think of the transition from past to future as the squeezed passage through the birth canal, from which difficult journey unknown, amorphous potential emerges in recognizable and meaningful form. And in a novel that demands reading as national allegory the birthing body is the body of the nation, the ideal subject of history. All possible pasts become meaningful as trails to its present. From that convergence it emerges battered but ready to embark upon a new chapter in its ongoing story.

Both content and form align the narrative perspective with the nation. We have seen at the level of content how characters are rendered exchangeable such that all are recognizable as monumental features of a single historical landscape. However diverse their stories prior to the moment marked as "present," they are not contradictory or irreconcilable. Rather, the present reveals them to have been fragments of one story all along. The novel underlines that reconciliation at the level of form by dividing history into "1948" and "Before": the narrative present is 1948; all else is not other discrete times, but the "Before" of this present. For Ermath, the medium of historical time, here exemplified by "Before," is "itself a representation of the first magnitude" (26). By analogy to single-point perspective she explains

> the view of time as a neutral, homogeneous medium like the space of pictorial realism in painting; a time where mutually informative measurements can be made between past, present, and future, and where all relationships can be explained in terms of a common horizon. In single-point perspective sight is rationalized by a pictorial space that extends from here to eternity without encountering any disturbing fractures. The temporal analogue that links past, present, and future involves a different faculty (consciousness) and a different medium (time), but the same formation inheres. In history, that is, consciousness

is rationalized by a narrative time that extends from here to eternity, perhaps encountering many disturbing warps but no disturbing fractures. In history all temporal perspectives, however widely dispersed, 'agree' in the sense that they do not contradict; in this powerful sense they achieve a consensus tantamount to the creation of a common horizon in time and hence of the power to think historically. (27)

Realised formally in the realist novel, the single-point perspective is evident in the omniscient, unnamed "'Nobody' narrators" that "literally *constitute* historical time by threading together into one system and one act of attention a whole series of moments and perspectives" (28). That threading together gives *Small Island* its shape as it follows its protagonists' stories, telescoping dizzyingly from vast historical and spatial reaches to one house, then one room, then one climactic scene.

Ermath is interested in the epistemological and literary consequences of what she calls "the triumph of historical time" (30), a world-shaping development traceable in "the metaphysics of presence"; in "the structure of the human sciences"; in "the definition of subjectivity as 'individuality'" (9); in "our laws, our experiments, our capital, and our knowledge" (30)–in short, in "all we hold dear" (30). All these accomplishments rely on a collective faith that "if each individual could see all the world [. . .], all would see the *same* world (30, emphasis in original). Although she writes from the vantage point of the literary postmodern and Hall from modernity's crumbling political architecture, the two share an epistemological hypothesis of modernity beseiged by postmodernity. To Ermath's list of things we hold dear, things that constitute our being and anchor us in a known world, we might add Hall's great collectives—an extrapolation consistent with Ermath's analysis of the fragmentation of modernity's structural scaffolding. In *Small Island*, we see the powerful results of the triumph of historical time as expressed by and in service to the nation. The novel's single-point perspective constitutes an implied spectator that coincides with the nation at the moment of its rebirth, or its transition from its "Before" to its future. To serve the present needs of that subject, time is conceptualised as empty, homogeneous, and linear, capable of containing all the stories that are organised into a known pattern of the past for the present that causes the future. The "subject function" identified by Ermath, "one evident in the implied spectator of realist painting and in the implied historian of realist narrative" (38), is in Levy fulfilled by the nation as telos of history.

Moreover, in Levy as in Hall it is the Black British who make possible the nation's suturing not by loss and decline but by rebirth and progress. The mechanism of interchangeability equalizes all characters' claims to national membership, delivering the homogenisation necessary for all to be citizens. But, as we have noted, this peculiar generalisation does not demand the erasure of difference and a consequent uniform Englishness. On the contrary, it requires diversity and celebrates multiple paths to national membership. Hence, the novel's opposing pulls of the idiosyncratic and the representative, figured as the heterogeneity of a multiracial society wherein race is the sign of the difference that must be respected and the difference that must be overcome. And therein, too, lies the continuing relevance of the nation at a time when, as Hall suggests, it is threatened by identities and affiliations that are shifting simultaneously to the local and the global. The nation that finds legitimacy as the political expression of an essential folk perhaps cannot survive the conditions described by Hall. But in this moment of possibly looming fossilisation it finds a new life as the necessary space where heterogeneity can be convivially lived. It provides the shape of the better world imagined by Gilbert, the form taken by the telos of progressive history. Rather than signifying its proper destiny, thereby suturing through loss in the manner of Thatcher, the imperial past can be reconceptualised as but one stage in the nation's history. National history is centrally about the protracted struggle between colonizer and colonised, and more specifically between white and black. The struggle is the shared heritage of black and white citizens, and the culture that results their co-creation.

In this rescripting heterogeneity, by populating an interiority, is the sign of national exceptionalism, not the end of English distinctiveness.[6] Although her notion of a jointly created culture echoes Hall, Levy diverges from Hall's insistence upon an unpredictable difference that remains a source of anxiety for the settlements of individual and national identity. For Hall, the past is not fully recoverable; it retains an improvised, at times invented quality, while he points to still visible narrative seams. If the alternative, that the accommodation of difference can supply an alibi for the nation, attends his account as an unwitting danger, in Levy that meaning is embraced as the device that can move the Black British from margin to center. When that content is coupled with the formal harmonisation of potentially irreconcilable multiplicity into a surveyable past existing in uniform time, it effects the closure required to harness the Black British to the historical project called the nation.

To be sure, the experience of a convivial multiculture, albeit one in the uneven process of becoming, is a great improvement upon social life experienced as a war of invasion and counter-invasion. For the previously disenfranchised there is the further advantage of being the heroes who rescue the nation in its time of duress. Their presence signals its newly reinforced foundations, and their successful struggle for inclusion its utopian capacity. Perhaps, then, it is petulant to note that the Black British are themselves sutured by nation in the story told by Hall and Levy. The nation is the condition of their possibility, and they find their significance in its meaning-filled history. The two entities—nation and national subject—are intertwined in a tautological loop, with the Black British conscripted to the destiny of the nation. Congratulated for their role in that destiny, they also are deprived of alternative outcomes. Certainly they are celebrated as monuments of British history, but thus monumentalised their impact also can be contained and any potential threat neutralised. For instance, in *Small Island* the exclusion they contest is simply deferred, rather than undermined. Assisted by the strongly unifying single-point perspective that renders all possible stories into one story, the nation continues to find its cause in deep history. The black-white encounter replaces the organic folk as the essence of that history—a gesture that includes the Black British, but closes the door behind them to all other, now nonessential claimants.

NOTES

1. This chapter owes a great deal to Ana María Sánchez-Arce for her persistence and patience. Thanks are also due to Priya Purohit, research assistant extraordinare.
2. For a fuller reading of the emblematic nature of the characters and events, see Fischer.
3. See Brophy for a persuasive reading of Queenie as more aligned with cosmopolitanism than with nation, simultaneously complicit with and dissenting from imperialism.
4. A quick, unsystematic browse of book titles on amazon.com reveals a dozen books with "Windrush" in their title (accessed 14 December 2012). The Windrush Foundation is located in Lewisham.
5. "The often repeated 'facts' of the *Windrush*, including the date of the vessel's arrival, the gendering of the migrants, the supposedly uncomplicated route of the *Windrush* from Kingston to Tilbury, the names and number of stowaways, and, most significantly, the number and nationalities of those on board are all disturbed by reference to the passenger log" (Mead 142).
6. My reasoning here is modelled after Kalliney's analysis of class relations as a sign of national exceptionalism.

REFERENCES

Brophy, Sarah. "Entangled Genealogies: White Femininity on the Threshold of Change in Andrea Levy's *Small Island*." *Contemporary Women's Writing* 4.2 (2010): 1–20. Print.

Ermath, Elizabeth Deeds. *Sequel to History: Postmodernism and the Crisis of Representational Time*. Princeton, NJ: Princeton University Press, 1992. Print.

Fanon, Frantz. *Black Skin, White Masks*. 1952. Trans. Richard Philcox. New York: Grove/Atlantic, 2007. Print.

Fischer, Susan Alice. "Contested London Spaces in Monica Ali's Brick Lane and Andrea Levy's *Small Island*." *Critical Engagements: A Journal of Criticism and Theory* 1.1 (2007): 34–52. Print.

Gilroy, Paul. *Postcolonial Melancholia*. New York: Columbia University Press, 2005. Print.

Hall, Stuart. "Ethnicity: Identity and Difference." *Radical America* 23.4 (1989): 9–20. Print.

Kalliney, Peter J. *Cities of Affluence and Anger: A Literary Geography of Modern Englishness*. Charlottesville and London: U of Virginia P, 2006. Print.

Levy, Andrea. "Biography." Andrealevy.co.uk. N.p. n.d. Web. 12 December 2012.

———. *Fruit of the Lemon*. London: Review, 1999. Print.

———. Interview with Blake Morrison. *Women: a Cultural Review* 20.3 (2009): 328–38. Print.

———. *Small Island*. NY: Picador, 2004. Print.

Lima, Maria Helena. "'Pivoting the Centre': The Fiction of Andrea Levy." *Write Black Write British: From Post Colonial to Black British Literature*. Ed. Kadija Sesay. Hertford, UK: Hansib, 2005. 56–85. Print.

Mead, Matthew. "Empire Windrush: The Cultural Memory of an Imaginary Arrival." *Journal of Postcolonial Writing* 45.2 (2009): 137–49. Print.

Thatcher, Margaret. "Speech to Conservative Rally at Cheltenham." Cheltenham Racecourse, U.K. 3 July 1982. *The Margaret Thatcher Foundation*. Web. 3 December 2012.

Vernon, Patrick. "Windrush Day." *Guardian*. Guardian, 24 January 2010. Web. 14 December 2012.

Williams, Raymond. *Marxism and Literature*. Oxford: Oxford University Press, 1977. Print.

Part II

Formal Prescriptions and Identity Politics

5   From the "other side"
Mimicry and Feminist Rewriting in the Novels of Beryl Bainbridge

Huw Marsh

In her review of Beryl Bainbridge's novel *Injury Time* (1977), Claire Tomalin makes an astute observation that has implications for Bainbridge's fiction more generally. Writing of Bainbridge's low-key, in some ways even
comic, depiction of a rape, Tomalin suggests that it is "believable, if not
what women are currently supposed to come up with" (58). This sense that
Bainbridge's writing is "not what women are currently supposed to come
up with" has undoubtedly affected its reception in an era during which
feminism and women's studies have played such a pivotal role in canon formation. And Bainbridge herself has not helped matters by repeatedly and
categorically stating that she is not a feminist:

> I've never been drawn to the feminist movement. I was brought up to
> believe that men had little to do with the home or children—except
> to bring in the money. I've never been put down by a man, unless I
> deserved it, and have never felt inferior. It seems to me that a mutually
> beneficial relationship between a man and a woman requires the man
> to be dominant. A sensible woman will allow the man to think he is the
> most important partner. (Bainbridge, "Art of Fiction" 259)

These sentiments echo Bainbridge's 1976 description of her background
in "a very matriarchal family": "My mother," she said, "treated men
with the utmost contempt. They were far more women's lib, in the worst
sense, than they are today" (Bainbridge, "Beryl Bainbridge Talks" 49).
And in a 2006 *Observer* article, Bainbridge told Nicki Sprinz: "I am not
a feminist in the slightest. I was brought up to believe that women were
much superior to men, only you kept it very quiet" ("What I Know" 22).
This seems emphatic, but Bainbridge's relationship with feminism is not
as clear-cut as it might at first appear. In interview after interview she
demonstrated an almost wilful ignorance of what feminism actually is
and what being a feminist might mean, an ignorance that seems largely
to emerge from a dramatic gift for overstatement and a belief that feminism has no relevance to her experiences: "I've never had to be [a femi-
nist]," she said in 2001, "[a]t home, my mother was always the dominant

one" (Bainbridge, "Femail" 52). These pronouncements reinforce her status as an outsider to the literary mainstream, and while other writers of roughly her generation (Angela Carter, Margaret Drabble, Eva Figes, and Fay Weldon, for example) engaged directly with the changing currents of thought concerning feminism and gender studies, Bainbridge determinedly took her own course. Indeed, when she commented publicly on her fiction, she seemed anxious to locate it firmly within her own life and experiences and to deny any conscious engagement with wider social or political issues (Warner; Gibbs; Bainbridge, "You Couldn't"). Like Doris Lessing or Anita Brookner, writers who have also distanced themselves from feminism, Bainbridge was anxious to shun labels and to remain "unclubbable."[1]

In *Post-War British Women Novelists and the Canon* (2010), Nick Turner notes how middle-aged and older women writers tend to be marginalised in a literary marketplace increasingly geared towards youth. He suggests that exceptions to this occur when the author "can be portrayed as a lovable eccentric," citing Bainbridge as an example (55). Turner's point is well made and may partly account for Bainbridge's high media profile, but this image of lovable eccentricity is not entirely positive. As Margaret Reynolds and Lisa Jardine suggest in a Nicholas Wroe profile of Bainbridge, the "cult of personality" has affected her critical reception and has tended to draw attention away from her writing. It is not hard to see how—in combination with her controversial attitudes on feminism and other issues— the casting of Bainbridge as an eccentric who bashed out equally eccentric novels from her Victoriana-filled Camden townhouse has contributed to a degree of neglect in academic criticism. Although D. J. Enright has suggested that Bainbridge "doesn't want to *look* serious, and people who don't look serious tend not to be taken seriously" (16), this role is one that she came increasingly to find frustrating (Bainbridge, "*Observer* Profile"). As Jardine has noted, it also marginalises Bainbridge and makes it easy for people to dismiss her work:

> Wearing my hat as chair of the Booker I'm faced with 100-odd authors and I ask myself whether some of the men look much like Beryl Bainbridge, except that no one comments on their eccentricities. And in that 100 you have to go a long way before you reach writing of Bainbridge's quality. (qtd. Wroe)

"If you think Bloomsbury in relation to Bainbridge," Jardine continues, "then she won't look nearly so odd. Look at her and think Virginia Woolf before she was canonised—an oddly dressed lady with funny tastes; that was Virginia Woolf" (qtd. Wroe). This is a useful comparison and highlights how ideas about Bainbridge's personal character have tended to overshadow her literary achievements. It is, however, as far as any significant affinity with Woolf goes.

In fact, Lorna Sage has drawn a distinction between Bainbridge's writing and that of Margaret Drabble, one of the authors Roberta Rubenstein describes as writing "in the wake" of Virginia Woolf. Sage argues that Bainbridge is "worlds away" from Drabble "in sensibility and style" and that "the neatness, economy and hard humour of the writing [. . .] are a tacit satire on the traditional women's novel, the mode of concern and other-centredness" (85). This tacitly satirical edge further distances Bainbridge's work from the dominant picture of recent women's literature, as does the fact that she used male narrators as often as female and wrote in a mode that eschews the psychological or overt sociological analysis embarked upon by so many writers who came of age during the same period. Yet, in Bainbridge's fiction at least, one is hardly presented with depictions of orthodox, patriarchal households or of superior masculinity. Her portraits of Robert Scott and his team of Antarctic explorers in *The Birthday Boys* (1991), for example, question and destabilise orthodox masculinities rather than reinforcing them. And when women have the central roles, they may, as in *The Bottle Factory Outing* (1974), be comic or even absurd figures, but underlying this are often are often serious subtextual critiques of patriarchal authority and the limited roles available to women. Therefore just as Lessing's and, to a lesser extent Brookner's work have inspired readings that persuasively situate them within feminist discourse, so with Bainbridge it is to the work that one must ultimately turn. It would be reductive to reclaim Bainbridge as a strident or actively engaged feminist, but a distinction can still be made between those writers who are card-carrying feminists whose work consciously and consistently engages with sexual politics, and those whose work is not consciously allied to feminism but who nevertheless engage with debates that can be described as feminist. One need not fit Bainbridge onto the procrustean bed of the standard picture of postwar women's letters in order to see how, notwithstanding her protestations, her work falls into the latter category.

This dimension to Bainbridge's work has been recognised by some, and although the entry on Bainbridge in Hodder and Arnold's *Literature in English Post-1914* (2005) describes how she "has been seen as different from other contemporary women writers such as Margaret Atwood and Angela Carter in that her novels do not present overtly feminist gender or sexual debates," it goes on to note that "gender and class debates are intertwined in her work" (Sánchez-Arce, "Beryl Bainbridge" 15). The word "overtly" is important here because in excluding Bainbridge from the context of feminism or gender studies, many critics gloss over an important aspect of her writing. Virginia Richter has acknowledged this and describes Bainbridge's novels as "feminist precisely in their refusal to underwrite the ideas of fullness, wholeness and meaning" (163). Similarly Elaine Showalter, who in the 1970s listed Bainbridge along with Iris Murdoch, Muriel Spark, Doris Lessing, and A. S. Byatt as a writer whose work was representative of "a renaissance in women's writing" (*Literature* 35). More recently, Helen Carr has argued that feminism could provide an important context for Bainbridge's work and describes how "her resistance to seeing women as victims has much in common with [Angela] Carter" (79). But in Carr's essay, as in the other texts cited above, the question of Bainbridge's relationship with feminism is left undeveloped. In fact, there are only two sustained attempts to place her work within the contexts of women's writing or feminism: in *Femicidal Fears* (2001) Helene Meyers describes *The Bottle Factory Outing* (1974) as an implicit critique of masculine violence, and in "The Prop They Need" (2001) Ana María Sánchez-Arce reads *Master Georgie* (1998) as a redress to the heroic, male-centred war narrative. These represent valuable contributions to the field, but there remains more to be said.

In "The Woman Writer and the Continuities of Feminism" (2006), Patricia Waugh provides a useful summary of trends in post-1960s women's writing:

> First, a pre-theorized and ambivalent phase beginning in the sixties and involving writers such as Iris Murdoch, Doris Lessing, Sylvia Plath, Simone de Beauvoir, and Muriel Spark. Second, a phase of explicitly 'writing as a woman,' and involving, above all, a quest to reconcile the collective with the personal voice, to explore the reverberations of the 'personal is political' as in the continuing work of Lessing, Greer, Millett, Rich; the 'midd-leground' [sic] or in the metafictionalized realism of writers such as Margaret Drabble, Anita Brookner, Pat Barker, A.S. Byatt, and early Margaret Atwood; as well as the Gothic and carnivalesque fiction of the early Fay Weldon and Angela Carter. Finally, emerging in the 1980s, a third phase of explicit engagement with the challenges of postmodernism and postcolonialism. (192)

Bainbridge could best be described as belonging to the first, "pre-theorized and ambivalent" stage of this schema, which, whilst making her feminism out of step with the times, should not be allowed to overshadow the ways in which her fiction engages with feminist debates. In the centralisation of Hester Thrale and her daughter Queeney in Bainbridge's "Samuel Johnson" novel *According to Queeney* (2001), and in the "carefully planned attack on the concept of the heroic war narrative" (Sánchez-Arce, "Prop" 93) that is *Master Georgie*, recent years have seen Bainbridge engage in a gendered critique of the past and its representation in historical discourse. The critique is implicit in these later works, but it is the small group of novels set in the era of their composition that express this engagement most fully: in *A Weekend with Claude* (1967) and *Another Part of the Wood* (1968) Bainbridge questions narratives of sexual liberation in the 1960s; in *Injury Time* (1977) and *Winter Garden* (1980) she satirises the effects of these changes in the decades that followed; and in *The Bottle Factory Outing* and *Sweet William* (1975) she describes the lives of women who may kick against the pricks, but who continue to be defined, and to define themselves, in relation to patriarchy. The sexual politics of *Sweet William* in particular suggest how Bainbridge's writing is imbricated and engaged with feminist debates, whether or not she would have defined it in those terms herself.

Bainbridge has described how when she began writing, "women were beginning to write about girls having abortions and single mothers living in Hampstead and having a dreadful time," but that she decided not to concern herself "with all that rubbish" (Bainbridge, "Art of Fiction" 258). Once again these comments are both a simplification and a dramatic overstatement, not least because her description of the archetypal women's novel sounds suspiciously like the plot of *Sweet William*, a novel featuring a botched illegal abortion and a woman living in Hampstead who is abandoned by the father of her child. The major difference is that in Bainbridge's hands the "dreadful time" had by her protagonist, Ann, becomes the stuff of laughter. As critics such as Judy Little, Regina Barreca, and Margaret Stetz have suggested, there is a significant body of comic writing by women that is often overlooked or read using what Barreca describes as "inherited critical structures which do not provide for the particularly insurgent strategies used by women writers" (9). Far from being either unserious or the preserve of men, comedy can provide the ground for subversive and challenging critiques, and if one is aware of the subversive quality of humour in Bainbridge's fiction, then her alliance with authors more readily described as feminist becomes clear. Like much of Bainbridge's fiction, *Sweet William* is unashamedly humorous and depicts Ann's travails as noir comedy, but although it works within conventionally male genre codes, it does so in a manner that challenges some of the assumptions about masculinity on which these codes are founded. It is a novel that undermines critical orthodoxies about Bainbridge's work by responding to the canon of postwar male authors in a way that strongly engages with certain strands of feminism. In fact, as archival evidence makes clear, *Sweet William* directly "writes back" to this literature, and particularly to the subgenre of "lad lit." In doing so it presents a critique of patriarchy that parallels many of the arguments found in second wave feminism of the 1960s and 1970s.

Sweet William opens with Ann saying goodbye to her safe, conventional fiancé, Gerald, who is moving to America, and quickly falling into a bohemian relationship with the mercurial William. William speaks the language of the 1960s liberalism when it suits him ("if only she would empty her mind of pride and ownership. Love was all that counted"), but also of the Western, where men could be men: "'That's where friendship began. Mates [. . .] In the West, when they didn't have any women'" (133; 44). William is like Joseph in Bainbridge's earlier novel *Another Part of the Wood* (1968), who also swaggers around like a cowboy, mouthing platitudes concerning free love but practising them only in regard to himself.[2] When Ann first meets William she lives alone and has independent means, but at his insistence she leaves her job at the BBC and has soon allowed him to block the hallway of her flat with his wardrobe, to hang his pictures on her walls, and to usurp her books with his own. It becomes clear to the reader, though not to Ann, that while William expects to be the sole locus of her affections, she can only ever be one of his many "compartments" (75). He becomes an author figure, dictating letters from Ann to Gerald and, it later transpires, to Ann from his wife, and intervening directly when it seems that she and Gerald might be reconciled. As Pamela, Ann's cousin and another of William's compartments, tells Ann: "'You're not leading anybody. You're following'" (84); Ann's freedom is illusory and she is forced to admit that she has been "'taken over, requisitioned'" by William (115). As David Punter writes in *The Hidden Script*: "Ann is presented, in the shape of William, with a text which she makes an attempt to read," but is ultimately forced to concede that "such completeness of comprehension is not possible" (68): she can read only the surface and not the subtext. But while Ann is unable to piece together the puzzle that is William, the reader is able to situate him within a specific context and literary tradition: Bainbridge's novel also engages in a form of re*writing*.

In her 2002 essay "Ladlit," Elaine Showalter delineates the evolution of a subgenre of literature, the founding text of which is Kingsley Amis's *Lucky Jim* (1954). Lad-lit features "anti-heroes" who are "often losers and boozers, liars, wanderers and transients," but who are also "attractive, funny, bright, observant, inventive, charming, and excruciatingly honest" (Showalter, "Ladlit" 60–61), a mould into which the eponymous hero of *Sweet William* fits nicely. His arrogance and occasional unpleasantness are balanced with a degree of charm, and he is both "excruciatingly honest" and a liar. *Sweet William* follows in the wake of *Lucky Jim* and a slew of other comic novels that appeared during the 1950s and 1960s, most prominent among which are perhaps Keith Waterhouse's *Billy Liar* (1959) and Bill Naughton's *Alfie* (1966).[3] These books advertise the focus of their attentions via the proper names in their titles and their protagonists tend to come of age within the pages, reaching a point of crisis and realising the need to change. They also tend to be more than a little sexist. As Richard Bradford argues in *The Novel Now*, both character and narrator in these texts tend to view women with "what might best be termed predatory heterosexual empathy":

> Women characters were respected, sometimes even portrayed as more complex, prescient figures than their male counterparts, but alongside this would come a degree of puzzlement, a sense of desire (unless the women in question were undesirable) as the overpowering inclination. (116)

The protagonists do, therefore, have a degree of self-aware empathy with women, but, as Bradford implies, this takes place within a narrow definition of what women can be.

In his introduction to *Lucky Jim*, David Lodge answers his own query as to the book's sexism by answering swiftly: "Of course it is!" (xvi). At one point in the novel, Jim speculates on the two women in his life and concludes that "if Christine looked like Margaret and Margaret looked like Christine his spirits would now be very much higher." Then, resigning himself to the less-favoured candidate, he laments the fact that "Margaret with Christine's face and body could never have turned into Christine" (Amis 203). This mix-and-match approach to courtship finds a correlative in Bainbridge's novel through William's aforementioned "compartments," each containing different women from whom he gets different things—there is Ann, Ann's cousin Pamela, Mrs Kershaw the landlady, his current wife Edna, his ex-wife Sheila, and quite possibly a number of others besides. Like Bill Naughton's Alfie, who "look[s] on an evening with just one bird as only half the menu, sausage and mash without the treacle pud" (16), William seems unable—or unwilling—to be monogamous and equally unable or unwilling to be honest about this or to allow his partners the same freedom. And like Billy Liar, William navigates his life by creating a series of improbable lies and covering untruths with yet more untruths. In Waterhouse's novel, which is perhaps the closest in style and content to *Sweet William*, Billy gets engaged to two women and struggles to keep them from talking to one another. Then, when Barbara and Rita discover his deception, he tries and fails to convince them that it has all been "'a bit of a mix-up'" (Waterhouse 180). William gets similarly caught out when Ann finds him burying a lock of another woman's hair on Hampstead Heath and when she discovers that he has two former wives rather than one, as she had assumed. Like Billy, William spins lies and diversions to cover up deceits, adapting to the situation by becoming "anything anyone wanted him to be" (63). So, as Krystyna Stamirowska has noted, whilst Ann believes that she has some degree of agency, "in fact it is William who always controls the situation" (448). But there are also crucial differences between Bainbridge's version of lad-lit and the thing itself. Returning to David Lodge's comments on *Lucky Jim*, he argues of Jim's spurned partner, Margaret, that her "story is potentially tragic, but it is not told here," adding that "it was to be told many times, and powerfully, by women novelists" (xxvi–vii). This is precisely what is achieved in *Sweet William*, which tells "Margaret's" (i.e. Ann's) story by reversing the perspective of the narration; Bainbridge reworks the lad-lit formula.

This attention to form and genre is borne out in a document found in the British Library's Bainbridge Papers. In a fragment of manuscript consisting of Bainbridge's doodles and sketched ideas relating to *Sweet William*, and amongst ideas like "Mistake 2nd wife for 1st wife" and "I am drawing a picture of a magnificent sod," is this note: "*Chapter Headings* / Just William format" (British Library Add. MS 83793, 199r). Bainbridge seems initially to have planned the novel as a series of linked short stories in the mode of Richmal Crompton's *Just William* books, which describe the exploits of the

mischievous and eternally eleven-year-old schoolboy William Brown. Crompton's stories have titles such as "William Goes to the Pictures," "William
and the Smuggler" and "William and the Policeman's Helmet," the latter
of which is included in a collection entitled *Sweet William* (1936), to which
the title of Bainbridge's novel seems directly to respond. The novel's title and
William's boyish character aside, however, the resemblances between Bainbridge's novel and Crompton's books are only passing in the published edition, which departs from the more faithful homage she originally envisaged.
In what appears to be the first in a projected series of vignettes, a surviving
manuscript fragment entitled "William at the Harvest Festival" describes
William's first eccentric overtures toward Ann.[4] The story survives as a por-
tion of the published novel's first chapter and shows that Bainbridge was
thinking carefully about form from the outset.

The second manuscript note reinforces this impression. It reads: "Lucky
Jim from other side. / Chaps writing about women" (BL Add. MS 83793,
199r). Bainbridge's comment makes explicit what is already implicit in the
text: that by writing a lad-lit narrative but "from [the] other side," she
is making a gendered, tacitly feminist gesture, whether or not she would
describe it in those terms herself. This finds an analogue in gender theory
in Teresa de Lauretis's idea of "feminist rewriting": "a development may
be seen to have taken place with regard to the understanding of feminism
as a radical *rewriting*, as well as a rereading, of the dominant forms of
Western culture," de Lauretis writes in *Technologies of Gender*, "a rewriting which effectively inscribes the presence of a different, and gendered,
social subject" (xi). Here, as throughout de Lauretis's work, the emphasis
is largely on philosophy, critical theory and semiotics, but the overarching
strategy she describes seems precisely to echo what Bainbridge attempts in
her reworking of male-centred narratives. And once one establishes this
link, it is possible to place *Sweet William* within a wider feminist project to "rewrite cultural narratives, and to define the terms of another perspective—a view from 'elsewhere'" (de Lauretis 25). As Randall Stevenson
has noted, this is "a tactic regularly employed by women writers" in order
to highlight the "patriarchal assumptions" of certain male-authored texts
and to "suggest alternatives" (476). Other examples include the versions
of fairy tales published in Angela Carter's *The Bloody Chamber* (1979)
and Margaret Atwood's reworking of Homer in *The Penelopiad* (2005),
a novel written from the points of view of Penelope and the twelve maids
hanged on Odysseus' return to Ithaca. In each instance, this "substitution or insertion of a female narrative draws attention to the remarkable
absence of the female in the originals" (Connor 169) and, in Bainbridge's
case, provides an alternative perspective on the lad-lit narrative ("Chaps
writing about women"). Indeed, there are further parallels with a group
of novels discussed by Susan Brook in *Literature and Cultural Criticism
in the 1950s* (2007). Brook adapts Homi Bhabha's idea of "mimicry," a
trope he identifies in the transposition of English culture to India, in order

to describe Lynne Reid Banks's *The L-Shaped Room* (1962) and Shelagh Delaney's *A Taste of Honey* (1959) as responses to the novels and plays of the "Angry Young Men," a group that included John Braine, Alan Sillitoe, John Osborne, and of course, Kingsley Amis. Brook suggests that the novels of Banks and Delaney destabilise some of the assumptions found in the "angry" text because:

> they are hybrid texts, both repeating and dislodging the familiar narrative concerns that emerge from the focus on the male protagonist. The texts show a similar tension between accommodation and rebellion, for example, as other angry texts, but insofar as they focus on *women* both struggling against and accepting their positions in society, they implicitly critique the way in which angry texts fail to treat women as agents. (107)

This implied critique is also apparent in *Sweet William*, which writes back to and decentres the lad-lit novel. Like Margaret in the other version of *Lucky Jim* imagined by David Lodge, then, Ann emerges as a deeper, more tragic figure than she would in the novel had it been written by Amis, Waterhouse or Naughton.

Bainbridge avoids creating a clear dichotomy between saints and sinners, perpetrators and victims and, whilst it is clear that she is more sinned against than sinning, Ann is not portrayed as a helpless victim. Rather, *Sweet William* is told largely from Ann's perspective so that the reader shares in her confusions and betrayals, her dilemmas and conflicts. In a repetition of the odd-couple relationships that recur in Bainbridge's fiction,[5] Ann is set against her mother, Mrs Walton, who exists on the other side of a seemingly unbridgeable generational divide. Ann's landlady, Mrs Kershaw, describes how she and Ann "'inhabit a different world'" to that of Ann's mother; a world in which sex outside of marriage is not taboo and in which new freedoms can be enjoyed (13).[6] But things are not as simple as they at first appear. Ann's mother is not "ordinary"; it is not an "adequate word" to describe the brassy Mrs Walton, who refers to men as "'persons'" and has a "dreadful," inflexible will (13). Mrs Walton's attitudes toward men are anything but those of the orthodox, submissive housewife:

> Men were alien. Her mother and Aunt Bea preferred the society of women: all girls together—leave the nasty men alone with their brutish ways and their engorged appendages. Men were there to pay the mortgages and mend the fuses when they blew. Send them out onto the path to clean the car and hose the drains, brush the lupins from the grass. (46)

This wonderfully cutting passage echoes Bainbridge's own memories of her mother's attitude toward men and the idea that she and her friends were "far more women's lib, in the worst sense, than they are today." There is

also an element of class-bound pride and obsession with keeping up appearances in Mrs Walton's attitudes, the brunt of which are borne by her put-
upon husband, Captain Walton, who is largely silent throughout and is
almost the archetypal browbeaten husband so long a staple of comedy. Yet
whilst media from Chaucer's "The Wife of Bath's Prologue" (c. 1387–1400)
to Sam Mendes's *American Beauty* (1999)—and beyond—have used this
figure as a foil against which to delineate a manipulative or shrewish version of femininity, in Bainbridge's novel a more nuanced point is made:
Captain Walton bears witness to the fact that his wife's happiness has been
substituted for an ordered and superficially successful petit-bourgeois existence. At one point Ann thinks that it was her mother "who should have
met someone like William" (86); that Mrs Walton was a strong enough
woman to have handled him and should never have settled for the life she
fell into. This tension, as well as Captain Walton's silent withdrawal, seems
precisely to echo Germaine Greer's description of the festering resentments
brought about by the marriage code:

> The housewife accepts vicarious life as her portion, and imagines that
> she will be a prop and mainstay to her husband in his noble endeav-
> ours, but insidiously her unadmitted jealousy undermines her ability
> to appreciate what he tells her about his ambitions and his difficulties.
> She belittles him, half-knowingly disputes his difficult decisions, taunts
> him with his own fears of failure, until he stops telling her anything.
> (*Female Eunuch* 287)

Therefore, whilst Bainbridge insists that she has "never had to be" a feminist because her mother "was always the dominant one" in her household,
Sweet William describes the underlying inequalities that can engender bitterness and resentment, as well as an ensuing need to assert dominance
in the home. Whether or not it is a conscious engagement, Bainbridge
describes, and satirises, a situation that was being identified and challenged
by second-wave feminism of the period.

Mrs Walton's confrontational and resentful attitude toward men also
works as a comic reversal that serves to question certain assumptions about
women's lives, and is similar to the attitude of Mrs Fiedke in Muriel Spark's
1970 novel *The Driver's Seat*. Having met her shortly before in a depart-
ment store, Mrs Fiedke aims a diatribe at the novel's (anti-)heroine, Lise,
bemoaning the fact that men "'are demanding equal rights'." She continues, "'That's why I never vote with the Liberals'":

> Perfume, jewellery, hair down to their shoulders [. . .] There was a
> time when they would stand up and open the door for you. They would
> take their hat off. But they want their equality today. All I say is that
> if God had intended them to be as good as us he wouldn't have made
> them different from us to the naked eye. [. . .] If we don't look lively

[. . .] they will be taking over the homes and the children, and sitting about having chats while we go out and fight to defend them and work to keep them. They won't be content with equal rights only. Next thing they'll want the upper hand, mark my words. Diamond ear-rings, I've read in the paper. (Spark 290–91)

Here, as in *Sweet William*, a reversal defamiliarises debates surrounding sexual equality: the power dynamic as it is usually presented is turned upside down so that men become the drones, forced outside to work and to endanger themselves, whilst the women—the queens—reside in the domestic, feminine, sphere and defend it against masculine invasion. This seems to echo what Betty Friedan describes as the "feminine mystique," in which the role of homemaker is sublimated into an ideal of femininity in order to maintain the status quo:

Beneath the sophisticated trappings, it simply makes certain concrete, finite, domestic aspects of feminine existence—as it was lived by women whose lives were confined, by necessity, to cooking, cleaning, washing, bearing children—into a religion, a pattern by which all women must now live or deny their femininity. (Friedan 39)

But neither Bainbridge's nor Spark's novels are reactionary pleas to continue this state of affairs, and instead they satirise attitudes in which the sexes are seen as alien to one another and the spheres of work and home life as impermeable, biologically essentialised spaces. This is the sort of "tacit satire on the traditional women's novel" described by Sage, but it is a form of satire that supports many of the arguments found in its own object, here taking a character's views to extremes in order to make them appear absurd. In Bainbridge's case, this satire is extended to Ann, whose position as part of a newly liberated generation is hardly unproblematic.

When Ann discovers that she is pregnant, Mrs Walton reacts to the news with a mixture of unexpected restraint and a certain degree of jealousy:

It was very difficult for her, under the circumstances. All those years of duty and conformity gone for nothing. Of no value. Twenty years later the old standards swept away as if they had never been. There was Ann, pregnant, unmarried, money in the bank, neither ostracised nor selling heather in the gutter. Unrepentant. One might say, unaware that there was anything to be unrepentant about. It was terribly unfair. (148)

Mrs Walton feels that she has been born in the wrong era and it is clear that, for all of her bluster, she has been hemmed in by "duty and conformity"; as Ann comes to realise, her mother has had a "disappointing life" (86). But William's treatment of Ann acts as a partial rejoinder to this image of new liberalism sweeping away old conservatism. Yes, unmarried motherhood has become more acceptable, but it is William's money in Ann's bank account, it is he who controls the relationship throughout, and it is he who is free to disappear, leaving Ann alone with her newborn baby. As Lynne Segal suggests in *Is the Future Female?* (1987), a "new wave of egalitarianism and permissiveness [. . .] transformed the lives of women" during the 1960s (75), but Bainbridge complicates any sense that this new wave simply swept away the old codes; she delineates how certain sexual inequalities continued into the permissive society. And although in the feminist circles recalled by Segal "it was not usually the men who initiated [. . .] erotic encounters" (78), in *Sweet William* it is always William who is in charge from the moment he barges into Ann's life at the harvest festival. In fact, as Segal herself notes in *Slow Motion* (1990), "something happened" when women attempted to join men and enjoy new freedoms and sexual possibilities:

> The tangled sense of sexual freedom, inferiority and confusion women felt then [. . .] pushed them ineluctably towards finding each other and finding a voice. The permissive moment of the sixties slowly prepared the stage for its major event, its last and lasting climax: the eruption and consolidation of the women's liberation movements of the west. (231)

The sexual revolution was, therefore, a significant staging post in the formation of more equal gender relations, but this was partially in a negative sense: women were brought together in reaction against the inequalities that continued into the permissive society. Indeed, in an essay cited by Segal, Sheila MacLeod is emphatic on this point. From the perspective of the 1970s, MacLeod writes in "A Fairy Story," "the sixties looked very much like a male invention based in power, promiscuity and self-abuse." Only later was it possible to see that "the false liberation of the sixties had paved the way for the subsequent struggle towards a true definition of what it meant to be female and at least relatively free" (182).

Although writing in the 1970s, Bainbridge does not depict the women's movement that was by then finding a strong voice, but rather delineates the background to this as described by MacLeod—an era in which male dominance continued despite a liberalisation of attitudes towards sex. Once again it is Ann's mother who perceives this: "'You haven't learnt anything,'" she tells Ann, "'All this permissiveness has led you young girls into slavery'" (150). There are parallels here with Hilary Mantel's novel *An Experiment in Love* (1995), which portrays a later generation of women but describes a similar tension between change and continuity. The narrator of Mantel's novel, Carmel McBain, recalls the women at her university halls of residence who had gained hard-won access to higher education but would still iron their boyfriends' shirts:

> If I could time-travel I would fly back, back in time to the ironing room; I would fly back to those girls and slap them. I would like to

bring them to their senses; say, how can it be, that after all these years of education, all you want is the wash-tub? Leave this, and go and run the country. (164)

As Margaret Atwood describes it, Mantel depicts "girls at the end of the 60s, caught between two sets of values, who had the pill but still ironed their boyfriends' shirts" ("Little Chappies").[7] In *An Experiment in Love*, as in *Sweet William*, aspects of the sexual revolution are revealed as a veneer under which a core of male hegemony still remains. In Bainbridge's novel, Ann can be seen as "a victim of sexual freedom rather than of sexual bondage" (Kermode 42).

The conclusion of *Sweet William* sees Ann left with few available options; she is isolated from her former friends and her family, with only her landlady at her side. William remains on her mind though, as her thoughts turn to the lock of hair that signifies his duplicity: "There must be an answer somewhere. An identification. One had to know the relationship between people. The whole secret of life was there, if only she could be given the clues." But Ann is not despairing and instead resolves that she does not "really want to know" where William has gone to (159–60). She is defiant rather than hopeless, something that the 1980 film adaptation makes more explicit when Ann, played by Jenny Agutter, bursts into laughter on realising that the baby to whom she has given birth bears an uncanny resemblance not to William but to her ex, Gerald. In both the film and the book, the juxtaposition of Ann's emotional confusion with the punchline about the identity of the father seems to encapsulate the combination of the tragic and the comic, the flippant and the historically incisive that one finds throughout Bainbridge's work.[8] It is not, as Brett Josef Grubisic indicates, that "Bainbridge encourages an ambivalent if not actively derisive response" to Ann (84), but that the reader is placed on the same plane as her and is not given an outside perspective from which to measure her actions. Neither is it that Bainbridge engages in "mockery of the would-be emancipatory politics of the sexual revolution" (Grubisic 81), but rather that she questions the degree to which the promises of this revolution have been fulfilled, showing how men like William were able to hijack cultural change.

Reading *Sweet William* in this way goes against the grain of Bainbridge's playful, sometimes disingenuous commentary on her own work, as well as many of the prevailing critical attitudes about it. The latter is no doubt partly informed by the former, but Bainbridge's disavowal of feminism and other critical contexts for her fiction should not be allowed to dominate the work or to contain it within too narrow parameters. Nor should the comic, tacitly satirical nature of the writing overshadow the serious critiques it often offers. Although the feminism in *Sweet William* is not, from a contemporary perspective (and perhaps even from the perspective of the mid-1970s), radical or politically engaged, its identifiably feminist subtext destabilises conventional readings of Bainbridge's fiction and suggests an aporia in the study of postwar women's writing. Her response to lad-lit is perhaps too close in style to the genre itself for this aspect to have been previously acknowledged, but by rewriting the genre from the "other side" Bainbridge suggests a critique of patriarchy comparable in form and political subtext to those of Margaret Atwood, Angela Carter, Emma Tennant, or Michèle Roberts. The sense that Bainbridge's writing is "not what women are currently supposed to come up with" remains, but this is part of what makes her novels so interesting and challenging to critical orthodoxies.

NOTES

1. Lessing has repeatedly disavowed any links with feminism and sees the academic focus on this aspect of her work as reductionist (see, e.g., Lessing), while Brookner "has explicitly distanced herself from feminist politics and declared that her aesthetic ideal is one of Enlightenment rationalism" (Waugh, *Feminine Fictions* 126). Nick Turner also comments on Brookner's anti-feminism and suggests that it has had a significant and negative impact on her reception and position within the canon (70). He makes similar claims for Iris Murdoch, whose reputation has varied greatly over the years (53). Turner's book provides a useful and insightful discussion of "canonicity" in postwar writing, with detailed discussions of four women writers—Murdoch, Brookner, Ruth Rendell, and Emma Tennant—and the factors affecting their positions within the canon.
2. Julian Symons has described Joseph as a "preliminary sketch for sweet William" (40).
3. In the lad-lit novel, a comic tone prevails over any out-and-out anger. This distinguishes it from the work of Alan Sillitoe, David Storey, and other authors of the same period with whose work these novels might otherwise be compared.
4. See British Library Add. MS 83797–83798, Bainbridge Papers Vols. LXIX-LXX for several different versions of "William at the Harvest Festival."
5. Antagonistic pairings are a staple of Bainbridge's fiction, from the embattled marriages in *A Quiet Life* (1976) and *Watson's Apology* (1984), to the mismatched lovers in *Injury Time* (1977) and *Winter Garden* (1980), to the unlikely housemates in *The Bottle Factory Outing* (1974), the resentful aunts in *The Dressmaker* (1972) and the mutually mistrustful Scott and Oates in *The Birthday Boys* (1991).
6. The precise timeframe of *Sweet William* is hard to establish definitively. The setting appears to be the 1960s, and Pamela's near-fatal home termination suggests a date prior to 1967 when abortion was legalised in Britain.
7. This attitude is reflected in an anecdote about the 1972 decision to admit women to King's College, Cambridge, recorded in Germaine Greer's *The Whole Woman* (1999). Greer reports that "a cynical Don was heard to remark, 'Now the men will get their laundry done free'" (122).
8. In the novel, the child is described as looking "like Gerald" (159) and as the "dark-haired baby, with the beaked nose" (160). He certainly is not the "blond and snub-nosed" (89) baby Ann expected from William.

REFERENCES

Amis, Kingsley. *Lucky Jim*. 1954. Harmondsworth: Penguin, 1992. Print.

Atwood, Margaret. "Little Chappies With Breasts." *New York Times* 2 June 1996. Web. 16 August 2012.

———. *The Penelopiad*. 2005. Edinburgh: Canongate, 2006. Print.

Bainbridge, Beryl. *According to Queeney*. London: Little, Brown, 2001. Print.

———. *Another Part of the Wood*. 1968. Rev. ed. London: Duckworth, 1979. Print.

———. "The Art of Fiction CLXIV." Interview by Shusha Guppy. *Paris Review* 157 (2000): 242–68. Print.

———. "Beryl Bainbridge Talks to Yolanta May." *New Review* 3.33 (1976): 48–52. Print.

———. *The Birthday Boys*. London: Duckworth, 1991. Print.

———. *The Bottle Factory Outing*. London: Duckworth, 1974. Print.

———. *The Dressmaker*. London: Duckworth, 1972. Print.

———. "Femail Interview: Beryl Bainbridge." Interview by Mary Riddell. *Daily Mail* 6 September 2001: 52. Print.

———. *Injury Time*. London: Duckworth, 1977. Print.

———. *Master Georgie*. London: Duckworth, 1998. Print.

———. "The *Observer* Profile: Beryl Bainbridge." Interview by Kate Kellaway. *Observer* 25 October 1998, sec. Review: 20. Print.

———. *A Quiet Life*. London: Duckworth, 1976. Print.

———. *Sweet William*. London: Duckworth, 1975. Print.

———. *Watson's Apology*. London: Duckworth, 1984. Print.

———. "What I Know About Men . . . : Beryl Bainbridge." Interview by Nicki Sprinz. *Observer* 15 January 2006, sec. Woman: 22. Print.

———. *Winter Garden*. London: Duckworth, 1980. Print.

———. "You Couldn't Make It Up: Why All My Novels Are About The Men In My Life." *Observer* 22 Feb. 1998, sec. Review: 1. Print.

Barreca, Regina. Introduction. *Last Laughs: Perspectives on Women and Comedy*. Ed. Regina Barreca. New York: Gordon and Breach, 1988. 1–12. Print.

Bradford, Richard. *The Novel Now: Contemporary British Fiction*. Oxford: Blackwell, 2007. Print.

British Library. Add. MS 83793, Bainbridge Papers Vol. LXV, 4.

British Library. Add. MSs 83797–83798, Bainbridge Papers Vols. LXIX–LXX.

Brook, Susan. *Literature and Cultural Criticism in the 1950s: The Feeling Male Body*. Houndmills, Basingstoke: Palgrave Macmillan, 2007. Print.

Carr, Helen. "'Unhomely Moments': The Fictions of Beryl Bainbridge." *Writing Liverpool: Essays and Interviews*. Ed. Deryn Rees-Jones and Michael Murphy. Liverpool: Liverpool University Press, 2007. 72–87. Print.

Carter, Angela. *The Bloody Chamber and Other Stories*. 1979. *Burning Your Boats: Stories*. By Carter. London: Chatto and Windus, 1995. 109–228. Print.

Connor, Steven. *The English Novel in History 1950–1995*. London: Routledge, 1996. Print.

Crompton, Richmal. 1936. *Sweet William*. London: Macmillan, 1986. Print.

Enright, D. J. "Just Going Outside." *London Review of Books* 30 January 1992: 16. Print.

Friedan, Betty. 1963. *The Feminine Mystique*. Harmondsworth: Penguin, 1992. Print.

Gibbs, Alison. *Writers on Writing*. London: Robert Hale, 1995. Print.

Greer, Germaine. *The Female Eunuch*. London: Paladin, 1971. Print

———. *The Whole Woman*. London: Anchor, 2000. Print.

Grubisic, Brett Josef. *Understanding Beryl Bainbridge*. Columbia, SC: University of South Carolina Press, 2008. Print.

Kermode, Frank. "Coming Up for Air." *New York Review of Books* 15 July 1976: 42–44. Print.

de Lauretis, Teresa. *Technologies of Gender: Essays on Theory, Film, and Fiction.* Houndmills, Basingstoke: Macmillan, 1987. Print.

Lessing, Doris. "The *Progressive* Interview: Doris Lessing." Interview by Jonah Raskin. Progressive June 1999. Web. 16 August 2012.

Little, Judy. *Comedy and the Woman Writer: Woolf, Spark, and Feminism.* Lincoln, NE: University of Nebraska Press, 1983. Print.

Lodge, David. Introduction. *Lucky Jim.* By Kingsley Amis. Harmondsworth: Penguin, 1992. v–xvii. Print.

MacLeod, Sheila. "A Fairy Story." *Very Heaven: Looking Back at the 1960s.* Ed. Sara Maitland. London: Virago, 1988. 175–83. Print.

Mantel, Hilary. *An Experiment in Love.* London: Viking, 1995. Print.

Meyers, Helene. *Femicidal Fears: Narratives of the Female Gothic Experience.* Albany, NY: State University of New York Press, 2001. Print.

Naughton, Bill. *Alfie.* 1966. London: Allison and Busby, 1993. Print.

Punter, David. *The Hidden Script.* London: Routledge and Kegan Paul, 1985. Print.

Richter, Virginia. "Grey Gothic: The Novels of Beryl Bainbridge." *(Sub)Versions of Realism: Recent Women's Fiction in Britain.* Ed. Irmgard Maassen and Anna Maria Stuby. Heidelberg: C. Winter, 1997. 159–71. Print.

Rubenstein, Roberta. "The Feminist Novel in the Wake of Virginia Woolf." *A Companion to the British and Irish Novel.* Ed. Brian W. Shaffer. Oxford: Blackwell, 2005. 45–64. Print.

Sage, Lorna. "Female Fictions: The Women Novelists." *The Contemporary English Novel.* Ed. Malcolm Bradbury and David Palmer. London: Edward Arnold, 1979. 67–87. Print.

Sánchez-Arce, Ana María. "Beryl Bainbridge." *Literature in English Post-1914.* Ed. Ian Mackean. London: Hodder and Arnold, 2005. 15–17. Print.

———. "The Prop They Need: Undressing and the Politics of War in Beryl Bainbridge's *Master Georgie.*" *Dressing Up for War: Transformations of Gender and Genre in the Discourse and Literature of War.* Ed. Aránzazu Usandizaga and Andrew Monnickendam. Amsterdam: Rodopi, 2001. 93–110. Print.

Segal, Lynne. *Is the Future Female?: Troubled Thoughts on Contemporary Feminism.* London: Virago, 1987. Print.

———. *Slow Motion: Changing Masculinities, Changing Men.* 3rd ed. Houndmills, Basingstoke: Palgrave Macmillan, 2007. Print.

Showalter, Elaine. "Ladlit." *On Modern British Fiction.* Ed. Zachary Leader. Oxford: Oxford University Press, 2002. 60–76. Print.

———. *A Literature of Their Own: British Women Novelists from Brontë to Lessing.* Rev. ed. London: Virago, 1982. Print.

Spark, Muriel. *The Driver's Seat.* 1970. *The Prime of Miss Jean Brodie, The Girls of Slender Means, The Driver's Seat, The Only Problem.* London: Everyman's Library, 2004. 239–318. Print.

Stamirowska, Krystyna. "The Bustle and Crudity of Life: The Novels of Beryl Bainbridge." *Kwartalnik Neofilologiczny* 35.4 (1988): 445–56. Print.

Stetz, Margaret D. *British Women's Comic Fiction, 1890–1990: Not Drowning, But Laughing.* Aldershot: Ashgate, 2001. Print.

Stevenson, Randall. *The Oxford English Literary History, vol. 12: The Last of England?, 1960–2000.* Oxford: Oxford University Press, 2004. Print.

Sweet William. Dir. Claude Whatham. Perf. Jenny Agutter, Sam Waterson and Anna Massey. Berwick Street, 1980. DVD.

Symons, Julian. "Threats of Violence." *New York Review of Books* 17 July 1980: 39–40. Print.

Tomalin, Claire. "Trite Finish." *New Review* 4.44 (1977): 57–58. Print.

Turner, Nick. *Post-War British Women Novelists and the Canon.* London: Continuum, 2010. Print.

Warner, Val. "Beryl Bainbridge." *Contemporary Novelists.* Ed. James Vinson. New York: St. Martin's, 1976. 79–81. Print.

Waterhouse, Keith. *Billy Liar.* 1959. Harmondsworth: Penguin, 1963. Print.

Waugh, Patricia. *Feminine Fictions: Revisiting the Postmodern.* London: Routledge, 1989. Print.

———. "The Woman Writer and the Continuities of Feminism." *A Concise Companion to Contemporary British Fiction.* Ed. James F. English. Oxford: Blackwell, 2006. 188–208. Print.

Wroe, Nicholas. "The Profile: Beryl Bainbridge." *Guardian* 1 Jun. 2002. Web. 16 Aug. 2012.

6 Affect and Authorial Performance in Angela Carter's "Feminist" Fiction

Michelle Ryan-Sautour

Works of literature that foreground questions of identity often place the persona of the writer at the forefront. The author is not simply inscribed in the text as the infamous "implied author," that is the set of values or orientations that transpire through narrative structure, ideology, characterisation, and so on. He/she also appears in the paratextual discourse of critiques, photos, book covers, marketing, and interviews, as perceived against the landscape of the author's collected writings. Such indications equip the reader with tools to construct a composite image of an author in her/his engagement with identity politics. Angela Carter's work typifies this process and, in fact, actually fosters a tension between reflections on authorial anonymity, evident in the intertextual character of her writing, and the paratextual militancy of the authorial persona that frames it. Many readers, for example, have read Carter's revisionist fairy tales in search of underlying "feminist" discourse, only to be disoriented by a complex orchestration of palimpsests and narrative techniques, indications of ideological strands that resist clear appropriation. This chapter will address this contradiction through a synthesis and study of critical commentary surrounding Carter's authorial performance. I will argue that Carter's problematic authorial identity places the reader at the core of controversy surrounding the tradition of the "death of the author" and reveals how the affect of a militant authorial will can be communicated to the reader and lead to politically productive forms of aesthetic engagement.

It is difficult to think about Carter without her statement, "I'm in the demythologising business" ("Notes" 71) coming to mind. Her socialist inclinations and increasing awareness of the quandaries associated with feminine identity have not only infused her fiction with a political awareness, but have also carried over into the fluctuating fiction of her identity as an author. As both a journalist and fiction writer, Carter has always blended the boundaries of fiction and nonfiction. Sarah Gamble has observed that many of her pieces, as "hybrid writings" (Gamble 2), can easily be inserted into either context, and can simultaneously appeal to different readerships. This is particularly true of autobiographically tinged texts such as "Flesh and the Mirror" (1974) or "The Quilt Maker" (1981), both published in

Carter's collected short fiction, *Burning Your Boats*, but resonating closely with Carter's nonfiction pieces, "The Mother Lode" (1976) and "Sugar Daddy" (1983), which appear in Carter's collection of nonfiction, *Shaking a Leg* (1997) (Gamble 2). Gamble, in *Angela Carter: A Literary Life* (2006), studies this play on boundaries closely, observing Carter's elusive autobiographical self, and the manner in which her writing resists confessional modes. Even towards the end of Carter's life, Gamble remarks how Carter "had retained control of the script of her life to the last" (195), and notes how the facts of Carter's life that have entered the public domain "were put there by Carter herself" (1). Carter's authorial persona appears to develop as a virtual work of art produced over time in a layered sedimentation of declarations and performances. Gamble comments on how Carter's "perennial fascination with masks, masquerade, theatricals and dressing-up, tropes that appear throughout her fiction, in this respect point to the endlessly shifting identity of the author herself" (9), and underlines the incredible consistency in Carter's personal "script" (8), resulting in an opaque, impenetrable version of the author that continues to baffle, as is evident in the glaring absence of any traditional biography concerning the author. Gamble studies Carter's persona in its reciprocity with her texts, preferring the interweaving of fiction and nonfiction in the blurred boundaries of the authorial self to any pretence at penetrating to the origins of Carter's creative persona.

Lorna Sage has also commented on Carter's stylisation of her self, referring to Margaret Atwood's perception of Carter as a "Fairy Godmother" and Carmen Callil's vision of her as an "oracle" of an "enchanted circle" (*Angela* 1). Sage describes how Carter developed the performance of "How to Be the Woman Writer" as a means to test the "distinction between art and life, so that she was inventive in reality as well as in creating plots and characters for the books" (*Angela* 1). Even her physical appearance was constantly shifting, reflecting, as Sage notes, "a way of looking at herself, and other people, as unnatural. She was, even in ordinary and relaxed situations, a touch unlikely on principle. Her hair went through all the colours of the rainbow, before becoming white at the moment when decorum would have suggested a discreet, still-youthful streaked mouse" (*Angela* 28). The 1992 Omnibus documentary, *Angela Carter's Curious Room* filmed shortly before Carter's death speaks of the author's heightened need for a last performance, an incomplete closure to many years of authorial posturing.

Her early death in 1992 has certainly heightened our perception of this authorial performance, as the numerous descriptions generated in her wake have painted a picture of a multifaceted author whom director David Wheatley has described as a "jigsaw" (235) saying that "you could never completely fathom where she stood on anything" (235). As her literary executor, Susannah Clapp, notes, she was hazy on and off the page: "Playing with style, making fairy tale and fantasy tell new truths, was part of the point of her work. 'Is she fact or is she fiction?' was Fevvers's slogan, and it would have been Angela's on the page, and in life" (viii). Carter cultivated this enigmatic presence, making herself appear as perplexing as the speculative schemes outlined in her fiction. As she commented in interview with Kerryn Goldsworthy in 1984, storytelling allows her to evade illusions of authorial transparency: "But if you're telling a story, then you're not telling somebody about yourself. And I've got quite a strong resistance to telling people about myself" (Carter, "Interview Goldsworthy" 6). The fragments of her authorial self emerge instead from rare pieces of personal narrative, impressions derived from her fiction, comments made by her editors and peers, and the words of the author herself.

The numerous quotations in this article attest to the resulting discourse surrounding her person, as various critics and friends observe the forms of her authorial masquerade. Salman Rushdie has described her affectionately as an unruly "wizard," "a thumber of noses, a defiler of sacred cows" who "demolishes the temples and commissariats of righteousness." Indeed, one cannot help but see this figure behind Carter's polemical work *par excellence, The Sadeian Woman* (1979) in which she declares that Sade encourages women to "fuck their way into history and, in doing so, change it" (*Sadeian* 27). Marina Warner has commented on how she found this work a bit frightening (252), and Lorna Sage observes how such writing alienated Carter, placing her on the margins of feminist movements contemporary to her work:

> She was not, either, able to repose securely in the bosom of the sisterhood, since her insistence on reclaiming the territory of the pornographers—just for example—set her against feminist puritans and separatists. [. . .] And, of course, she was in general an offence to the modest, inward, realist version of the woman writer. (*Angela* 40–1)

It is perhaps one of the most powerful ironies of Carter's work that her feminist impulse is so clearly underlined both within and outside of her writing, only to be in conflict with what Denise Riley describes as the "ossified massifications" of feminism (*Words* 176). Carter's 1977 novel, *The Passion of New Eve*, undeniably submits the phenomenon of "'women' en bloc" (*Words* 176) to a slippery game of parody and irony, presciently suggesting a will for "demassification" and heterology, a solidarity concomitant with a recognition of differences. Certainly declarations such as "In Japan, I learnt what it is to be a woman and became radicalized" (Carter, *Nothing* 29) have been integrated into the rich and varied strata of Carter's commentaries on feminist politics, serving to many critics as an entryway into her aesthetics in what is, perhaps, an inadvertent fetishisation of "authentic" feminism. Ana María Sánchez-Arce has commented extensively on political appropriations of the concept of authenticity in relation to authorship, and notes, in reference to Gayatri Chakravorty Spivak, how "Authenticity is called upon, summoned as it were, in much the same way that God or the Muses would have been in the past. This is unsurprising given the close links between authenticity and Romanticism. The fact that authenticity is 'invoked' highlights its status as—to use Michel Foucault's terminology—a discourse of truth" (142). Carter appears to harness this mechanism of invocation; she troubles the "truths" of authentic feminism through a potent, complex interplay between fictional matrices and nonfictional, authorial affirmations. Like her fiction, which hovers on the fringes of metafiction, the gothic, science fiction, fantasy, magical realism, and so on, Carter was a difficult figure to categorize. Called "feminist" by some, yet rejected by certain factions of the movement, her enigmatic presence is intertwined with the cryptic political ideas embedded in her fiction. Robert Coover observes her "appetite for irony and parodox," explaining how her "narratives do not surrender easily to neat allegorical and interpretive schemes" ("Introduction" 243). Despite overt declarations about "demythologising," or comments about language as "power, life and the instrument of culture, the instrument of domination and liberation" (Carter, "Notes" 77), it is strikingly difficult to establish a set agenda in Carter's writing beyond an obligation to, as she states in interview with John Haffenden, "explicate and to find about things" (96).

Clapp has also commented on the connection between Carter's speech performance and the complexity of Carter's prose which she characterizes as "allusive, parodic and playful" (viii). It is fascinating to observe the number of commentaries made about Carter's voice. Clapp describes her "exceptional verbal sharpness" and how Carter "surrounded her trenchancies with long pauses, huge wheezes of silent laughter, verbal flutters in which south London slang took over from her usual piping tones" (viii). Robert Coover marvels at her range of inflections: "Her voice was unforgettable, and above all her telephone voice, a reed instrument of marvelous versatility and emotional range, chimelike in its bold ringing of metaphors, saturated with wry self-deprecating humor, and utterly compelling" ("Passionate" 9). Marina Warner notes Carter's biting illocution, "But Angela specialised in provocation; she had a way of tilting her head, lifting the corner of her lips on one side and lowering her eyes as she delivered softly, in her near stammer, some delicious, poisoned barb at the pieties or thoughtless prejudices of her interlocutor" (251). Kerryn Goldsworthy has commented on Carter's "soft and beautifully modulated voice," and describes the experience of watching Carter give a reading at Deakin University, "holding the audience still and silent with an ethereal performance that called to mind her early ambition to be an actress" (qtd. Carter, "Interview Goldsworthy" 4). It is, in fact, the theatricality of this storytelling voice that dominates Carter's authorial persona towards the end of her career with her emphasis on editing the fairy tale.

As Lorna Sage comments, this shift had already appeared with the publication of *The Bloody Chamber* (1979): "The fairy tale idea enabled her to *read* in public with a new appropriateness and panache, as though she was *telling* these stories" (*Angela* 40). This leads Sage to perceive her as performing in turn the roles of "Fairy Godmother," mentioned above, and also playing with the originary image of tale-telling, Mother Goose in the 1980s, "she read aloud with increasing pleasure and style, she wrote introductions, edited anthologies—a Woman of Letters in the mocking mould of Mother Goose" (*Angela* 42), roles that have since been submitted to the critical lens of multiple academics. According to Sage, Carter's experimentation with her role as a writer allowed her to "ally herself in imagination with the countless, anonymous narrators who stood behind the literary redactors like Perrault, or (much later) the brothers Grimm" (*Angela* 40). The result is the development of a "robust political and performative role" (*Angela* 40) which, as Stephen Benson has observed, appears as a "feminist strategy" in her "distinctly un-Blooming conception of literary tradition and influence," and her "pantomimic notion of authorship" (47). Benson reads Carter's performance in the role of oral narrator as "deliberate" and "staged in part to deflate the myth of paternal authority" (47).

Indeed, as Lorna Sage remarks, Carter's politically charged experimentation with these "tale-telling models that date from the time before the author was an individual" ties in with her "personal transformation" of Roland Barthes' famous "Death of the Author" (*Angela* 43), a now familiar association with Carter's writing. Sage's comment highlights a diffuse political militancy at the heart of Carter's fiction, evident in rewriting practices and a foregrounding of multivoiced representations. Carter's political territories foreground the variegated lives of all utterance, be it those of literary allusion, cliché, stereotypes, or colloquialisms, and her texts display a self-consciousness of the amassment of ideological layers in language. Sage identifies the "nostalgia for anonymity" evident in Carter's work, yet also notes Carter's attraction to the "whiff of original sin" apparent in Carter's use of the "grandmother-guise of the yarn spinner" ("Introduction" 2). Sage's emphasis on hybridity, on the demystification of the individual self ("Introduction" 3), as predominant utopian promises in Carter's work, raises the polyvocality of Carter's work to the foreground, indicating a dissemination of authorial authority in her fiction, and the potential liberation in the activity of "talking about the self as socially determined" (*Angela* 44).

According to Cheryl Walker, this corresponds to a heightened consciousness in feminism of the advantages of a poststructuralist vision of authorship: "theoretically informed feminist critics have recently found themselves tempted to agree with Barthes, Foucault, and the Edward Said of *Beginnings* that the authorial presence is best set aside in order to liberate the text for multiple uses" (142). Amongst Carter's aesthetic declarations can be found a consistent celebration of the reader's creativity, and an emphasis on the power of reading: "Reading is as creative an activity as writing" (Carter, "Notes" 69). According to Carter, the main authorial moral imposed upon the reader in her fiction is "curiosity": "But the moral function should not be hortatory in any way—telling people how to behave. [. . .] I would regard curiosity as a moral function" ("Interview Haffenden" 96). In the framing of her own work, there is an insistence on creating new configurations of reading. It is certainly for this reason that she drew attention to the work of Milorad Pavic, as he "isn't interested in a new way of writing. He is interested in a new way of *reading*" ("Milorad Pavic" 497).[1] By liberating the author, Carter was indeed also liberating the reader, and thus releasing her feminism to a plurality of viewpoints.

However, as Walker observes, this multiplicity is not without constraints, and the "who is speaking" question underlined by Foucault in "What is an Author" is exceedingly relevant for a rethinking of authorial presence, particularly in relation to the reader:

> Ideology will also govern our construction of the author, especially but not only if the author becomes *un sujet à aimer*, a someone to love. Yes, I want to ask like Foucault 'What difference does it make who is speaking?' But I want to answer, the difference it makes, in terms of the forces I can persuade you are speaking, occupies a crucial position in the ongoing discussion of difference itself. (157)

The republication of Walker's 1990 essay in William Irwin's 2002 collection attests to its relevance, as it brings the question of authorship to the fore of feminist criticism. Instead of adhering to complete authorial erasure, or an easy return to a common sense approach to treatments of the author, Walker calls for what she labels "persona criticism":

> My own brand of *persona criticism* assumes that to erase a woman poet as the author of her poems in favor of an abstract indeterminacy is an act of oppression. However, every version of the persona will be a mask of the author we cannot lightly remove. When one discovers the proliferation of a certain kind of mask in a given poet (the mask of the passionate virgin in Sara Teasdale, for instance) it is interesting to ask: What social configurations of the feminine might have led to this mask? (157)

The "who is speaking" question indeed appears exceedingly apposite for a study of Carter's shifting facades. Her apparent nostalgia for anonymity and professed aversion to Romantic authorial individualism coexists paradoxically with the militancy of her persona in the realms of both literary and extra-textual performance. Walker does not further develop her concept, but rather suggests it as a path towards future reflection, proposing that we rethink our role as readers in relation to the masks of the author. We might take this a step further in conceiving of these masks as a fluctuating amalgam with its own temporality, an author continually "becoming" in the reader's mind. As she suggests in her historical contextualisation of Sara Teasdale's writing, one might also examine the figure of the author in light of the temporality of the literary object and the shifting horizon of expectations of the reading public. Until now, the "feminist" mask has appeared as the most pervasive element in relation to Carter's aesthetics, as is evident in the numerous articles dealing with the question of literary aesthetics and sexual identity, but this is gradually giving way to other questions such as the problematic question of "who is speaking." Carter's staging of the author-text relationship indeed places the reader at the heart of critical tensions and ambivalence regarding authorship and the woman writer. Mary Eagleton gives a striking overview of this process in *Figuring the Woman Author in Contemporary Fiction* (2005), underlining what she calls a "twin impulse both to give birth to the woman author and to bury her" in reaction to Barthes's "Death of the Author" (3). However, this does not simply occur through the use of author-characters, or even authorial personas, but also in the reading mechanisms set into play through structure. Just as the lay reader's initial reflex in entering a work of fiction is to seek out a story,[2] so does the reader's perception of the author affect his/her entry into a fictional work. Carter's fiction, particularly her work with short narrative, plays upon such normative reflexes in relation to the authorial mask; it triggers reading pragmatics associated with images of the author "god," impressions that persist in contemporary relationships to the author, and feed the reader's need for an authorial figure to validate one's reading. Jean-Jacques Lecercle, in his *Interpretation as Pragmatics* (1999), comments on how "the reader needs an author to play with, to authorise her reading and grant it the weight of his authority" (14). Angela Carter's work, with its overt militancy, and performance-oriented pragmatic structures, accompanied by the politically charged image of the "real" author, displays an exploitation, and even subversion, of this need for authority which is consequently, and unexpectedly, transformed into an additional zone of speculation.

The narrator figure is often portrayed in Carter's fiction, for example, with an overt didactic function, and interpellation of the reader is foregrounded. Monika Fludernik has commented on the "pronominal acrobatics" that predominate in Carter's short fiction, and how these intensify the reader's interpretive engagement with the text: "Temporal and pronominal changes such as those employed by Carter in the two stories therefore ultimately serve as shifters and as metatextual clues to the need for interpretative sophistication" (216). Such a phenomenon is particularly evident in one of Carter's most well-known stories, "The Company of Wolves," where the overt play with the slippery hypotext of "Little Red Riding Hood," intensifies the reader's interaction with the processes of "demythologising," as is evident in the amount of critical attention the story has received:

> She saw how his jaw began to slaver and the room was full of the clamour of the forest's Liebestod but the wise child never flinched, even when he answered:

All the better to eat you with.

The girl burst out laughing; she knew she was nobody's meat. She laughed at him full in the face, she ripped off his shirt for him and flung it into the fire, in the fiery wake of her own discarded clothing. The flames danced like dead souls on Walpurgisnacht and the old bones under the bed set up a terrible clattering but she did not pay them any heed. (Carter, *Bloody* 118)

Echoes of familiar versions of the tale with "all the better to eat you with," along with explicit revisions of the role of Red in the character's laughing, "freely" giving a kiss, and the narrator's comment, "she knew she was nobody's meat," invite the reader to adopt the detective mode of recognising shifts in the fairy tale, along with perceiving the ideological function of such revision. Terms such as "Liebestod" teasingly ask the reader to interpret their relationship to the wolf/Red as a "couple" and a nexus for critical investigations. A political agenda hovers in the background of such open rewriting strategies, an effect that is heightened by narrative interpellation that intensifies the reader's involvement:

The blizzard will die down.

The blizzard died down, leaving the mountains as randomly covered with snow as if a blind woman had thrown a sheet over them, the upper branches of the forest pines limed, creaking, swollen with the fall.
[...]
Midnight; and the clock strikes. It is Christmas Day, the werewolves' birthday, the door of the solstice stands wide open; let them all sink through.

See! Sweet and sound she sleeps in granny's bed, between the paws of the tender wolf. (118)

This is accentuated by the multiple temporal shifts in the narration, as the future mode of the above example gives way to the past, and then shifts to the present in the same passage, a typical practice in Carter's aesthetics that, in addition to the pronominal shifts underlined by Fludernik, disconcerts, and exerts a force upon the reader, an imperative to stretch his/her mind into intellectual acrobatics in order to maintain a mental "footing" in the text. The use of the imperative in the last line, with "See!" emphasizes the illusion of a hectoring author.

Many of Carter's works begin with forceful imperatives. "The Cabinet of Edgar Allan Poe," for example, begins with "Imagine Poe in the Republic!" (Carter, *Saints* 71). "Overture and Incidental music for *A Midsummer Night's Dream*" begins with "Call me the Golden Herm" (Carter, *Saints* 85), and "Alice in Prague *or* The Curious Room" begins with "Outside the curious room there is a sign on the door which says 'Forbidden'. Inside, inside, oh, come and see! The celebrated Dr. Dee" (Carter, *American*

Ghosts 121). The examples are numerous in Carter's fictional aesthetics where a didactic narrator appears to pull the strings of the reader upon the stage of fiction as a "system of signification."[3] These are just a few examples of how the reader is openly invited into Carter's "theatre" so as to participate in the performance of language and ideology at play. There appears to be an ongoing dialogue between the "I" of the narrator and the "you" of the reader. The following passage taken from "The Werewolf" typifies this practice in Carter's fiction:

> To these upland woodsmen, the Devil is as real as *you* or *I*. More so; *they* have not seen *us* nor even know that *we* exist, but the Devil *they* glimpse often in the graveyards, those bleak and touching townships of the dead where the graves are marked with portraits of the deceased in the naïf. (Carter, *Bloody* 108 emphasis added)

The complicity of the narrator and the reader as the "we" and the "us" as opposed to the "they" of the "upland woodsmen" who have not seen "us" (the reader and authorial figure) accentuates a general bond with the authorial figure in Carter's writing. In "A Souvenir of Japan," a fictionalised love affair with autobiographical resonances (the story is about a Japanese lover, and Carter's experiences in Japan are openly referred to in her "Afterword" to the collection) (Carter, *Fireworks* 132–133), the "I" of an authorial narrator appeals to the "you" of the reader: "Well, then, you must realize that I was suffering from love and I knew him as intimately as I knew my own image in a mirror. In other words, I knew him only in relation to myself. Yet, on those terms, I knew him perfectly. At times, I thought I was inventing him as I went along, however, so you will have to take my word for it that we existed" (Carter *Fireworks* 9).[4] In another prominent pseudo-autobiographical story from the same collection, "Flesh and the Mirror," the text simultaneously resists and cultivates autobiographical appropriation, and the reader's attempts to capture the "real" Carter give rise to unanticipated forms of speculation:

> The magic mirror presented me with a hitherto unconsidered notion of myself as I. Without any intention of mine, I had been defined by the action reflected in the mirror. I beset me. I was the subject of the sentence written on the mirror. I was not watching it. There was nothing whatsoever beyond the surface of the glass. Nothing kept me from the fact, the act; I had been precipitated into knowledge of the real conditions of living. (Carter, *Fireworks* 71)

The trope of the mirror as a metonymy for identity crises, and the grammatical games with the shifting pronouns/subjects of "I" and "Me" openly foreground a reflection on the quandaries of identity, and intertwine the questionable status of fiction with that of the author as character.[5] These are well known textual manifestations of the boundary blurring practices of Carter's writing and life. Such semi-fictional life scripts, along with extra-textual performances, amplify the reader's reflex to seek out the figure of Angela Carter.

Sarah Gamble perceives in Carter's multilayered fictionalised autobiographies such as that of Fevvers in *Nights at the Circus* (1984) and Dora and Nora Chance in *Wise Children* (1991), an echo of the veiled "I" in Carter's autobiographical writings: "Carter is mimicking in fiction what she was also doing with her own life story. Her autobiographical essays are similarly, not a means of revelation, but rather of disguise, creating a crafted persona for public display" (197). As Gamble observes, the result is the perception of an author as a "screen of words," suggesting that authenticity is only an illusion, as Carter is thus "concealed from public view" (197). Gamble focuses a particular attention on Carter's national identity, particularly her "Englishness" in relation to her family background, and observes the resulting "tensions" Carter habitually returns to between "north and south; proletariat and petit bourgeois; charm, and the madness that charm conceals" (199); her "literary persona" is therefore based on "the conflation of opposites that exist side by side, unreconciled into a seamless whole" (201). Although "seamless" does not best describe the disjunctions that appear in Carter's juxtapositions and staging of tensions, the idea of contradictory forces at work in her fiction as well as her nonfiction are evidently interlaced with her authorial performance. Of particular interest is Gamble's discussion of the shifts in persona following Carter's death, wryly summarised by Pat Barker:

> she dies untimely, and everyone suddenly bursts out weeping. The obituaries give her better notices than anything she ever wrote received in her lifetime. Her books sell out within three days of her death. She becomes the most read contemporary author on English university campuses. Her last story, finished during her final illness, sells 80,000 copies in paperback. She has arrived. But she is dead. (Barker qtd. Gamble 203)

What Gamble ultimately, yet inadvertently, underlines in her subsequent summary of the myriad visions of Carter in the wake of her death, in the mass of obituaries issued by friends, writers, critics, editors, is the metamorphic potential of Carter's persona, as she suggests the "fairy godmother role" gives way to that of the "tragic image of the writer who died too young" (204). As the script Carter authored for herself is gradually released to the forces of time, it indeed leaves the question of her identity open, as Gamble notes: "Complete closure is impossible in the case of a literary life, for such a life continues as long as an audience for that author still exists" (204–5). However, this persona is not only open ended, but also, because of the wilful manipulations demonstrated by Carter, and the structure of her fiction, remains an essential aspect of the reading pragmatics associated with the work, as the seeking out of her figure, behind the "screen" of works highlighted by Gamble, remains an important force in the politics of her writing practices, an effect that has not yet received sufficient critical attention. There appears to be a celebratory trend in Carter criticism that colours essays with the "intentions" of the author by either seeking out the threads of Carter's own critical commentary in her fiction, or attempting to exemplify Carter's demythologising. Gamble comments, for example, on the tendency of critics to avoid conclusions (Gamble 204) in deference to Carter's own resistance to closure, showing that Carter's persona, as changeable as it might be, persists as a forceful shadow in both the reading and criticism of her work.

Carter's well-known predilection for self-conscious modes fuels this process. Laurent Lepaludier observes how metafiction fosters links between the author and the fictional exchange: "The literary text can present an analogical effect between the elements of the narrative and the different aspects of the literary communication act. A character or a narrator can be considered as the figure of the writer and stimulate a reflection about the act of writing, the process of writing, the text's aesthetics, or the status of the writer" (31 my translation).[6] The most classic example is when the narrator is cast in the role of the author, such as in Carter's rewriting of Shakespeare's Puck character in "Overture and Incidental Music for a Midsummer Night's Dream": "Puck is no more polymorphously perverse than all the rest of these submicroscopic particles, his peers, yet there is something particularly rancid and offensive about his buggery and his undinism and his frotteurism and his scopophilia and his—indeed, my very paper would *blush*, go pink as an invoice should I write down upon it some of the things Puck gets up to down in the reeds by the river" (Carter, *Saints* 90). Such asides are familiar territory in the postmodern realm of fiction Carter's fiction tends to occupy. Analogy is also a powerful tool for creating links between other art forms to reflect back upon fiction. The theatre is a favourite trope of Carter's, and one cannot help but perceive a veiled discourse about characters as puppets in the author's theatre of fiction in the following statement from "The Loves of Lady Purple," "The puppeteer speculates in a no-man's limbo between the real and that which, although we know very well it is not, nevertheless seems to be real. He is the intermediary between us, his audience, the living, and they, the dolls, the undead, who cannot live at all and yet who mimic the living in every detail since, though they cannot speak or weep, still they project those signals of signification we instantly recognize as language" (Carter, *Fireworks* 24–25). The reflection on language evident in the segment, "signals of signification," can also be perceived in the intertextual games in Carter's texts, as words appear in multiple guises, and are placed in surprising combinations within the same phrase. The reader is interpellated by the elusive political project present behind such practices.

Relations with the author in Carter's texts are indeed slippery, as Carter's staged performance as a writer is intricately intertwined with the political thrust of reflections on language and society set forth in her aesthetics. Her militant yet changeable authorial persona affects the illocutionary force of her fictional texts, if we treat them, as Jean-Jacques Lecercle suggests, as "extended speech act[s]": "I mean systematically to operate a metaphorical extension from *speech act* to *text*, from *linguistic interlocution* to *textual interpretation: interpretation is a language-game in which a text is treated as an extended speech act*, involving the five actants [speaker (author), text, language, encylopaedia, hearer (reader)] already mentioned, and rules or maxims that remain to be formulated" (34). Sage has commented on the dispersal of authority in Carter's text: "It's a paradoxical authority, because it involves the multiplication and dispersal of the narrative voice ('power is everywhere'). This is performative and political writing, writing that means to *work*" ("Introduction" *Flesh* 2). Despite the hybrid, shifting nature of her texts, the image of the real author, with her political declarations and her play with persona, haunt the texts, encouraging the reflex, underlined by Lecercle, to ascribe intentions to an authorial figure, in our case that of Carter, who in turn is transformed by the reader:[7] "The process of interpretation both needs to ascribe meaning to an author's *intention* [. . .] and to *ascribe* such intention, which is therefore an effect of construction. The author is not only Victor Frankenstein creating a monster that turns against him, he is also the monstrous creation of the reader, who acquires a life and a will of his own" (Lecercle 149). Lecercle makes a distinction between the real author, and the position in relation to language that is accorded him/her in reading/writing. Recognising the power of language to exert force upon the speaker, Lecercle demonstrates how texts, and in particular literature, can stage our consequent struggle for autonomy in relation to language: "my interpellation as a subject may fail, and my self be shattered. This maxim [. . .] insists on the *fragility of interpellation*. Because the stability of a self is obtained by composition and summation, it is always threatened with return to the original fragmentation [. . .] It is the role of literature to stage such processes" (183).

Carter juxtaposes diffuse authority, that is the image of Carter that flickers in her fiction, in what Gamble sees as "narrative that functions as a hall of mirrors reflecting multiple images" (197), with the affect of authorial political will. This affect is conveyed through the interpretative scheme set into action through the reading of her fiction. According to Lecercle, the author is both master and slave, both subjected and subjecting, (150) reflecting what Denise Riley has described, in a perhaps less agonistic portrayal, as the impersonal of language being made personal: "Language is impersonal: its working through and across us is indifferent to us, yet in the same blow it constitutes the fiber of the personal" (*Impersonal* 1). Riley, in her introduction to *Impersonal Passion* (2005) comments on the perceived tension between individual autonomy and the impersonal forces at work in language, exploring how such forces work "with" the speaker:

The following essays are pragmatic, their emphasis not so much on How to Do Things with Words, as Austin's title had it, but How Words Do Things with Us. And that 'with us'—as distinct from 'to us'—is pivotal. [. . .] [These essays] fray at the edges of that usual antithesis (crudely, in 'continental' versus analytic philosophy) between language as speaking us, and our status as freely choosing users of language. As a result they'll come closer to apprehending language's affect as that outward unconscious which hovers between people, rather than swimming upward from the privacy of the heart. (3–4)

Carter's fiction, with its dense, multilayered intertextual structures, stages what Riley identifies as the "ventriloquy of inner speech" (*Impersonal* 7) as a sort of individual communion with the exterior forces of language in the spirit of "as if" they had been individually produced. It is this concept of "as if" that predominates in a reading process where Carter appears as a "fantasy" to the reader, as a construction through interpellation: "The term 'fantasy' points out that the status of the author is that of the subject of ideology, subjectified by ideology, who has an *imaginary* relation to his real conditions of existence. At the very moment when we construct the figure, we treat the author 'as if' he were a real subject" (Lecercle 149). It is in the entertainment of this "as if" connection that the perlocutionary effects of the Carterian utterance can emerge to the reader.

The realm of the imaginary in our relation to subjectivity is therefore placed at the forefront of the textual communication situation staged in Carter's fiction. Carter's tricky authorial figure, as she appears in a cumulative form through the commentaries that frame her fictions, resonates with textual and narrative structures laden with political affect. This compels readers to creatively seek out reflections concerning identity, producing multiple forms of engagement with the issues embedded in her writing, entering into a process of interpellation that works with and through the reader in his/her play with the figure of Carter. In her exploitation of the reader's imagined relationship to the author on both textual, paratextual, and extratextual levels, Carter inadvertently creates varied forms of interaction with the power of language as an "instrument of culture" through each individual reading experience. As her collected works are submitted to the temporality of literary history, this process will certainly remain in the foreground, undergoing gradual shifts as the memory of her physical presence and performances are sifted through layers of critical framing and commentary. As Mary Eagleton observes, corporeal death produces subtle alterations in the sense of life attributed to the author, "Thus, death is both the 'final signified'—there will be no new work from this author—and the event that permits the most open and flexible reading," and she underlines the "paradox" that in the author's physical death "we always have the strongest sense of the life while the metaphorical death of the author is unable to escape from a sense of the insistent presence of the author" (21). In June 2006, the South Bank Centre organised a day of talks to pay homage to Carter, and her novel, *Nights at the Circus* was brought to the stage by Emma Rice the same year, all signs, as Christina Patterson observes, that the life of Carter as author is far from over: "For much of her far-too-short life, her books were remaindered and out of print. Less than 14 years after her death, however, she seems set for a whole new lease of life." It is indeed in our reaching for the metamorphic, shape-shifting figure of Carter that her image will live on in the minds of readers and critics alike, attesting to her insistent presence, however unfixed and impalpable it might be.

NOTES

1. Carter highlights the capacity of Pavic's text to influence the reader's participation, "If the text is a constant, then the ways of reading it are not. Pavic's reader is invited, via the formal device of a crossword puzzle and its clues, to read the book 'not in order of succession and across (as the river flows) but *down*, as the rain falls'" (Carter, "Milorad Pavic" 497).
2. Susan Lohafer, in reference to the work of cognitive scientists, insists upon the inherent reflex of each reader to seek out "storyness" in a narrative: "Each chapter revolves around an experiment in which one or more readers identify sentences within a short story where the text *could* end. In doing so, readers tap a deeply ingrained ability to recognize narrative wholeness, which I call *storyness*. [. . .] However, I am making no formal claim for a transgender, transethnic, or transracial Ur-model. All I am asserting is that preclosure study brings assumptions about storyness to light, no matter how relative they may be to their corner of the world" (3).
3. As Carter comments in relation to her novel *Nights at the Circus* (1984): "it does seem a bit of an imposition to say to readers that if you read this book you have got to be thinking all the time; so it's there only if you want it. From *The Magic Toyshop* onwards I've tried to keep an entertaining surface to the novels, so that you don't have to read them as a system of signification if you don't want to" (Carter, "Haffenden" 87).
4. I have commented extensively on the reading pragmatics associated with three of Carter's fictionalised pieces with autobiographical overtones in "Autobiographical Estrangement in Angela Carter's "'A Souvenir of Japan,' 'The Smile of Winter' and 'Flesh and the Mirror'" (Ryan-Sautour).
5. Mary Eagleton has commented on this process: "Though not everyone is as mischievous as Muriel Spark who uses her fictional author, Fleur Talbot, to respond to critiques made of her own writing and one would not want to present all fiction as merely veiled autobiography, the figure of the woman author provides the living woman author with opportunities to explore, to some extent at least, her own situation, her aspirations and anxieties. A number of texts play on the notion of the creation of a 'real' authorial life by their use of biographical and autobiographical modes" (4–5).
6. "Le texte littéraire peut présenter en effet des analogies entre des éléments du récit et des aspects de l'acte de communication littéraire. Un personnage ou un narrateur peut-être considérée comme figure de l'écrivain et provoquer une réflexion sur l'écriture, sa production, son esthétique ou le statut de l'écrivain" (Lepaludier 31).

7. I have studied this phenomenon in "Revisiting the 'Intentional Fallacy' as a Political Mechanism in Angela Carter's 'The Loves of Lady Purple.'" (Ryan-Sautour)

REFERENCES

Benson, Stephen. "Angela Carter and the Literary *Märchen*: A Review Essay." *Angela Carter and the Fairy Tale*. Ed. Danielle M. Roemer and Cristina Bacchilega. Detroit, MI: Wayne State University Press, 2001. 30–58. Print.

Carter, Angela. *American Ghosts and Old World Wonders*. 1993. London: Vintage, 1994. Print.

———. *The Bloody Chamber*. 1979. New York: Penguin, 1993. Print.

———. Carter, Angela. *Burning Your Boats*. 1995. New York, Penguin, 1997. Print.

———. *Fireworks*. 1974. New York: Penguin, 1987. Print.

———. Interview. *Angela Carter's Curious Room*. Dir. Kim Evans. BBC 2. 15.9.1992. Film Documentary, BFI Film archives, London.

———. Interview by Kerryn Goldsworthy. *meanjin*. 44.1 (1985): 4–13. Print.

———. Interview by John Haffenden. *Novelists in Interview*. London: Methuen, 1985. 76–96. Print.

———. "Milorad Pavic: Landscape Painted with Tea." 1991. *Shaking a Leg*. Ed. Joan Smith. London: Chatto and Windus, 1997. 496–8. Print.

———. "Notes from the Front Line." *On Gender and Writing*, Ed. Michelene Wandor London: Pandora Press, 1983. 69–77. Print.

———. *Nothing Sacred*. 1982. London: Virago, 1992. Print.

———. *The Passion of New Eve*. 1977. London: Virago, 1995.

———. *The Sadeian Woman*. 1979. New York, Penguin, 2001. Print.

———. *Saints and Strangers*. 1985. New York: Penguin, 1986. Print.

———. *Shaking a Leg*, Ed. Jenny Uglow. London: Chatto & Windus, 1997. Print.

Clapp, Susannah. 1996. Introduction. *The Curious Room*. London: Vintage, 1997. vii–x. Print.

Coover, Robert. "Introduction to 'Entering Ghost Town'." *Angela Carter and the Fairy Tale*. Ed. Danielle M. Roemer and Cristina Bacchilega. Detroit, MI: Wayne State University Press, 2001. 242–9. Print.

———. "A Passionate Remembrance." *Review of Contemporary Fiction*. 14.3 (1994): 9–10. Print.

Eagleton, Mary. *Figuring the Woman Author in Contemporary Fiction*. Houndmills, Basingstoke: Palgrave, 2005. Print.

Fludernik, Monika. "Angela Carter's Pronominal Acrobatics: Language in 'The Erl-King' and 'The Company of Wolves.'" *European Journal of English Studies* (EJES) 2.2 (1998): 215–37. Print.

Foucault, Michel. "What Is an Author?" 1969. *The Norton Anthology: Theory and Criticism*. Ed. Vincent B. Leitch. New York: W.W. Norton & Company, 2001. 1622–36. Print.

Gamble, Sarah. *Angela Carter: A Literary Life*. New York: Palgrave Macmillan, 2006. Print.

Lecercle, Jean-Jacques. *Interpretation as Pragmatics*. New York: St. Martin's Press, 1999. Print.

Lepaludier, Laurent. "Procédés métatextuels et processus cognitifs." *Métatextualité et Métafiction: Théorie et Analyses*. Rennes: Presses Universitaires de Rennes, 2002. 25–38. Print.

Lohafer, Susan. *Reading for Storyness*. Baltimore, MD: Johns Hopkins University Press, 2003. Print.

Patterson, Christina. "Angela Carter: Beauty and the Beasts." *The Independent*. 18 January 2006. Web. 10 July 2010.

Riley. Denise. *Impersonal Passion: Language as Affect*. Durham, NC: Duke University Press, 2005. Print.

———. *The Words of Selves: Identification, Solidarity, Irony*. Palo Alto, CA: Stanford University Press, 2000. Print.

Rushdie, Salman. "Angela Carter, 1940–92: A Very Good Wizard, a Very Dear Friend." *New York Times on The Web*. 8 March 1992. Web. 25 August 2012.

Ryan-Sautour, Michelle, "Autobiographical Estrangement in Angela Carter's 'A Souvenir of Japan,' 'The Smile of Winter' and 'Flesh and the Mirror'." *Etudes britanniques contemporaines*. 32 (2007): 57–76. Print.

———. "Revisiting the 'Intentional Fallacy' as a Political Mechanism in Angela Carter's 'The Loves of Lady Purple'." *Journal of the Short Story in English*. 54 (2010). Print.

Sage, Lorna. *Angela Carter*. Plymouth, Northcote House Publishers, 1994. Print.

———. Introduction. *Flesh and the Mirror*. Ed. Lorna Sage. London: Virago, 1994. 1–23. Print.

Sánchez-Arce, Ana María. "'Authenticism,' or the Authority of Authenticity." *Mosaic*. 40.3 (2007): 139–55. Print.

Walker, Cheryl. "Feminist Literary Criticism and the Author." 1990. *The Death and Resurrection of the Author?* Ed. William Irwin. Westport, CT: Greenwood Press, 2002. 141–59. Print.

Warner, Marina. Introduction. "Ballerina: The Belled Girl Sends a Tape to an Impresario." *Angela Carter and the Fairy Tale*. Ed. Danielle M. Roemer and Cristina Bacchilega. Detroit, MI: Wayne State University Press, 2001. 250–3. Print.

Wheatley, David. Interview by Cristina Bacchilega. "In the Eye of the Fairy Tale: Corinna Sargood and David Wheatley Talk about Working with Angela Carter." *Angela Carter and the Fairy Tale*. Ed. Danielle M. Roemer and Cristina Bacchilega. Detroit, MI: Wayne State University Press, 2001. 225–41. Print.

7 The Role of Jeanette Winterson's Sexual Identity in the Academic Reception of Her Work

Zita Farkas

LITERARY RECEPTION AND THE WRITER'S IDENTITY

Contemporary writers are often engaged in debates around the reception of their work based on their identity. Writers such as Zadie Smith, Irvine Welsh, Arundhati Roy, Jeanette Winterson, and Jackie Kay object to what they see as the reduction of their work to the expression of their ethnicity or sexuality. However, this connection between the writer's identity and her/his work is intensified by several literary practices such as publishing and marketing. Within the field of academic criticism, feminist, lesbian or queer readings are dismissed as interpretations driven by the gender and/or sexuality of the writer.

Literary reception is formed by the complicated interconnection of a multiplicity of practices. The positioning of a writer's work within the vast field of literature is influenced by the processes of marketing and publishing, by interpretations constructed through the academic discourse, by interviews and reviews appearing in the media, by university syllabi, literary prizes, readings and appearances at literary festivals. Looking at literary reception as a process incorporating all these practices implicates the understanding of literature as an institution defined by the social and cultural discourses constructed by these practices.

Considering "literature as a cultural apparatus" involves the exploration of "the social genesis of the literary field—of the belief which sustains it, of the language game played in it, of the interests and the material or symbolic stakes engendered in it" (Bourdieu xix). One of the main interests in this field is the relationship between the writer and his/her work since the way authorship is conceptualised influences the way we approach and interpret literature. This relationship has undergone several changes during the centuries from the Romantic author who was the embodiment of genius and originality to the postmodern author who lost his/her supremacy and vanished into textuality. The "death of the author", proclaimed by Roland Barthes, became one of the governing ideas in structuralist and poststructuralist literary analysis of the twentieth century. However, there has been a resurrection of the author by several critics such as Nancy K. Millner, Sara Ahmed, and

Rita Felski who contest the complete denial of the author's existence. In their readings, the author is no longer cut off from the text. Instead, the author, the "embodied subject," is part of a complex interplay between work, auto-biography and social/cultural formations. I distinguish between "author" and "writer." I apply the term "author" to the discursive construction of the writer. In Foucauldian terminology, I reflect upon the "authorial function." The "writer" refers to the individual person.

This complex interplay between writer and work expressed through the concept of the author extends beyond the field of literary theory. The way writers are authored is the product of several social and cultural prac-tices defining the literary field. Thus "authorial identities [. . .] have been shaped interactively by the conditions under which texts are produced, dis-seminated and consumed" (Hadjiafxendi and Mackay 2). Publishing and marketing are social and cultural practices that produce and disseminate literary texts and also influence their consumption. Since producing and disseminating texts involves the negotiation of the relationship between writer and work, these two practices, besides literary theory and criticism, contribute to the construction of the authorial figure.

How the publishing industry and marketing strategies determine and form contemporary British literature is examined by Claire Squires in her *Marketing Literature: The Making of Contemporary Writing in Britain*. In her view, in recent years the changing culture of publishing and book retail environment have intensified the role of marketing in publishing. Market-ing has become "in a very real sense, *the making of contemporary writing*" (Squires 3). These changes have also affected the patterns of authorship "[f]or the authors high in the hierarchy of marketability, the authorial role is expanded far beyond that of the writer of the text" (Squires 37). The writer guided by her/his literary agent who acts "as the author's business manager" (Squires 35) embarks on the promotion of her/his work. S/he takes part in a series of events *performing* the role of the author: "give[s] readings at bookshops, attend[s] events at literary festivals, appear[s] in the media and embark[s] on promotional tours that can last months" (Squires 37). The work is promoted by and through the image of the writer. This author-centred promotion together with a literary journalism increasingly focused on the life of the writer contribute to a direct and "false" con-nection between the writer and her/his work in which the work becomes identified as an expression of the writer's identity. The work is read through the writer's identity.

The role of marketing and literary journalism in the conflation of writer and work is most evident in the several marketing stories analysed by Squires. By looking at the promotion of the novels such as Irvine Welsh's *Trainspotting* and Arundhati Roy's *The God of Small Things*, Squires pres-ents how in the process of promotion and reviewing these novels become representatives of one of the many aspects of the writer's identity. These novels were framed by the writer's nationality. Welsh's Scottishness was exploited in the novel's marketing and reception in the same way as Roy's Indian origin played a central role in the discussions about her novel as representative of Commonwealth literature. Squires considers that this kind of publishing and marketing has a negative impact on the reception of the writer's work. It narrows down the interpretative strategies as it "locks authors and their work into stereotypes" (Squires 122).

Squires' discussion focuses on the practices of publishing, marketing and literary journalism so she does not take into consideration that this foreclosure of "interpretive horizons" (Squires 122) could be overcome within the field of academic reception. The writer is at the centre of the marketing process since it is through his/her name, face, and life that the product—the book—is advertised. In the process of marketing the writer's work is branded by the writer's identity. In the urge to label and sell, the identity of the writer frames the book and the writer's persona can easily overshadow it. According to Lorna Sage, in contemporary literary life, the writer "becomes even more ubiquitous" (267) as s/he has to make a multitude of public appearances such as readings, book-signings, interviews. The writer's prevalence can also be discerned in the art of literary journalism. Reviews function as the immediate barometer as to whether (the marketing of) the book is going to be successful or not. The reviewer is driven by "zest, curiosity, voyeurism, vicarious *paper*-living" (Sage 264). In the presentation of their readings of the newly published book, reviewers easily shift their focus from the book to the writer: "Reviewers collude with authors as they always did. Even when they abuse them, they single them out, pay them attention, characterize them and make a noise about them" (Sage 263).

The news media contribute to the reception of a writer by constructing a particular image. While the academic reception addresses theoretical questions and engages in close readings of the text positioning the writer within a literary tradition, the news media tend to approach the work from a biographical perspective and intertwine biographical/lifestyle information with a discussion of the writer's work. In this articulation of the writer's image a certain life story narrative is constructed. Some elements of the biography are highlighted. These particular elements are continuously reiterated and thus become the trademark of the writer's image by which the audience identifies her and situates her in the cultural arena.

One of the main differences between literary journalism and academic criticism that made these two forms of interpretive practices grow apart is the role of the writer. While reviews zoom in on the writer, academic criticism tries to take a more detached position. According to David Lodge, literary journalism has a completely different approach to a writer's work than the academic: "While post-structuralism has asserted the impersonality of creative writing in the most extreme theoretical terms—the so-called 'death of the author'—literary journalism has never been so obsessed with the personality and the private life of the author" (144). This kind of distinction based upon detachment and involvement between literary journalism and academic criticism is, however, questioned by disputing the "death of the author" (Millner, Ahmed, Felski) and by highlighting the academics' emotional involvement in their interpretations. Lynne Pearce's reader-autobiography, for example, in which she reflects upon her reading of Winterson's novel *Written on the Body* (89–90, 140–3) shows how academics are entangled in an emotional relationship with their texts which in turn can influence their approach. This emotional aspect of reading, however, is rarely acknowledged. Rather, it tends to be sublimated as the discourse of academic interpretation requires detachment and a clear argument to support a particular line of interpretation. However, as the examples of Pearce's explorations of the affective nature of professional reading demonstrate, academic interpretation has been opened up to recognise the emotional involvement of the academic critic.

The academic debate on the reception of Jeanette Winterson's work has often been fueled by the emotional involvement of academics and the writer herself. Jeanette Winterson has expressed, as have many of her contemporaries (e.g., Zadie Smith, Monica Ali, Andrea Levy, A.L. Kennedy,[1] Jackie Kay, Carol Ann Duffy, and Hanif Kureishi), concerns about reading and interpreting her work through the prism of her identity, particularly of her gender and sexual identity. This approach could be condemned as damaging to the work as the writer's identity overshadows the work and reduces the variety of interpretations. While writers are concerned by this process, they unwillingly contribute to it when taking part in the marketing of their books since marketing, as Squires' analysis of marketing contemporary British writing suggests, is often based upon the writer's image by highlighting one of the aspects of the writer's identity. The media being a useful tool of marketing also strengthens the connection between the writer's identity and her/his work. Thus the contemporary writer often finds her/himself in an ambiguous situation when s/he partakes in practices such as marketing and media appearances that have the effect of forcing and reinforcing the writer's identity upon the work. While taking part in it, writers try to dismantle and to undermine this unwanted relation between life and work.

This "unwanted" relation between writer's identity and work is articulated across the different practices of literary reception such as literary criticism, marketing and the media. Within the area of literary criticism, the conceptualisation of the author incorporates the elucidation of the role of the writer in the construction of his/her work. While the nature of academic interpretation is often described in opposition to the style of literary journalism free of any interest in the writer's life(style) and identity, it is questionable if academic reception manages to evade the tension arising from reading the work through the writer's identity by turning the writer into a concept, the author.

Academic interpretations defined by a feminist, lesbian, gay and queer theoretical framework have been contested and often criticised for their narrow approach to texts. Feminist interpretations, for example, are regarded as motivated by the ideological zeal of the feminist critic to unmask the oppression of patriarchy. In her/his pursuit, the feminist critic loses sight of the aesthetic value of the text and sacrifices the text's literary values on the altar of ideology. Harold Bloom regards criticism that focuses on ideological issues as a "flight from the aesthetic" (17). Any such kind of criticism "reduces the aesthetic to ideology, or at best to metaphysics" (18). The essence of the literary work of art—its aesthetic value—is diminished since "[a] poem cannot be read *as a poem*, because it is primarily a social document, or, rarely yet possibly, an attempt to overcome philosophy" (18). Furthermore, according to John Ellis, "work by feminist critics is shaped so completely by the notion of patriarchy that an *intelligent* contribution to the understanding of literature becomes impossible" (74; my emphasis). This critique of feminist interpretations implicates the belief that there is a non-ideological position solely determined by universalist aesthetics. In order to demonstrate that there is no such completely ideologically free reading, Rita Felski refers to branches of literary theory such as hermeneutics and reader-response criticism that particularly focus on the reading process and the interaction that happens between the reader and the text. According to these theories, Felski suggests "[r]eaders *always* come to a work equipped with beliefs, assumptions, and prejudices" (9, my emphasis) and "claiming to possess a non-ideological viewpoint is a very ideological act" (10).

Besides not being able to perceive the "pure" aesthetic value of a literary work of art, feminist/lesbian and queer critics also have to defy and confront the criticism of reading the gender and/or the sexuality of the writer onto or into the work of the writer. It is assumed that women's writing is solely the territory of women writers and that the sexuality of the writer defines lesbian, gay, or queer writing. This assumption derives from the fact that most women's writing/*l'écriture féminine*[2] are indeed written by women and many writers who are lesbian, gay, or queer transpose their life experience into their writings. However, this does not inherently mean that the definition of a text as feminist, queer, or lesbian is determined by the gender and the sexuality of the writer. Any definition of a text should be primarily determined by the characteristics of the text itself: its style and topic.

In the 1980s and 1990s, but especially during the first half of the early 1990s, lesbian-feminist critics were engaged in a debate about defining the parameters of lesbian-feminist fiction. The major question addressed by several lesbian-feminist theoreticians was the formulation of the notion of "lesbian" in connection with texts and writers. For example, Patricia Duncker's standpoint on the role of the sexuality of the writer in the interpretation of the work coincides with Winterson's opinion that her sexuality should not influence the reception of her work:

> So far as writing is concerned, I believe that it must remain irrelevant to the reader whether the author herself lives as a Lesbian, committed in 'blood, breast and bone' to the other women. It is writing itself which

reveals or conceal [*sic*], is successful or not, on its own terms. For writing has its own rules, and can be remote from a writer's life, a life lived on different terms and in different ways. (171)

While accepting the differentiation Duncker asks for between the writer's everyday life and her fiction, the question that Duncker's comment raises is what those terms are on which we evaluate lesbian fiction or even call a particular text lesbian fiction. Gabriele Griffin identifies the problematics of automatically ascribing lesbian fiction to lesbian writers by pointing out that not all lesbian writers necessarily write fiction with lesbian topics (*Heavenly Love* 3). Some lesbian writers find the denotation as limiting their creativity and the reception of their work and are therefore reluctant to identify themselves with the "cause."

Besides the explanation of a work through the identity of the writer, this relation is also problematic because it operates with a narrow and simplified understanding of identity, in this case the writer's identity. When we are talking about a woman writer, a Scottish/Welsh/English or an Indian writer, a lesbian/gay/or queer writer, the identity of the writer is not only reduced to just one segment but also completely defined by it. The complexity of identity construction is erased. In this context, identity operates as an essentialist concept. This identity concept has been criticised by many theorists[3] primarily because its "tendency to posit one aspect of identity (say, gender) as the sole cause or determinant constituting the social meanings of an individual's experience" (Moya 3). The woman writer's identity is determined by her gender and the lesbian/gay/or queer writer's identity is marked by her/his sexuality.

How can these writers' avoid a reception of their work marked by their identity? Is it possible for them to overcome to be authored as woman/lesbian/gay/queer writer? Is the "universal" position open for them? Is it desirable at all? Toril Moi considers that women writers are subjected to a double bind. The frequently encountered statement "I am not a woman writer" is usually a defensive statement in "*response* to a provocation" (265). In this case the writer tries to evade the entrapment of her identity and work by her gender. However, Moi's most important contribution to this conundrum is that the universal position is as problematic as the gendered one because it requires from the woman writer to deny her gender: "[I]t can just be as frustrating for a woman writer to feel that she has to write as a generic human being, since this opens up an alienating split between her gender and her humanity" (266).

The issue of the universal and the particular is also at the core of Monique Wittig's contemplation of the reception of Djuna Barnes' work and her reluctance to be considered a lesbian writer. Wittig argues that in order to be part of literature "one must assume both a particular and a universal point of view" (67). The work is an important piece of literature if it "succeeds in making the minority point of view universal" (64).

However, how does a text achieve this? What would make a text "universal"? According to Wittig, it is through style, form and "textual reality" that texts manifest their literary value. These are texts "which are of the greatest strategic importance both in their mode of appearance and their mode of inscription within literary reality" (62) regardless of their topic and theme, I should add.

From amongst the contemporary British writers, the academic reception of Winterson's work has been caught in the debate between the universal and the particular. In the following section, I shall explore this discussion in order to question the influence of Winterson's sexual identity in defining the reception of her work. Firstly, I present the main approaches to her work. Then I shall focus on the way several critics (e.g., Helene Bengtson, Marianne Børch, Cindie Maagaard, Louise Horskjær Humphries, Margaret Reynolds, and Jonathan Noakes) regard the academic reception of her work as dominated by lesbian-feminist interpretations. Following the arguments of these academic critics, I shall examine how this debate articulates the meanings of lesbian-feminist and postmodern interpretations into a binary opposition of sexual identity (the particular) versus universalism.

Further on, by examining the "'[u]n-sexing' of the Wintersonian *ouevre*" (Humphries 3) proposed by these critics, I consider the role Jeanette Winterson's stance on the relationship between a writer's sexual identity and her work has in this debate. Since she rejects being regarded a lesbian writer, her affirmation is often used to legitimise universalist readings in opposition to lesbian-feminist interpretation.

THE ACADEMIC RECEPTION OF
JEANETTE WINTERSON'S WORK

A variety of interpretations of Winterson's novels has been produced since the beginning of her career as a writer. Out of this diversity two major trajectories can be delineated: lesbian-feminist criticism that shifted from the end of the 1990s towards postmodern lesbian and queer readings of her works and postmodern readings discussing issues of storytelling and the concept of love. There are also some readings of her work (Pressler, Onega) that heavily rely on the intertextuality of her novels with modernist or "canonical" writers. These kinds of interpretations, however, compared to the number of lesbian-feminist and postmodern interpretations, are so few that they do not form an extended separate "interpretative community" (yet). This division of the academic reception of Winterson's work into lesbian-feminist and postmodern approaches is also indicated by Merja Makinen and Sonja Andermahr in their guide to academic interpretations of Winterson's novels.

Lesbian-feminist and postmodern receptions of Winterson's work are articulated in relation to each other. They may be regarded in terms of binary oppositions. They are separated by the inclusion or exclusion of gender and sexuality as the main analytical focus. The common element between them is postmodernism. This constitutes an overlap between the two different academic receptions. At the beginning of the 1990s, lesbian-feminist criticism incorporated postmodernism into its theoretical conceptions which then became part of the formation of queer theory. The postmodern perceptions of identity as unstable and contradictory are not only aspects of postmodern readings of Winterson's novels but also form the basis of postmodern lesbian readings. These postmodern *lesbian* readings of Winterson's work presented by critics such as Laura Doan, Lisa Moore, Marilyn R. Farwell, and Paulina Palmer investigate the consequences of this unstable identity concept for the lesbian subject whereas the postmodern readings focus on the analysis of the construction and deconstruction of identity through narrative (Gade, Onega). In this kind of interpretation gender and sexuality does not play such an important role as in lesbian-feminist interpretations. Identity is treated as "universal."

According to Bengtson, Børch, and Maagaard, the editors of *Sponsored by Demons: The Art Of Jeanette Winterson*, Winterson's work has been misread. This misreading is due to the prevalence of lesbian-feminist interpretations of her novels that limit the acknowledgment of the diversity of the Wintersonian *oeuvre*. They argue for the need for interpretations that depart from lesbian-feminist approaches in order to present the complexity, versatility, and universalism of her work. They therefore want "to read [Winterson's] writing so as to *illuminate* aspects of her art that have been *overshadowed* by critical focus on feminist and lesbian issues" (1). This illumination can be achieved if academics turn their interest towards "universalist" topics such as:

> love, subjectivity, and the problems of giving voice to singular experience through language; postmodern and premodern aspects of Winterson's art; the role of the feminine for notions of identity; Winterson's place within, and stance toward, tradition; and her imaginative visions of the worlds and beings which attest to the power of the creative word to test—and expand—the reader's conceptions of what is real, what is possible, and what is desirable. (1)

Bengtson, Børch, and Maagaard's "Preface" to *Sponsored by Demons* casts the division between lesbian-feminist and postmodern readings in the light of the debate between the old universalist "traditional" literary studies and the new literary schools that no longer believe in the sanctity of a time-less aesthetics. The postmodern interpretations within this context become interpretations that are regarded as "universalist" in comparison with lesbian-feminist readings as they evaluate Winterson's work based upon "pure aesthetics" and not from one ideological point of view such as the lesbian-feminist approach. This ideological character of lesbian-feminist readings is seen as its main weakness since it limits the reading to one point of view and also because the ideology and political character of this approach is seen as an imposition upon the text. The irony is that postmodern theories are the ones that promulgated the subversion of the grand narrative based upon the idea of "universalism." In comparison with and in opposition to lesbian-feminist approaches, however, the postmodern/poststructuralist interpretations of Winterson's work represent exactly the idea they should undermine. Instead of undermining the idea of "universalism," they become the advocates of "universalism."

Yet, Humphries also considers that the "feminist-lesbian approach—partly by force of its sheer dominance—actually results in the depreciation of the 'vastness' of Winterson's fictional universe" (4). According to Humphries, lesbian-feminist criticism on the whole is an area that "is highly perceptive and clever" but when it comes to analysing Winterson's work "this specific interpretative key encourages an approach which is *at best* partial and *always* reductive" (4, emphasis added). What Humphries overlooks is that all approaches, not only lesbian-feminist interpretations, tend to be reductive. This characteristic is due to the rules that govern (academic) interpretation. The novel is analysed from a certain theoretical perspective focusing on a specific topic. The interpretation is then formulated in such a way as to create a coherent argument that sustains the focus of what the academic reader explores. Thus it is in the nature/method of interpretation to be reductive. However, the versatility of academic interpetations of a text is sustained by the acceptance of the possibility to interpret one text from multiple points of view. The problem arises when one angle is declared to be the dominant one, limiting the versions of the text.

It seems that lesbian-feminist criticism does not measure up to the all-inclusive aims of the universalists. It fails to do so because, as Felski points out, one of the main arguments against feminist literary theory is that it kills the literary value of the texts as it focuses solely on gender-ideological issues. These critics (Bengtson, Børch, Maagaard, Humphries, Reynolds, and Noakes) view postmodern interpretations not as a group that complements lesbian-feminist readings but as a group representing an opposition to lesbian-feminist approaches.

Humphries does not see a "universalist" reading as another interpretative group besides the lesbian-feminist one in the academic field or in Winterson's reception, but she views it as the one type of interpretation that provides readings that reflect the complexity of the Wintersonian literary universe and thus the "right" interpretation. Besides the legitimisation of an all-encompassing reception of Winterson based upon universal aesthetic values, Humphries draws our attention to another important feature of this "universalist" discourse. The title of the article speaks for itself: "*Listening for the Author's Voice*: 'Un-Sexing' the Wintersonian Oeuvre" (my emphasis). Here it is actually the author, Jeanette Winterson, who legitimises the universalist readings since she rejects lesbian-feminist readings. Humphries frequently uses the author's voice as an argumentative tool that sustains her position against lesbian-feminist readings. The little incident told by Winterson in her essay "The Semiotics of Sex" is one of the favoured anecdotes used to exemplify that Winterson does not really appreciate being included in the Lesbian Canon but rather prefers to be part of the Universal Canon:

> I was in a bookshop recently when a young woman approached me. She told me she was writing an essay on my work and that of Radclyffe Hall. Could I help? 'Yes', I said. 'Our work has nothing in common.' 'I thought you were a lesbian.' [sic] she said. (103)

> I was in a bookshop recently and a young man came up to me and said 'Is *Sexing the Cherry* a reading of *Four Quartets*?' 'Yes', I said, and he kissed me. (118)

When her work is read in comparison with Hall's by lesbian-feminist critics such as Griffin ("Acts of Defiance"), Winterson's work image is viewed in opposition to Hall's. The comparison between them can only show the differences in their work. In the case of T. S. Eliot, critics (Onega, Finney, and Pressler) highlight those intertextual elements in Winterson's novels that refer to T.S. Eliot's work. So actually the connections that are made between these two writers and Winterson's work are in accordance with Winterson's wish to detach her work from Hall's and to be acknowledged for its affinity with T.S. Eliot's. However, the two incidents juxtaposed in Winterson's essay (the first one is the opening story and the last one is the closing one) underline Humphries' point. It is the author herself who wishes not to be read as a lesbian author. Humphries comments on these anecdotes in the following way:

> [T]he anecdotes at once provide a clue to what kind of *reader/critic Winterson respects*—someone who pays attention to the language as well as the literary tradition which are always echoed in her writing, and what kind of *reader/critic she disrespects*—someone who confuses the writer's biography with her work of art. (6; my emphasis)

Humphries' reading of the anecdotes illustrates the way literary critics are enclosed into opposing interpretative communities. The defining trait of the lesbian-feminist critic is that she reads the writer's life into her work of art. Following the logic of this binary opposition, the lesbian-feminist critic does not "pay attention to the language as well as the literary tradition" as other "respectful" critics do. My main concern with this distinction between critics who only see the work of art as a pure aesthetic object and critics who only read it as a reflection of the writer's life is the extremities and labels it creates. Aesthetic issues or literary tradition are also part of the interests of lesbian-feminist interpretations.

Humphries' aim is to rescue Winterson's work from lesbian-feminist interpretations as her "article arises, in part at least, from a regret that so much academic criticism approaches Winterson's *oeuvre* as strictly lesbian literature; that is, sees Winterson as a political riter [sic] whose principal merit is her promotion of the lesbian-feminist cause" (3). She suggests that aesthetic readings are the appropriate approach when analysing Winterson's novels simply because this approach is favoured by the author herself and the lesbian-feminist ones are misreadings because they go against the author's wishes. Her statement also implies that lesbian-feminist critics allow themselves to read Winterson's work from such a perspective simply because Winterson is a lesbian, thus suggesting that their readings have nothing to do with the topics of the novels themselves. In the cases of *Oranges Are Not the Only Fruit* and *Written on the Body*, as the topic of lesbianism and gender are at the core of these novels, it is not surprising that many lesbian-feminists read these novels from a gender perspective. While she declines lesbian-feminist readings as unprofessional because they seemingly align the work and the writer's private life, Humphries legitimises her approach, which I would term "universal aesthetic," by invoking the authorial voice in her article. If critics are not allowed to take into consideration the author's life when analysing her novels, why is their reading measured against what the author says? Humphries revives the influence of the author, handing her the power of authority to prescribe the interpretation of her own work.

Reynolds and Noakes in their "Critical Overview" expressed the same concern in connection with the academic reception of Winterson's work as did Bengtson, Børch, Maagaard, and Humphries. The high interest of lesbian-feminist criticism in Winterson's work was, according to Reynolds and Noakes, due to two factors. One was the particular "historical convergence of her arrival on the scene, as a new writer, with the relatively early stages of a recognisable 'lesbian' criticism, growing out of the theoretical frames of feminist theory" (157). The other factor was Winterson's lesbianism: "Winterson was a well-known lesbian. Therefore her works were examples of 'lesbian writing'. *Ergo*, it was perceived that her works were ripe for 'lesbian criticism'" (157). In this line of argument, lesbian criticism is faced with the charge of imposing a lesbian reading on the text simply because the author of the text is known to be a lesbian. From among Winterson's novels, Reynolds and Noakes regard *Oranges* as the only novel that "can be read in the terms of 'lesbian criticism'"(157). With this affirmation they acknowledge a third factor that contributed to the high interest of lesbian criticism in Winterson's first novel. As a new writer, she became famous with a lesbian novel.

Reynolds and Noakes' criticism of regarding Winterson as a lesbian writer is confusing in light of the fact that Reynolds was the editor of *The Penguin Book of Lesbian Short Stories* that included one of Winterson's short stories. One has to assume that Winterson's inclusion in a lesbian collection was based upon the consideration of her writing as in some way "lesbian" and was done by Reynolds herself as editor of the lesbian collection. Thus, while in 1994 Reynolds recognised Winterson as a lesbian writer, in 2003 she objected to naming her as a lesbian writer: "Winterson is not and has never been a 'lesbian writer'. She is a writer" (15).

THE WRITER'S VOICE

The attitude of lesbian writers towards the reception of their work through the lens of lesbianism can vary from reluctance to be seen as "only" a lesbian writer (Jeanette Winterson) to the desire to be seen above all as a lesbian writer (Adrienne Rich). Like Winterson, Jane Rule also felt that the label "lesbian writer" limited her work "because [. . .] I hold and express many concerns as well" (10). However, after many years, she no longer regards it as a "discrediting stigma, hardly worse than being a woman writer or a Canadian writer or a lady academic" (10). Contrary to Winterson and Rules' attitude, Adrienne Rich saw her lesbianism as an essential element for the understanding of her poems. Lillian Faderman relates Rich's reaction to the reading of her poems that appeared in the volume *Twenty-One Love Poems* by two women readers who considered the poems to show the "universal" nature of love: "I see that as a denial, a kind of resistance, a refusal to read and hear what I've actually written, to acknowledge what I am" (qtd. Faderman 409). Contrary to Rich, Winterson aspires in her work to imbue lesbian love with universal character, the love of *Written*'s genderless narrator being the best example of this.

In the argument against (the predominance of) lesbian-feminist interpretations of Winterson's work, Humphries, Reynolds, and Noakes invoke Jeanette Winterson's rejection of being named a lesbian writer. Jeanette Winterson's statement "I am a writer who happens to love women. I am not a lesbian who happens to write" (104) is actually often quoted as her affirmation on the relation between a writer's sexual identity and her work. This affirmation is reiterated in a recent interview with Sonja Andermahr. When asked "does your work address lesbian readers and women readers in particular ways" (Andermahr 128), Winterson disassociates her work from lesbian, queer and women audiences since she does not want her work to be used for sexual politics:

> The sexuality of a writer is not the business of literary criticism; to make it so is a cheap way of dealing with a work on its terms and in its own right. *Oranges* is not a 'gay' book and neither is anything else that I have ever written. I will always stand up for tolerance and honesty, I really won't stand up for all this PC sexual politics stuff which buries the energy of the work under the incredibly dull and simple-minded concerns of queer theory. (qtd. Andermahr 128)

Lesbian-feminist criticism is accused by the above mentioned critics and by Winterson of regarding the writer as a lesbian writer only because of her sexuality. There is a slight problem with this argument which is "Winterson is a lesbian" ergo "She is a lesbian writer." This false conclusion is due to the fact that most lesbian and gay writers are lesbian and gay but they are not considered lesbian and gay writers because of their sexuality but because of what they write about and how. In my line of thinking, Winterson can be considered as a queer writer not because of her sexual identity. She is a queer writer because her novels "invite" queer/lesbian and feminist readings that consider her work from the perspective of "the incredibly dull and simple-minded [. . .] queer theory."

Felski suggests that some creative writers make conscious use of theories in their fiction writing. She considers the influence of Judith Butler's theory of gender presented in *Gender Trouble* on literature, literary analysis and particularly on the feminist allegories of authorship and fiction writing. The Butlerian axioms: "gender as performance," "drag as parody" of the heterosexual gender matrix and "gender is a kind of imitation for which there is no original" have had effects not only on literary theorists but also on certain writers.

> Among contemporary writers, the works of British novelists Jeanette Winterson and Angela Carter were an ideal pairing for this kind of analysis; indeed, they often foreshadowed the ideas of their critics with remarkable prescience. Informed by feminist ideas, infused with a postmodern sense of the textuality of everything, such works of fiction reveled and glorified in the artifice of gender. (Felski 77)

In the case of Jeanette Winterson, Felski draws attention to *Written* which besides *Oranges* has received particular attention from lesbian-feminist critics (Lindenmeyer, Børch, Kauer, Stowers, Duncker). This interest is due to the way the novel does, or pretends to do away with gender since the gender of the narrator is never revealed. It is an interesting language and narratological game that Winterson plays as she avoids any possible word, phrase and story line that would give away the gender of the narrator. By focusing on this gender issue the novel invites interpretations that make use of the theory of gender as performance.

Catherine Belsey considers that a novel that has certain affinity with a theory "allows the text to invite certain readings and consider specific positions to its addressee" (163). Most of Winterson's novels such as *Oranges, Sexing the Cherry, The Passion,* and *Written on the Body* invite lesbian-feminist and queer readings. Thus the lesbian-feminist reception of Winterson's work explores one of the aspects of her novels contributing to a versatile academic reception. Lesbian-feminist interpretations are not based upon Winterson's sexuality. They are inspired by the style, the topics, and the issues raised by her novels.

CONCLUSION: BEYOND THE WRITER'S IDENTITY

In literary criticism, it is the work itself that (pre)dominates the reception of the writer's work and not her/his (sexual) identity. Literary analysis, even in case of queer/lesbian/feminist criticism that is accused by its opponents of being driven by identity politics, follows the prescription of evaluating the work on its own terms without reading the writer into it. Writers such as Jeanette Winterson, Sarah Waters, or Alan Hollinghurst are not queer writers due to their sexuality but rather to the topics and forms of their work. The difference between their personal identity and the identity of their work that gives form to it is, however, very easily erased. This erasure is due to the underlining assumption that one can only write about one's gender, culture, and sexuality. Thus women's writers tend to write about women's issues, queer writers about lesbian and gay topics, minority writers about their own culture, and so forth. Moreover, they are expected to write about the issues that are considered to be at the core of their identity/experiences. Their identity prescribes them as "authentic" voices of the groups they belong to or are assigned to. Ana María Sánchez-Arce explores the influence of the authentic discourse "that legitimizes knowledge on the grounds of it originating from essential identity characteristics or subjectivities" (143) in literature and literary criticism. Within the field of literature, this "authority of authenticity" leads to categorising books based on the writer's identity. This categorisation "compartmentalizes knowledge in subject areas neatly and diffuses the idiosyncratic qualities of literature" (152). Futhermore, "[i]t also creates the conditions for interpreting literature in an authenticist way and neglecting writing that does not follow these parameters" (152). From this perspective, the contemporary writer and his/her work are almost imprisoned by her/his own identity. Then it is understandable the desperate way writers try to reject any denomination at all and want to be recognised only as writers. We should recognize that this approach to literary works not only limits the writer but also limits the literary critic.

The close analysis of the academic reception of Winterson's work presented in this article illustrates the way critics can also fall into categories that (pre)determine the expectations of their interpretations. These categorisations, like the categorisations of writers' work based on their identities, erase the complexity and versatility of literary interpretations. Lesbian-feminist critics are accused of being blindsided by their identity politics and consequently reading Winterson's novels through the prism of her sexuality. In this debate for "appropriate" readings of Winterson's work, lesbian-feminist literary interpretations are reduced to this kind of narrow definition, not taking into consideration that lesbian-feminist readings can also incorporate issues of aesthetics, textuality and literary tradition. Furthermore, aesthetics is named as the prerogative of "universalists," postmodern interpretations. Winterson's opposition to the label "lesbian writer" assists "universalist" critics in legitimising their own interpretations and their disapproval of lesbian-feminist criticism.

The issue of identity is present thoughout the field of literary reception and constructs a complex web of interconnections. The relation between the writer's identity and her/his work is part of several practices of literary reception such as marketing, literary journalism, and academic criticism. While each practice articulates this relation differently, they also inter-cross and influence each other. Marketing the work through the image of the writer, extensively describing his/her lifestyle and presenting his/her detailed biography, show an increasing interest in the writer. This preoccupation with the writer might overshadow the work and perpetuate a "false" relation between the writer and her/his work by considering the writer's identity/bibliography to offer an understanding of the work. However, it is not only the writer that should be released from the constraints of her/his identity. Lesbian-feminist interpretations are not just identity-driven readings. Their interests go beyond the writer's identity and they engage with the texts themselves. The lesbianism of any author is not determined by the sexuality of the writer, but it is primarily determined by the text: its queer aesthetics and lesbian topics.

NOTES

1. A. L. Kennedy, for example, expresses her disapproval of approaches to her work based on her gender, sexuality and ethnicity by writing excellent parodies of these kinds of interpretations. Considering her novels as exemplary of Scottish writing would induce a set of stereotypes about Scottish identity imposed upon her work: "A. L. Kennedy is Scottish—we soft Southern fools can't even begin to understand how Scottish. She's gritty. She writes about death and sex and murder and grit—grit we can never understand. Post-industrial malaise—that's her middle name" (Home Page). In the same way, her gender, her woman-ness, can overshadow her writing. Moreover, her writing is seen as an expression of her gender: "A. L. Kennedy is a woman—she writes like a woman, she spells like a woman, the way she uses commas is essentially female. No one without a vagina could string paragraphs together the way that A.L. Kennedy does. Every word is a reaction to the oppressive patriarchal dead hand of penis waving which has for so long clouded our thoughts, throttled our voices and caused the silvery sugar ball bearings to drop off our gingerbread" (Home Page).

2. Women's writing is generally considered to be writing by women, for women and about women. The term *l'écriture féminine,* coined by the French feminist literary critic Hélène Cixous in her essay "The Laugh of the Medusa," has often been used to embody the idea that gender and a particular style of writing are intertwined. Cixous urges women to express themselves through writing: "Woman must put herself into the text—as into the world and into history—by her own movement" (875). Through its applications in feminist literary discourse the term has come to signify a special kind of feminine writing that operates outside the logic of phallocentric language. Feminine writing desires to articulate the female body, female difference, and female sexuality through nonlinear and cyclical writing. So it is most of all a form/a

style of writing. However, one of the intriguing questions is whether this style is the 'privilege' of women writers or can male writers also engage in its production. How does the writer's gender relate to feminine writing? By asking this question I would like to indicate the difficulties of separating the form/style of writing from the writer's gender. It is regularly assumed that the writer of feminine writing is a woman although there are some exquisite pieces of feminine writing employed by male authors. For example, there is Molly Bloom's monologue at the end of James Joyce's *Ulysses* or the novel *Seventeen Swans/Tizenhét hattyúk* written by the Hungarian writer Péter Esterházy. Still, male writers rarely venture into the field of feminine writing. Readers approach the text with certain preconceived notions, developed as a consequence of gender stereotypes, once they know the gender of the writer. In other words, one expects a female-authored text to read in a particular manner and embody a certain set of aesthetic and political values.

3. Stuart Hall's essay "Who Needs 'Identity'?" presents an overview of the multitude of debates around the concept of identity "subjected to a searching critique" (15). He engages with the theoretical work on identity of critics such as Foucault, Derrida, Laclau, Althusser, Butler, Bhabha, Heath, and Rose. Through his dialogue with these critics, Hall articulates an identity concept highlighting that identity is always in process and is composed by the intersection of several discourses: "Identities are thus points of temporary attachment to the subject positions which discursive practices construct for us" (19).

REFERENCES

Ahmed, Sara. *Differences That Matter: Feminist Theory and Postmodernism.* Cambridge: Cambridge University Press, 1998. Print.

Andermahr, Sonja. *Jeanette Winterson.* Basingstoke: Palgrave Macmillan, 2009. Print.

Belsey, Catherine. "Textual Analysis as a Research Method." *Research Methods for English Studies.* Ed. Gabriele Griffin. Edinburgh: Edinburgh University Press, 2005. 157–75. Print.

Bengtson, Helene, Marianne Børch, and Cindie Maagaard, eds. *Sponsored by Demons: The Art of Jeanette Winterson.* Agedrup: Scholar's Press. 1999. Print.

Bloom, Harold. *The Western Canon: The Books and The School of Ages,* London: Macmillan, 1995. Print.

Børch, Marianne. "Love's Ontology and the Problem with Cliché." Bengtson, Børch and Maagaard, 1999. 41–55. Print.

Bourdieu, Pierre. *The Rules of Art: Genesis and Structure of The Literary Field.* Trans. Susan Emanuel. Palo Alto, CA: Stanford University Press, 1996. Print.

Butler, Judith. *Gender Trouble: Feminism and the Subversion of Identity.* London: Routledge, 1990. Print.

Cixous, Hélène. "The Laugh of the Medusa." Trans. Keith Cohen and Paula Cohen. *Signs: Journal of Women in Culture and Society* 1.4 (1976): 875—93. Print.

Doan, Laura. "Jeanette Winterson's Sexing the Postmodern." *The Lesbian Postmodern.* Ed. Laura Doan. New York: Columbia University Press, 1994. 137–55. Print.

Duncker, Patricia. *Sisters and Strangers: An Introduction to Contemporary Fiction.* Oxford: Blackwell, 1992. Print.

Ellis, John M. *Literature Lost: Social Agendas and the Corruption of the Humanities.* New Haven, CT: Yale University Press, 1997. Print.

Faderman, Lillian. *Surpassing the Love of Men*. London: The Women's Press, 1981. Print.

Farwell, Marilyn R. "The Postmodern Lesbian Text: Jeanette Winterson's *Sexing the Cherry* and *Written on the Body*." *Heterosexual Plots and Lesbian Narratives*. Ed. Marilyn R. Farwell. New York: New York University Press, 1996. 168–99. Print.

Felski, Rita. *Literature after Feminism*. Chicago: The University of Chicago Press, 2003. Print.

Finney, Brian. "Bonded by Language: Jeanette Winterson's *Written on the Body*." *Women and Language* XXV. 2 (2002): 23–32. Print.

Gade, B. "Multiple Selves and Grafted Agents: A Postmodernist Reading of *Sexing the Cherry*." Bengtson, Børch and Maagaard, 1999. 27–41. Print.

Grice, Helene, and Tim Woods, eds. *"I'm Telling You Stories": Jeanette Winterson and the Politics of Reading*. Amsterdam: Rodopi, 1998. Print.

Griffin, Gabriele. "Acts of Defiance: Celebrating Lesbians." *It's My Party: Reading Twentieth Century Women's Writing*. Ed. Gina Wisker. London: Pluto, 1994. 80–103. Print.

———. *Heavenly Love: Lesbian Images in Twentieth-century Women's Writing*, Manchester: Manchester University Press, 1993. Print.

Hadjiafxendi, Kyriaki, and Polina Mackay. "Introduction: Authorship and its Contexts." *Authorship in Context: From the Theoretical to the Material*. Eds. Kyriaki Hadjiafxendi and Polina Mackay. New York: Palgrave Macmillan, 2007. 1–12. Print.

Hall, Stuart. "Who Needs 'Identity'?" *Identity: A Reader*. Eds. Paul Du Gay, Jessica Evans, and Peter Redman. London: Sage, 2000. 15–31. Print.

Humphries, Louise Horskjær. "Listening for the Author's Voice: 'Un-sexing' the Wintersonian Oeuvre." Bengtson, Børch and Maagaard, 1999. 3–17. Print.

Kauer, Ute. "Narration and Gender. The Role of the First Person Narrator in *Written on the Body*." Grice and Woods, 1998. 41–35. Print.

Kennedy, A.L. Home Page. Web. 24 August 2012. http://www.a-l-kennedy.co.uk/index.php/assistance.

Lindenmeyer, Antje. "Postmodern Concepts of the Body in Jeanette Winterson's *Written on the Body*." *Feminist Review* 63 (1999): 48–63. Print.

Lodge, David. "Literary Criticism and Literary Creation." *The Arts and Sciences of Criticism*. Eds. David Fuller and Patricia Waugh. Oxford: Oxford University Press, 1999. 137–51. Print.

Makinen, Merja. *The Novels of Jeanette Winterson*. New York: Palgrave Macmillan, 2005. Print.

Millner, Nancy K. "Changing the Subject: Authorship, Writing, and the Reader." *Feminist Studies/Cultural Studies*. Ed. Teresa de Lauretis. Bloomington, IN: Indiana University Press, 1986. 102–20. Print.

Moi, Toril. "'I am not a Woman Writer': About Women, Literature and Feminist Theory Today." *Feminist Theory* 9. 3 (2008): 259–71. Print.

Moore, Lisa. "Teledildonics: Virtual Lesbians in the Fiction of Jeanette Winterson." *Sexy Bodies: The Strange Carnalities of Feminism*. Eds. Elizabeth Grosz and Elspeth Probyn. London: Routledge, 1995. 104–26. Print.

Moya, Paula M. L. "Reclaiming Identity." *Reclaiming Identity: Realist Theory and the Predicament of Postmodernism*. Eds. Paula M. L. Moya and Michael R. Hames-García. Berkeley, CA: University of California Press, 2000. 1–29. Print.

Onega, Susana. *Jeanette Winterson*. Manchester: Manchester University Press, 2006. Print.

Palmer, Paulina "Jeanette Winterson and the Lesbian Postmodern: Story-telling, Performativity and the Gay Aesthetic." *The Contemporary British Novel since*

1980. Eds. James Acheson and Sarah C. E. Ross. Edinburgh: Edinburgh University Press, 2006. 189–203. Print.

———. "Lesbian Fiction and the Postmodern: Genre, Narrativity, Sexual Politics." *Just Postmodernism*. Ed. Steven Earnshaw. Amsterdam: Rodopi, 1997. 157–77. Print.

———. "Postmodern Trends in Contemporary Fiction: Margaret Atwood, Angela Carter, Jeanette Winterson." *Postmodern Subjects/Postmodern Texts*. Eds. Jane Dowson and Steven Earnshaw. Amsterdam: Rodopi, 1995. 181–97. Print.

Pearce, Lynne. *Feminism and the Politics of Reading*. London: Arnold, 1997. Print.

Pressler, Christopher. *So Far, So Linear: Responses to the Work of Jeanette Winterson*. London: Pauper's Press, 2000. Print.

Reynolds, Margaret, ed. *The Penguin Book of Lesbian Short Stories*. London: Penguin Books, 1994. Print.

Reynolds, Margaret, and Jonathan Noakes. *Jeanette Winterson: The Essential Guide to Contemporary Literature*. London: Vintage, 2003. Print.

Rule, Jane. *Lesbian Images*, London: Pluto Press, 1989. Print.

Sage, Lorna. "Living on Writing." *Grub Street and the Ivory Tower: Literary Journalism and Literary Scholarship from Fielding to the Internet*. Eds. Jeremy Treglown and Bridget Bennett. Oxford: Oxford University Press, 1998. 262–77. Print.

Sánchez-Arce, Ana María. "'Authenticism', or the Authority of Authenticity." *Mosaic* 40.3 (2007). 139–55. Print.

Squires, Claire. *Marketing Literature: The Making of Contemporary Writing in Britain*. Basingstoke: Palgrave Macmillan, 2007. Print.

Stowers, Cath. "The Erupting Lesbian Body: Reading *Written on the Body* as a Lesbian Text." Grice and Woods, 1998. 89–103. Print.

Winterson, Jeanette. *Art Objects: Essays on Ecstasy and Effrontery*. London: Vintage, 1996. Print.

———. *Oranges Are Not the Only Fruit*. 1985. London: Vintage, 2001. Print.

———. *The Passion*. 1987. London: Vintage, 2001. Print.

———. *Sexing the Cherry*. 1989. London: Vintage, 2001. Print.

———. *Written on the Body*. 1992. Toronto: Alfred A. Knopf, 2000. Print

Wittig, Monique. "The Point of View: Universal or Particular?" *The Straight Mind and Other Essays*. Boston: Beacon Press, 1990. 59–67. Print.

8 Why Kazuo Ishiguro Is Stuck to the Margins
Formal Identities in Contemporary Literary Interpretations

Ana María Sánchez-Arce

By most criteria used to define canons of contemporary literature, Kazuo Ishiguro has made it. Nevertheless, the interpretive frameworks used to discuss Ishiguro's work are narrow. He is seen as, for example, a "postcolonial," "migrant," "new international," and "world" writer and placed under the umbrella term "Black British." For instance, John Skinner shoehorns him in his essay "Black British Interventions" despite saying that "the label does not seem quite right" for him (129). Ishiguro is included in a group of writers "whose work is informed by other national traditions" (Childs 221). These interpretive categories have forestalled readings of Ishiguro other than through the lenses of marginality. Despite being an English and British writer, Ishiguro is always being critically labelled as "almost the same, but not quite" to use Thomas Babbington Macaulay's famous phrase in "Minute on Indian Education" (1835). Ishiguro's background—he was born in Japan and brought to England at the age of five—and the fact that his first two novels were set in Japan, invite these distinctions and affect the way his fiction is read. At the beginning of his career, his background was also used cleverly to tap into the growing market for "exotic" writers, hence the persistent categorisation of Ishiguro as a postcolonial or world writer.

Ishiguro's association with these categories exemplifies the contemporary need to define and label writers according to their supposed identity. Since Ishiguro is not seen as being "quite" British (and certainly not English, hence the use of British as an umbrella term), he is automatically included in the default categories reserved for "almost," "but not quite" British writers such as migrant, second generation, Black British, postcolonial, and world writers, regardless of whether his background, writing, or concerns actually make this plausible, and also regardless of his British passport. At the heart of these problems with nomenclature is a battle over the definitions of writers' identities and their authenticity. Note the slippage between English and British, and consider which writers are automatically considered "British" and which are "English," "Northern Irish," "Scottish," or "Welsh." The assumption is that "British" writers are either non-English writers co-opted into the English Literature tradition, or qualified Britons.

The articulation of the latter is usually British[+], meaning that they belong to other cultures as well. However, under British[+] can lie its opposite, British[-], and the feeling that a superscript or hyphen is necessary to define these writers is a sign of their precarious status as simply British.

It is extremely difficult to do without the superscript—the hyphen—because identity has become the way to think and write about writers perceived as "other." What started as a drive to privilege what Jean-François Lyotard has called *petit récits* has turned into a totalising grand narrative itself that looks for "otherness" in writers' backgrounds and links it to resistance to metanarratives (cf. Sánchez-Arce 144,154). However ethically right, politically defensible, and aesthetically relevant it is to study literature in relation to cultural diversity, postcoloniality, or hybridity (to name a few of the issues), we need to rethink their relationship to writers and writing since labels such as "postcolonial," "migrant," and "Black British" are also critical shortcuts that have become *de rigueur* terms for writers and writing who do not fit established (formalised) ways of thinking about identity. By treating them not just as interpretive or politically inflected terms, but also as forms in themselves, we will be able to exit the *cul-de-sac* that they sometimes become.

Realising that established critical labels are forms will allow us to analyse how they can be used prescriptively to interpret texts by superscripted or hyphenated writers. Writers whose names and backgrounds mark them as ideal for readings based around politics of difference find themselves up against strict definitions of what they should be writing about and in which way they ought to do it. Their work is either made to fit an interpretive angle or found at fault if it does not. In order to explore how these interpretive forms can become a straight-jacket, I will focus on Kazuo Ishiguro's career.

Stanley Fish writes about the role of what he calls interpretive communities. These are groups of people and institutions who control the production of knowledge, including teachers and academia. Different ways of interpreting (or writing, as Fish would say) texts are the product of each interpretive community's strategy. Fish concludes that:

> [i]nterpretive communities are made up of those who share interpretive strategies not for reading (in the conventional sense) but for writing texts, for constituting their properties and assigning their intentions. In other words, these strategies exist prior to the act of reading and therefore determine the shape of what is read rather than, as is usually assumed, the other way around. (171)

Critical approaches are the combination of the interpretive strategies adopted by particular interpretive communities and the reception of texts is a result of the application of these strategies that "exist prior to the act of reading and therefore determine the shape of what is read." Fish sees the reader as a writer since form—including interpretation as form—exists in the mind of the reader before reading the book. Therefore form as interpretation is not inherent in texts but co-produced with the reader.

It used to puzzle me when students referred to the postcolonial as a genre, but I realise now that the postcolonial can be seen as form, perhaps even a genre, insofar as postcoloniality is the principal idea by which interpretations of that work are produced. To use Fish's terminology, postcolonial reading strategies enable readers to write texts as postcolonial. Therefore, postcolonial texts are not just content; they are also form in the traditional sense derived by the Latin meaning of "forma," which is the equivalent to the Greek "idea." Interpretation could therefore be seen as the actualisation of particular forms in specific texts as they are produced using a community's interpretive strategies, their reading/writing moulds.

Ishiguro's work is not seen as postcolonial on the grounds of the postcoloniality of Britain or Japan, but because his name and background mark him as an alien, an "other" who is automatically included in the framework of postcoloniality instead of English (or British) literature. Consequently, Ishiguro scholarship has been moulded around the interpretive strategies pertaining to postcolonialism and alterity studies. Mike Petry complains about this, arguing that "all kinds of 'Centre/margin approaches' to Ishiguro's writing strike me as missing the point" (15). Ishiguro's attempts to distance himself from such labels have paradoxically been used to reinforce them. For example, Barry Lewis justifies applying "postcolonial ideas to Ishiguro" on the grounds that Ishiguro himself "believes he is '*stuck on the margins*', thereby aligning himself with the postcolonial emphasis on the marginal, the liminal, the excluded" (13). However, the context of the statement (not provided by Lewis) makes it clear that Ishiguro is not referring to himself or to his writing when he discusses marginality, but to the British literary tradition after the Second World War which he felt was "*stuck on the margins*" because it refused to accept that it was no longer the centre of the world. Ishiguro aligns himself with writers such as V. S. Naipaul, Julian Barnes, and Ian McEwan and lists two ways of bypassing this sense of irrelevance: "either you go out there physically and start searching around [. . .] or you have to use your imagination" (Ishiguro 1993, 11). Therefore, the phrase "*stuck on the margins*" has less to do with identity than with writing style:

> [T]here's a natural instinct to write realism. It takes much more to start thinking of other ways to write. It's when you're actually *stuck on the margins*. Then you start to become conscious that you are stuck on the margins and the things that you know intimately on that concrete, documentary level just won't do. [. . .] What can you do? You know about English life and the texture of English society, but it's something you feel you can't use that well. You have to start looking for other ways in which to work. I think here you start to move, not so much into out-and-out fantasy, but you start to create a slightly more fabulous

world. You start to use the landscape that you do know in a metaphorical way. Or you start to create out-and-out fantastic landscapes.
(Ishiguro 1993, 12)

Ishiguro includes himself without question in "English life and the texture
of English society." Why then is marginality to Englishness deduced from
his words if not because the interpreter is already looking for it in the first
place? Lewis's and Ishiguro's uses of "marginality" are related in that they
emphasise a sense of irrelevance, but Ishiguro does not see himself as marginal; on the contrary, he has made a conscious effort to use his knowledge
of "English life" in order to appeal to readers beyond Britain.

Lewis's lead has been followed on numerous occasions. Cynthia F. Wong,
for example, refers to Lewis's description of Ishiguro "as neither Japanese
nor English" to identify the theme of displacement in his novels:

> Barry Lewis deems Ishiguro's cultural identity as 'neither Japanese nor
> English, somewhere in-between departure and arrival, nostalgia and
> anticipation,' and calls the author 'a displaced person, one of the many
> in the twentieth-century of exile and estrangement' (2000: 1). Such a
> displacement may account for Ishiguro's own declaration that he is an
> international writer, for such a detail is relevant when examining the
> contexts of his five novels up to 2000 [. . .]. (493–4)

The problem here stems from the assumptions that go with nationality
labels. Both "English" and "Japanese" conjure up a series of imaginary
qualities and interpretive forms that are difficult to break. In an interview
with Kenzaburo Oe, Ishiguro refers to himself as "a homeless writer" in
relation to fitting these national identity moulds:

> My very lack of authority and lack of knowledge about Japan, I think,
> forced me into a position of using my imagination, and also of think-
> ing of myself as a kind of homeless writer. I had no obvious social role,
> because I wasn't a very English Englishman, and I wasn't a very Japa-
> nese Japanese either. And so I had no clear role, no society or country
> to speak for or write about. Nobody's history seemed to be my history.
> ("The Novelist" 115)

Ishiguro's lack of confidence in both his Englishness and his Japaneseness
lies in his perception that he "wasn't a very English Englishman, and [he]
wasn't a very Japanese Japanese either." He lacks "authority" because, in
his view, he lacks authenticity. That is to say, his identity is compromised in
relation to his origins and experience. This relates to the current emphasis
on literary interpretation in relation to the writer's identity, to the expectation that the work will provide a representation that reflects the writer's
"authentic" reality in relation to his origins (cf. Sánchez-Arce). Ishiguro

feels that he is not in a position to offer this. The qualification of Englishman and Japanese with "very English" and "very Japanese" emphasises the view that there is a truer way of being English and Japanese. Ishiguro (more than likely influenced by reactions from those surrounding him) seems to have adopted the popular way of thinking about nationality as a category that is unchanging and stable and this shuts him out of both Englishness and Japaneseness. Rather than rethink the labels, he refers to himself in negatives, as having no role, no society and no country.

Although this feeling of unbelonging is common, the interpretive categories that make it possible have also been challenged. Yasmin Alibhai-Brown remarks: "It is astonishing to hear pundits and politicians speaking of the 'four nations' of Britain. *Windrush* and its aftermath is not even an afterthought in this discourse. [. . .] where do we, the black Britons go? Perhaps we can put in a bid for London, please?" (271). Her humour should not obscure her critique of outdated nationalist rhetoric which may make a large section of the population feel that they have no role, no society and no country. National labels must be rethought and redefined, likewise concepts such as national literatures that derivate from nationalist discourses. If Ishiguro was not perceived as "not quite" British or English, his inclusion in the English canon would not have to be qualified.

My argument here follows Benedict Anderson in conceiving of the nation as "an imagined political community" (15), a frame of reference that is now so established that "the national state is the overwhelming norm" (123). However, whereas Anderson is optimistic about the lack of relationship between racism and nationalism, arguing that racism does not "derive from nationalism" but from "ideologies of class" (135;136), I believe that nationalism's inherent drive to unify populations and repress difference may go hand in hand not just with classism, but also with other discriminatory practices such as racism. Edward Said's *Orientalism* already analyses how orientalist discourse helped form an idea of what European nations and nationals were supposedly not, providing a definition by negatives and aligning the Oriental with undesired elements in Western societies (cf. 206). In European nations citizenship may have become more open to racial difference, but the imagined communities that Anderson describes based on nationalism are still to be tackled successfully. This may account for the problems with nomenclature regarding writers like Ishiguro, who do not fit the imagined racial make up of the nation, even if it is Britishness rather than Englishness. Ishiguro's homelessness is therefore a result of him being part of interpretive communities that not only take for granted nationality as a category to judge identity, but whose frameworks to interpret identity are modelled on nineteenth-century nationalist discourses imbued with Orientalism.

Besides being seen as "neither Japanese nor English," Ishiguro's work has also attracted interpretations in the West on the basis of his supposedly authentic Japaneseness. These have ranged from Orientalist readings of his novels to an insistence that he write about his experiences as an immigrant in Britain and thus record his "authentic" self. For the former, Ishiguro is providing explanations about Japan and Japanese sensibility whether his books are set there or elsewhere in the world; for the latter, Ishiguro is a renegade who performs "whiteness" and represses his "authentic" self in search of mainstream audiences. However opposed these interpretations may appear, they share a belief in an essential character for the writer based on his perceived identity which is then translated into appropriate themes and style. They treat writers and literature as artefacts to be valued in relation to their origins rather than in their own right. This is based on authenticist premises that attach authority to representation on the basis of the author's identity (in Ishiguro's case, his identity as Japanese, Anglo-Japanese, or "a displaced person"). Authenticism is "the discourse or grand narrative that legitimizes knowledge on the grounds of it originating from essential identity characteristics or subjectivities. It permits and precedes the 'celebration' of difference whilst enforcing a repressive discourse that restricts the articulation of those differences" (Sánchez-Arce 143).

Authenticism fosters the idea that origins are paramount to identity and helps the nationalist-inflected tendency to repatriate writers figuratively, insisting on seeing Ishiguro as Japanese. It creates the demand that Ishiguro's work provide access to an exotic or marginalised subjectivity regardless of the content of the books. Gabriele Annan exemplifies this position when she states that Ishiguro's first three novels—*A Pale View of Hills* (1982), *An Artist of the Floating World* (1986), and *The Remains of the Day* (1989)—"are explanations, even indictments, of Japanese-ness [. . .] He writes about [. . .] duty, loyalty, and tradition. Characters who place too high—too Japanese—a price on these values are punished for it" (3). Annan places Ishiguro in the role of the informant siding against his own culture. Not only is Ishiguro "explaining" Japaneseness, he must also be indicting it. Yet there is nothing in the novels to suggest that the values of "duty, loyalty, and tradition" are essentially Japanese. Ironically, what Annan identifies as Japanese is also associated with Englishness. Besides, in these three novels it is only the English Stevens who is unequivocally loyal and obsessed with duty and tradition. Etsuko in *A Pale View of Hills* has left her first husband and moved to England and Ono in *An Artist of the Floating World* keeps changing ideology as he sees fit.

Pico Iyer's review of *The Remains of the Day* further illustrates the perception of Ishiguro as a native informant. Iyer places a considerable emphasis on Ishiguro's name and background in order to interpret the novel as being ultimately about Japan but dressed in English clothes:

> [Ishiguro] shows us how unreasonable it is for us to expect those
> trained—or even hired—to be self-annulling, to act otherwise; and
> how unreasonable, for them, to expect us to renounce impulse or

emotion. In the process, he begins to explain how the Japanese can be highly sophisticated, yet innocent as toddlers; refined, yet seemingly by reflex; extraordinarily considerate and in spite—indeed *because*—of that, apparently unfeeling. Translating the most Japanese of virtues into terms we recognize as our own, he brings their foreign features home to us. (Iyer 1991, 588)

This reading is conditioned by Iyer's use of an "us" and "them" logic, the "us" being supposedly Western and the "them" clearly other and Japanese. Iyer's logic is that of the Orientalist who stresses

the fact that the Oriental lived in a different but thoroughly organized world of his own, a world with its own national, cultural, and epistemological boundaries and principles of internal coherence. Yet what gave the Oriental's world its intelligibility and identity was not the result of his own efforts but rather the whole complex series of knowledgeable manipulations by which the Orient was identified by the West. (40)

Iyer's review demonstrates that names and origins matter, that Ishiguro's name and supposed nationality can affect some readers to the extent that they see Japan even when it is not there. It does not occur to Iyer that Ishiguro might instead be portraying the English and Englishness, or simply self-deception through a character who happens to be English. Ishiguro's name and background mark him out for interpretations that place the author's ready-made identity at the heart of reading/writing texts. This authenticist approach to interpreting literature pins writer and writing to fixed moulds that are determined by (also fixed) identity labels attributed by the reader to the writer. Writers like Ishiguro are thus put in their identity box regardless of what they actually write.

Despite relying on the supposed correlation between "reality" (the author's identity) and fiction (what the author writes about), critics like Anan and Iyer do not question Ishiguro's representation of Japan. Ishiguro's works are appropriated by an authenticist discourse which uses them as representatives of his supposed "native" culture. Thus Ishiguro becomes a translator of Japaneseness. Readers familiar with Japanese culture are aware that Ishiguro's early fiction simulates Japan. Yoshifumi Saito details what he calls "blatant error[s]" (176) in Ishiguro's (mis)use of Japanese forms of address, descriptions of objects, people and rooms, and customs.[1] For example, Saito analyses Ishiguro's use of bowing in *A Pale View of Hills*:

the custom of bowing seems very bizarre to the Japanese eye. They bow all too frequently. For example, Etsuko makes a bow to express her acceptance of Sachiko's request to borrow money [. . .]. Bred in England, Ishiguro must have been convinced that the Japanese would bow anytime they need to show politeness and must have fallen into the error of making his characters bow to answer in the affirmative, approve of others' requests or apologise, whilst they do in reality virtually only for greeting. (176)

It is extremely unusual to find a critique of Ishiguro's authenticity in relation to the accuracy of his Japanese novels and characters. Saito is right in pointing out all these inaccuracies as a healthy corrective to many Western critics' insistence on Ishiguro's "Japanese" credentials. Whether his analysis is seen as too pernickety or an overdue assessment of Ishiguro's right to be seen as a Japanese writer, it is impossible to maintain after reading it that Ishiguro writes accurately about Japan or the Japanese. As Saito states, "the factual correctness of his description, or even the evocativeness of Japanese culture through his description, does not matter so much in his literary enterprise" (184).

Ishiguro has often said that reading for authenticity in his settings or in relation to his life will not get readers very far. For instance, Mark Lawson relates Ishiguro's experiences as a child in England to the "isolation" of his narrators. However, Ishiguro insists that he "felt exotic, but not isolated," and goes on to explain that "[i]f people want to [. . .] make these links between my autobiography and my narrators, I'm perfectly open to that. It's all part of the fun. Whether it will necessarily help you to a deeper reading I don't know" (Interview). Ishiguro has also talked about how the Japan in his novels is an attempt to record his imaginary version of Japan:

> I grew up with a very strong image in my head of this other country [. . .] Of course, I didn't know Japan, because I didn't come here. But in England I was all the time building up this picture in my head, an imaginary Japan, if you like. And I think when I reached the age of perhaps twenty-three or twenty-four I realized that this Japan, which was very precious to me, actually existed only in my own imagination, partly because the real Japan had changed greatly between 1960 and later on. I realized that it was a place of my own childhood, and I could never return to this particular Japan. (Oe and Ishiguro 1991, p.110)

Ishiguro's position as an intermediary between Japan and England is complicated by the fact that his first two novels are not just set in this imaginary Japan but also attempt to imitate the effects of an English translation from Japanese. Ishiguro has commented on how they

> were written as though they were written in Japanese. Of course I wrote them in English but the characters are Japanese. [. . .] I was having to portray characters talking in English but I had to create the impression that they were actually talking in Japanese. It had to almost be like a subtitles effect. (Interview)

The effect of this narrative technique, which Ishiguro goes on to call "English as translationese" (Interview), is similar to that of the commercial paintings Masuji Ono makes:

> We were also quite aware that the essential point about the sort of things we were commissioned to paint—geishas, cherry trees, swimming carps, temples—was that they look 'Japanese' to the foreigners to whom they were shipped out, and all finer points of style were quite likely to go unnoticed. (*An Artist* 69)

Ishiguro's first two books have "look[ed]" as "Japanese" as Ono's paintings. His portrayal of postwar England as a mythical place drawing on the country-house novel in *The Remains of the Day* follows a similar pattern of simulation and mock-realism. The emphasis on what seems to be portrayed—postwar Japan and England—has nevertheless obscured other "points of style" apart from the unreliability of the narrators which has been extensively discussed.

All of Ishiguro's narrators seem to be translated in the sense that they mimic social roles and the language that goes with them. This can be seen in Christopher Banks' obsession with tropes from detective fiction or Kathy's acknowledgement that the clones copy gestures and expressions from television programmes. But it is most obvious in Stevens's use of a convoluted prose style and his insistence that he reads romances to improve his command of English:

> it was an extremely efficient way to maintain and develop one's command of the English language [. . .]. It has never been my position that good accent and command of language are not attractive attributes, and I always considered it my duty to develop them as best I could. One straightforward means of going about this is simply to read a few pages of a well-written book during odd spare moments one may have. (*The Remains* 167–8)

Stevens argues that a "command of language" is to be learnt not from human interaction, but by reading "sentimental romance[s]" (167) with their hyperbolic use of language and improbable situations. Stevens's own narrative is itself exaggerated and baroque. This is characterised by the use of impersonal constructions such as "one may have" instead of the more straightforward "I have," and an over-reliance on negative statements instead of less elaborate, positive ones.

These linguistic tics point towards Stevens's aspirational use of language and his fear of misusing it. Stevens knows that being a butler is a role that he performs continually:

> 'dignity' has to do crucially with a butler's ability not to abandon the professional being he inhabits. Lesser butlers will abandon their

professional being for the private one at the least provocation. For such persons, being a butler is like playing some pantomime role; a small push, a slight stumble, and the façade will drop off to reveal the actor underneath. The great butlers are great by virtue of their ability to inhabit their professional being and inhabit it to the utmost; they will not be shaken out by external events, however surprising, alarming or vexing. (42–3)

Stevens refuses to acknowledge that being a butler is just a role, not the defining characteristic of his being. More importantly, his definition of a "great butler" uses stereotypes of butlers as impervious beings. Stevens's absorption of his father's story about the butler in India who deals with a tiger in the dining room without much fuss illustrates this. Stevens strives to become like the butlers in stories, a butler without a real counterpart. Interestingly, being phlegmatic is also associated with the gentleman,[2] the epitome of Englishness and a figure that Stevens alludes to frequently and aspires to be. Englishness and "butler-ness" could both be said to be simulations.

The fact that Stevens is acquired together with the house and displayed for Farraday's American guests to see is just one more step towards his definition as a simulation, as a "mock-butler" (124). Farraday's expectations that Stevens be an authentic English butler cruelly make Stevens's aim possible: "[T]his *is* a genuine grand old English house, isn't it? That's what I paid for. And you're a genuine old-fashioned English butler, not just some waiter pretending to be one. You're the real thing, aren't you?" (124; emphasis in original). Farraday's insistent questions point to the constructed, artificial nature of the reality he craves. Stevens's persona has finally caught up with him and from now on he is expected to play up to it. Mike Petry makes a similar point about the novel, stating that it is "a 'mock' version of an England gone past and of certain types of the English novel gone past. And the England that is depicted in the novel [. . .] is certainly not even a country that has once really existed" (102).

And yet Ishiguro's name and contested nationality still colour critical interpretations of his work. Whereas he has been celebrated for his representations of Japan by critics who read his work for difference, negative reactions have come from those who feel betrayed because they read Ishiguro's books for sameness and cannot find in them a mirror where they can look at themselves. For example, Sheng-mei Ma complains that Ishiguro's writing is dominated by his desire to transcend his own ethnicity (71) and attacks *The Remains of the Day* and *The Unconsoled*, which she interprets as failed attempts by Ishiguro to pass as white:

[S]urely no one would dispute the simple fact that being figments of the imagination, characters could be viewed as a novelist's projection of his or her unique conditions of existence, ethnicity being one of them. [. . .] This is to assume, in an essentialist manner, that there is such a thing—a particular kind of ethnicity—to be represented. But to assume otherwise is a luxury enjoyed by 'the haves,' who have moved beyond the basic struggles for civil rights, whose ethnicity is no longer an impediment to success, whose ethnicity, in an ironic twist, is the key to success in a West fond of tokenized minorities. (71)

Ma's argument relies heavily on a conflation of author and characters and the assumption that there is a direct relationship between the former and the latter. She labels Ishiguro "Anglo-Japanese" and then demands that he use narrators who occupy this particular subject position. The writer's context is seen as the unproblematic origin of the writing and acts merely as a projection or representation of it. Yet turning Ishiguro into an "ethnic" writer who should only concern himself with "ethnic" topics could be felt to "tokenise" him as much as the "West" does. The authenticist demand for coherence between texts and the author's cultural background does not only occur in Orientalist or reactionary discourses. It is employed as a way to control individuals by all sides, including those who pride themselves on fighting against reactionary politics. Paradoxically, this makes the author the ultimate authority over the text without allowing for any deviation from his/her "authentic" formal identity in terms of themes or style. Ishiguro's transplanted, ambiguous nationality is seen not simply as unusual or anomalous, but is subject to an insidious moral disapproval.

Although Ishiguro's early novels have been interpreted following realist conventions, Ishiguro writes in an idiosyncratic mock-realist style that combines a veneer of plausibility with a metaphorical emphasis on characters, settings and events. The expression of these themes is what makes Ishiguro's writing unique and, paradoxically, what puzzles a great many readers who rely on "naively mimetic premises" to interpret texts. The stories could be written as page-turning, realist novels with a chronological plot, but Ishiguro's thickly layered narrative structure keeps the reader guessing. As Miss Lucy says to the students in *Never Let Me Go*, "you've been told and not told" (73). This might almost be Ishiguro's motto. He tells and does not tell by means of recursive metaphors, the impact of which widens as one reads on. These metaphors are at times limited to one of the novels (such as the Bridge of Hesitation in *An Artist of the Floating World*) but the most powerful ones recur in several of them. This is the case of the lines of trees in desolate landscapes which figure in *A Pale View of Hills* and *Never Let Me Go*, or the image of the wound that Etsuko uses to talk about her trauma on her daughter's suicide. In *The Unconsoled* Brodsky also talks about a wound in metaphorical terms to refer to trauma, although by the end of the novel it is discovered that he has a literal wound as he has lost a leg. This physical wound, however, is more than that. It is not certain whether it is the belated expression of his mental wound or the cause of it. Nevertheless, like Etsuko's, Brodsky's life revolves around his wound and the search for a "consolation":

You realise soon enough when a wound's not going to heal. The music, even when I was a conductor, I knew that's all it was, just a consolation. It helped for a while. I liked the feeling, pressing the wound, it fascinated me. A good wound, it can do that, it fascinates. It looks a little different every day. (313)

The wound that does not heal and the different things that people use as "a consolation" for their particular wound are at the heart of Ishiguro's fiction and his other work. Consolations are different for each narrator. Etsuko's grief is far too recent for her to have found one, but her need to tell stories could be the beginning. Ono's vain insistence on prestige and fame is his way out of painful memories about his collaboration. For Stevens it is duty and dignity. This consolation in a public role is shared by Ryder and Christopher Banks, who delude themselves (as Ono does) into believing their efforts can save the world and themselves. Music features prominently in *The Unconsoled* as a way of saving the city and all the family relationships in the book, which in a way are all Ryder's own displaced thoughts about his own life and that of his parents. It is also the main element linking the short stories in Ishiguro's *Nocturnes* (2009). Kathy and the other "students" believe in love and creativity as a way out of their fate, and they are encouraged to value artistic output above all else by their guardians at Hailsham. These different "consolations" are used to attempt to create a stable identity and fend off the uncertainty that a wound—a liminal space between outside and inside, public and private, trauma and healing—conveys as a metaphor.

Ishiguro has spoken about writing itself in exactly these terms:

Writing is a kind of a consolation or a therapy. Quite often, bad writing comes out of this kind of therapy. The best writing comes out of a situation where I think the artist or writer has to some extent come to terms with the fact that it is too late. The wound has come, and it hasn't healed, but it's not going to get any worse; yet, the wound is there. It's a kind of consolation that the world isn't quite the way you wanted it but you can somehow reorder it or try and come to terms with it by actually creating your own world and own version of it. [. . .] I think serious writers have to try, in some way or the other, to keep moving in a direction that moves them toward this area of irresolution and lack of balance. ("Stuck" 30–1)

For Ishiguro, writing is "a consolation" rather than an answer. His emphasis is on "creating your own world" rather than the wound and its origins, whereas some readers would prefer it if he were to focus on specific biographical traumas. This would fit him into a "ready-made" identity and would provide a more satisfactory "consolation," one that allows for a reassuring reproduction of certainty. Yet implication and inference are bywords for his writing and readers are confronted by stories where neither the situation nor its outcome are ultimately fully explained. They are offered a pale view of the narrators' lives and thought processes, asked to read between lines and, just like Ishiguro's ideal writer, "keep moving in a direction that moves them toward this area of irresolution and lack of balance." For an interpretive community that looks to texts for resolution and balance in relation to the author's ready-made (marginal) identity and the interpretive forms that go with it, books like Ishiguro's are not a consolation but a challenge to these forms.

It is therefore unsurprising that the novel that has proved most divisive among readers and critics is titled *The Unconsoled*. Boasting an omniscient yet unaware first person narrator, *The Unconsoled* is a radically experimental novel that takes Ishiguro's previous mock-realism a little further to unravel assumptions surrounding mimetic representation of reality. It would be very difficult to interpret *The Unconsoled* following authenticist tenets and it leaves little space for analysis in relation to Black British writing or postcoloniality. This narrative strategy should have warned readers that Ishiguro is not and never has been a realist. Judging by Ishiguro's comments in 1989, he could be daring readers to interpret an experimental novel following conventional ways of reading:

> These stereotypes are all right as part of a publicity game. Where it starts to get irritating is when people read your work in a sort of way: it seems my Japanese novels are so exotic and remote that I could have written bizarre Márquezian or Kafkaesque stuff and people still would have taken it as straight realism. (qtd. Lewis 9)

Could this be at the heart of experimentation in *The Unconsoled* and *When We Were Orphans*, two novels where Ishiguro stretches the limits of credibility in a way that makes it impossible for them to be read in an authenticist way? *The Unconsoled* in particular deprives readers of the cultural, identity and genre markers they expect, making it extremely difficult to employ one set of stable (formal) interpretive strategies and leaving readers who are not able or willing to adapt literally "unconsoled." *When We Were Orphans* does something similar but reverts to a non-omniscient first person narrator and puts back setting, cultural and genre markers to trick readers into thinking themselves safe in a detective story when it is anything but.

It is particularly difficult to read *The Unconsoled* as realistic since Ishiguro decides to transform his already unreal backgrounds into a fully surrealist world. The novel depicts a nightmarish world in which the narrator—Ryder, who is allegedly "the world's finest pianist" (11)—is in a city to give a concert which never takes place. The rules of space and time are subverted as events that should last a few seconds are made to last long enough for an extended conversation and places that are apparently distant are connected by doors and passages. Ryder is subject to other characters' whims, but at other times his thoughts dictate the way other characters behave. He appears not to have a structured memory and never finishes what he sets out to do, distracted by polite requests that he is unable—or unwilling—to refuse. His memory seems blocked and his past haunts him in narrative chaos. Other characters float in and out of his narrative as if they were ghosts of his past—Mr and Mrs Hoffman—or aspects of his former or future selves—Boris, Stephan, Brodsky (cf. Adelman). Ryder's troubled past, vacuous present and possible futures are hinted at in a novel that also addresses its own function in a meta-narrative way as discussions of music echo debates along the lines of those on Modernism and Postmodernism. *The Unconsoled* pushes narrative conventions and characterisation to the limit, challenging every authenticist tenet on the correspondence between reality and fiction, the author and his work.

Just as Ryder appropriates other characters to project his life, so Ishiguro appropriates names to suggest a setting without settling for a particular one. There seems to be a consensus that the novel is set in an undetermined town in Central Europe but it is clear that Ishiguro has been careful not to provide a clear correlation between his imaginary town and a real place. Richard Robinson discusses this but argues that "the novel is only superficially ahistorical. Central European history is a latent content which we can profitably ascribe to the dreamwork of the narrative" (118). Robinson's clever interpretation, putting real space and history "back" in the book as it were, is proof of how readers' interpretive strategies are key to the way they think about texts. He argues for "the Central European character of the novel" (111) on the basis that being "nowhere, in particular" (title) is distinctly Central European. In Central Europe, he says, "[s]tatehood has often been felt to be merely the temporary occupation of 'arbitrary slices of latitude and longitude'. For example, it was possible in the twentieth century to have lived under Austria, Poland, the Soviet Union, and Ukraine— while not moving an inch" (113). Robinson emphasizes central Europe's mutability in terms of states and nationhood in order to make a case for its importance to *The Unconsoled* as "a latent content which we can profitably ascribe to the dreamwork of the narrative" (Robinson 2001, 118). This is a compelling argument, although I would like to consider here the unspecified central European location as a way for Ishiguro to undermine our reliance on nationality, history and geography. By using an array of names that guide readers towards conflicting or undetermined nationalities, the novel raises the issue of whether the nationality of its characters and setting (and by extension, of the writer) is important at all. History and geography are vague and this allows for mythology to develop. The central European location could also be mining the ignorance surrounding central Europe's history and geography, using it as another colonisable space for "otherness" that is "almost, but not quite" like home. Like Ryder's hotel room or the flat he visits with Boris, location is both familiar and alien to the Western European reader. This may lead to a replication of Ryder's anxiety in readers who fit this interpretive framework.

The setting of *The Unconsoled* shows Ishiguro's mimicry at its most experimental level. Mimicry is key to Ishiguro's settings—including his imaginary China, England, Japan and other European locations—and to his style, for just as Ishiguro acknowledges that he was "deliberately using a kind of 'Japanese' (in quotes) aesthetic in my early works" (Interview), one can say that he then moves on to cannibalise other styles or genres such as the historical novel, the country-house novel, the detective novel, the sci-fi or dystopian novel and even the boarding school novel. None of these accurately describe his work although it partakes and feeds on all of these genres. Ishiguro uses recognisable genre markers, settings, historical events and even character types as metaphors to convey ideas and emotional states. More disturbingly, the clones in *Never Let Me Go* are versions of untraceable originals and treated as "almost, but not quite" human by society. Their lack of family names—they are known by name and, if need be, a letter in place of a surname—is as significant as the proliferation of central European-sounding settings in *The Unconsoled*.

Like satire, mimicry is sometimes dependent on being understood as such. Just like a satire can be taken at face value, particularly if the reader agrees with what is being satirised, mimicry can also be interpreted as mimetic rather than showing up the lack of authenticity of the models it imitates. Ishiguro's style, his "realism" with a non-mimetic intent, together with his supposed otherness embodied in his name, is what creates the confusion; it defies the logic promoted by authenticism that there is a one-to-one correspondence between reality and representation, identity and literary output. It is this logic, together with the distinction between "us" and "them" (where "them" is knowable through writing), that makes possible identity-centred readings. Edward Said mentions this interdependence:

> the kind of language, thought, and vision that I have been calling Orientalism very generally is a form of *radical realism*; anyone employing Orientalism, which is the habit for dealing with questions, objects, qualities deemed Oriental, will designate, name, point to, fix what he is talking or thinking about with a word or phrase, which then is considered either to have acquired, or more simply to be, reality. (72; emphasis added)

Although Said does not call it authenticism, his insistence that "a form of radical realism" legitimises Orientalism points to this. For what is the premise of a "radical realism" if not authenticism? Furthermore, this "radical realism" extends beyond Orientalism to many other ways of interpreting literature and the world. It is more than an approach to literature; it is a "vision" of the world.

The reception and interpretation of Ishiguro's work throws light onto authenticist reading practices and their failure to cope with non-overtly representational literature, or literature that presents something other than otherness as oppositional politics. These readings can foreclose other interpretations. Authenticism is a monologic system based on opposites like true/false, accurate/inaccurate, real/unreal. It textualises otherness, prescribes themes and styles of writing for it, and polices both style and subject matter by authors whose background labels them as other to a delusional norm. The prescription of content and either prescription or neglect of form for texts by authors whose names and/or backgrounds attract authenticist readings is at play in the reductive effect of this type of interpretive formalism. This prescription is at times a far cry from the actual content and form of the text. Therefore, the invocation of the authenticity of writers and texts may connote freedom for the individual in self-expression but it either does not tolerate freedom when writers deviate from acceptable forms or is used to justify interpretive strategies that interpret/write the text following accepted critical forms.

Theodor Adorno expresses doubts about the progressive aspects of authenticity as coming from what the subject *is* rather than what the subject *does*:

> In the jargon [of authenticity], finally, there remains from inwardness only the most external aspect, that thinking oneself superior marks people who elect themselves: the claim of people who consider themselves blessed simply by virtue of being what they are. Without any effort, this claim can turn into an elitist claim, or into a readiness to attach itself to elites which then quickly gives the axe to inwardness. A symptom of the transformation of inwardness is the belief of innumerable people that they belong to an extraordinary family. The jargon of authenticity, which sells self-identity as something higher, projects the exchange formula onto that which imagines that it is not exchangeable; for as a biological individual each man resembles himself. (61)

Adorno spells out the dangers of authenticity's essentialism. The emphasis on the individual is hollowed out, subsumed into the individual belonging to "an extraordinary family." This claim can be empowering in situations where a particular group has been singled out for discrimination. However, it quickly turns into a binding law in itself which "gives the axe to inwardness." Interpretive strategies based on politics of difference inflected through authenticism may lead to a predisposition to interpret texts according to the author's supposed identity concentrating on established ideological forms. This does a disservice to the "extraordinary families" that these interpretive communities believe to be championing and promotes a totalisation of experience neatly packaged into distinct forms of cultural identification.

The common denominator in all of these totalising *petit récits* that erect themselves as alternative norms is their reliance on authenticism to celebrate their difference and repress any deviations. This repression, as seen in Ishiguro's case, takes the form of critiques based on the correlation (or not) between the supposed identities of writers and the content and form of their work. Some writers are conveniently adopted by some "extraordinary family" and their works read and policed accordingly. They are therefore, literally, stuck to the margins. Ishiguro has not so much been adopted by the Japanese as one of their own as thrust into the exotic, Japanese and postcolonial drawers, to mention a few. Identity in this case is imposed from outside as a shorthand to understanding a writer's work. It is one thing to go along with Ishiguro's initial simulation of Japan and later simulation of England and other locations as long as we are aware that it may not be accurate. It is something else altogether to rely on someone's name, ethnic origin and place of birth to interpret their work in a way that turns them into native informants, and to use their origins to deny them full status as English writers.

NOTES

1. Many thanks to Gen'ichiro Itakura for drawing my attention to Saito's essay and providing a copy of his translation.
2. A figure much used in colonial discourse as (English) gentlemen were portrayed as better than those they ruled and therefore right to do so. See, for example, the repeated use of "phlegmatic" to describe Phileas Fogg in Jules Verne's *Around the World in Eighty Days* (1873).

REFERENCES

Adelman, Gary. "Doubles on the Rocks: Ishiguro's The Unconsoled." *Critique: Studies in Contemporary Fiction* 42:2 (2001): 166–79. Print.

Adorno, Theodor. *The Jargon of Authenticity*. Trans. Knut Tarnowski and Frederic Will. London: Routledge, 2003. Print.

Alibhai-Brown, Yasmin. *Who Do We Think We Are? Imagining the New Britain*. London: Penguin, 2001. Print.

Anderson, Benedict. *Imagined Communities. Reflections on the Origin and Spread of Nationalism*. London: Verso, 1983. Print.

Annan, Gabriele. "On the High Wire." *New York Review of Books* 7 December 1989: 3–4. Print.

Childs, Peter. "The English Heritage Industry and Other Trends in the Novel at the Millennium." Shaffer 210–224. Print.

Fish, Stanley. *Is There A Text in This Class? The Authority of Interpretive Communities*. Cambridge, MA: Harvard University Press. Print.

Ishiguro, Kazuo. *An Artist of the Floating World*. London: Faber and Faber, 1997. Print.

———. *A Pale View of Hills*. London: Faber and Faber, 1991. Print.

———. Interview by Mark Lawson. Front Row. BBC Radio 4. 17 February 2005. Radio

———. *Never Let Me Go*. London: Faber and Faber, 2005. Print.

———. *Nocturnes. Five Stories of Music and Nightfall*. London: Faber and Faber, 2009. Print.

———. "The Novelist in Today's World: A Conversation." Interview by Kenzaburo Oe. *Boundary* 2, 18 (1991): 109–122. Print.

———. *The Remains of the Day*. 1989. London: Faber and Faber, 1993. Print.

————. "Stuck on the Margins: An Interview with Kazuo Ishiguro." *Face to Face. Interviews with Contemporary Novelists*. Ed. Allan Vorda. Huston, Texas: Rice University Press, 1993: 1–35. Print.

————. *The Unconsoled*. 1995. London: Faber and Faber, 1996. Print.

————. *When We Were Orphans*. London: Faber and Faber, 2000. Print.

Iyer, Pico. "Waiting Upon History." *Partisan Review* LVII:3 (1991): 585–89. Print.

Lewis, Barry. *Kazuo Ishiguro*. Manchester: Manchester University Press, 2000. Print.

Ma, Sheng-mei. "Kazuo Ishiguro's Persistent Dream of Postethnicity: Performance in Whiteface." *Post Identity* 2:1 (1999): 71–88. Print.

Petry, Mike. *Narratives of Memory and Identity. The Novels of Kazuo Ishiguro*. Frankfurt: Peter Lang, 1999. Print.

Robinson, Richard. "Nowhere in Particular: Kazuo Ishiguro's The Unconsoled and Central Europe." *Critical Quarterly* 48:4 (2006): 107–30. Print.

Said, Edward. *Orientalism*. New York: Vintage, 1994. Print.

Saito, Yoshifumi. "Japan in English. Three Novels by a Japanese British Author." *Teaching and Learning English: Integrating Language, Literature and Culture*. Trans. Gen'ichiro Itakura. Tokyo: Tokyo University Press, 2003: 171–85. Print.

Sánchez-Arce, Ana María. "'Authenticism', or the Authority of Authenticity." *Mosaic* 40:3 (2007): 139–55. Print.

Shaffer, Brian W., ed. *The British and Irish Novel 1945–2000*. Oxford: Blackwell, 2007. Print.

Skinner, John. "Black British Interventions." Shaffer 128–43. Print.

Wong, Cynthia F. "Kazuo Ishiguro's The Remains of the Day." Shaffer 493–503. Print.

9 "Not yet not yet . . ."

Forms of Defiance, Forms of Excess in the Poetry of Alice Oswald

Kym Martindale

I came to this chapter with the desire to prove that the literary, at its best, offers, in Wordsworth's words from "Tintern Abbey" (1798), "a presence that disturbs me with the joy / Of elevated thoughts; a sense sublime / Of something far more deeply interfused" (lines 95–97). While this desire haunts me in any discussion or dealings with the literary, whether I am teaching, studying, or simply reading, it is the desire itself which chiefly intrigues, constituting as it does, a paradox. I urgently want to be assured of the value, in some lasting and transcendent way of what I am doing, but, as with all desire, it is unclear how satisfactory it would be to have such proof, for the bleak danger of the closure that it might bring. The desire also presumes that one of the purposes of the "literary" is to unsettle, to make us feel, and think in excess of the work itself, to confront us with being part of something much larger than the ordinary round.

In "Tintern Abbey," Wordsworth was writing more directly about the spiritual significance of nature amongst other things, but indirectly, as ever, about poetry and the imagination. Immediately prior to the lines quoted, he reflects that he has come to "look on nature" not with the hedonism of youth, but instead, "hearing oftentimes / The still, sad music of humanity" that is "of ample power / To chasten and subdue" (lines 91–93). There is an inherent violence in the poet's epiphany that undercuts yet magnifies his experience of the sublime—a violence that arguably threatens the speaker's sense of being, even as it is reaffirmed; a violence that haunts too the work of Alice Oswald. The tension is between dissolution and union or perhaps, an anxiety that the trajectory from dissolution to union will lose its way, and result only in rupture. Isobel Armstrong discusses this passage in her longer analysis of Wordsworth's entire poem (97–107). As I will show, her argument functions usefully as a point of departure from which to read the work of Alice Oswald. The poetics of place is always, too, the poetics of self, but in Oswald's case, self is the matter beyond identity, and thus her work prompts a reevaluation of boundaries, categories, and materiality itself.

Oswald is commonly read as a poet of place, landscape, and nature; although academic responses are more cognisant of recent contestations of the label "nature," in reviews and interviews, "nature" is understood in essentially post-Romantic terms, with little critical attention to that position's ideological and historical basis. The emphasis on Oswald as a writer of place and landscape is, however, understandable, and not entirely inaccurate. Her first collection, *The Thing in the Gap-Stone Stile* (1996) examines a world largely removed from the urban or metropolitan, and her subsequent work continues to scrutinise specific landscapes, which, while they are not exactly "wilderness," are rural or pastoral. *Dart* (2002) and *A Sleepwalk on the Severn* (2009) are both book-length poems which interpret and perform the respective rivers, Dart and Severn, through the voices of those for whom the rivers are essential, those who both claim and are claimed by them.[1] *Woods etc.* (2005) is, like her earlier collection, deeply interested in place: sea, woods, fields, and their nonhuman inhabitants, and even her latest piece, *Memorial* (2012), an intense revisioning of Homer's *Iliad*, is far from ignoring the Homeric landscape.

Oswald herself rejects the category "nature poet," qualifying it: "[i]f the phrase must be used, then a nature poet is someone concerned with things being outside each other." She continues, "How should extrinsic forms, man and earth for example, come into contact?" (qtd. Pinard 26). More scholarly reception of her work intuits and is drawn to her pleasure and interest in form, shape-shifting, and the value of process over arrival: Tom Bristow, for example, highlights how the end of *Dart* "has the poet turn into the seal watcher, who in turn merges into both the animals and the voice of the mutating river-sea" (179). He further observes that "withdrawal from the human and the propensity to name is the key intellectual impulse at the end of [. . .] *Dart*" and that Oswald's work "resists the desire for recognisable order and relinquishes force" (170, 181). Bristow encourages an understanding in which Oswald's work moves deliberately away from a trajectory towards resolution, upon which the uncovering and promotion of identity/ ies is arguably dependent. Indeed, Oswald exhibits an apparent lack of allegiance to any specific identity as formulated out of race, class, or gender (although this need not detract from analyses foregrounding how racial, gender, or social politics might operate in her work). This is despite the presence, in both *Dart* and *A Sleepwalk on the Severn* of local, historically real voices; other readings of these poems might offer such voices as evidence of a project to recover a regional identity. But Oswald's larger project proposes a self constituted through *listening* rather than through an insistence on being heard and/or seen, two aims which drive identity politics.

Mary Pinard emphasises the importance and function of listening in her discussion of Oswald. She notes that Oswald's poetry is both "multivocal" and "shaped by sound" (26) and cites Oswald's own description of her *modus operandum*: "Poems are written in the sound house of a whole body [. . .] so [. . .] before putting pen to paper, I ask myself, 'Am I listening? Am I listening with a soft, slow listening that will not obliterate the speaker?'" (qtd. Pinard 26). It is essential that the poetry is equally concerned to engage its reader in such listening: in *Dart* the reader is urged to "put your ear to it" to hear "water / cooped up in moss and moving" (Oswald, *Dart* 10); in *Woods etc.*, the poem "River," similarly commands us so that with our ear to the trees we will "hear the widening / numerical openings of the river" (Oswald, *Woods etc.* 41).[2] But Oswald goes further: the poetry must enact this process, to reveal how sound is integral to being itself: thus in "Birdsong for Two Voices," a "song [. . .] assembles the earth / out of nine notes and silence" (*Woods etc.* 5). The reader is now exhorted not merely to be a liste*ner*, but to understand, and to experience coming into being through sound, through listen*ing*. The shift from the passivity of the noun to the dynamism of the verb is critical, and recalls Jean-Luc Nancy's sense of listening as being "always on the edge of meaning" (7).

This runs counter to identity-based writing and criticism, which cries out against that which has silenced or ignored it; identity is anxious to establish itself, to voice *its own* story, which is then fenced off, and carefully policed against identities otherwise imposed from outside.[3] These anxieties, while understandable, certainly at times necessary, are nevertheless problematic as the fierce debates around gender and race in response to queer theory have demonstrated. Judith Butler's observation that identity politics continued to be based on exclusion, and thus, being hostage to ontological thinking, shored up the very norms they sought to overturn, was the most radical element of a theory that proposed the elimination of categorisation altogether (Alsop et al. 94–113). Categories and boundaries are essential to articulations of (racial, gender/sexual, or class) identity, formulated as they are, as narratives of origin and/or arrival, at resolution and "truth." It is therefore pertinent and significant that both of Oswald's river poems do much to undermine the apparently inevitable narrative of "river" that moves from source to finish, by repeatedly emphasising the plurality, or the instability of this natural phenomenon. In *Dart*, different bodies of water converge and merge; they in turn enter the sea. There is no arrival at being *this* or *that*, simply a series of entities clashing, "at loggerheads [. . .] wrangling away into this valley of oaks" (*Dart* 11) rather than an identity seeking and finding place. Note the struggle, however, as pluralities continue in friction. The Dart sustains difference, and in fact, would not be the river it is without its tributaries. Even as it enters the sea, which might seem the obvious *telos* of "river," it continues in a multiplicity of selves, to be "all names, all voices [. . .] Proteus /[. . .]/ driving my many selves from cave to cave . . ." (*Dart* 48). But difference and dis-unity are recognised as abrasive as well as possibly desirable. *A Sleepwalk on the Severn* more evidently rejects the "river" narrative, focusing wholly on the Severn Estuary, a place of shifting mud banks and tides, and accordingly, a landscape subject to that other shape-shifting phenomenon, the moon.

Such strategies as, to borrow again from Bristow, a resistance to a "recognised order" or force, are especially powerful in poetry, the most invested in order and force of all the literary genres; they are similarly potent in writing that, whatever Oswald says, does explore "nature," so taxonimised as that is.[4] However, it is not Oswald's more obviously "nature" writing that I want to discuss here, but work in which she deliberately explores being as both physical and metaphysical. This is precisely because her definition of a "nature poet" as "someone concerned with things being outside each other" drives her aesthetic in such a way that it can offer a gesture that is also radical, if, through listening, we grasp the supreme importance of communicability itself. Oswald's poetics offer a discourse that relinquishes identity as a practice to suggest a mode of being that, in Giorgio Agamben's sense, unsettles "for its being-*such*, for belonging itself" (Agamben 2).

To return to "Tintern Abbey," it is listening that Wordsworth attempts, and in which he partly succeeds, "hearing oftentimes/The still, sad music." Isobel Armstrong's reading of this passage further reveals a poetry that is both thought and emotion, and suggests an intuition that resonates with Agamben's: "[l]ove [that] is never directed toward this or that property of the loved one [. . .] but neither does it neglect the properties in favour of an insipid generality (universal love): The lover wants the loved one *with all of its predicates*, its being such as it is" (Agamben 2). Agamben continues that the "Lovable" is not the "intelligence of some thing [. . .] but only the intelligence of an intelligibility [. . .] the movement that transports the object not toward another thing or another place, but toward its own taking-place—toward the Idea" (2).

There are several key words in Wordsworth's much-discussed lines: "disturbs"—oddly and disturbingly placed in relation to "joy"; "something," "the sense sublime," and for Armstrong, the repeated use of "of." The first word, "disturbs," captures that epiphanic jolt out of self that art or nature can prompt, and which here implies a self welcoming its dissolution as a necessary precursor to union. The second word, "something," as Armstrong notes, has unsettled and teased critics for years (96–7). By not naming that "something," Wordsworth might be accused of abdicating poetic and spiritual accountability in the face of the "unrepresentable." Instead, he has made us a gift, Armstrong argues: for "by the time we come to the much disputed "sense sublime / Of something far more deeply interfused," Wordsworth has built up so many appositional phrases that the lines of erasure form an "infinite number of possible connections" and that is partly the point" (99–100).[5] That "something" is not visited externally upon the poet, nor is it only sensed; it is *thought* by him. Armstrong pushes us to see that Wordsworth recognises the intellectual labour necessary to the existence of the "sense sublime" as well as its apprehension; that "something" is made out of sky, sun and sea, yes, but also "the mind of man."[6]

The intricacy of this process is significant for any aesthetic that seeks to be engaged politically, and yet cognisant of, and responsive to affect. Wordsworth's wonder is at Agamben's "intelligence of an intelligibility" which both includes and exceeds "the mind of man": the "motion and spirit that impels/All thinking things [. . .] rolls through all things" is an affect which prefigures Agamben's "movement that transports toward [. . .] the Idea." (Agamben 2) Affect has also lately been so distrusted in literary scholarship where the priority has been to uncover the text's cunning in making us feel rather than think. Thus Armstrong insists that we recognise Wordsworth's gift: the possibility of sense and thought being dialectic rather than in opposition:

> The categories of sense and thought are constructed out of one another as the subsuming of thought by matter creates an interactive universe. Thus, the sense sublime is not about being overpowered [. . .] or about the despotic subject/object relationship, but about the possibility of the transformation of categories, new knowledges.
>
> [. . .]
>
> The excess of the signifier is not about the unrepresentable, but the creation of new meanings. (99–100)

Such a dialectic also reinvigorates the material, the corporeal, as the site of a much more complex and nuanced process than confirming one's worth in terms of gender, race, or sexual orientation. We now move towards a realisation of Agamben's "whatever singularity" where "such-and-such being is reclaimed from having this or that property which identifies it as belonging to this or that set [. . .] class [gender, race et al]" (1). Accordingly, the literary can now be defined as that which consoles yet unsettles, not through certainty/ies as they arise of out of "this or that property" but from the sheer fact of already belonging. Wordsworth's "sense sublime" foresees Agamben's belonging which values difference (as does Oswald's river, the Dart) as essential to the energy of the "being in common" that "whatever singularites" or "beings" share (Agamben 86–7). Similarly, in "Tintern Abbey" that which is "far more deeply interfused" remains crucially unnamed, unplaced, and inclusive of the animate/inanimate; human/nonhuman; subject/object. However, where Wordsworth sees the binding factor as "the motion" which "rolls through all things," for Oswald, and Agamben, it is the boundary itself which is the nexus.

Oswald has expressly stated that as a poet, she seeks to excise her presence from the poem, so that poetic persona or identity is itself undermined in any fixing sense. In an interview with Kate Kellaway, she tells us that, "I almost feel that I am not part of it. I believe the poet shouldn't be in the poem at all except as a lens or as ears." For Oswald, unsurprisingly, the emphasis is on the ear:

> What's important is that listening [. . .] is a way of forcing a poem open to what lies bodily beyond it. Because the eye is [. . .] tuned to surfaces, but the ear tells you about volume, depth, content [. . .]. The

ear hears into, not just at what surrounds it. And the whole challenge of poetry is to keep language open, so that *what we don't yet know can pass through it*. (qtd. Pinard 17; my emphasis)

This immediately posits the corporeal as matter to be wielded and understood, both intellectually and emotionally; it also stresses the participation of mind and matter. Her work also shows in its un-/re-doing of poetic form, the significance of form to content, meaning, and being as process. The result is a poetry that scrutinises the sheer materiality of existence and of language for the potentiality of both.

Echoing perhaps, the imperative of Agamben's "whatever being," Thomas Docherty has asked that metaphor should be a practice of thought, a thinking that is always hospitable to otherness—or difference (Docherty 31). The two poems discussed here, "Five Fables of a Length of Flesh" and "The mud-spattered recollections of a woman who lived her life backwards" (Oswald, *Woods etc.* 32–5; 49–51) engage with this maxim. The former achieves precisely that play of form and being that is, in Docherty's words "culture [as] the activity of becoming" (24); the latter demonstrates why such play is important, or what results in an "I" confined by her attachment to narrative.

"Five Fables of a Length of Flesh" has at its core, a consciousness which experiences form/s in terms of struggle, as if escape from form were the true desire. The poem's "I" variously inhabits a man, a frog, a ferret, an ass, and a sheep. There are parallels in this to the idea of creative force seeking formal, artistic expression, yet being simultaneously thwarted by the dilution that rendering into language brings. With this in mind, it is useful to read this poem through its references to a poetic genre of some vintage, the body-soul dialogue. To do so awkwardly invokes the theological and spiritual, and the status of poetry in relation to those; but Oswald's poem, though expressive of the discontinuities between the physical and the metaphysical, flattens the moral and aspirational hierarchy inherent in the body-soul dialogue. It also makes problematic the dichotomies upon which that form's ideology is dependent, dichotomies which identity-based criticism can also reinstall. This returns us to the paradigm which proposes reason and emotion, or knowledge and affect as oppositional.

Yet reason and emotion are equally valid in any understanding and analysis of an artwork, and/or the aesthetic that names it thus. Armstrong urges that we must:

[dissolve] the traditional distinction between affect, or the emotions, and knowledge [. . .]. Indeed, it is necessary to include affect under the sign of cognition and enable it to be comprehended in the definition of knowledge. [. . .] This opposition needs to be undone [so that w]e think of artwork as a form of thought as well as a form of feeling. (59)

The medieval and later early modern body-soul dialogue offers itself as almost the foundation for such gendering: the body as the fleshly seat of carnal appetite is the feminine; while the soul, aspiring to and capable of transcending its gross prison is masculine. But, clearly in its form—that of debate and argument, reason in fact—the genre is concerned with being a "form of thought" as much as it is with being a "form of feeling."

The genre, typically, functions around two voices, representing the Body and the Soul who alternately castigate each other for their respectively frustrated desires. Michel-André Bossy further notes that "body and soul debates can be thematically divided into two categories: either the Soul argues with the Body from a position of moral superiority or it shares guilt with the Body (and often deserves more blame)" (145). The Soul chiefly regrets its corruption by the Body for the Body's defilement of the former's likeness to God: "I who was created so noble, shaped in the Lord's likeness, and cleansed of all guilt by baptism, am thus again blackened [. . .] and thanks to you, wretched Flesh, I am a reprobate" is one famous and anonymous medieval example (qtd. Bossy 146).

Andrew Marvell's "A Dialogue Between the Soul and the Body" (1681) is an unusual example of the genre in that it concedes the last word to the otherwise much-maligned Body; Marvell's Body also castigates the Soul's part in the Body's awareness of itself and its sinful desires: "What but a soul [it asks] could have the wit / To build me up for sin so fit?" (Aitken 43) The poem leaves the Soul equally culpable. The Body's question also highlights the paradox of the conceit: how can the Body act without the Soul's agency and volition, and how does the Body have a voice and will that are clearly its own? The Body reasons, it debates, it defends itself and is witty, yet according to the logic of the body/soul dichotomy, it should be inert, animated only by coarser appetites.

Some suspension of disbelief is necessary for the dramatisation of this conflict to work, but we can also understand the Body as the Soul gone astray, abusing as it does, its considerable powers of reason, to defend its own wickedness. This is the moral core of the device. There is too, in the Body's self-serving wit and abdications, an intimation of the diabolical. But if we reverse the conceit, we note the Soul's fundamental dependence on the Body, as sparring partner and moral foil: the Body is the Soul's testing ground.

This is germane to my reading of "Five Fables of a Length of Flesh." Angela Leighton observes how the word "form" seems to require an other for completion: thus the pairings "form and content," "form and meaning," "form and poetry," suggest "something unfinished, even unformed about form" as if form would be "disembodied" altogether without its "shaping partner," despite its definitions as "body, shape, or matter" (Leighton 2). Oswald must also reckon with this paradox, and does so by making a feature of it. However, where the conventional body-soul dialogue retains a moral core that is secure, even didactic in its theology, Oswald secularizes the form to offer a moral structure that is diffuse or horizontal as opposed to the vertical structure of a moral framework handed down by a deity; Oswald is intent that the onus is passed on to the reader. Such a manoeuvre should prod us out of intellectual inertia, and remind us of our part in Agamben's "coming community," summarised by Alex Murray, as "a way of referring to or naming the collective potentiality of beings, a possible form of human belonging which will result in a dwelling, to which Agamben gives the name ethos" (51).

Oswald initially alludes to the split between "soul" and flesh by beginning the poem, "I was *once* a man" (32; my emphasis); at this point, and until the third stanza, the speaker might simply be reminiscing bitterly on finer points of masculinity. But the split is confirmed and becomes the principle of the poem, as "I" yearns to force a separation between the corporeal and noncorporeal: "I was dying to ditch his head," it continues (32).

These lines, and the refrain "not yet not yet," echo St Augustine, who is central to the Christian doctrine concerning the body-soul conflict. First in the fatigue of Oswald's "I," we might hear Augustine's desolate belief that "in this present life, the corruptible body weighs down the soul" (Saint Augustine 551); the poem's "I" is resigned to the cycle of life/death/regeneration, rather than invigorated by it—"what happens once will happen all over again" it sighs wearily three times (32, 33); it is also agitated at the body's inevitable decline: as Frog, "I" is heard "grieving being born and grown / and rotted down and born" (34). But in the refrain "not yet not yet" there is too, an evocation of Augustine's youthful, and in retrospect, disingenuous plea: "But I wretched, most wretched, in the very commencement of my early youth, had begged chastity of Thee, and said, 'Give me chastity and continency, only not yet'" (Pusey 397–98).

Augustine's plea is often quoted for its honesty and the speaker's acknowledgement of his own frailty. The confession continues however:

> For I feared lest Thou shouldest hear me soon, and soon cure me of the disease of concupiscence, which I wished to have satisfied, rather than extinguished. [. . .] For I was afraid that you would answer my prayer at once and cure me too soon of the disease of lust, which I wanted satisfied, not quelled. (Pusey 397–98)

The young Augustine understood that "not yet" was a deferral of an ending, which is what Oswald's "I" hopes to fend off in two of its manifestations, each exiting the poem "muttering to himself not yet not yet" (32, 35). But the fear of the absence of desire altogether is another aspect of our encounter with the imagination and the schism it reveals between the real and what is desired or imagined; to imagine being other, and to be able to desire, are both essential to potentiality, and are the marks of the chaotic, restless business of being human.

Marvell's "Dialogue" is most obviously recalled in the fourth stanza of Oswald's "Five Fables": "so done in I was from carrying everything / lungs bones hands belonging to this man" (32). These lines almost rewrite the Soul's opening stanza of Marvell's "Dialogue":

O, who shall from this dungeon raise
A soul, enslaved so many ways
With bolts and bones, that fettered stands
In feet, and manacled in hands. (43)

Thus Oswald arguably signals the poem's intention to renegotiate the body-soul model in terms much more messy and unsettling, in a modern contemplation of anxieties concerning faith in presence and being. The poem introduces that dualism and the hierarchies of the body-soul dialogue, which in modern parlance might be expressed as "the real me/the wrong body/story," only to confound, refute, and secularize these new pieties.

If we return briefly for example, to the poem's title, it is evident from the outset that dualism is to be at least under scrutiny: "Five Fables of a Length of Flesh" at once indicates an agency—the "I" who will recount the fables—and the inescapable corporeality, the flesh of that "I" which is sustained in further graphic anatomical references throughout the rest of the poem: "wetlands of the womb"; "the two-chambered holt of the heart" to note two instances (32, 33).

However, while the poem might seem to act out a dualist model, keeping body and "soul" separate as "I" flits from one body to another, Oswald's emphasis on the fleshliness of the body, recalls the conventional Soul's despair to different effect. Where that Soul looks to Christ for salvation, this "I" harbours the dream of escape into lightness and sound, into disembodiment in fact, in a secular transcendence. This diverges from Christian doctrine, at least that which looks to Augustine, in which the body and soul are ultimately reunited. Another theological line of thought, from Aristotle to Thomas Aquinas, defines the soul as only the form of the body, unable to survive death. According to John W. Cooper, Aquinas thus maintains that, "the soul is both the form of the body and an intellectual substance in its own right. It can exist separate from the body but is then deficient in two ways. Metaphysically it is only potentially, not actually, the form of the body. And functionally it cannot be conscious in any way that would require bodily organs" (13). Both models require the body's integrity, but in the latter model, there is less separation, and the soul is incomplete without the body. The "I" of "Five Fables" seems to acknowledge the Aquinas model, in its lack of debate, and in the oxymoronic statement "I died" (34); these are points to which I will return.

Like the conventional Soul of the dialogue, however, "I" repeatedly experiences the body (form) as clumsy and unpleasant weight, driven by gross appetites to eat, copulate, scratch and defecate. Early on, as noted earlier, "I" longs to "ditch" its body and but adds that "I would sing then I would sing if I could" (Oswald 32); later, in its incarnation as "Ass," "I" hears the crickets:

> persistently telephoning and glorying in their
>   lightness

> saying 'Singing is who we are in this place.
> We are made of digital sounds [. . .]' (34)

This moves "I" closer to realising its aspiration towards being sound: the crickets presumably have a material existence, but seem to inhabit some intermediate state between the earthly and the celestial, or death and resurrection. The delightful allusions to modern technology anchor the poem to modernity, ironically so often held responsible for an increasingly materialist creed, yet here harnessed to the possibility of transcendence. The crickets all but realise Oswald's ambition, as they try to "unconceal things" (34) through singing, "the whole challenge of poetry [. . .] to keep language open, so that what we don't know can pass through it." (Oswald qtd. Pinard 17) The contrast with the current host body of the ass, hostage to its bodily needs and functions, implies the desire to be free entirely of the corporeal, which is compounded by the speaker's resolve "From that day" thereafter to "eat nothing but dew" (34, 35). The consequence, of course, is death, as this "I" recounts, and here the poem both proves and disproves, the soul's dependence on the body, bringing both Augustine's and Aquinas's models into crisis. The claim "I died" is oxymoronic, and the poem recognises this too: "I" dies in full view and in contradiction of "my own huge eyes / that stared at me from behind" (35).

I noted previously that poetry is the most formal of literary genres, which brings me to Oswald's strategies in relation to questions of form, and self. "Five Fables of a Length of Flesh" is in free verse, which as a rewriting of the body-soul dialogue is significant. The Marvell poem for example, is typical of the genre in that it is tightly rhymed and paced; Body and Soul are equally represented, with two stanzas each; each participant and their argument are contained in those separate stanzas. This form recalls both the Socratic dialogue (Armstrong's "form of thought") and the dramatic text. Yet, while these blocks of verse outline and enact the separateness of each entity, the form of the whole also contains the two warring entities, so that the conflict remains utterly within, and defining that entity as the human. The scansion and rhyming scheme confirm such definition by insisting on boundary, as if essence must agree to, and be given *particular* form. Finally, more often than not, the dialogue is concluded in proper moral (Christian) terms.

Oswald's lineation and stanzas on the other hand, her scansion and refusal to rhyme enact the impossible desire for formlessness, or a freer form at least, of self—and possibly too, of both poetry and of something we might call "spirit" freed now of doctrinal baggage. The poem ends, like *Dart* with ellipses and the refrain "not yet not yet . . ." as if it too would fend off its own determining finality. This un/re-doing of form and boundary is undergone also by "I": not only does "I" slip from man to ferret to ass and sheep, but even within those manifestations, the category is unstable, as is the distinction between the human and the nonhuman: the "Ferret" section for example states that "I was next a woman" who, however, "began, like a ferret"; the "Ass," though labelled thus, with descriptions fitting that creature's physical appearance, is also a man of sorts; the "I" in the "Sheep" section, similarly begins "Crashed over backwards buried under all the layers / of my body," but concludes, "I lay in my last self, stricken, like a sheep on its back" (32–33, 34, 35). There is a shift from metaphor to simile, but it is the shift into the simile which startles us into noticing the metaphor as we lose it, as if the poem would alert to us to the intrusion of its own devices, that is, its form. The blurring of the human/nonhuman is additionally integral to the poem's democratisation of form, as "I" seems to propose itself not as a soul any longer, but a life principle, an energy that seeks to return to, or become pure energy (light or sound). It is vital that we feel the poem believes in there being such purity: thus the bodies here are clumsy, unpleasant, even unwell, and too "bodily." This flesh is highly susceptible to corruption.

Similarly, there must be a focus on the ostensible promiscuity of "I": traversing species as it does, this "soul" or essence challenges the natural and divinely ordained order of being that underpins the body/soul dichotomy: if man is made in the Lord's likeness, to be *once* a man, and then carelessly a ferret, frog, or sheep, is to defile that likeness. But the lack of apparent purpose with which "I" inhabits each form is what decentres the poem's moral structure, as well as the absence of actual debate. For the poem's most radical departure from the body-soul dialogue is that "I" (the possible "soul") debates with and of nothing. It simply observes, with dissatisfaction, the unhappy experience of form altogether, and suggests in the final lines, somewhat despairingly, that ultimately there is no separation. "I" is condemned to remain fast in the rotting, corrupting body.

The metaphor however, is this: it is not so much the literal body/flesh, but our fetishisation of the corporeal that is in danger of over-determining us as this or that, above and beyond the simple sheer fact of Agamben's "belonging," or "being such." Oswald's light and sound are perhaps a more abstract or poetic version of Agamben's "being in common": a transcendence which arises out of that ability simply to be. In each case, it is broadly "this or that property" of being, whether that is Man, Ass, Ferret or Sheep, that "I" abandons.

In this ending of sorts, we might hear the poem mourning its own inevitable "death." One consequence of form is that it threatens to make finite that which it contains. As a narrative of arrival from which deviation is problematic, identity is also finite and fearful of process. In "The mud-spattered recollections of a woman who lived her life backwards" we see this closure at its most chilling.

The poem's conceit is that the speaker is dead, but rises to live her life over again, this time in reverse. Horribly, she is pulled from her grave "at the appointed hour / and rushed to the nearest morgue to set out yet again" (49). This repeats the weariness expressed by "I" in the previous poem where "what happens once will happen all over again" (32). But that "I" exceeds and extends indefinitely, its narrative whose ending is "not yet not yet"; here, narrative is the form that imprisons, and literally reduces "I." The speaker goes on, or back, to experience her children "racing towards me getting smaller and smaller" until "one terrible morning for maybe the hundredth time / they came to insert my third child back inside me" (50). Tellingly, this "was death it was death" not least for the physical pain of having the child forced back into her body, but also for her loss of the child: "I'd never see my darling daughter again" (50). Her marriage is then undone, until finally, "they came to insert me feet first back into nothing / complete with all my missing hopes" (51).

This confusion between death and birth, or death and living haunts the poem, and is noted as a limbo, in which "I was or was not either living or dead / in a windowless cubicle of the past" (50). This might have offered, in its liminality, a place of potential, but the mud-spattered woman is unable to negotiate such a place, and experiences it only in terms of deprivation. In contrast, the "I" of "Five Fables" sees form as limit to be overcome, or as possibility, "going in and out of the swing door of the body" (33), playing with the permeability that boundary can mean. Crucially, though, boundary is also essential to the metamorphosis, the becoming other, of "I."

In Agamben's sense, the "I" of "Five Fables" enables potentiality by treating boundary as threshold. As Agamben argues, "what is in question in this bordering is not a limit [. . .] that knows no exteriority, but a threshold [. . .] that is a point of contact with an external space that must remain empty" (67). It is Agamben's insistence on border as that which recognises its "outside" as is important, recalling as it does Oswald's statement, quoted earlier: "a nature poet is someone concerned with things being outside each other." Agamben further observes that "the notion of 'outside' is expressed in many European languages by a word that means 'at the door'. The *outside* is not another space that resides beyond a determinate space, but rather, it is the passage," and the threshold is the "experience of limit itself, the experience of being-*within* and *outside*" (68). In the title poem of her first collection, "The Thing in the Gap-Stone Stile," Oswald's speaker is exactly that, crouched in the stile, her "pose [becomes] the pass across two kingdoms/before behind antiphonal, my cavity the chord" (32). The "I" of "Five Fables" similarly recognises limit as that which should nourish the imagination, rather than be a barrier to it.

The figure of the mud-spattered woman contradicts "Five Fables of a Length of Flesh." She experiences what could be threshold or passage as boundary painfully breached, and "outside" as that which confirms the need to remain inside. The poem begins with "I" stating ownership of the narrative, but her claim serves only to announce the anxiety of policing this "I": "*I'll* tell you a tale" (49; emphasis mine), she says, and repeats this in various formulations. The urgency with which the speaker attempts to stamp the narrative as hers suggests a self fixedly held to, (falsely) reassured by linearity, and the particular properties that identify her as wife and mother. In other words, these are the properties which constitute this "I" as woman; as they are taken away through a process of reversal, the speaker is left with nothing but her "missing hopes" (51) and a self eroded.

The statement of ownership with which the poem opens is compromised by its being made from the grave (49). "I" is already measured and oddly completed, yet as frustrated as she is assured of the rightness of her "too short-lit / life both fruitful and dutiful." (49) She is then "pulled from the ground at the appointed hour / and rushed to the morgue to set out yet again" (49). Her narrative is subject to forces beyond her control. Even the telling of her tale, which "is like a rose, once opened" has no choice to but blossom to death as it were, (50), becomes a performance she is unable to abandon, to the extent that ultimately, the narrative performs her in an eerie echo of Coleridge's Ancient Mariner. Like that compelled narrator, and in terms that recall Butler's idea of gender as "stylised repetition" (Butler 141), the mud-spattered woman's tale is marked by a lack of agency, no matter how she insists on her authorship.

Yet the speaker has to endure the bitterness of frustrated desire, which signals her sense of there being "more." The rose that is her tale, now recalls Baudelaire's "vieux boudoir plein de roses fanées" where "I" is that boudoir, and earlier "un cimetière" (252). This is a life staged as a series of deaths rather than births, by repetition rather than novelty, and by entrapment rather than freedom. The form of the poem stresses the desire for conclusion: each quatrain, unlike the enjambment that enacts the speaker's form-shifting in "Five Fables" is self-contained, describing a moment or event that is resolved before the next occurs. "I" is also clearly identified by specific attributes: the speaker is dead, yet paradoxically aware that her life was both "fruitful and dutiful"; she is too, a consciousness seeking a listener: "I'll tell you" she insists. But in the irony of the life both "fruitful and dutiful" we hear the conflict that is inevitable in the construction of and adherence to identity, if we agree that identity is founded on exclusion and containment. The mud-spattered woman recognises her particular state as one of completed incompletion, but her attachment to that state, and her anxiety concerning its preservation, condemns her to relive it. The "I" here is always already "dead"; she thus has no opportunity of becoming, but must constantly relive, so to speak, a series of endless returns "into nothing" (51).

For this reason, the poem's trajectory of reversal is especially significant. The poem offers an undoing that is not sufficient: reversing order only confirms order itself as a practice, rather than relinquishing it. Reversal is therefore as likely to smother possibility as its counterpart, *telos*.

The quest for identity is one often concerned with return and origin out of a need to right a wrong, to reclaim place whether that is geographical, historical or social. The tragedy of the mud-spattered woman can be read in feminist terms, as the history of one who cries out against the restraints of being merely wife and mother, but this reading is itself reductive. When the speaker is divested of children and husband, she is diminished. While this suggests a self construed out of this or that aspect of one's existence is in itself diminishing, it also warns, as Agamben does, against mistaking aspect for the whole at all.

How does this help us read Oswald's work for its aesthetic metal while hearing its political or ethical engagement? Isobel Armstrong's idea is that by reinstating poetry as thought, and giving back the power of affect its intellectual fibre, we return to poetry (and perhaps by extension all literature and art) both its aesthetic and political value. Refusing to turn suspiciously away the "seductive power of affect" altogether, Armstrong redefines that power as the "limit case of thought in erasure." (101) Thus, she can "look to the text for what thought does—to examine and create categories" (101). Overall, there is a "political struggle for the sign, as erasure suggests and contends with new possibilities: to belong to this struggle is one of the ways we speak to literature" (101), and I would add, how literature should speak with us. It is about a relationship based on the need to enter into a relationship—not unlike Agamben's "belonging"—in which "the answering need to understand accepts the displacement understanding requires" (Armstrong 102). This is much more than mere empathy, Armstrong argues. And indeed, it requires a strenuous effort to surrender certainty as it is characterised by this or that aspect or attribute, and to move towards the "taking-place" in itself of the text, or any entity (Agamben 2) There is in this surrender, an allowance for, and a recognition of the transcendent as "not the supreme entity above all things; rather, *the pure transcendent is the taking-place of every thing*" (Agamben 14, 15).

The political potential and philosophical richness of Oswald's aesthetic as it applies to identity and form can be discerned in the two poems just discussed, amongst others. The transcendent that Agamben describes, is not ungraspable or other worldly; in fact, its real potential lies precisely in its "being irreparably in the world" (15). It is rooted irrevocably in the material. It is the being-such of each entity that we must allow for its own sake, or as Agamben says, "good [. . .] is the taking-place of the entities [. . .] the point at which they grasp the taking-place proper to them" (15).

That moment does not occur for the mud-spattered woman, and in her failure, there is Agamben's idea of "evil" as "the reduction of the taking-place of things to a fact like others" (15). On the other hand, in "Five Fables of a Length of Flesh" Oswald offers being as in itself possibly transcendent, if we allow it its "taking-place," its belonging for itself. But this can only happen if we read the poem as yet another opening, another potentiality, so that, in Oswald's words, "what we don't yet know can pass through it."

NOTES

1. The course of the Dart is over Dartmoor, a large area of moorland, owned and protected in part by the National Trust, in Devon, South West England; the Severn rises in mid-Wales, to run the remaining length of the border between England and Wales, and enter the Bristol Channel at the Severn Estuary. The Bristol Channel joins, ultimately, the Atlantic Ocean.
2. I have used page numbers to reference Oswald's poetry rather than line numbers.
3. Both Pinard and Bristow discuss Oswald's poetics in terms of the auditory, but read this in terms of how it positions the human/nonhuman, broadly speaking.
4. Oswald's strategy goes further, to suggest the possibility of the collapse of the subject/object divide that keeps nature "other"; as Timothy Morton has argued, in *Ecology without Nature: Rethinking Environmental Aesthetics* (2007), in order for nature to be not-other, we should erase it altogether as a category. This particular issue, however, is beyond the scope of this chapter.
5. Armstrong's quotation is from Emmanuel Lévinas's 1949 essay, "The Transcendence of Words."
6. Armstrong clarifies her interpretation through attention to Wordsworth's placing of "of," which occurs five times in this passage; "of" can mean simply "about," but it can also mean "made out of" or "constructed from," or "possessing." Wordsworth creates uncertainty as to which "of" his "sense sublime" refers, by earlier stating that the "still, sad music of humanity" is "of [possesses] ample power/To chasten and subdue."

REFERENCES

Agamben, Giorgio. *The Coming Community.* Trans. Michael Hardt, Minneapolis, MN: University of Minnesota Press, 1993. Print.

Aitken, G. A., ed. *The Poems of Andrew Marvell.* London: Routledge, n.d. Print.

Alsop, Rachel, Annette Fitzsimmons, and Kathleen Lennon. *Theorizing Gender: An Introduction.* Cambridge: Polity Press, 2002. Print.

Armstrong, Isobel. *The Radical Aesthetic.* Oxford: Blackwell, 2000. Print.

Baudelaire, Charles. *Les Fleurs du Mal.* Trans. Richard Howard. Jaffrey, NH: Godine, 1983. Print.

Bossy, Michel-André. "Medieval Debates of Body and Soul." *Comparative Literature*, 28.2 (1976): 144–63. Print.

Bristow, Tom. "'Contracted to an eye-quiet world': Sonic Census or Poetics of Place in Alice Oswald." *Symbiosis: A Journal of Anglo-American Literary Relations* 10.2 (2006): 167–85. Print.

Butler, Judith. *Gender Trouble: Feminism and the Subversion of Identity.* London: Routledge, 1990. Print.

Cooper, John W. *Body, Soul and Life Everlasting: Biblical Anthropology and the Monism-Dualism Debate.* 2nd ed. Grand Rapids, MI: Eerdmans, 2000. Print.

Docherty, Thomas. 2003. "Aesthetic Education and the Demise of Experience." *The New Aestheticism.* Ed. John J. Joughin and Simon Malpas. Manchester: Manchester University Press, 2003. 23–35. Print.

Kellaway, Kate. "Into the woods." *Observer*, 19 Jun. 2005. Web. 26 August 2009. http://www.guardian.co.uk/books/2005/jun/19/poetry.features.

Leighton, Angela. *On Form: Poetry, Aestheticism and the Legacy of a Word.* Oxford: Oxford University Press, 2007. Print.

Morton, Timothy. *Ecology without Nature: Rethinking Environmental Aesthetics.* Cambridge, MA: Harvard University Press, 2007. Print.

Murray, Alex. *Giorgio Agamben.* London: Routledge, 2010. Print.

Nancy, Jean-Luc. *Listening.* Trans. Charlotte Mandell. New York: Fordham University Press, 2002. Print.

Oswald, Alice. *The Thing in the Gap-Stone Stile.* London: Faber. 1996. Print.

———. *Dart.* London: Faber. 2002. Print.

———. *Woods etc.* London: Faber. 2005. Print.

———. *A Sleepwalk on the Severn.* London: Faber. 2009. Print.

Pinard, Mary. "Voice(s) of the Poet-Gardener: Alice Oswald and the Poetry of Acoustic Encounter." *Interdisciplinary Literary Studies: A Journal of Criticism and Theory*, 10.2 (2009): 17–32. Print.

Pusey, Edward B., trans. *The Confessions of Saint Augustine.* Calvin College, MO: Christian Classics Ethereal Library. 397–98. Web. 28 July 2010. http://www. ccel.org/ccel/augustine/confess.html.

Saint Augustine (Bishop of Hippo). *City of God.* Trans. Henry Bettenson. Rev. ed. London: Penguin, 1972. Print.

Wordsworth, William. "Lines Composed a Few Miles Above Tintern Abbey on Revisiting the Banks of the Wye During a Tour, July 13, 1798." *The Norton Anthology of Poetry.* 4th ed. Ed. Margaret Ferguson, Mary Jo Salter and Jon Stallworthy. New York: Norton, 1996. 699–703. Print.

Part III
Physical Forms, Formal Identities

10 The Confessional Other
Identity, Form, and Origins in Confessional Poetry

Marsha Bryant

When we hear the words *confessional poetry*, we tend to think (if we stop to think at all) of autobiographical, artless forms of writing. The *I*'s have it, and they have it all the time. They cast their long shadows across the line, the page, the book. And presumably, such IMAX[1] modes of authorship offer instant access to the poets themselves, whether we see them merely as amplifiers of their own emotion (David Yezzi) or mostly as representative victims (Paul Breslin). Even if, like Jo Gill, we see confessional poets as consummate performers, the I-dentity still occupies center stage. When the cast of characters expands, we think of the usual suspects: parents, spouses, offspring. Indeed, the default settings for confessional poetry assume a social unit no larger than the nuclear (and Freudian) family. Diane Middlebrook enriches this standard perspective with class identity: "Confessional poetry investigates the pressure on the family as an institution regulating middle-class private life, primarily through the agent of the mother" ("What Was" 636). Here the *I*'s may still have it, but they speak from and through their households. And Mommy dearest is the deep source of personal (and social) identity. Zoom out further, and we can see the national family superimposing itself over the nuclear family, the State over the suburb. Deborah Nelson's analysis of American confessional poetry shows that its penchant for airing the family linen says more about postwar surveillance than self-disclosure because the home was "the most common metaphor of privacy in the cold war" (75). Here the house of confessional poetry takes on the legislative dimensions of the House, Senate, and Supreme Court. And yet the *I*'s still have it, flanked by the eyes of the law and the ayes of consent.

But there is another occupant in the house of confessional poetry: *the confessional other*. This generative figure appears behind the spotlight, lies deeper than formative families, spreads further than American geographies. Its sudden appearances dislodge the *I*, pushing past the poem's default settings toward other racial formations. In white confessional writing, the confessional other usually appears as Asian, African, Middle Easterner, or Native American—although the figure does not always confine itself to a single racial or ethnic identity. Trafficking in and moving beyond Edward Said's Orientalism, Toni Morrison's Africanism, and Hollywood's "magic

Negro," the confessional other spreads across a global sphere of ancient civilisations and modern empires. As we shall see, invoking the confessional other is and is not "playing in the dark." In the generative spaces before the page, in the geographies before America, the confessional other is confessional poetry's secret sharer.

This chapter focuses on three poets that engage the confessional other in texts that signal stylistic breakthroughs: Robert Lowell (*Life Studies*, 1959), Sylvia Plath (*Ariel*, 1965), and Ted Hughes (*Birthday Letters*, 1998). Other contemporary poets employ the figure, including John Berryman and Anne Sexton. All five of these white writers invoke dark figures to articulate the vexed enterprise of making a new kind of poetry. But the trio I have selected shows that, at its most fundamental level, the confessional other is more than an alter ego or foreign destination. While race proves crucial to the figure's cultural meanings, form trumps identity in its manifestations. In fact, we might see the confessional other as a *form-problem* in Fredric Jameson's sense—in this case, as a rich amalgam of literary movements and geopolitics. A textual trigger-point, it functions as a shared point of origin for each writer's originality. The confessional other underwrites the protean family portraits that haunt Lowell's "91 Revere Street," the five-line flights that bring forth Plath's bee sequence, and the harrowing intimacies that colour Hughes's reanimations of Plath. As we move across these three writers, the confessional other will shift from Asia and Africa to the Americas, moving closer to the country that generated the confessional poetry movement. And as we move closer to our own cultural moment, we will see the confessional poet become the confessional other.

The figure marks a cross-Atlantic form-problem within confessional poetry that reflects an *aesthetic* rather than personal identity. Jameson adopts George Lukács's term to designate the re-articulation of earlier styles, tropes, and images in the face of new cultural conditions (*Signatures* 133; *The Geopolitical* 33, 45, 133). In the case of the confessional poetry movement, postwar geopolitical realignments of British and American power undergird a literary recalibration of preceding movements in Anglo-American poetry. Our genealogies of confessional poetry tend toward American literature (Lowell and his contemporaries, Allen Ginsberg and the Beats, and their forebear Walt Whitman). But the generative figure I assess here has origins in Thomas De Quincey. Because contemporary confessional poets inherited both American modernism and its aesthetic other, British Romanticism, the confessional other serves as a mechanism for reworking literary relations between authenticity and innovation. William Blake and William Wordsworth voiced racial others to heighten sentiment and claim a folk authenticity in their respective poems "The Little Black Boy" (1789) and "The Complaint of a Forsaken Indian Woman" (1798). Such "authenticism," as Ana María Sánchez-Arce argues, proves "as constructed as that which is other" because the textuality of otherness "dictates how these 'others' are allowed to speak" (141). For Blake and Wordsworth, fashioning such faux-genuine voices did not require breaking the protocols of poetic form. Under modernism, racial ventriloquism transforms into the "Boomlay BOOM" poetry that Susan Gubar finds in Vachel Lindsay, T. S. Eliot, Wallace Stevens, and (in England) Edith Sitwell. Rather than performing a coherent subjectivity through a black (or brown) mask, these modernist poets employed "ersatz African rhythms," nonsense, and "anarchic incomprehensibility" to further fracture poetic form, moving beyond voice (139, 143). Yet even as this generation of poets rebelled against Romanticism through formal innovation, they continued their forebears' tropographies of empire to authenticate new styles. By the time Lowell would publish *Life Studies*, American expansionism had shifted the Anglo-American domains of poetic invention.

Three decades before the expansive speaker of Whitman's *Song of Myself* (1855) uttered the American prototype for confessional poetry's self-proclaiming *I*, *Confessions of an English Opium-Eater* (1821) emerged as the ur-text of its confessional other. This uncanny chronology suggests the fundamental role that otherness plays in a poetic mode we assume to be primarily autobiographical. While De Quincey violates literary decorum by "breaking through that delicate and honourable reserve" that inhibits unseemly self-disclosures, his "dark alliance" with the Malay shifts the memoir's character relations and disrupts its form (1, 2). In the "Preliminary Confessions" section, the narrator crosses class and gender lines to ally with sustaining characters that compel his sympathy (an abandoned child, a fallen woman). But the confessional other compels fascination and horror. Entering the text in its turn toward extreme experience, the Malay appears suddenly at the narrator's cottage door—as if spliced into the English mountains. More incongruous than Coleridge's person from Porlock, there is no apparent motivation for his arrival. De Quincey fashions the Malay as a strange amalgam of Orientalist attributes: he is a "tiger-cat" in "loose trowsers," a fiery-eyed "demon" with a complexion "veneered with mahogany" (50). Anticipating the Asian, African, and racially ambiguous confessional others that will follow in his wake, the Malay reroutes De Quincey's text from the Classical origins of Western literature to the older cultural origins of Asia and Egypt.

Like all confessional others, the Malay utterly transforms the text. In the culminating part ("The Pains of Opium"), he wreaks havoc on the narrator's dreams—and De Quincey's form. The figure multiplies into "other Malays" that relocate the narrator to "Asiatic scenes" of "vast empires," orchestrating "nightly spectacles" of "insufferable splendor" (64–5, 60). Said points out that "the vision of Orient as spectacle, or *tableau vivant*" constitutes a major motif in Orientalist discourse (158), and we certainly see that in De Quincey's excessive images of landscapes, architecture, and pageants. Yet his hyper-expansive dream passages also distort time, extending it backward to ancient origins and forward to D. W. Griffith (as if the Romantic writer is dreaming the birth of Hollywood epic cinema).

Here the confessional other as form-problem reveals itself most fully. De Quincey's Malay prompts a return to "the cradle of the human race" in primal scenes of empire where the narrator is overwhelmed by the "enormous population" and "vast age" of pre-Classical antiquity. Most horrifyingly, he is "laid, confounded with all unutterable slimy things, amongst reeds and Nilotic mud" for centuries (64–5). These muddy origins will become the primordial soup of confessional poetry. For in such fraught passages the writer confesses a dilemma as formal as it is experiential: "I have not been able to compose the notes for this part of my narrative into any regular and connected shape" (55); the Malay's reentry to the text triggers its structural breakdown. As Rajani Sudan asserts in her postcolonial reading, De Quincey's memoir "loses its formal integrity as an autobiographical narrative" in this section, "becom[ing] a series of dream fragments, fantasies, and journal entries" (390). Put another way, De Quincey's confessions approach a level of disjunction that anticipates modern poetry. The confessional other ushers in such breakdowns of identity and form at crucial junctures: when the text voices extremities of experience or insight; when the text, volume, or career veers into a new style.

I have spent time with *Confessions of an English Opium-Eater* because it provides vital clues about the malleable figure that underwrites Anglo-American confessional poetry:

- The confessional other is a trigger, an image, and an origin.
- The confessional other often appears as a non sequitur.
- The confessional other is a portal figure.
- The confessional other ushers in transitions between intimacy and innovation.
- The confessional other disrupts the space-time continuum.
- The confessional other opens the text to altered states, other geographies, alternative genealogies.
- The confessional other brings stylistic excess in its wake.
- The confessional other reveals proximities of breakdown and breakthrough.

De Quincey's ur-text also requires us to make adjustments to standard models of representing racial otherness in white writing. Like Freudian recapitulation, the confessional other can transport the text to childhood's primal scenes and civilisation's primal origins. Yet we cannot contain the confessional other within the Freudian unconscious, psycho-sexual development, or the nuclear family. Neither can we limit the figure to doubles, alter egos, or interlocutors (analogues that work well for the Tambo figure in Berryman's *Dream Songs*). For the confessional other taps *and* exceeds psycho-biographical contexts. Like Said's Orientalism, the confessional other's Middle Eastern and Asian inflections can appear as exotic, bestial, and duplicitous. As we see in De Quincey, such figures reinforce Orientalist plots of falling into altered states through contact with a corrupt East. But the gendered dualisms that Said identifies in Orientalist figures do not always hold with the confessional other, which is not always feminised. It can be male, female, androgynous, or ambiguous. Morrison's model of representing racial otherness is closer to the multiplicities we find in the confessional other. *Playing in the Dark* shows how "black presence" in the white literary canon underwrites the co-emergence of American literature and American national identity. Anticipating Hollywood's "magical, mystical Negro" that Spike Lee and others would identify (Gonzalez), the "Africanist character" that Morrison finds in Poe, Faulkner, Cather, and others can be the white protagonist's "surrogate and enabler." Yet Morrison's figure is also "an informing, stabilizing, and disturbing element." Indeed, in its latter iterations the black presence manifests in "explosive, disjoined, repetitive language," signaling "a loss of control in the text" (5; 51; 13, 69). Here we see a dynamic similar to De Quincey's "dark alliance" that will migrate to Lowell, Plath, and Hughes.

In Lowell's *Life Studies,* the figure manifests first as an African American soldier, then as the poet's dark-toned European ancestor. In Plath's *Ariel,* Africanised bees signify the "black mind" of the poet's creative process. The confessional other reaches its apotheosis in Hughes's *Birthday Letters*, where Plath becomes a multiracial woman. What we find at stake in these multicultural confessional others is not only "the invention and implications of whiteness" (Morrison 52), but the nature of literary inventiveness itself.

Lowell's *Life Studies* marks the official beginning of the confessional poetry movement, ushering in the controversial self-disclosures of his late signature style. This breakthrough volume builds to its title sequence of family poems that situate the poet in three households: his maternal grandparents', his parents', and his current abode with wife and daughter. If De Quincey displayed altered states of addiction and his own "moral ulcers or scars" (1), his American inheritor exhibits altered states of madness and airs his family's marital tensions. Indeed, Lowell lets us peer into the psychiatric hospital where he is among the "thoroughbred mental cases" (82)—a public disclosure that paved the way for Sexton's and Plath's hospital poems. (All were patients at McLean psychiatric hospital in 1958, 1973, and 1953, respectively.) Lowell's critical induction as father of confessional poetry is a familiar story: M. L. Rosenthal tagged postwar America's preeminent poet with the confessional label in an unflattering review of *Life Studies* ("Poetry" 154–55). Rosenthal was accounting for "a great change of direction" from the poet's former "sublime, impersonal authority," as Michael Hofmann puts it (xiii–iv). For the first time, Lowell spoke unabashedly as himself.

Less familiar is Lowell's reliance on the confessional other to make his confessional turn. We find this protean figure at a key threshold of *Life Studies*: the transition between the more impersonal Part One and the memoir constituting Part Two. Assuming two guises, the volume's confessional other manifests in texts that break from dominant forms. It debuts in the volume's only quatrain poem and reappears in the only prose section. Lowell's encounters with the confessional other offer vital means of reconfiguring cultural origins, family genealogies, and aesthetic identity.

The four poems in Part One bid farewell to Lowell's old style and influences, shifting from European to contemporary American inflections. The poet's parade of historical figures signals this key transition: Pius XII, Mussolini, Henri IV, Marie de Medici, President Eisenhower. In "The Banker's Daughter," Lowell crosses gender lines to voice de Medici, one of two drag performances in *Life Studies*. The volume's penultimate poem, "'To Speak of Woe That Is in Marriage,'" will cross the boundaries of propriety by performing his second wife's (Elizabeth Hardwick) commentary on his alcoholism and infidelity. Although such intimate disclosures shocked Lowell's contemporary readers, the poem transitions smoothly from its immediate predecessor "Man and Wife" (from his point of view). These paired poems follow the generational progression of the "Life Studies" section (Part Four). By contrast, Lowell's racial ventriloquism at the end of Part One becomes a form-problem that throws the section off kilter.

A portal poem to the volume's self-disclosures, "A Mad Negro Soldier Confined at Munich" confesses serial trysts with a raw frankness that pressures the quatrain stanzas and exact end-rhymes.[2] Lowell performs this rapid-paced monologue through the persona of a manic African American soldier in a military hospital. Through this confessional other, Lowell launches the volume's interplay of authenticity and extremity through a series of dualisms: American/European, black/white, violence/submission, vulgarity/restraint. The poem also displaces images of black power and psychiatric treatment: hospital orderlies become "two black maniacs" that subdue the speaker; sexual relations with his German "girl-friend" carry an "electric shock." Unlike the previous poems—including the sonnet on Eisenhower's inauguration[3]—Lowell Americanizes this one with slang ("set the town on fire"). Yet turning to America is not enough; the poet must turn his voice into a racial other's to authenticate unrestrained diction. The mad Negro soldier extols that "lieutenants squawked like chickens" in his lover's "skirts." One-upping Eliot's canoe confession in *The Waste Land*, he declares that he hired a canoe and "had her six times" in a public garden (8). Lowell presumably motivates his visceral vernacular with stereotypes of black virility, yoking the Romantics' language-really-used-by-men with white modernists' hypersexual depictions of African Americans. Through his mad Negro soldier, Lowell can break from Eliot's impersonal poetry while maintaining modernism's tropes of racial otherness. Gubar points out "the major role racial ventriloquism played in poetic experimentation" following the wake of Lindsay's 1914 poem "The Congo" (139–40). Lowell's black manic speaker and loosened diction also point forward to Berryman's black-face performances.

How might we account for the poem's peculiar status in *Life Studies*? Lowell's mad Negro soldier is the volume's sole black speaker and one of only two African American characters. "A Negro boy" jailed for marijuana possession appears briefly in "Memories of West Street and Lepke" (85), but Lowell does not develop this figure. Some may view the mad soldier as representative victim of a world gone mad, sharing Rosenthal's sense that he dramatizes "the breakdown of traditional meanings and cultural distinctions" ("Poetry" 155). Yet his mental state and sexual escapades hardly make him an Everyman figure. At the biographical level, Lowell's African American speaker does share the poet's "debility of mind," as Anthony Lane put it (86). Lowell suffered a manic episode at the Salzburg Seminar in American Studies in July 1952, prompting his own Munich confinement in a ward of mentally disturbed soldiers; biographer Ian Hamilton mentions no African American patients (188–95). Structurally, "A Mad Negro Soldier Confined at Munich" foreshadows the asylum poems in Part Four: "Waking in the Blue" and "Home After Three Months Away." In effect, Lowell's black manic speaker grants him poetic license to move closer to an autobiographical *I*.

Not exactly an alter ego, this confessional other is Lowell's black-face run at baring his own mental illness—and airing his bedroom linens. Lowell holds his mad Negro soldier at a strategic distance from his new poetic voice: segregated by race ("the colored wards"), sequestered by quotation marks. Acknowledged influence Elizabeth Bishop[4] made a parallel move by adding "Songs for a Colored Singer" to her debut volume, *North and South* (1946). Warping her default diction with forced rhymes (Varella/umbrella) and poor imitations of *Porgy & Bess* ("when I earns I spends"), Bishop's "attempt to get the Otherness right" falls flat (Bishop 47; Curry 94). Rather than emulating blues songs, Bishop fashions blue women singing the whites. Yet through these poems she makes her breakthrough to female speakers, bringing us one step closer to a notoriously un-confessional poet (Travisano 84). Lowell's blackface performance packs more punch. Uttering the volume's most unabashed language, "A Mad Negro Soldier Confined at Munich" launches a preemptive strike on readers' sense of propriety before they encounter the unseemly intimacies of family and psychological disclosures. Lowell recounts his own conjugal relations in relatively restrained poems, but these Bostonian bedroom confessions depend on the blackface poem's linguistic freedom. Through his carnal confessional other, postwar America's preeminent poet breaks free of his old style—and his readers' expectations.

The second confessional other in *Life Studies* serves as portal to the past—specifically, Lowell's childhood in Boston. The image of Major Mordecai Myers frames the prose memoir "91 Revere Street," which sets the stage for the "Life Studies" section. This figure bears closer proximity to Lowell because Myers shares lineage as well as nationality (cf. Hamilton). By invoking an inherited family portrait, the father of the confessional poetry movement darkens his paternal ancestor to fashion an exotic father. As Michael Thurston argues, the Myers portrait reinforces the memoir's interplay of "monuments and apotheoses" through its historicity and otherness; Mordecai Myers is "a Jewish ancestor, an Other within the family and so within Lowell himself" (94). Yet curiously, Lowell grafts multiple ethnicities onto Myers. Like De Quincey's Malay, Lowell's dark forebear occupies a shifting spectrum that alters the writer's identity and the memoir's form. The Myers portrait reroutes bloodlines with other geographies and detours the memoir's narrative with ekphrasis. Mordecai Myers is the prime mover of *Life Studies*, presiding over origins and entrances.

Disrupting "91 Revere Street" with false starts, Mordecai Myers dominates the memoir's first section as Lowell attempts to locate him historically, racially, and emotionally. These multiple starting points rupture continuity like a textual tic. Lowell's first sentence retrieves Myers from Cousin Cassie's "privately printed" museum catalogue, but the poet soon finds this approach unsatisfactory: "The account of him is platitudinous, worldly and fond, but he has no Christian name and is entitled Major M. Myers" (11). Tenuous and truncated, Mordecai Myers enters his descendant's text as a slight figure, despite his martial title and service in the War of 1812. But Lowell quickly abandons the historical person for Myers's image: finding the "name-plate" under his "gallant" portrait, fleshing him out with epaulets and "a scarlet frogged waistcoat" (11). Here Lowell accomplishes two things. He elides personal, family, and national history—a key element of his emergent signature style. And he begins to refashion his personal and aesthetic identity, "imagining the modern self to be composed not only of flesh and blood but also of text and image," as Nelson astutely notes (59). This early sign of his postmodern turn reminds us that even Lowell's most confessional writing is never strictly autobiographical. Cousin Cassie's account reveals Mordecai's military experience and ten children, links to the mad Negro soldier's virility. But the Myers portrait proves more malleable than the monologue. By the end of the memoir's first paragraph, we get our first hint of Mordecai's ethnic ambiguity: his "full-lipped smile" (11).

In Lowell's second start to his memoir, Mordecai Myers acquires an "almond eye" and becomes a man of more colour (and less refinement). He also activates spatiotemporal expansion, another sign of the confessional other: "Undoubtedly Major Mordecai had lived in a more ritualistic, gaudy, and animal world than twentieth-century Boston." Now "gaudy" instead of "gallant," the protean portrait takes on primitive trappings as it gravitates from New England to the Mediterranean. There Mordecai is in turn "a dark man, a German Jew," and "Moorish-looking." He also troubles time by appearing "both *ci-devant* and *parvenu*." The first rebel figure in Lowell's "adolescent war" on his parents, Mordecai Myers upstages the poet's bland father (11–12).

In takes three and four on Mordecai's portrait, Lowell returns to its looming presence in the Revere Street house, authenticating the memoir's primal image even as he confesses fabrications. The third assay backpedals on Mordecai's gaudiness, assigning him a more gentlemanly and domesticated identity. Now "my Grandmother Lowell's grandfather," the Major led a "tame and honorable" life and "shunned the outrageous." Despite Lowell's attempts to render him dangerous ("a true wolf"), Mordecai is but a "poor sheepdog in wolf's clothing." Yet even so, his portrait's "scarlet vest and exotic eye" stir Lowell's passionate mother "to warmth" (12). Just as Major Mordecai Myers retains virility, he retains his procreative power for *Life Studies*. Following in his wake, ancestors on both sides of Lowell's family acquire multiethnic traits in the pages that follow. The portrait of Theodorus Bailey Myers (Mordecai's son) appears "vaguely Middle-Eastern." Colour crosses over to the Winslow-Stark side in the "Life Studies" poems, where Lowell's maternal grandmother remarkably acquires "a Mohammedan" appearance in "Grandparents" (44, 68). Such racial transformations replay turn-of-the-century fears of Jewish "mongrel" mobility and hyper-fertility, a social anxiety Rachel Blau DuPlessis has traced in American modernist poetry (136–7). They also reflect Lowell's desire for a new identity that breaks from the New England strictures of his fabled family history, as well as from the psychological confines of his nuclear family. In the section's final paragraph (the fourth assay), Lowell relocates the ancestral portrait from his parents' home to his memory, admitting that the actual object is now "mislaid past finding." The poet has reconstructed Mordecai's image, claiming authenticity for his multiple versions of it (12). Fixed and malleable, familial and foreign, Mordecai Myers is the fecund figure poised at the threshold of Lowell's fraught childhood.

In the memoir's closing paragraphs, the portrait presides over another unbearable dinner scene. Here Lowell pushes ekphrasis to the breaking point by animating Myers' portrait, refracting the memoir's definitive statement through what "Mordecai would have said" if the image could speak: "'My children, my blood, accept graciously the loot of your inheritance. We are all dealers in used furniture'" (45). Lowell's parents inherited the family portraits and Edwardian furnishings from Cousin Cassie, but Lowell the writer inherits a well-used source for his memoir: the regenerations of the confessional other. If Lowell's confined Negro soldier liberates the language of *Life Studies*, Mordecai Myers offers the poet an alternative ancestry—and a "coloured in" past.

Plath (and Sexton) took Lowell's workshop in Boston, taking the confessional other in new directions for her signature work. As if superimposing Lowell's mad soldier and paternal ancestor, her breakthrough volume renders a "black man" as alternate father in her most notoriously confessional poem, "Daddy." But her ultimate figure of dark generation is the "Black / Mind" (*Ariel* 76, 90). In her *Ariel* poems, the confessional other marks altered mental states and manifests the creative process. It becomes the flashpoint between writer's block and breakthrough, turning on images of the active hand.

Although Plath's early poems lack confessional others, they make brief appearances in *The Bell Jar* when Esther Greenwood feels most at variance with herself. Anticipating her own colourisation in Hughes's *Birthday Letters*, the poet sometimes renders her novel's protagonist as Asian or Native American. Early in the novel Greenwood sees her reflection as "a big, smudgy-eyed Chinese woman staring idiotically into my face"; the literal image of smeared cosmetics expands geographically, suggesting kohl-lined Egyptian eyes. As the novel moves from the hectic New York sequence to the stasis of home, depression, and writer's block, Esther perceives that the face in her compact "looked like a sick Indian" (18, 112). Plath's racial augmentations in these mirror scenes magnify her protagonist's sense of losing identity, functionality, and creativity. Rather than De Quincey's intruding Malay or Lowell's foreshadowing figures, Plath's dark others in *The Bell Jar* bear closer proximity to the self—and the poet herself.

In *Ariel*, Plath turns to exoticised female figures in poems that many find her most revelatory, often turning toward the East through the veil motif. This recurring image reminds us of two key things. First, the American confessional poetry movement did not rely solely on Africa and African heritage for its confessional others; Plath proves closer to the Beats in incorporating so many Asian figures. Second, confessional poetry's stance of figurative nakedness plays differently across the gender divide, as Kathleen Lant argues in her discussion of self-disclosure, performance, and power in Plath's signature poems. For Plath, daring to bare often figures as a literal exposure of skin; her confessional poems are "flamboyantly revealing—if not *self*-revealing" (623). "Only let down the veil, the veil, the veil," Plath writes in "A Birthday Present," employing the triple repetition that inflects her signature style (68). Donning what Sally Bayley and Tracy Brain dub "ethnographic costumes" in "Lady Lazarus" and "Purdah" (5), the poet changes bodily and textual form as her *I* shifts across a spectrum of colours. All of these unveiling poems employ the free, three-line stanza that breaks from her earlier terza rima poems (such as "Full Fathom Five"). Lady Lazarus unwraps in a "big strip tease," while the speaker of "Ariel" "unpeel[s]" before ascending. Invoking Lady Godiva, the latter figure signifies whiteness, but Lady Lazarus accrues the darker hues of her Biblical forebear.

In the Japanese-inflected "Fever 103°," the speaker invokes Isadora Duncan's scarves to veil herself with the "yellow sullen smokes" emanating from her "gold beaten skin." She will shed these accoutrements, along with the "petticoats" of her "selves," when she rises in "pure"—and presumably selfless—form (*Ariel* 15, 33, 78–80). Augmenting the volume's interplay of disclosure and performance, this golden ascension marks Plath's emergent aesthetic identity as the female Yeats, echoing his transformation to a golden form "out of nature" in "Sailing to Byzantium" (96). Plath felt a strong spiritual connection to Yeats, citing him frequently in her journals. With Hughes she visited Coole Park and Ballylee to reignite her marriage and her writing. Living in Yeats's London house during the last months of her life, where she composed several *Ariel* poems, she felt his spirit would sustain her work (Paul Alexander 291–3). Like Yeats, Plath was a cultural outsider determined to enter the British canon.

Plath Orientalises the domicile to reconfigure volatile marital relations in "Purdah," speaking as a veiled Eastern woman in a transition to the volume's final homeward turn. Through this brown-face performance, she utters a prophetic voice foretelling how she will "unloose" herself in vengeance: a play on confessional poetry's figurative nakedness and an assertion of power. In the closing stanza, Plath draws on figurative nakedness as her speaker threatens to "unloose" from herself "the lioness"—the same mythic figure that energises the volume's title poem ("God's lioness"). Ultimately, Plath asserts poetic prowess from beneath her speaker's "mouth / Veil" and "eye / Veil," reinforcing rhetorical doubleness and split subjectivity with her cagey line breaks (*Ariel* 62–4, 33). As Bayley and Brain assert, the poem "unsettles" because its confessional performance renders the poet "so visible and yet so hidden"—as enigmatic as her Asian other (7). Plath's masking becomes a form of self-musing: she fathoms a state of mind, and she taps a hidden source of inspiration.

Along with the veil motif, "Purdah" continues the volume's generative image of the active hand. Its closing stanzas shift the repeated word *attendants* from noun phrases to one-word imperatives ("Attendants!") when the speaker summons servants to witness her furious prophesy—and Plath commands her audience's attention "for the explosive show that is to come" (Bayley and Brain 4). The implied hand-claps link with images of active hands that propel the poet's creativity. In *Ariel* this writerly figure moves ultimately to the page, initiating in the kitchen of "Lesbos" and culminating in the bee sequence. Plath's dark Muse makes a surprising appearance in "Lesbos," a signature poem of domestic delirium. The speaker addresses another housewife in her hellish kitchen, complete with smog and hissing potatoes. "Doped and thick" from sleeping pills, the speaker's altered state migrates eastward in a fantasy of wearing "tiger pants" by the sea. In the poem's third section, she recalls the two women on the beach scooping up "handfuls" of sand: "Working it like dough, a mulatto body, / The silk grits" (*Ariel* 38–9). Suddenly Sappho's island merges with *Island in the Sun*, a jarring superimposition of interracial erotica and food preparation, Hollywood and housewifery. Plath's tactile trope of physical intimacy disrupts a poem of distances: in "Lesbos" friendship is fraught, spouses are estranged, a child is face-down. The confessional other's appearance as a mulatto manifests the working hand as the speaker works through domestic frustrations—and Plath workshops domesticity for a new kind of poetry.

The culmination to *Ariel*, Plath's bee sequence, figures the creative process through the confessional other in a breakthrough from formal confinement to stylistic freedom. Karen Jackson Ford's nuanced reading stresses the poems' role in coming to terms with stylistic excess, noting their concern "with self-assessment and redefinition, both personal and poetic" (21). Employing a form of five-line, unrhymed stanzas, the sequence bears biographical contexts of Plath's beekeeping in Devon and the breakup of her marriage; she composed it during an especially productive period in October 1962. In "The Bee Meeting" the hesitant speaker enters the English countryside as an outsider, interlacing her heightened observations with increasingly hysterical questions. As she watches the villagers smoke the bees out, she compares the "smoke rolls" to "scarves" (a vestige of the veil motif) and contemplates "the mind of the hive" that will propel her writing. While most critics see the queen bee as the sequence's generative figure, it is the black mind that rises at the end of "Wintering"—a flight that does not end in death, but in seasonal and artistic renewal. In the sequence's portal poem, the writerly hand manifests itself through a figure of manual dexterity: "fingerjoint cells" that house the hive's "new virgins" (*Ariel* 82).

The bees accrue African and Roman identities in "The Arrival of the Bee Box," the poem that poises Plath on the edge of breakthrough. The bees are confined in the "clean wood" as Plath had been contained within standard forms in her pre-*Ariel* poetry. Alone with her "box of maniacs," the speaker peers into the "dark, dark" space. She perceives a "swarmy feeling of African hands" within the "locked" container, a "Black on black." As Ford, Curry, and others have discussed, this problematic image evokes at one level the hold of a slave ship; Curry finds that "blackness connotes enslavement, entrapment, and suffocation" in the sequence's framing poems (Plath, *Ariel* 84; Ford 147; Curry 161). To be sure, the confessional other in "The Arrival of the Bee Box" bears these colonialist meanings. Yet Plath's domination of black is a richer signifier than that; she does not restrict it to race (or even to human figures). For Christina Britzolakis, the bee box signifies "the unconscious itself, linked with the threat of racial and class otherness" that ultimately "threaten[s] the speaker with loss of sovereign control over words and meaning" (120). In other words, the bee box contains an art of darkness as well as a heart of darkness.

Ultimately, Plath's black bees signify a primal chaos that triggers her writer's frenzy and fosters her emergent style, a deep cultural past that does not fit squarely within Freud's Africanised unconscious of Europe. They do not even remain African. For in the din of the container, Plath sounds the origins of Western language. Here the confessional other shifts to another imperial geography, crossing the ancient Mediterranean where the "noise" and "unintelligible syllables" become a "furious Latin" (*Ariel* 84). Because Plath attempts to break through to Britishness in *Ariel*, the Latinate underpinnings of its poetry constitute a literary commodity as precious as the English landscape. When the speaker wonders if she can "let them out," Plath means more than liberating black bodies; she means unleashing the confessional other's power on the page. Anticipating her own artistic liberation, Plath breaks the poem's (and sequence's) form with a single-line stanza at the end: "The box is only temporary" (*Ariel* 84; see Ford 149). By the next poem ("Stings"), the now "bare-handed" speaker asserts: "I am in control" (87). Yet like the brown hands that clap commands in "Purdah," Plath's "swarmy" African hands compel her own. In her assessment of literary whitewashing in critical discourse, Morrison insists on the active role "the racial other" plays in shaping American literature's "imaginative and historical terrain." She asserts that "pouring rhetorical acid on the fingers of a black hand may indeed destroy the prints, but not the hand" (46). Our critical responses to *Ariel* can effect a similar erasure of the confessional others that underwrite Plath's self-musing.

In "Wintering," identity and form become one: the speaker has filled her honey jars, and Plath has completed her sequence (and volume). Here the poet manifests a black mind that extends beyond autobiographical confession and cross-racial performance; we cannot reduce it to clinical depression, and we cannot contain it within racial otherness. Significantly, the poem's speaker has made a second descent to darkness to store her yield, entering the cellar where "the black bunched [. . .] like a bat;" Ford points out the "explosive" alliteration that heightens suspense (*Ariel* 89; Ford 159). Tropes of the confessional other colour and distort Plath's descriptions of this fraught space: the flashlight's feeble beam is "Chinese yellow," the persistent darkness becomes a "black asininity." These pejorative images carry over the previous poems' racial (and sometimes racist) meanings. They also appear in "the heart of the house," Plath's katabatic cave of making (*Ariel* 89). At the poem's major turn, the speaker leaves the cellar's "appalling objects" to imagine the bees' flight over the snowscape. Forming "a mass," they appear as "Black / Mind against all that white" (*Ariel* 89–90). This image echoes the culminating figure of the bees as "a black intractable mind" in "The Swarm," which Plath discarded from her sequence (*Collected* 217). In "Wintering," the only monosyllabic line in the poem ("Black") is the fulcrum between chaos and form, bringing the poem's latent words to white paper. In feeding her bees, the speaker has also fueled the act of writing. The hive survives, the speaker recovers, and Plath overcomes the blank page.

Unlike Lowell's, Plath's black mind does not require black-face. The relationship between form and identity in *Ariel* is more shadowed, more complicated. Many of Plath's confessional others bear closer proximity to the poet by manifesting in domestic space and sharing her gender; these qualities can make some poems seem self-revelatory in ways we have come to expect of her. At the same time, the confessional other's fundamental difference from the poet proves equally crucial to the self-musing that Plath enacts in *Ariel*. At the heart of her bee sequence—and volume—lies an identity that proves fundamentally aesthetic and process oriented. Outflanking writer's block with the black mind, Plath's signature volume generates the poet's own reincarnation in contemporary British poetry's most famous confessional breakthrough.

The series of secret poems that Ted Hughes began writing to Plath in 1972 would become one of the best-selling volumes of poetry in the twentieth century, *Birthday Letters*. For years he had considered them "unpublishably raw and unguarded" (qtd. Wagner 4), although he did include one in the American edition of *New Selected Poems* (1982) and eight in the "Uncollected" section of *New Selected Poems, 1957–1994*. Released for publication during his last year of life, *Birthday Letters* incarnates a dark spectre of Sylvia Plath in harrowingly intimate accounts of their relationship, her personality, and her poetry. Rather than poems per se, Hughes saw the pieces as "occasions [. . .] in which I tried to open a direct, private, inner contact with my first wife" (qtd. Sagar 84). Daring to bare far more than Plath, Hughes aimed to "strip myself child-naked and wade in," writing in stripped-down style and addressing her directly as *you* (qtd. Middlebrook, *Her Husband* 276). In these acts of resurrection Hughes extends time by taking Plath out of it, fixing her (and their relationship) within Fate. But his figurations of Plath often prove far more fluid than fixed, especially when he transforms her into a woman of colour. And in the process, the twentieth century's most famous confessional poet becomes the confessional other. Significantly, these racial transformations take place in three poems that revisit formative events in their relationship: their first encounter, their first lovemaking, and their honeymoon.

Hughes relays these respective events chronologically in *Birthday Letters* ("St Botolph's," and "18 Rugby Street," "You Hated Spain"), giving prominence to his "coloured in" Plath in the opening eighteen poems. But he aired the latter poem first in the "enlarged"[5] American edition of *New Selected Poems*, which misidentifies "You Hated Spain" as part of *Crow* (1971). Thus Plath's first appearance as Hughes's confessional other disrupts his emerging canon of self-selected poems. A writer may mislay the confessional other, but it will return and proliferate as its darkened hand compels the writer's own.

Like *Birthday Letters* more generally, "You Hated Spain" utters the pain of early misreadings and belated recognitions. Hughes mistakes Plath as too much the "bobby-sox American"—that is, too white bread—to fathom the deep, generative otherness he perceives in Spanish culture. It "frightened" her, but he "felt at home" there (39). Like Lowell, Hughes darkens his origins with Moorish-Mediterranean ancestry. (The poet did, in fact, have Spanish heritage through his father's side.) But lacking the equivalent of Mordecai Myers's portrait, Hughes imports Goya's paintings to distill this essence. The poem begins by separating Plath from Spain's blood, dark complexions, and "African / Black edges to everything." Presumably, the college-coddled American poet cannot handle Europe's other. The poem turns when Hughes recognises the darkness within Plath and concedes that Spain was "the land of your dreams," something she could not escape rather than not enter. The poem returns to Africa, inscribing it on Plath's face and in her psyche: Spain is now "the juju land behind your African lips" (39).

Fetishising Plath as it mourns her, the poem begins Hughes's multiethnic reconstruction of the poet as an intimate otherness. She is "African-lipped" again in "St Botolph's," which recounts their now legendary first meeting at a Cambridge party. He reframes the event as "That day the solar system married us." Here, too, Hughes marks Plath as stereotypically American, a vivacious young woman "swaying" on "long, perfect" legs (14–15). The poem marks the portal to their fateful relationship, the "suddenly you" of Plath's—and the confessional other's—appearance.

She is "Beautiful, beautiful America!" in "18 Rugby Street," which refers to the couple's first night together. Hughes gives his version of their vigorous lovemaking in London before Plath traveled to Paris, reaching back through his memory and her journals—where he read her account "years after" her death. The poem shuttles back and forth across time, flashing forward to their child Nicholas (who acquires her "Slavic Asiatic" eyes), to her final days, her afterlife in her journals, then to her ascent up the Rugby Street staircase, before focusing on her body: "And now at last I got a good look at you" (24, 21, 182, 22). Hughes zooms in on her face, embellishing it as a "spirit mask" of a composite confessional other. Merging multiple continents and ethnicities, this figuration of Plath spans Asian, African, European, and North American identities. Her lips have an "aboriginal thickness" like the African lips in the other "coloured in" poems, while her nose broadens with "Apache" features. No longer a "bobby-sox American," Plath and her "boxer's nose" shift again as she acquires a "nose from Attila's horde," becoming at last "a prototype face" that could peer "through the smoke / Of a Navajo campfire" (23, 39). Hughes no longer needs to travel to Spain or tap his paternal bloodline for the otherness that fuels these confessions.

The young Plath may be Hughes's multiethnic "new world" (24), but Plath the confessional other is hardly fixed within its geographies. The critical conversation on these three poems gravitates toward Plath's symbolic status as Hughes's America. In the *New Yorker* issue that previewed *Birthday Letters*, A. Alvarez noted that Hughes "seems never quite to have lost his sense of her foreignness" (64). But following the wake of the other writers and racial embellishments that I have discussed here, Hughes's "coloured in" Plath proves far too familiar. Only the confessional other can usher him through the thresholds of haunted spaces and intimate agonies these poems articulate. And so Hughes fashions one from the same figure that is his subject: Sylvia Plath his wife, Sylvia Plath his text. And he finds a new Americanness in the bare candour of his conversational style.

If Lowell became the father of confessional poetry, Plath has become its most potent afterimage. Like the confessional other, the cultural composite "Sylvia Plath" is a portal between America and England, past and present, person and text, domestic and foreign, whiteness and darkness. Indeed, she has enabled a refashioning of confessional race relations by appearing in

Elizabeth Alexander's "The Female Seer Will Burn Upon this Pyre," where Plath becomes an exotic white ghost of postwar domesticity. Reinventing the tribute poem through her white confessional other, Alexander summons Plath in her kitchen as a "key female poetic forebear" for African American poetry (Pereira 285). Uttering prophecy like the speaker of "Purdah" and sweeping up "bumblebee husks" from her creative emergence, this magical, racialised Plath fixes hair, bakes cake, and types poems before she vanishes (34). Elusive and protean, the confessional other hovers at the space between dreaming and waking, conjuring and writing. It emerges from the cultural unconscious to reconfigure family, creativity, and remembrance. Recovering this neglected figure troubles our usual sense of poet/speaker relations by introducing a third party to confessional utterance. We expect confessional texts to show writers at their most authentic, autobiographical, and original. Yet the confessional other shadows the *I*, underwriting the writer's signature style. For at the most heightened , unstable, and distinctive parts of the text, we find that the confessional writer is never truly alone.

NOTES

1. For more on super-sized poetic persona or IMAX authorship, see Bryant. My term derives from Kate Moses's discussion of "the IMAX version of Sylvia Plath" in her review of *Unabridged Journals* (web).
2. Lowell employs flexible quatrains in "A Mad Negro Soldier Confined at Munich": ABBA, AABB, and ABAB. As Rosenthal notes, all but one pair of end words are exact rhyme (*New Poets* 63); "guards" and "wards" in Stanza Three are slant rhymes.
3. "Inauguration Day: January 1953," the third poem in Part One, is a truncated Italian sonnet of tetrameter lines.
4. Lowell dedicates the volume's culminating poem ("Skunk Hour") to Bishop.
5. Harper's *New Selected Poems* (1982) was an enlarged edition of Faber's Selected Poems: 1957–1981, also published in 1982. Faber's expanded New Selected Poems, 1957–1994 appeared in 1995.

REFERENCES

Alvarez, A. "Your Story, My Story." (Life and Letters). *New Yorker* 2 February 1998: 58–65. Print.
Alexander, Elizabeth. *Antebellum Dream Book*. St. Paul, MN: Graywolf, 2001. Print.
Alexander, Paul. *Rough Magic: A Biography of Sylvia Plath*. New York: Penguin, 1991. Print.
Bayley, Sally, and Tracy Brain. "Introduction: 'Purdah' and the Enigma of Representation." *Representing Sylvia Plath*. Ed. Sally Bayley and Tracy Brain. Cambridge: Cambridge University Press, 2011: 1–10. Print.
Bishop, Elizabeth. *The Complete Poems: 1927–1979*. New York: Farrar, Straus, and Giroux (Noonday), 1983. Print.
Berryman, John. *The Dream Songs*. New York: Farrar, Straus, and Giroux, 2007.

Breslin, Paul. *The Psycho-Political Muse: American Poetry Since the Fifties*. Chicago: University of Chicago Press, 1987. Print.

Britzolakis, Christina. "*Ariel* and Other Poems." *The Cambridge Companion to Sylvia Plath*. Ed. Jo Gill. Cambridge: Cambridge University Press, 2006. 107–23. Print.

Bryant, Marsha. "IMAX Authorship: Teaching Plath and Her *Unabridged Journals*." *Pedagogy* 4.2 (Spring 2004): 241–61. Print.

Curry, Renée R. *White Women Writing White: H.D., Elizabeth Bishop, Sylvia Plath, and Whiteness*. Westport, CT: Greenwood, 2000. Print.

De Quincey, Thomas. *Confessions of an English Opium-Eater*. 1821. Introd. William Bolitho. New York: Heritage, 1950. Print.

DuPlessis, Rachel Blau. *Genders, Races and Religious Cultures in Modern American Poetry, 1908–1934*. Cambridge: Cambridge University Press, 2001. Print.

Ford, Karen Jackson. *Gender and the Poetics of Excess: Moments of Brocade*. Jackson, MS: University Press of Mississippi, 1997. Print.

Gill, Jo. *Modern Confessional Writing: New Critical Essays*. London: Routledge, 2006. Print.

Gonzalez, Susan. "Director Spike Lee Slams 'Same Old' Black Stereotypes in Today's Films." *Yale Bulletin & Calendar*. 2 March 2001. Web. 20 December 2012.

Gubar, Susan. *Racechanges: White Skin, Black Face in American Culture*. New York: Oxford University Press, 1997. Print.

Hamilton, Ian. *Robert Lowell: A Life*. New York: Vintage, 1982. Print.

Hofmann, Michael, ed. *Robert Lowell*. Poet to Poet. London: Faber and Faber, 2001. Print.

Hughes, Ted. *Birthday Letters*. New York: Farrar, Straus, and Giroux, 1998. Print.

———. *New Selected Poems*. New York: Harper, 1982. Print.

———. *New Selected Poems, 1957–1994*. London: Faber, 1995. Print.

Jameson, Fredric. *The Geopolitical Aesthetic: Cinema and Space in the World System*. Bloomington, IN: Indiana University Press, 1992. Print.

———. *Signatures of the Visible*. New York: Routledge, 1990. Print.

Lane, Anthony. "The Fighter: Reading Robert Lowell." *New Yorker* 9 June 2003: 80–9. Print.

Lant, Kathleen Margaret. "The Big Strip Tease: Female Bodies and Male Power in the Poetry of Sylvia Plath." *Contemporary Literature* 34.4 (1993): 620–69. Print.

Lowell, Robert. *Life Sudies/For the Union Dead*. New York: Farrar, Straus, and Giroux. 1964. Print.

Middlebrook, Diane. *Her Husband: Hughes and Plath—A Marriage*. New York: Viking, 2003. Print.

———. "What Was Confessional Poetry?" *Columbia History of American Poetry*. Ed. Jay Parini and Brett Millier. New York: Columbia University Press, 632–49. Print.

Morrison, Toni. *Playing in the Dark: Whiteness and the Literary Imagination*. Cambridge, MA: Harvard University Press, 1992. Print.

Moses, Kate. "The Real Sylvia Plath." Part 1. *Salon*. Web. 20 May, 2000. Web. 22 Dec. 2012.

Nelson, Deborah. *Pursuing Privacy in Cold War America*. New York: Columbia University Press, 2002. Print.

Pereira, Malin. "Sister Seer and Scribe: Teaching Wanda Coleman's and Elizabeth Alexander's Poetic Conversations with Sylvia Plath." *Plath Profiles*. Vol. 1 (Summer 2008), 280–90. Web. 22 Dec. 2012.

Plath, Sylvia. *Ariel: The Restored Edition*. New York: Harper Collins, 2004. Print.

———. *The Bell Jar.* New York: Harper Perennial, 2005. Print.

———. *The Collected Poems.* Ed. Ted Hughes. 1981. New York: Harper, 1992.

Rosenthal, M. L. *The New Poets: American and British Poetry Since World War II.* London: Oxford University Press, 1967. Print.

———. "Poetry as Confession." Rev. of *Life Studies*, by Robert Lowell. *Nation* 19 Sept. 1959: 154–55. Print.

Sagar, Keith. *The Laughter of Foxes: A Study of Ted Hughes.* Liverpool: Liverpool University Press, 2000. Print.

Said, Edward. *Orientalism.* New York: Vintage, 1979. Print.

Sánchez-Arce, Ana María. "'Authenticism,' or The Authority of Authenticity." *Mosaic* 40.3 (Sept. 2007): 139–155. Print.

Sudan, Rajani. "Englishness 'A'muck': De Quincey's Confessions." *Genre* 27.4 (Winter 1994): 377–94. Print.

Thurston, Michael. "Robert Lowell's Monumental Vision: History, Form, and the Cultural Work of Postwar American Lyric." *American Literary History* 12.1&2 (2000): 79–112. Print.

Travisano, Thomas J. *Elizabeth Bishop: Her Artistic Development.* Charlottesville: University Press of Virginia, 1988. Print.

Wagner, Erica. *Ariel's Gift: A Commentary on* Birthday Letters, *by Ted Hughes.* London: Faber, 2000. Print.

Yezzi, David. "Confessional Poetry and the Artifice of Honesty." *New Criterion* (June 1998): 14–21. Print.

11 Writing the Self into Being
Illness and Identity in Inga Clendinnen's *Tiger's Eye* and Hilary Mantel's *Giving Up the Ghost*

Amy Prodromou

Looking at the construction of self in autopathography[1] both proves and problematises Paul John Eakin's view that the autobiographical self is whole, stable, and continuous, as argued in his book, *Living Autobiographically*. On the one hand, the loss of a stable self through the disorienting experience of illness acts as catalyst for the search for a unified, whole self. However, the same experiences can be so destabilising that writers' sense of a core being is left damaged in many ways and identity as a shifting, flexible concept becomes necessary to understanding the complex nature of recovery within the subgenre of narratives of loss that I call "memoirs of textured recovery."[2] This kind of complex recovery calls for theories of subjectivity that allow for the performance of a shifting, fluid self even as it strives for wholeness and continuity. While Clendinnen and Mantel on the one hand engender a whole, solid sense of self through the autobiographical act, the tension between self as either fragmented and discontinuous or whole and continuous—a tension never fully reconciled, and these selves juxtaposed—is the basis for this nuanced, "textured recovery" that I'm arguing forces us to rethink theories of the self, narrative, and healing.

This chapter traces the complex process of recovery throughout Mantel's misdiagnosis of endometriosis and Clendinnen's liver transplant. As Mantel and Clendinnen "write [themselves] into being" (Mantel 222) they attest to the fact that writing can heal a fragmented or destabilised self. Writing allows Mantel and Clendinnen to make sense of things, construct themselves, discover what they are thinking and feeling, find themselves and their lives—in short, it is "a weapon for the preservation of the self" (Clendinnen 168); it in turns emancipates, protects, identifies, memorialises, sustains, saves, creates, orders, and recuperates the self. These writers do much to build a solid sense of self from the fragments left by the experience of illness, and on one level conform to what studies between writing and healing show: narrative can heal. However, they also problematise the narrative self and complicate the recovery process by challenging the assumption that writing the self is always necessarily a healing enterprise.

The autobiographical act—writing the self—challenges postmodern theories of fragmented subjectivity by offering the possibility of the creation of a unified self through a process Eakin calls "doing self, doing consciousness" (85). It therefore potentially has enormous implications for female autonomy because it leads to "more self, more agency, not less" (Eakin 85), and chimes with what Nancy Miller has argued is "our desire to assert agency and subjectivity after several decades of insisting loudly on the fragmentation of identity and the death of the author" (12). This chapter tests Eakin's theory of autobiographical subjectivity against Inga Clendinnen's *Tiger's Eye* and Hilary Mantel's Giving *Up the Ghost* and examines the interplay between multiple identities and whole selves in a context where "[w]omen writers are beginning [. . .] to construct an identity out of the recognition that women need to discover, and must fight for, a sense of unified selfhood, a rational, coherent effective identity" (Waugh qtd. Cosslett et al. 6).

Eakin's recent research into identity and autobiography uses Antonio Damasio's focus on homeostasis (the body's ability to maintain a condition of equilibrium or stability through its physiological processes—e.g., constant body temperature) as an analogy for the act of autobiographical writing itself: "I would extend this view of the human organism's homeostatic regulatory activity to include our endless fashioning of identity narratives" (154). Ultimately, this "neurobiological story" translates into the creation of a whole, stable self: "As self-narration maps and monitors the succession of body or identity states, it engenders [in Damasio's words] 'the notion of a bounded, single individual that changes ever so gently across time but, somehow, seems to stay the same'" (155).

This desire or need for a whole, stable self at first sounds much like the traditional male autobiographical quest for autonomy when Eakin describes "our need for a stable sense of continuous identity stretching over time" (77). He says that "When we talk about ourselves, and even more when we fashion an I-character in an autobiography, we give a degree of permanence and narrative solidity—or 'body' we might say—to otherwise evanescent states of identity feeling" (77). The language Eakin uses to describe this "need" for a particular type of identity is telling: it is "stable," "continuous," "permanen[t]," "solid," within a "narrative anchor" (8). Furthermore, it is not so much a quest as a natural, biological, "largely unconscious" (22)—in comparing it to homeostasis—need to regulate our sense of self in autobiography. It's a process that seeks continuity—even in its "ever so gentl[e] [. . .] change [. . .] across time"—a "regulatory activity" that creates an identity made up of "a bounded, single individual that [. . .] stay[s] the same" (Damasio qtd. Eakin 155). On the surface, Eakin's original and exciting use of neurological processes to understand identity seems vaguely oppressive, serving only to shackle us to a view of identity as permanent and fixed, perhaps not unlike an ideal self or a "private Platonic essence" (Johnson 87) which could be misinterpreted as isolationist and individualistic.

However, there are several reasons that suggest this is not the case (beyond the fact that he discusses in depth the social and cultural forces that shape identity). Rather, Eakin also posits an idea of self that, while desiring stability, is nevertheless composed of multiple identities. This is because Eakin talks of the autobiographical process as an "endless fashioning of identity narratives" (154), and in this way suggests that we have many identities—an idea he repeats throughout, though does not elaborate on: he refers to "autobiography's tracking of identity states across time" which "maps and monitors the succession of body or identity states" (155). If "self adheres in [. . .] narrative" (74), then we have an "unending succession" of narrative identities that make up that self.

Secondly, this apparent contradiction is reconciled by Eakin's use of "identity" and "self" as different terms, and not interchangeably as is often the case: "Whenever I variously think of myself, for example, as a literary critic, as a father, a Midwesterner, a bourgeois suburbanite, and so forth, I am thinking of myself in terms of identity. *Self*, then, is the larger, more comprehensive term for the totality of our subjective experience" (xiv). Thus, the autobiographical act is the "maintenance of stability" (155) from this "unending succession of identity states."

This theory of subjectivity reconciles the dichotomy inherent in these different concepts of self as either whole or fragmented. It is also important for the construction of female subjectivity because it necessarily grants agency—in "the political imperative for women to constitute themselves as subjects"—while at the same time allowing for "multiple subjectivities" (L. Anderson 90) which has been so essential to theories of female selfhood. Instead, the two need not be mutually exclusive: we have many identities, and yet the self of the autobiographical act as Eakin refers to it is the whole self, Neisser's extended self: "the self of memory and anticipation, the self existing continuously across time" (3). It is a self that claims the same key features as Damasio's "core consciousness": "Individual first-person perspective, ownership, agency—these primary attributes of core consciousness are also key features of the literary form of self, the 'I' of autobiographical discourse" (Eakin 71).

Just as the autobiographical act engenders a whole, stable, self, Judith Harris argues that personal writing can "be a means of creating a stable identity and regaining ego strengths" (xv). Harris melds apparent contradictions in these two opposing notions of self within the field of psychoanalysis:

> With its emphasis on the unconscious and on what one does not yet know about one's self until it is uttered or written down, psychoanalysis offers a view of the writing subject in process. Rather than seeing the writer as someone who is chameleonlike and changing with each protean discourse he adopts, the more holistic approach of psychoanalysis enables us to view the individual as a *core being* whose identity is *fluid, mercurial, but self-constant.* (xiv; emphasis added)

This view of subjectivity is somewhat akin to Virginia Woolf's in *Moments of Being*, a view of the self which "emphasizes simultaneously the *change and continuity* of the individual identity" (Schulkind 14; emphasis added) and echoes Eakin's "endless fashioning of identity narratives" (154) in its "ceaseless transformation of personality" (Schulkind 12). It too somehow collapses dichotomies: "That self was an elusive will o' the wisp, always just ahead on the horizon, *flickering and insubstantial*, yet *enduring*" (Schulkind 12; emphasis added). The autobiographical act is one that "help[s] us to *anchor* our *shifting identities* in time" (Eakin xi; emphasis added).

In his review of Eakin's work, David McCooey writes that the analogy to homeostasis, "which aims to create a sense of stable identity" (347), although exciting, is also problematic:

> If identity is indeed 'part of' homeostasis, and therefore biological, then presumably it would make sense to consider those events and literary forms that mark and narrate a *loss* of stability. If identity is homeostatic, then bodily and psychological crises, conversions, and traumas would be the main challenges that a homeostatic model of identity would face. (347)

It is certainly true that these kinds of crises threaten to destabilise self, and often do fragment or negate sense of self. Yet paradoxically, in narratives of loss, where the self experiences a loss of stability, the impulse towards creating a stable self is actually more immediately apparent. The very nature of loss, which McCooey argues "challenges" Eakin's theory, actually goes a long way to confirming it. If the search for a whole self is neurologically "hard-wired" in us as Eakin has argued, then nowhere is this more manifest than in illness narratives.

Many critics have argued that experiences of illness, where the self is under threat, act as catalyst for the search for stable identities. Indeed, G. Thomas Couser has argued that it is "only by reference to [an] ongoing interior autobiography that many writers of illness and disability narratives can assure themselves of a sense of self" (*Recovering* 84). In her article, "Pathography and Enabling Myths: The Process of Healing," Anne Hunsaker Hawkins gives a possible reason for this:

> In narratives describing illness and possible death, the reader is repeatedly confronted with the pragmatic reality and *experiential unity* of the autobiographical self. The self of pathographical writing is the self-in-crisis: When confronted with serious and life-threatening illness, that fictive "ghost" of the self is contracted into a defensive ontological reality. (227; emphasis added)

For Hawkins, these kinds of crises force what may be an insubstantial or fragmented self into a concrete, unified one. In this sense, it echoes and reinforces theories of subjectivity where two apparently contradictory sense of selves are united. In "What Can Narrative Theory Learn from Illness

Narratives?" Shlomith Rimmon-Kenan recognises this contradiction and suggests that it is more apparent within illness narratives: "Autobiographical writing about illness may be an attempt to control the uncontrollable, and hence it can become a battleground between two competing principles" (244). She says further that "The tension between a thematization of disintegration and a writing that preserves qualities of narrative order may be a dramatization of the struggle between an acceptance of fragmentation and the need to overcome it by creating a coherent narrative" (244). However, in order to understand how writers create a stable identity, and the ways in which the self is made an "experiential unity," we need to first consider how illness contributes to a loss of stability in the self.

In our culture, illness itself is destabilising for a number of reasons. One is that it is regarded as a stigma, as discussed at length by critics, theorists and practitioners of illness narratives.[3] One reason for why illness is stigmatised stems from Hawkins's observation that in our culture more than in previous ones, illness is separated from daily life: "in earlier times, illness seems to have been considered an integral and inseparable part of living (and dying). [. . .] It is only in the twentieth century that serious illness has become a phenomenon that can be isolated from an individual's life" ("Pathography" 223). It is largely the fault of modern scientific medicine and how "it tends to focus on the disease process and on ways in which this process can be interrupted and reversed," rather than on the individual, who is "only peripherally, or secondarily" considered ("Pathography" 223). In her narrative about undergoing a liver transplant, Clendinnen gives a chilling description of how hospitals are set up to dismantle one's sense of self. The process begins with "that initial submission" (22) of admitting oneself into a hospital. Then:

> Abruptly naked, you are thrust into a vestigial smock. [. . .] When you move, your buttocks show. It is at once lewd and sexless, an outfit designed for depraved choirboys [. . .]. Then you are labelled. It is unnerving to be tagged around the wrist, more unnerving to be tagged around the ankle as well, as if you might come unstuck and they will have to match up the parts. (22–3)

The result is that illness carries with it feelings of isolation, shame and humiliation—indeed, of the self fragmented, interrupted from the goings-on of everyday life. Both Mantel and Clendinnen identify themselves in opposition to those who are healthy. Their memoirs "display a kind of postcolonial impulse—the impulse to define oneself in resistance to the dehumanising categories of the medical and health-service institutions" (Couser, *Signifying* 46). In describing the long, painful years before her diagnosis, Mantel tells us that "[e]ach day I was taking, though I didn't know it, a small step towards the unlit terrain of sickness, a featureless landscape of humiliation and loss" (167). In a discussion panel with Fay

Weldon titled, "Autobiography and Fiction," Mantel adds that "the process is humiliating" and calls it "a negotiation with shame." In this way, Mantel and Clendinnen "recognise [. . .] and write against the social and cultural isolation of disabled [or in their case—chronically ill] people" (Couser, *Signifying* 178).

Although the medical profession may be responsible for sidelining the individual in the illness process, Mantel's story of medical neglect is particularly horrifying, especially given that much of her misdiagnosis was due to gender-specific prejudices of the time. In Mantel's narrative, illness does more than fragment and destabilise self. It goes beyond this by robbing her of her sense of self and entirely negating self. She develops feelings of helplessness: "I was an invalid now, and I wasn't entitled to a policy, not a policy of my own" (176–7). In 1979, at twenty-seven years old, Mantel describes her complete lack of agency: "having my fertility confiscated and my insides rearranged" (185). After her operation, during which they remove her womb and "a few lengths of bowel" (209), she finds she has lost the decision to choose; she has lost her autonomy: "Neglect—my own, and that of the medical profession—had taken away my choices. Now my body was not my own. It was a thing done to, a thing operated on. I was twenty-seven and an old woman, all at once" (211). Unable to perform to society's expectations, Mantel feels even further robbed of self because of the gender implications associated with her illness:

> It used to be fashionable to call endometriosis 'the career woman's disease': the implication being, there now, you callous bitch, see what you get if you put off breeding and put your own ambitions first. I was no good for breeding, so what was I good for? Who was I at all? [. . .] I was old while I was young, I was an ape, I was a blot on the page, I was nothing, zilch. (211–12)

Clendinnen echoes this sense of absolute negation of self. After her transplant, she says "I am one of those shreds of silk, streaming, tearing in the wind" (185) and "held together by shadow knitting" (186). Two months after her transplant operation she says, "what then is this observing and commenting 'I'?, I answer that it is a shred, a nothing: a sliver of shattered silk whirling in the wind, without anchor or destiny, surviving only because the wind happened to drop" (188).

Loss culminates in the destabilising experience of the self—fragmented, negated, interrupted, discontinuous. It's hardly the picture of Eakin's whole, stable self that stays the same over time. However, the destabilising experience of loss does not necessarily challenge Eakin's theory if loss proves motivation for the construction of a whole, stable self.

One of the outcomes of this fragile, fragmented sense of self, which is particularly amplified in narratives of illness, is that it fuels a strong desire for agency. Mantel says that "[f]or a long time I felt as if someone else were writing my life" (71) and that "The book of me was indeed being written by other people: by my parents, by the child I once was, and by my own unborn children, stretching out their ghost fingers to grab the pen" (71). This is especially true of the medical sector, which often labels writers and rewrites their story for them: in an interview, Mantel says: "When I wrote my story, I re-experienced the shame of being disbelieved. I relived old feelings of futility. I was conscious that it was doctors who had written it first—in a very different version, recorded in my medical notes" (qtd. Blake 7). Pathography, as Hawkins says, "restores the person ignored or cancelled out in the medical enterprise, and it places that person at the very center" (Hawkins, "Pathography" 223).

Mantel and Clendinnen illustrate Eakin's argument that the autobiographical act leads to "more self [. . .] more agency." As Mantel succinctly says: "I began this writing in an attempt to seize the copyright in myself" (71). Similarly, Clendinnen refers to "the Olympian authority of writing" (73) which emphasises the power of writing to heal a violated sense of self. Towards the end of her narrative, Mantel says, "I have been so mauled by medical procedures [. . .] that sometimes I feel that each morning it is necessary to write myself into being" (222). For Mantel, writing equates to constructing the self; she says in an interview, "As I write, pieces of the past fall into place. Sense emerges where there was no sense. And I begin to construct myself, complete with the missing bits" (qtd. Blake 8). Similarly, in the rehabilitation hospital, Clendinnen writes on a notepad in order "to find myself and my life again" (22).Writing is remedy for the dissolved self: for Mantel, "When you have committed enough words to paper you feel you have a spine stiff enough to stand up in the wind" (222–3). She further attests to the close connection between writing and the self: "I am writing in order to take charge of the story of my childhood and my childlessness; and in order to locate myself" (222).

The new interest in autobiography for what it "does" as opposed to what it "is" (L. Anderson 91), perhaps accounts for, in part, the increasing interest in the potential of writing to heal. In 1985, Suzette Henke coined the phrase "'scriptotherapy' [. . .] the process of writing out and writing through traumatic experience in the mode of therapeutic re-enactment" (xii). Since then, numerous studies have been carried out in the field of trauma studies,[4] as well as more recently in medicine[5] and psychology with results showing that "[w]hen people put their emotional upheavals into words, their physical and mental health improved markedly" (Pennebaker 3). Such studies emphasise the importance of translating experience into language, an idea that lies at the heart of Kristeva's theory of mourning: "for the normal subject it is recognition of this loss which creates the possibility of symbolisation, as words come to stand in for the lost object" (Hanson 90).

However, the ability to transform loss into words, and the healing this act can at times produce, is in theory easier to understand than in practice. It's not a simple process, as Clendinnen points out: "to try to understand any of this [the experience of illness] by transforming inchoate, unstable emotion and sensation into marks on paper is to experience the abyss between fugitive thought, and the words to contain it" (1). In her attempt to articulate the experience of illness, Clendinnen creates a hybrid form, mixing fiction, non-fiction, and historical biography along with pathography. Each mode becomes important *"as a weapon for the preservation of the self"* (168; emphasis added) in the attempt to garner a whole self; however, for the purposes of this chapter, I will focus on the use of metaphor.

The articulation of loss necessarily involves heavy use of metaphor and imagery to restore the self. Rimmon-Kenan discusses *Love's Work: A Reckoning With Life*, by British Professor of Philosophy Gillian Rose, who writes about the problem of communicating the experience of a colostomy. Rose is concerned with two dangers inherent in writing about illness: (a) using the language of medical discourse, which is ultimately separate from the embodied experience of illness, and (b) using illness as metaphor, a subject famously highlighted by Susan Sontag, who as early as 1978 pointed out the detrimental effects of seeing illness as metaphor, as "a doom deserved or brought upon oneself" (Sontag qtd. Rimmon-Kenan 246). Sontag compares attitudes surrounding TB with those surrounding cancer and HIV: "it was still thought that a certain inner disposition was needed in order to contract the disease" (qtd. Stacey 46). In her book, *Teratologies*, Jackie Stacey argues that "the cultural taboos surrounding cancer continue to reproduce a sense of blame and shame with considerable potency" (45) and that not much has changed since Sontag's observation that "there is mostly shame attached to a disease thought to stem from the repression of emotion. [. . .] The view of cancer as a disease of the failure of expressiveness condemns the cancer patient: expresses pity but also conveys contempt" (Sontag qtd. Stacey 47). Stacey points out that "according to this belief system, cancer is a *disease of the self* [. . .] the disease is a physiological expression of the person's helplessness, hopelessness, or lack of self-love" (191). In *Signifying Bodies*, Couser also points out damaging metaphors that attack character, referring to Georgina Kleege's *Sight Unseen*, where she gives examples of damaging metaphors of blindness: "If you want to talk about stupidity, prejudice, weakness, or narrow-mindedness, no other word will do" (qtd. Couser 173). In first reading Lauren Slater's *Spasm*, I was disturbed by some of the descriptions and assumptions about epilepsy that come through in her use of epilepsy as a metaphor, such as her equating "epilepsy" with the adjectives "dirty" and "spastic" (39): "Epilepsy does not mean to be possessed, passively; it means to need to possess, actively. You are born with a hole in you, genetic or otherwise, and so you seize at this, you seize at that, your mouth so hungry you'll take your own tongue if you have to" (156).[6] As Couser says, "In claiming to have epilepsy and an epileptic personality [. . .] she may not only have misrepresented herself, she has perpetuated a harmful notion of epilepsy as entailing a character defect" (*Signifying* 128).

However, using metaphors to describe illness is not always detrimental. Sontag's own metaphor of illness as a "kingdom" has been often quoted, and Sontag herself acknowledges in later writing that "one cannot think without metaphors" (qtd. Stacey 48). Hawkins argues that even Sontag's admonition not to use illness as metaphor is nevertheless "organised around a mythic formulation; in this case, what might be called the myth of 'meta-phorlessness' [because] even if we agree with Sontag that illness should be stripped of metaphor, myth, and symbol, it is an expectation that few could live up to" ("Pathography" 230). Indeed, in this chapter there have already been numerous examples of metaphors used by both Mantel and Clendinnen outside of those I will shortly hold up for discussion. Perhaps, then, we need to look not only at metaphors themselves, but beyond to their cultural construction. As Stacey argues,

> It is thus not metaphor of which we should be wary *per se*, but the cultural uses to which its heightened applications may be put. If [. . .] metaphorical readings of illness are inevitable because of the ways in which language works, what we need to focus on in careful detail is how metaphors might serve the purposes of constructing particular illnesses as shameful. (63)

So while this requires diligence and a certain exploding of metaphor to reveal hidden assumptions, it can also open up the discussion towards positive uses of metaphor in opposition to those that are detrimental. As Hawkins argues: "mythic formulations of illness [can be] empowering" ("Pathography" 240). We have seen how Mantel and Clendinnen use narrative to cope with illness, make sense of things, or "bring it under control" (Anatole Broyard qtd. Hawkins, "Pathography" 229). Hawkins argues that metaphors are "heuristic devices that give meaning to the illness, organizing and interpreting it" ("Pathography" 230). Clendinnen, while describing the hospital itself as "a child's nightmare" (1), nevertheless likens falling ill to falling in love: "'Fall' is the appropriate word; it is almost as alarming and quite as precipitous as falling in love" (1), and also to "falling down Alice's rabbit hole" where "like Alice, you are subject to unscheduled and surprising transformations" (1). This (initial) world is markedly different from Mantel's "unlit terrain of sickness, a featureless landscape of humiliation and loss" (167). Even at the end of the narrative, while Clendinnen acknowledges that as liver-transplant survivors, "We will remain guinea pigs, experimental animals, for as long as we live" (281), she amends this image: "Or, if you prefer, angels borne on the wings of our drugs, dancing on the pin of mortality" (281–3).

Clendinnen also uses the "mythic construct" (Hawkins, "Pathography" 232) of the tiger. Early on in her hospital stay she remembers a nearby zoo and the tigers there. She describes her experience in the hospital as "the kaleidoscope of the horror of helplessness" (21), but she acts as the tiger does and refuses to acknowledge it. There's no doubt that the image of the tiger has a healing effect: "Thereafter, whenever I felt the threat of *the violation of self*, I would invoke the vision of the tiger and the freedom that vision gave me, to be at once the superb gaze, and the object of the gaze: an incident in a tiger landscape" (21; emphasis added); in other words, directly illustrating how imagery can sustain the self.

The significance of transforming experiences of loss into words is highlighted in the extreme when Clendinnen experiences nightmarish hallucinations just after her liver transplant. The hallucinations come in the form of a film, controlled by a malicious camera that has developed particularly nasty human traits. If Clendinnen refuses to accept what she is being shown, then "There is a furious blur like a hive gone mad: the camera is angry. Then it squats down, eyes me. Pure malevolence" (178). Clendinnen's example illustrates vividly Hawkins's argument that "The subject of pathographies is generally something that is so destructive and disorienting to the experiencing self that it stimulates a counter impulse towards creation and order" ("Pathography" 231). The images become more and more horrific the more she denies their truth. Only by transforming the moving images into words is she able to regain control of them, and thus control of her self, only then can she read the "cryptic history of the unknown self which had unspooled behind my eyelids" (189).

The importance of putting the image—the experience of illness—into words, is also illustrated in Mantel's narrative. Just before her surgery—when doctors are still unsure of her diagnosis and believe the growths in her abdomen might be malignant—she remembers the hymn, "Litany for a Happy Death" which she had read in the back of a prayer book as a child. The affliction in the prayer reads much like the symptoms of akathisia; in a relatively short-lived episode, shortly after being given antipsychotic drugs, Mantel develops this condition (marked by restlessness and an inability to lie or sit quietly), where: "The patient [. . .] wrings her hands; she says she is in hell" (181). The plea repeated throughout the prayer—"*Merciful Jesus, have mercy on me*" (206)—evokes a healing refrain absent in the tortured description of akathisia. Importantly for this discussion of writing and healing, Mantel is moved by language—by the bodily detail of language in the prayer: "I admire particularly the phrase about the hair stiffening on the head" (207); she's moved by the use of the semi-colon: "Note that excellent semi-colon. People ask how I learned to write. That's where I learned it" (207); in other words, by the power of language to express experience, to articulate loss.

However, Charles Anderson reminds us that though "[w]riting, as one of our richest and most powerful symbolic acts, naturally creates the conditions within which healing may take place [. . .] it is important to understand that writing is not healing nor does writing about difficult experience guarantee healing" ("Editor's Column" x). Although he hastens to add that "this does not invalidate its effects or diminish its importance" (xi), this complicates assumptions of healing the self through narrative, especially when "the power of narrative is not always enough to pull us through" (Stacey 9). At times, as well, it is questionable whether the whole self which Mantel and Clendinnen achieve through writing can indeed sustain itself, and whether it is indicative of a "healed" self.

To some extent, Clendinnen conforms to Eakin's theory of a self that "changes ever so gently across time" yet still "somehow, seems to stay the same": she talks about "the development of a conscious narrative of the self—which [. . .] will change through time" (239). However, in direct contrast to his theory, she says after her transplant operation that "I was beginning to suspect [. . .] that we are [. . .] *not coherent and continuous objects in a changing sea,* but half-illusory creatures made out of the light and shadows cast by that sea, articulated by our own flickering imaginings" (191; emphasis added). Very close to the end of the narrative she seems unsure of the "self" she has performed throughout. When she goes back to write of her childhood, she continues her analogy of "falling down Alice's rabbit hole" (1) in language that seems to echo Alice's conversation with the caterpillar: "I was troubled, first, by the unreality of the person invoked as 'me', and then by the implicit claim that I still was that person merely grown larger. Am I that person? Is my consciousness really continuous?" (238). This is certainly not the whole, stable self of which Eakin speaks, that changes over time but largely remains the same. In questioning whether the self is at all continuous, Clendinnen questions the whole basis of autobiographical writing as a homeostatic process, upon which Eakin's theory rests.

Furthermore, despite what she has said about the "Olympian authority of writing" and the power of writing to recover the self, in the last chapter of the narrative, titled "Now," she still does not have a particularly solid or continuous sense of self, describing herself as "a fiction" (282). It does not seem as though she has regained a solid sense of self at the end of the narrative; in fact, the attempt has, in the end, made her less sure of her self. In the "Epilogue," she all but shatters everything that we have seen her work for through writing:

> This stuck-together 'I' is tired of introspection, that interminable novel of the invention of the self. I am tired of the 'I,' with its absurd pretensions to agency, so elegant, so upright, moving so serenely through the thickets of lesser words, surveying them from such a height. Poised on so narrow a base. It is difficult to take that preposterous pronoun seriously when you know it to be a fabricated, chemically supported, contingent thing. (286)

This admission, detrimental as it is to feminist theories of subjectivity and agency, detrimental as it is to Eakin's theory of a stable self, nevertheless illustrates complex, textured recovery, ambiguous and shifting in nature. In the "Epilogue," Clendinnen tells us how she feels at the end of her narrative: "battered, possibly wiser, certainly wearier and, oddly, happier" (289). The narrative ends on a positive note, yet there is this play on "possibly," and "oddly" which, as well as carrying ironic undertones, allows for a certain openness of interpretation which we don't see with other memoirs driving home a pre-determined agenda for the reader. It allows for many conflicting emotions at once: ("battered, wiser, wearier and happier"). Although perhaps *Tiger's Eye* is in many ways less ambiguous than *Giving Up the Ghost*, it still departs from "the typical trajectories [of] crisis, rescue and recovery" (Stacey 7). The experience of loss, then, becomes much richer in all its complex nuances.

Mantel's narrative highlights its complexity towards recovery most obviously in its title. "Giving Up the Ghost" in the negative sense can mean to die, to give up a struggle or to give up on life. But in Mantel's case, where she is haunted by many ghosts of the past, giving up the ghost may mean more positively, giving up the past and its ability to haunt her. Mantel's attitude to mourning is also ambivalent when she says: "Mourning is not quick; when there is no body to bury, mourning is not final" (230). This could be interpreted in two ways: it could mean that mourning is not final, as in mourning is not "The End"; it is not a finality, it goes on and on, it never ends, there is no relief. Or it could mean mourning is not final—it's not the final word, not the be-all and end-all but rather, there are possibilities beyond mourning, the chance that you can get beyond it to somewhere else.

Despite Mantel's recovery of self through writing, her use of the present tense problematises this. Towards the end of the narrative, she says "I was (*and am*) unsure about how I am related to my old self, or to myself from year to year" (221; emphasis added). At the time of writing—more than twenty years after her experience at St. George's hospital—Mantel says, "everything about me—my physiology, my psychology—feels constantly under assault: I am a shabby old building in an area of heavy shelling, which the inhabitants have vacated years ago" (222). This problematises Eakin's theory of a solid sense of self we have seen her create through writing.

At the end of their narratives, both Clendinnen and Mantel remake their lives. Mantel moves to a new house. In the beginning of the narrative, Owl Cottage housed the ghost of her stepfather, and at the end her second house holds the ghost of her unborn child, Catriona. It is important that she be rid of both ghosts. They move to an apartment in a converted lunatic asylum, built in the 1860s in London. When people ask her "Aren't you afraid of ghosts?" her response suggests recovery from her past and the ghosts who have haunted her: "But I smile and shake my head; I say, not I. Not I: not here: not now" (250). Again, it's important that Mantel doesn't choose to end the narrative on this note, which clearly indicates recovery. There are other incidents she chooses to include after this. At the end she sees a figure that is herself: "a figure shrouded in a cloak" (251), carrying "books that, God willing, I am going to write. But when was God ever willing? And what is this dim country, what is this tenuous path I lose so often—where am I trying to get to, when the light is so uncertain?" (252). Here, writing seems more of a burden instead of a path to healing, and there is no grand understanding of self reached at the end. She moves "back from the window, [it's] dawn or dusk" (252), hope or hopelessness in equal measure, laying the table for her ghosts, once again inviting them in.

Emily Nye says "Once a thought or story is written down, its memory and value are preserved, and one's mind is at peace" (394), but in assumptions like this there can be a danger of smoothing over complexity. I do not wish to diminish the important connection between writing and healing, nor detract from the fact that many writers such as Anne Lamott find that "[t]his page held some space, perhaps for whole scenes, in the way that—after a loss—a great friend holds some space for you in which to grieve or find your bearings" (qtd. Anderson, Holt and McGady 58). However, after wielding the "Olympian authority of writing," Clendinnen maintains her frustration with the "I" and its "absurd attempts at agency," and Mantel remains "a figure in a shrouded cloak," showing that the relationship between writing and healing is no simple process, and indeed the relationship between writing and the construction of self no straightforward enterprise. After experiencing terrible complications from a recent operation, Mantel remains "fascinated by the line between writing and physical survival" (Mantel, "Diary"). She reasserts the importance of writing as a vehicle for agency: "The black ink, looping across the page, flowing easily and more like water than like blood, reassured me that I was alive and could act in the world" ("Diary"). She argues as well that "Illness strips you back to an authentic self"; however, she is quick to add, "but not one you need to meet" ("Diary"). Her uncertainty about self at the end of this latest trauma is clear when the voice of her hallucinations ask, "Are we somebodies?" and the reply comes: "Yes, we are somebodies [. . .] But very few of us are saved" ("Diary"). Through resisting the compensatory paradigms of illness narratives, these texts, in showing recovery to be ambiguous and shifting in nature, successfully avoid "dilut[ing] a special truth into the reassuring terms of therapy" (Caruth vii) by honouring the rich texture of the experiencing self.

NOTES

1. In a note to the Preface of the 2nd edition of *Reconstructing Illness*, Anne Hunsaker Hawkins says: "Unfortunately, I did not know about the special issue of *a/b: Auto/Biography Studies*, 'Illness, Disability, and Lifewriting,' which was published in the spring of 1991, while I was in the final stages of preparing *Reconstructing Illness* for publication. Couser and I, independently, seem to have arrived at the term 'pathography' to delineate autobiographical narratives of illness" (228).

2. See also Prodromou, "'That Weeping Constellation': Navigating Loss in Women's Memoirs of Textured Recovery" in *Life Writing* 9.1 (2012).

3. Such as Susan Sontag, Anne Hunsaker Hawkins, G. Thomas Couser, Nancy Mairs, Jackie Stacey.
4. See Judith Herman's *Trauma and Recovery* (1992).
5. Such as the publication of a landmark series of studies into the relationship between writing and healing in *JAMA* (*Journal of the American Medical Association*) in which the authors concluded "This is the first study to demonstrate that writing about stressful life experiences improves physician ratings of disease severity and objective indices of disease severity in chronically ill patients" (C. Anderson, "Editor's Column" xi).
6. Since writing this, confirmation of my ideas have surfaced in Couser's *Signifying Bodies*, specifically in his chapter titled, "Disability as Metaphor: What's Wrong With *Lying*."

REFERENCES

Anderson, Charles M. "Editor's Column: Writing and Healing." *Literature and Medicine* 19. 1 (2000): ix–xiv. Print.

Anderson, Charles M., and Marian M. MacCurdy. "Introduction." Anderson and MacCurdy 1–22. Print.

———.eds. *Writing and Healing: Toward an Informed Practice*. Urbana: NCTE, 2000. Print.

Anderson, Charles, Karen Holt, and Patty McGady. "Suture, Stigma, and the Pages that Heal." Anderson and MacCurdy 58–82.

Anderson, Linda R. *Autobiography*. London: Routledge, 2001. Print.

Blake, Fanny. "P. S. Ideas, Interviews, Features." *Giving Up the Ghost*, by Hilary Mantel. London: Harper Perennial, 2004. Print.

Caruth, Cathy, ed. *Trauma: Explorations in Memory*. Baltimore, MD: Johns Hopkins University Press, 1995. Print.

Clendinnen, Inga. *Tiger's Eye*. Melbourne: Text Publishing, 2000. Print.

Cosslett, Tess, Celia Lury, and Penny Summerfield, eds. *Feminism and Autobiography: Texts, Theories, Methods*. New York: Routledge, 2000. Print.

Couser, G. Thomas. *Recovering Bodies: Illness, Disability, and Life-Writing*. Madison, WI: University of Wisconsin Press, 1997. Print.

———. *Signifying Bodies: Disability in Contemporary Life Writing*. Ann Arbor, MI: University of Michigan Press, 2009. Print.

Eakin, Paul John. *Living Autobiographically: How We Create Identity in Narrative*. Ithaca, NY: Cornell University Press, 2008. Print.

Hanson, Clare. "Bestselling Bodies: Mourning, Melancholia and the Female Forensic Pathologist." *Women: A Cultural Review* 19.1 (2008): 87–100. *Academic Search Complete (EBSCO)*. Web. 22 November 2008.

Harris, Judith. *Signifying Pain: Constructing and Healing the Self through Writing*. Albany, NY: State University of New York Press, 2003. Print.

Hawkins, Anne Hunsaker. "Pathography and Enabling Myths: The Process of Healing." Anderson and MacCurdy 222–45. Print.

———. *Reconstructing Illness: Studies in Pathography*. 2nd ed. West Lafayette, IN: Purdue University Press, 1999. Print.

Henke, Suzette A. *Shattered Subjects: Trauma and Testimony in Women's Life-Writing*. London: Macmillan, 1998. Print.

Herman, Judith Lewis. *Trauma and Recovery*. New York: BasicBooks, 1992. Print.

Johnson, T. R. "Writing as Healing and the Rhetorical Tradition." Anderson and MacCurdy 85–114. Print.

Mantel, Hilary. *Giving up the Ghost.* London: Harper Perennial, 2004. Print.

————. "Diary." *London Review of Books.* 32.21 (2010). Web. 20 November 2010.

Mantel, Hilary, and Fay Weldon. "Fiction and Autobiography." *Dissecting the Self* series, Centre for Life-Writing Research. King's College, London. 17 December 2009. Discussion Panel.

McCooey, David. Rev. of *Living Autobiographically: How We Create Identity in Narrative*, by Paul John Eakin. *Biography: An Interdisciplinary Quarterly* 33.2 (Spring 2009): 345–8. *Project Muse.* Web. 12 January 2010.

Miller, Nancy. *But Enough About Me: Why We Read Other People's Lives.* New York: Columbia University Press, 2002. Print.

Nye, Emily. "The More I Tell My Story: Writing as Healing in an HIV/AIDS Community." Anderson and MacCurdy 385–415.

Pennebaker, James W. "Telling Stories: The Health Benefits of Narrative." *Literature and Medicine* 19.1 (2000): 3–18. Print.

Prodromou, Amy. "'That Weeping Constellation': Navigating Loss in Women's Memoirs of Textured Recovery." *Life Writing* 9.1 (2012): 57–75. Print.

Rimmon-Kenan, Shlomith. "What Can Narrative Theory Learn from Illness Narratives?" *Literature and Medicine* 25.2 (2006): 241–54. Print.

Schulkind, Jeanne, ed. Introduction. *Moments of Being*, by Virginia Woolf. London: Sussex University Press, 1976. Print.

Slater, Lauren. *Spasm: A Memoir with Lies.* London: Methuen, 2000. Print.

Stacey, Jackie. *Teratologies: A Cultural Study of Cancer.* London: Routledge, 1997. Print.

12 Materiality and Manipulation
Trauma, Narrative, and the Body in Anne Enright's *The Gathering*

Ulrike Tancke

Anne Enright's novel *The Gathering* focuses on recurring contemporary preoccupations: the fascination with trauma and the concern with storytelling. The protagonist, Veronica Hegarty, delves into her Irish Catholic family's past on a quest to find out the truth about her recently deceased brother Liam's sexual abuse by her grandmother's landlord at the age of nine as she was looking on. While this topical subject matter may be part of the reason why the novel has attracted considerable attention and even won the 2007 Man Booker Prize, *The Gathering* is more than just another story of a blighted childhood in the "mis lit" genre that fills the shelves of high street chain bookstores (cf. Barnes). Rather, the novel pursues a complex agenda, summarily contained in Veronica's seemingly contradictory statement on her journey into the past: "History is only biological—that's what I think. We pick and choose those facts about ourselves—where we come from and what it means" (Enright 162). This profoundly equivocal pair of sentences gives the cue to my discussion of *The Gathering*, as it contains the essence of the larger questions the novel raises. The passage initially equates history and biology, in other words, it puts on a par the material reality of human lives and the cognitive, if not imaginative processes of deriving meaning from human experience. At the same time, it highlights the selective interpretive operations at work in any human attempt to record and give meaning to the past. While this interest in the construction of history is in tune with the oft-repeated postmodern doctrines of the conflatability of history and stories and the unattainability of fixed meaning, situating history in biology goes against these very beliefs. It counterpoints the necessarily slippery nature of storytelling with the stable material basis of human affairs and thus moves beyond the common postmodern interventions. In effect, the novel points towards the inherent aporia of postmodern narratives: how can we reconcile the human inclination to storytelling with the tangible material reality of the body?

The novel's setup as a quest story-*cum*-trauma narrative is emblematic of this interrogative venture. From the very start, the novel's first-person narrator ostensibly sets up a quest plot—a search for "some ideal, forbidden, lost, or otherwise unreachable state or condition" (Murfin and Ray

446)—to reveal her problematic childhood memory, yet immediately undermines its fundamental impulse of revealing truth. Determined to unveil Liam's childhood trauma, Veronica states: "I would like to write down what happened in my grandmother's house the summer I was eight or nine, but I am not sure if it really did happen. I need to bear witness to an uncertain event. I feel it roaring inside me—this thing that may not have taken place" (Enright 1). This is a narrative voice which is unreliable from the very start, self-consciously drawing the reader's attention to the uncertainty of the event she says she only half remembers, and the murkiness of her own memory. Veronica is aware that the "truth" about the incident resides in its narrative (re-) production: "I do not know the truth, or I do not know how to tell the truth. All I have are stories, night thoughts, the sudden convictions that uncertainty spawns" (Enright 2). By aligning the "truth" with the imaginary process of storytelling, she questions the very concept of truth. In a sense, as this insight occurs in the novel's very first chapter, it puts into perspective the purpose of the novel as a whole. *The Gathering* is thereby set apart from the traditional conceptualisation of the genre as tracing the protagonist's gradual progress towards greater understanding, a clearer sense of self and a more coherent identity (cf. Watt 86).

Of course, abandoning these tenets is not a recent literary intervention. Rather, the passage must be read as a self-conscious nod towards the postmodern deconstruction of truth, the critique of identity and meaning and the disillusionment with conventional quest plots—concepts which have been widely endorsed by writers and literary critics ever since the poststructuralist turn. Yet, as we shall see, the novel does more than simply reiterate postmodernist assumptions about the inherently unreliable nature of any textual account of reality. It situates the impossibility to attain meaning and get to the truth as a condition that is inherently linked with the traumatising nature of the experiences that it deals in, and with the material nature and biological condition of human life and relationships, but also with the human impulse to tell stories and to diverge from a faithful account of events if this is deemed advantageous to manipulate others. While it plays with the postmodern catchphrase that stories are unreliable and telling the truth is impossible, *The Gathering* is situated at the very nexus at which postmodern credentials collapse and give way to an appreciation of the material dimensions of identity on which any attempt at meaning-making is necessarily based, and the novel thereby invites us to question the narrative structures on which this process is founded.

In order to fully grasp the complex manner in which the narrative proceeds, it is crucial to understand that the novel operates on two levels. The first level, Veronica's quest to find out and tell the truth about Liam's childhood abuse and her role in it, most immediately grabs the reader's attention because of the emotional shock value of its subject matter, and because it is the issue that the narrator emphasises in the very first chapter. Beneath this, however, is a second level, namely Veronica's underlying urge to establish a stable and coherent sense of self, which is intertwined with her inquiry into Liam's fate and her own past, and in which she negotiates especially her roles as a daughter, wife, and mother. This latter quest takes various forms, most notably her lengthy forays into the past as she reconstructs her grand-mother Ada's life, her musings on her mother, her memories of her childhood and adolescence, and her thoughts on her relationships with her husband and daughters. What is striking about this narrative setup is the persistent manner in which Veronica makes herself the centre of the various narratives strands that she weaves, even when—as is most prominently the case with Liam's abuse—the events she recounts are not primarily about herself. In this sense, the novel seems to literalise and take to their extreme the principal tenets of dominant contemporary theory of identity and narrative.

As Paul John Eakin argues, narrative—in the broadest sense of "talking about ourselves" (cf. Eakin 1–59)—is a fundamental, indispensable com-ponent of identity formation: in "talking about ourselves [. . .], we per-form a work of self-construction" (Eakin 2). Conversely, "[w]hen it comes to our identities, narrative is [. . .] a constituent part *of* self" (Eakin 2). More broadly, this observation can also be made about human experience as such, because "we organize our experience and our memory of human happenings mainly in the form or narrative—stories, excuses, myths, rea-sons for doing and not doing, and so on" (Bruner 4). According to Jerome Bruner, this process also has a reverse effect; that is, our perception comes to mirror the narrative structures commonly used to capture it: "just as our experience of the natural world tends to imitate the categories of familiar science, so our experience of human affairs comes to take the form of the narratives we use in telling about them" (Bruner 5).

While this may sound convincing enough—after all, there is something very reassuring about the idea that stories give meaning to our lives, and that our lives are, in fact, stories of their own—the latter point in particular also highlights the problems inherent in this approach. In response to the widespread belief that narrative is pervasive as regards identity formation, Galen Strawson draws attention to the dangers of narrative construction: "the Narrative tendency to look for story or narrative coherence in one's life is, in general, a gross hindrance to self-understanding: to a just, gen-eral, practically real sense, implicit or explicit, of one's nature" (Strawson 447).[1] This is because stories are, by nature, amenable to manipulation and falsification—human experience may not resemble the stock narratives we commonly believe in, and the attempt to make reality match the story may result in streamlining and misrepresenting that reality. In Strawson's words, "the more you recall, retell, narrate yourself, the further you risk moving away from accurate self-understanding, from the truth of your being" (Strawson 447).

The Gathering highlights this danger of the narrative approach to identity in a particularly salient fashion because it is a trauma narrative, which by definition refuses any straightforward integration into a coherent storyline. Susannah Radstone's broad definition of trauma underscores this point: trauma is an experience that is "elusive and impossible to grasp," and that frustrates "sense making and the assignment of meaning [and that hence] cannot be integrated into memory, but neither can [. . .] be forgotten" (Radstone 117). With its position outside of the "normal" processes of meaning-making, trauma foregoes any rational grasp and cognitive analysis. As a corporeally immediate experience, trauma cannot be adequately rendered in conventional narratives featuring a beginning, middle and end, but calls for narrative strategies and modes that include the body and its materiality (cf. Etherington 28; Vickroy 10).

Moreover, this inescapability of the human corporeal reality is valid beyond the domain of the trauma discourse. Trauma merely crystallises the inadequacies of the prevalent perception—central to Western culture since the antiquity, cemented by the Cartesian Enlightenment and embraced by much contemporary theory—of the material as a phenomenon outside of and apart from the self. This is the second point at which the novel asks us to rethink dominant critical perspectives: it highlights the necessity to understand materiality as a quality intrinsic to the self—as "embodied materiality," so to speak. This perspective:

> emphasises the difficulty, even impossibility, to separate the material and the spiritual, mind and matter. Such an embodied materiality performs us, as it were: we are at the mercy of an intricately complex organism of whose operations we are often not aware and which we are only now beginning to understand. (Müller-Wood 15)

Taking seriously this "embodied materiality" as the starting ground of any human activity means that we acknowledge the body as the basis from which we think. Human beings are a species whose bodies work according to the same principles than those of other animals, and their ability to reflect on their status as beings in the world "is in itself a material capacity, which we possess *because of* our bodies" (Müller-Wood 15). In other words, the body is the very precondition of any human attempts to transcend it—narrative, of course, being one way of moving beyond and leaving behind the material, while at the same time exposing the limitations inherent in the very attempt.

However, a particular variant of the mind versus body debate is at play in narratological theory: there is considerable controversy as to whether the body and narrative ought to be conceptualised antithetically, or in parallel, as mutually constitutive. According to the dominant mode of thought—bound up with the legacy of Cartesian dualism that pervades Western modernity—the body is seen as "whatever is outside of the narrative ordering of experience. [. . .] The body exerts demands that work against the kinds of cultural and intellectual construction inherent to narrative" (Punday 88–9). Yet there is also a reverse view, which claims that "the body itself can be the promoter of a story. The body situates a 'beginning' and after its course an 'end'" (Mangold 39). The fixed temporality of a life span, which the body cannot transcend, translates into a structured and reassuringly complete narrative formation. Rather than siding with either of these views, *The Gathering* situates the body in-between these theoretical positions: the body (especially the traumatised body) intrudes in and disrupts the narrative, it is also these disruptions—moments beyond narratorial control—that are central to the narrative and propel it forward. My subsequent analysis is fundamentally concerned with this duality, which is at the core of the novel's questioning of postmodern credentials and its alternative reworking of materiality as a foundation for human lives and their fictional rendition. In the following, I will chart the novel's textual strategies of exposing the complex interactions of narrative control and its opposite, surrendering or losing that control.

Set up as a quest plot combined with an account of traumatic experience, *The Gathering* exposes the hazards intrinsic to the narrative approach to human life and selfhood. With her focal position at the centre of the narrative, Veronica Hegarty crystallises the dangers of manipulation and misrepresentation at the heart of storytelling. This is visible early on in the novel, when she sets out to recover her grandmother Ada's story, which she returns to periodically throughout the novel. At the start of her retelling of Ada's past, Veronica explains her motivation to do so and embeds it in her primary quest, to find out the truth about Liam:

> if I want to tell Liam's story, then I have to start long before he was born. And, in fact, this is the tale that I would love to write: history is such a romantic place, with its jarveys and urchins and side-buttoned boots. If it would just stay still, I think, and settle down. If it would just stop sliding around in my head. (Enright 13)

This passage is emblematic of Veronica's approach to the past, and of her stance vis-à-vis her narrative as a whole. Her grandmother's love story is deliberately constructed as an antidote to Liam's abuse, which suggests that Ada's life will be rendered in romanticised terms. The sentimental vision of history in the following sentence, by which the past is reduced to the cutely diminutive notion of "jarveys and urchins and side-buttoned boots," is, of course, undercut straight away: history refuses to be fenced in by a comforting narrative, it cannot be streamlined or nailed down to a wished-for version of itself.

Subsequently, the narrative oscillates between Veronica's conscious assertion of the artificiality of her story and her presentations of past events as believable (and, this is the assumption, verifiable) facts. As she lurches into the story of Ada's initial encounter with her first suitor Lamb Nugent—later her landlord, who abuses Liam—Veronica self-consciously states that "[t]his is the moment I choose" (Enright 13). She takes up on this stance when, towards the end of the chapter, she reiterates the point that "[t]his is all *my* romance, of course" (Enright 21; emphasis added). It is significant that Veronica dubs Ada's story—or rather, her version of it—a "romance": she thereby evokes notions of fantasy and exoticism and explicitly relegates the story to the realm of wishful thinking. What is more, thus drawing attention to the subjective and, by implication, unreliable nature of her tale is a way of legitimising the act of storytelling: as she frames Ada's life story with these assertions, Veronica renounces any responsibility for the veracity of its content and the implications of truth or fiction—a gesture of letting herself off the hook, as it were.

At the same time, there are tentative indications that this disavowal of narrative responsibility may not work, or rather may be overridden by what could be called a usurpation of narrative responsibility. Looking at Ada's wedding photo, Veronica observes: "She has my feet. Or I have hers: long, with scraggly toes. Also the large-boned ankles and endless, flat shins that made me feel so gawky at school" (Enright 21). Biology—the unmistakeable effects of genes and inheritance—interferes with storytelling. The passage foregrounds a dimension of the narrative that has thus far been submerged: the inescapable impact of biology on human affairs, which no storytelling can eliminate and which therefore necessarily coexists with any attempt to exert narratorial control. This recognition is also marked by the curious change of perspective at the beginning of this passage: symbolically, Veronica has to yield her grasp on the narrative to the more powerful grip exerted by biological legacy. In such moments of narrative impasse, the novel unveils the essentially biological core of human consciousness and charts the conflicting impulses that ensue, to both accept biological conditions and strive to transcend them.

A version of this shift of narrative focus—the inevitable presence of biological givens—can be found in the frequent entry of the material into the narrative Veronica purports to control.[2] Such intrusions—not always in the sense of biological facts, but also in the form of references to physical objects or corporeal sensations—are detectable in multiple side remarks at various points in the novel. For instance, in the second chapter, when Veronica has come to her mother's house to break to her the news of Liam's death, the material reality of her surroundings intrudes on Veronica's account of her interaction with her mother and her grief: "The kitchen smells the same—it hits me in the base of the skull, very dim and disgusting, under the fresh, primrose yellow paint. [. . .] It makes me gag a little, and then I cannot smell it any more. It just is. The smell of us" (Enright 5). In one sense, with its physically intrusive interruption, the material threatens to undermine Veronica's control of her story, entering unwanted.

However, there is a sense in which the material can be read as a means of grounding her narrative, in spite of its initially negative connotations. This function as a reassuring, solidifying device is also at the core of passages such as the following:

> I walk to the far counter and pick up the kettle, but when I go to fill it, the cuff of my coat catches on the running tap and the sleeve fills with water. I shake out my hand, and then my arm, and when the kettle is filled and plugged in I take off my coat, pulling the wet sleeve inside out and slapping it in the air. (Enright 5)

While such passages may at first glance appear superfluously detailed and confusing in their frequency, I believe that to understand them as a strategy of grounding the narrative—and, by extension, the self that it constructs—is a fruitful angle from which to approach the interconnections between narrative and the material in *The Gathering*. Moreover, this angle allows for a broader perspective on how identity, narrative and materiality can be conceptualised, which points to an inclusive (rather than oppositional) understanding of these categories. Paradoxically, the material is both a threat to a solid sense of self and the very means by which the self can approach anything like a firm and rooted identity, and it is this duality which Veronica's narrative charts.

With its frequent allusions to the physical presence of bodies and objects, *The Gathering* prompts a reading along the lines of "embodied materiality." Beyond its noticeable preoccupation with material detail, in particular those parts of the novel that develop the primary level of the plot (Veronica's inquiry into her memory of Liam's abuse) are suffused with the corporeal in a noticeable and quantitatively predominant fashion. Tracing the physical and psychological impact of traumatic experience—most centrally, that of Veronica as a witness of Liam's abuse—these passages exemplify the centrality of materiality and the body in relation to trauma.

The most immediately recognisable instance of trauma, Liam's sexual abuse as a nine-year-old boy, is characterised by a disturbing corporeality which comes to dominate its narrative representation. Veronica's recall of the scene starts with her fiercely declared determination to acknowledge and reveal the truth about the past: "It is time to put an end to the shifting stories and the waking dreams. It is time to call an end to romance and just say what happened in Ada's house, the year that I was eight and Liam was barely nine" (Enright 142). And yet the depiction of the scene that follows—domestic life in Ada's home that Veronica remembers from holidays spent there as a child—initially smacks of a nostalgia for the past similar to her previous remarks about history as something sweetly reassuring, which, in effect, glosses over the disturbing emotional cruelty underneath the traditional family scenario. This is itself a first indication that the narrator does not succeed in "call[ing] an end to romance." It prepares the reader for the way in which Veronica gradually relinquishes narratorial control in her retrospective account of Liam's abuse. She accidentally witnessed the incident as she walked in on Liam forcibly masturbating Lamb Nugent; significantly, she slips back into the perspective of her eight-year-old self as she recounts the scene:

What struck me was the strangeness of what I saw, when I opened the door. It was as if Mr Nugent's penis, which was sticking straight out of his flies, had grown strangely, and flowered at the tip to produce the large and unwieldy shape of a boy, that boy being my brother Liam, who, I finally saw, was not an extension of the man's member, set down mysteriously on the ground in front of him, but a shocked [. . .] boy of nine, and the member not even that, but the boy's bare forearm, that made a bridge of flesh between himself and Mr Nugent. (Enright 143–4)

The naïve perception of the little girl has a dual effect: while it clearly registers the "wrongness" of the scene, it also attenuates its violent impact as it coats the image in the reassuring terms of a kind of fairy tale—somewhat mysterious, but ultimately unthreatening. Even the monstrosity of the exposed penis is alleviated as it is merely mistaken for Liam's arm creating a "bridge of flesh." With its slippage into a comparatively banal set of images, the passage outlines the workings of repression, immediately activated in order for the event not to even be hardwired in the girl's memory (cf. Luckhurst 8–11; Adami 12). Veronica's childhood self is reactivated as she recounts the scene, yet fails to connect with her adult self. With this separation of her chronologically distinct identities, the passage can be read as an example of the way in which "[t]rauma undoes the self by breaking the ongoing narrative, severing the connections among remembered past, lived present, and anticipated future" (Brison 41).

To extend the argument, Veronica's self-imposed quest to unearth the truth about Liam's abuse is a way of re-establishing her coherent self with the help of the narrative. Recovering from trauma is commonly identified with regaining narrative control: "Piecing together a self requires a working through, or remastering of, the traumatic memory that involves going from being the medium or object of someone else's (the torturer's) speech to being the subject of one's own" (Brison 48). In fact, rather than Veronica's memories unwittingly intruding into consciousness, the narrative oscillates between her conscious decision to "put an end to the shifting stories" (Enright 142) and falling prey to them. And yet, it is also clear that all she can do is replace the "shifting stories" of her memory with yet more stories—stories of the kind that assist her search for her self. This is all too visible in the paragraphs following Veronica's recall of the rape scene (which was already focalised through her, of course), in which her focus gradually shifts to her own life as she compares Lamb Nugent to different men that she has had abusive or at least dysfunctional relationships with and tries to link her memory of Liam's abuse with her own experience of desire (cf. Enright 144). The reason why Veronica never manages, as she says from the start, to clearly say what did happen to Liam is a result of the way in which it is a function of narrative in a double sense: her story is distorted due to the nature of the events she recounts, and also because it is part of a larger narrative of self-construction (even after her lengthy narrative forays into the past, she states: "I know that my brother Liam was sexually abused by Lambert Nugent. Or was *probably* sexually abused by Lambert Nugent" (Enright 224; emphasis added)).

This ambiguity is heightened towards the end of the novel, where Veronica voices blurred and confused memories which suggest that she, too, may have been abused by Lamb Nugent. Her snapshot memories of "the 'eye' of his penis" (Enright 221) and "Nugent's come spreading over my hand" (Enright 222) are consistently called in question by her own narrative gestures of casting doubt on the truth value of these thoughts: "This comes from a place where words and actions are mangled. It comes from the very beginning of things, and I cannot tell if it is true. Or I cannot tell if it is real" (Enright 221–2). In one sense, the corporeal nature of these memories is suggestive of a traumatic experience that foregoes expression via language and undermines the commonly assumed split between mind and matter by bringing back bodily sensations. At the same time, the passage relies on the reader's awareness of the ways in which Veronica consciously strives to render the events of her own and her family's life a coherent story of cause and effect. Thus she concludes her fragmentary memories of her own possible abuse by repeating the pattern of seeking straightforward answers: "I know he [Nugent] could be the explanation for all our lives" (Enright 224). She subsequently admits that things might be more complex than a simple sequence of cause and effect, with Nugent as perpetrator: "I know something more frightening still—that we did not have to be damaged by him in order to be damaged" (Enright 224). Disturbingly, this acknowledgement is undercut yet again as her line of argument channels back to Nugent immediately: "It was the air he breathed that did it for us. It was the way we were obliged to breathe his second-hand air" (Enright 224). Here Nugent again assumes the central explanatory function in Veronica's life story. As he is credited with a physically tangible effect, we simply cannot tell whether Veronica confronts us with traumatic memories that are beyond her conscious recall and traceable only corporeally, or whether her narrative is geared towards a deliberate, conscious imposition of blame.

The novel consistently charts this two-fold contingency of corporeal constraints on memory and the narrative manipulation working against it. Most strikingly, the passage following Veronica's recall of Liam's abuse reads as the narrative voice of the adult Veronica expressing her clear awareness of the mechanism by which her unwitting repression has distorted her memory of the abuse and has foreclosed any possibility of establishing retrospectively "what really happened":

> I am trying to remember what [Liam] looked like, but it is hard to recall the face of your brother as a child. And even though I know it is *true* that this happened, I do not know if I have the true picture in my mind's eye [. . .] I think it might be false memory, because there is a

terrible tangle of things that I have to fight through to get to it, in my head. And also because it is unbearable. (Enright 144)

While Veronica is able to articulate the unreliable nature of her younger self's memory, she also perpetuates the evasiveness with which she then dealt with the incident. The mental images she recovers are couched in the same terms as her perceptions at the time, producing the ameliorating, if not euphemistic visions of a "peculiar growth" and a "bridge of flesh." Yet, strikingly, Veronica attaches the catchphrase of "false memory" to her experience, which suggests her awareness of popular discourses surrounding the issue of childhood sexual abuse in which she is consciously placing herself (cf. Luckhurst 73). Thus, at the same time as she relinquishes responsibility for her narrative and has to succumb to the material immediacy of the traumatic experience, she also seeks to control it and assert herself as an agent of her narrative self-construction.

In order to fully grasp the implications of this dual impulse, the first train of thought—Veronica's surrender of narrative authority—requires closer examination. What her remark about the "terrible tangle of things" suggests is that the "truth" in a factual sense is not really at issue here. Rather, Veronica expresses the unsettling nature of traumatic experience: what marks an event as traumatic is precisely the fact that it resists being disentangled, categorised and thereby explained. Trauma is essentially "unbearable"; as a result, the ostensive quest plot that Veronica sets up is undermined by her immediate declaration of its futility. This thwarted quest, however, also opens up other ways of conceptualising narrative and identity that do not transcend, but start from the body. Veronica's retrospective account of the abuse and her coping strategies suggest such an "embodied" narrative. Thinking back to her girlhood self, she muses: "I think you know everything at eight. But maybe I am wrong. You know everything at eight, but it is hidden from you, sealed up, in a way you have to cut yourself open to find" (Enright 147). This violent imagery is indicative of the corporeal immediacy of the traumatic incident, but also of the violence involved in its retrieval. It dovetails with the way in which biology is, in fact, crucial in another respect: as the narrative depiction of Veronica's witnessing of the abuse scene suggests, trauma has a manifest corporeal dimension, not just for the victim who is physically abused, but also for the witness (cf. Felman and Laub 1–5, 57–74). Her memories are predominantly physical—she remembers the cold of the room, the smells, which she has imported from the moment as "the smell of things going wrong" (Enright 146), and both the adult Veronica writing about the incident and the girl who witnessed it react with physical urges that are disgusting and disturbing by ordinary standards. The adult Veronica remembers (or at least believes she remembers): "I closed the door and ran to the toilet upstairs, with an urge to pee and look at the pee coming out; to poke or scratch or rub when I was finished, and smell my fingers afterwards. At least, I assume that this is what I did if I was eight years old" (Enright 146). Revisiting the scene in the narrative present, she says: "I pause as I write this, and place my own hand over my face, and lick the thick skin of my palm with a girl's tongue. I inhale. The odd comforts of the flesh. Of being me" (Enright 146). Again, her adult self merges with her adolescent one ("a girl's tongue"), suggesting a blurring of identities and an unsettling chronological indeterminacy. Yet there is a sense of continuity in spite of the unreliability of her thoughts and her memory. Significantly, it is the body (rather than the mind or her thoughts) that provides comforts and a reliable sense of self. At this moment, far from being external to or even disruptive of the narrative rendition of the experience, the body fulfils a meaning-giving, ordering function (cf. Damasio, *Descartes* 134–5, 141–3).

This is where my earlier observations on the simultaneity of Veronica relinquishing and asserting control of the narrative dovetail to create a network of mutually determining conditions. Ostensibly, in her narrative, Liam's abuse dominates Veronica's sense of self; at the same time, her sense of self dominates her narrative rendition of the event. Similarly, her search for the truth is constructed as superior to the material; yet the material continually thwarts her quest. And lastly, her quest for the truth about Liam's abuse overshadows her inquiry into her own sense of self, both for Veronica herself within the narrative, and for the reader. She foregrounds Liam's trauma in order to divert attention away from the fact that the sources of her pain, guilt and insecurity lie elsewhere. The traumatic intrusion of the body is indicative of this displacement—or rather, of its futility—and at the same time provides the nexus where these two interlocking levels of narrative meet.

The second, underlying narrative level, Veronica's struggle to establish a coherent sense of self, is most significantly played out in relation to her mother and birth family. Here, too, Veronica is caught in a double bind: while she acknowledges the biological ties that continue to emotionally bind her to her mother, she also engages in a process of storytelling through which she creates her own identity and self-image, consciously styling herself as the offspring of the clichéd Irish Catholic family. This simultaneity of biological inevitability and narrative construction permeates Veronica's portrayal of her relationship with her mother. Visiting her with the news of Liam's death, Veronica gives vent to her disillusionment with her mother. At first glance, her anger seems to be bound up with a stereotypically Irish Catholic family dynamic:

> My mother had twelve children and—as she told me one hard day—seven miscarriages. [. . .] Even so, I haven't forgiven her any of it. I just can't. [. . .] I do not forgive her the whole tedious litany of Midge, Bea, Ernest, Stevie, Ita, Mossie, Liam, Veronica, Kitty, Alice and the twins, Ivor and Jem. [. . .] I don't forgive her those dead children either. The way she didn't even keep a notebook [. . .] No, when it comes down to

it, I do not forgive her the sex. The stupidity of so much humping. Open
and blind. Consequences, Mammy. *Consequences*. (Enright 7–8)

In Veronica's angry tirade, blame-laying is almost a mantra (in the full
passage, the anaphoric "I don't forgive her" returns even more often). In
a sense, Veronica creates a "tedious litany" of her own as she depicts hers
as the stereotyped Irish Catholic childhood, in which she felt deprived, if
not of actual sustenance, then at least of emotional nurture, intellectual
stimulation, cultural sophistication and social standing. And yet, precisely
because of the clichéd nature of her perception, it is easy to overlook the
more complex dimensions of Veronica's outburst. This is very obviously an
exercise in self-construction: rather than genuinely examining her mother's
decisions and motivations, Veronica consistently returns to her own point
of view ("I don't forgive her"). Her self-centred claim on her mother's past
is also behind the curious role reversal Veronica stages between mother
and daughter: the final admonition in the quoted passage ("Consequences,
Mammy. *Consequences*") sounds like a mother's standard nagging, and the
passage in its full length contains oddly diminutive interspersions such as
"My sweetheart mother. My ageless girl" (Enright 8). At first glance, such
expressions of endearment seem to be out of tune with the scathing criticism that Veronica directs at her mother. The apparent ambiguity begins
to make sense, however, if it is viewed as part of the narrator's deliberate
construction of her family as a cliché and of her mother as an immature,
irresponsible person. At the same time, the discourse of family and motherhood is nevertheless intrinsically shaped by the intrusion of the biological
ties that continue to bind Veronica to her mother and family. This is the
reason why Veronica can, without contradiction, on the one hand feel emotionally and physically bound to her family and express this in no uncertain
terms, and on the other hand poignantly declare that she herself and her
relatives bear "the wound of family," and that "being part of a family is the
most excruciating possible way to be alive" (Enright 243).

The corporeal dimension of the "wound of family," which is at the core
of its unbreakable spell, becomes most drastically visible when Veronica
describes her own and her mother's reaction to Liam's untimely death. Just
as her mother responds to the news of Liam's death with "a grief that is biological, idiot, timeless" (Enright 11), Veronica herself reacts with a physical
immediacy which seems to replace the emotional dimension of mourning
with unmediated, abject corporeality: "I am a trembling mess from hip
to knee. There is a terrible heat, a looseness in my innards that makes
me want to dig my fists between my thighs. It is a confusing feeling—
somewhere between diarrhoea and sex—this grief that is almost genital"
(Enright 7). The disturbing identification of grief with a breakdown of corporeal boundaries collapses any boundaries between cerebrally mediated
responses to an unsettling event, and instinctual emotional reaction as a
corporeal mechanism (cf. Damasio, *Descartes* 280). The terminological

parallel that Veronica creates between her description of her own grief and her mother's is indicative of a further merging, between her mother and herself. With this collapse of boundaries on various levels, which is substantially related to the fusion of the corporeal and cognition, the novel reiterates the point that family relations are, first and foremost, biological, and hence cannot be shaped at will.

Predictably, this insight, too, is subject to narrative distortion in Veronica's project of self-constitution. Her depiction of her relationship with her own family, her husband Tom and daughters Rebecca and Emily, is set up as a conscious and self-reflexive exercise in storytelling. This becomes obvious when Veronica recalls a lengthy car journey during which her daughters questioned her, with typical children's stubbornness, about how she and Tom became a couple. In her answers, Veronica consciously creates a fairy-tale version of events, deliberately manipulating the truth ("This is probably not true, but they like it," "Which is true—but not in the way they might expect" [Enright 69]) in favour of a streamlined tale of boy-meets-girl complete with "happily ever after." Consciously diverting from the real course of events, she omits less palatable truths, such as the fact that Tom had yet to end his current live-in relationship to be with her, and that the initial sexual attraction she felt for "the curve to his top lip" and "the dent in his chest as he stooped" (Enright 70) triggered in her the irrational conviction that "he did not belong to her [the other woman], [. . . but that] he belonged to me" (Enright 69).

Beyond the obvious reason that this is a version of events told to befit small children's range of understanding, Veronica is aware of the fact that she is telling the glossed-over story as much for her daughters' sake as for her own. The real course of events signals another intrusion of the corporeal—in the form of sexual desire—into her life story, and this corporeality involves "ruthlessness" (Enright 70) towards the woman Tom was living with, even, metaphorically, "a spill of blood" (Enright 70). It triggers a sense of guilt that has to be narratively remedied:

> Because we [Tom and Veronica] each knew we had met our match, [. . .] we knew we would put it all right one day with this: two beautiful daughters in two beautiful bedrooms. Tall, no doubt, and clever. Who would attend their destined private school, and who would each be mapped, discussed, mulled over, well loved. (Enright 70)

Once again, stories—in this case, the narrative of cosy, comfortable middle-class prosperity—are employed to contain the uncontrollable nature of biology. As this passage indicates, Veronica uses the narrative of her family to construct the story of her self, turning her daughters into elements that can be functionalised for the sake of her own sense of self. This narrative force is literalised in a disturbing side remark when Veronica almost enforces her daughter Rebecca's affection to respond to her own need for tenderness and cosy mother-daughter closeness: "I get a daughter on the sofa and manhandle her into loving me a little" (Enright 38). The physical force with which Veronica manipulates Rebecca's feelings parallels the figurative violence she exerts on the narrative in order to present herself as a model middle-class mother. Enforcing her daughter's affection is a means for Veronica to reassure herself of her self-image as the loving mother of a close-knit nuclear family, in deliberate contrast to what she perceives as her own mother's emotional absence and inaccessibility. Yet again, the material returns, for all Veronica's efforts of self-construction: her "manhandling" of Rebecca suggests that family relations inevitably boast an undercurrent of violence that has basic corporeal effects and is relentlessly perpetuated.

Veronica's account of her relationship with her husband takes this intrusion of the material to its extreme. From the start, her difficulties in her marriage—ostensibly due to Tom's long working hours and their continual squabbles over household chores and child-rearing duties—are consistently presented in corporeal terms: "There he is now, in our bed, still alive. The air goes into him and the air comes out. His toenails grow. His hair turns silently grey. [. . .] And I don't know what is wrong with me [. . .], but I do not believe in my husband's body any more" (Enright 73). Veronica even goes so far as to project the disturbing uncontrollability of the material onto Tom's body. Waking up to him lying prostrate on his back and noticing his erection, her thoughts spiral towards the potentially destructive underbelly of desire: "the thing my husband is fucking in his sleep [. . .] might be me. Or it might not be me. [. . .] it might be a child—his own daughter, why not? There are men who would do anything, asleep, and I am not sure what stops them when they wake. I do not know how they draw a line" (Enright 134). What Veronica acknowledges here is the capacity for violence that is innate to human beings and that potentially erupts at random. Earlier on in her narrative, in the context of her recall of the abuse scene, Veronica comments on Tom's sexuality in a similar vein: "This is the way his desire runs. It runs close to hatred. It is sometimes the same thing" (Enright 145). It is crucial that this observation should occur in relation to the allegedly traumatic events of witnessing Liam's abuse: this parallel situates trauma within the banal, the everyday, ordinary relationships. What this means, in effect, is that the genuinely traumatising dimensions of human experience are not primarily or exclusively the extraordinary and instantly recognisable ones, but the violence, pain, and suffering humans inflict on one another on a day-to-day, even trivial basis. Violence is a capacity inherent to any human being, it cannot be safely projected onto easily identifiable perpetrators. Significantly, however, Veronica voices this disturbing insight in relation to another person, and hence is able to keep at a safe remove from her own sense of self. As her narrative rendition of her feelings towards her daughters has revealed, however, it is not a capacity that can be controlled by means of narrative construction of a reassuring storyline and hence easily diverted away from the self. Rather, the attempt to transcend the basic materiality of the human may work in such a way as to deceive oneself about the violence innate to any human individual.

The novel's final chapter charts this double bind as Veronica, waiting at Gatwick Airport, contemplates travelling to some random exotic destination rather than returning to Dublin and to her family. Her confused train of thoughts captures the peculiar nature of family ties: "I have run away from my daughter. I have left her behind. But there is no leaving the girls, they are always with me" (Enright 257). In a sense, Veronica's quest has come full circle: she started her narrative with the professed aim of disentangling her family's history and, by extension, releasing some of its oppressive grip on her, yet at the end she is forced to realise that the very premises of her quest were futile: "I think we make for peculiar refugees, running from our own blood, or towards our own blood; pulsing back and forth along ghostly veins that wrap the world in a skein of blood" (Enright 258). Veronica here clearly voices the point that her narrative has consistently made: that there is a primary biological core to human existence that cannot be overcome. Kinship is a matter of blood, not conscious decision. At the same time, as the remainder of the chapter suggests, her narrative fails to fully register this point—or maybe this failure is in itself the novel's very essence: the final paragraphs construct a sugar-coated ending that verges on the unconvincing. Veronica's interior monologue painfully records her urge to impose narrative coherence on her memory; and while she does acknowledge her inability to do so, this coherent identity seems to be the sense of self that she aspires to. The phrase "If I could" punctuates her thoughts (Enright 260), poignantly exposing the underlying awareness that there is no such thing as coherent memory as a self-explanatory tool, however much we may desire it.

Veronica's off-the-cuff suggestion to have another baby, in her imaginary conversation with Tom, at first glance smacks of a regressive naivety that is hard to swallow: "A boy. Hey, Tom, let's have this next baby. Just this one. The one whose name I already know. Oh, go on. It'll cheer you up no end" (Enright 260). The consciously ironic stance of this passage, conveyed by the childishly enthusiastic phrases, cannot obscure the bleak truth luring underneath: there is no escape from the corporeal ties of family. The imaginary baby boy's name Veronica already knows—it will be Liam, we can guess, thus perpetuating the succession of thwarted Hegarty lives that Liam's fate exemplifies.

The novel's final sentences are equally ambiguous. Veronica explicitly situates herself within the quest that her narrative has self-consciously set off to trace: "I have been falling into my own life, for months. And I am about to hit it now" (Enright 261). On the surface, these sentences convey a sense of closure, the search for meaningful and coherent identity coming to an end. While the image of "falling into my own life" initially suggests a reassuring identity of the self and its outward conditions, at a closer look this is a profoundly disturbing image. The imagery of "falling" and "hit[ing]" has an obviously violent and destructive dimension, suggesting that to acknowledge the conditions of one's own life requires a brutal honesty that does not shy away from the disconcerting realities of biological power, violence, and traumatic memory.

Thus, with its complex setup and interlocking concerns, *The Gathering* makes a fundamental point (or two related ones) about human identity. At this point I would like to return to Veronica's curious statement on history that I used as a starting point for my analysis: "History is only biological—that's what I think. We pick and choose the facts about ourselves—where we come from and what it means" (Enright 162). The novel suggests that the gist of this seemingly contradictory observation is that human life *is* and *is not* mere biology, constantly manipulated by the attempt to deliberately mould biological givens to fit the stories we tell about ourselves. It communicates this ambiguous attitude towards our material selves: we tend to approach the material with disgust and rejection and seek to transcend it, although we are aware of the futility of any such endeavour. And yet it is also the material that provides a firm grounding and a reliable core of selfhood. A similar ambiguity accrues to narrative: it is a necessary and welcome tool for self-reliant identity formation, and we tend to rely on narrative structures to give meaning and coherence to our lives. At the same time, narrative is fundamentally unreliable, manipulable, and hence beyond our control. Creating such quandaries, *The Gathering* suggests that human beings are inevitably caught in these double binds, leaving us with a sense of humility in the awareness that, ultimately, the stories of our lives *are* and *are not* ours to tell.

NOTES

1. Strawson uses the term "Narrative" (capitalised) to refer to those strands of theory which regard narrativity as the defining marker of human identity.
2. In my usage the material denotes the external object-world, whereas the body refers to the human organism. Both terms are, of course, related in that they both refer to "matter," but the body cannot be wholly externalised as it is always bound up with the consciousness of the person it helps constitute.

REFERENCES

Adami, Valentina. *Trauma Studies and Literature: Martin Amis's Time's Arrow As Trauma Fiction.* Frankfurt: Peter Lang, 2008. Print.

Barnes, Anthony. "Mis Lit: Misery is Book World's Biggest Boom Sector." *The Independent,* 4 March 2007. Web. 6 June 2010. http://www.independent.co.uk/arts-entertainment/books/news/mis-lit-misery-is-book-worlds-biggest-boom-sector-438812.html.

Brison, *Susan* J. "Trauma Narratives and the Remaking of the Self." *Acts of Memory: Cultural Recall in the Present.* Eds. Mieke Bal, Jonathan Crewe, and Leo Spitzer. Hanover, NH: University Press of New England, 1999. 39–54. Print.

Bruner. Jerome. "The Narrative Construction of Reality." *Critical Inquiry* 18.1 (1991): 1–21. Print.

Damasio, Antonio R. *Descartes' Error. Emotion, Reason and the Human Brain.* New York: Grosset/Putnam, 1994. Print.

Eakin, Paul John. *Living Autobiographically. How We Create Identity in Narrative.* Ithaca, NY: Cornell University Press, 2008. Print.

Enright, Anne. *The Gathering.* New York: Black Cat, 2007. Print.

Etherington, Kim. "Trauma, the Body and Transformation." *Trauma, the Body and Transformation: A Narrative Inquiry.* Ed. Kim Etherington. London: Jessica Kingsley Publishers, 2003. 22–38. Print.

Felman, Shoshana, and Dori Laub. *Testimony: Crises of Witnessing in Literature, Psychoanalysis, and History.* London: Routledge, 1992. Print.

Luckhurst, Roger. *The Trauma Question.* London: Routledge, 2008. Print.

Mangold, Manuela. "The Body's Twist: How Does the Body Construct a Story?" *Picturing America: Trauma, Realism, Politics and Identity in American Visual Culture.* Ed. Antje Dallmann, Reinhard Isensee and Philipp Kneis. Frankfurt: Peter Lang, 2007. 37–48. Print.

Müller-Wood, Anja. "Being Me and *Being Dead*: Jim Crace's Embodied Materialism." *"Hello, I Say, It's Me": Contemporary Reconstructions of Self and Subjectivity.* Ed. Jan Kucharzewski, Stefanie Schäfer and Lutz Schowalter. Trier: Wissenschaftlicher Verlag Trier, 2009, 13–31. Print.

Murfin, Ross, and Supryia M. Ray. *The Bedford Glossary of Critical and Literary Terms.* New York: Bedford/St. Martin's, 3rd ed. 2009. Print.

Punday, Daniel. *Narrative Bodies: Towards a Corporeal Narratology.* Basingstoke: Palgrave Macmillan, 2003. Print.

Radstone, Susannah. "The War of the Fathers: Trauma, Fantasy, and September 11." *Trauma at Home: After 9/11.* Ed. Judith Greenberg. Lincoln, NE: University of Nebraska Press, 2003. 117–23. Print.

Strawson, Galen. "Against Narrativity." *Ratio (New Series)* 17.4 (2004): 428–52. Print.

Vickroy, Laurie. *Trauma and Survival in Contemporary Fiction.* Charlottesville, VA: University of Virginia Press, 2002. Print.

Watt, Ian. *The Rise of the Novel: Studies in Defoe, Richardson and Fielding* (1957). London: Pimlico, 2000. Print.

13 Queer Early Modern Temporalities and the Sexual Dystopia of Biography and Patronage in Jeremy Reed's *The Grid*

Goran Stanivukovic

Published in 2008, *The Grid*, a novel by British novelist, essayist, poet, and biographer Jeremy Reed belongs to the genre of post-AIDS fiction. That fiction imagines homosexuality after medical advances in the treatment of HIV/AIDS in the industrial world have changed the way we think about HIV/AIDS, no longer as a disease but as a controlled condition that allows an HIV-stricken body to live a long life, possibly even without developing AIDS. *The Grid* is also another instance of Reed's rewriting of history as erotic past. In previous novels like *Boy Caesar* (2004), which fictionalises the sexual life of the young Roman emperor Heliogabalus, and *Dorian* (1997), which reimagines the sexual afterlife of Dorian Gray, Reed revises imperial and literary history, respectively, as fictions of homosexuality. He stylises the intersection of history and the male body in poetry as well. In a series of historical sonnets entitled "Byzantine Sonnets," included in the collection *Engaging Form*, Reed's subject is the fall of Constantinople to the Turks. He transforms the opulence of Byzantine ornamentation into contemporary camp poetics and juxtaposes the destructive masculinity of "the blood shrieking" Turks with the anti-militant masculinity of the castrati, the new heroes since "vasectomy makes them into athletes,/gold-dust sprinkling their armpits and their feet" (130). Reed experiments with gender, sexuality, and history in different literary forms by reconfiguring and altering the definitions of these forms.

By taking up the novel as the main form of his experimentation with gender and literary representation, Reed turns historical fiction around and makes sexual difference a challenge to history and to the writing about history. In his novels, the homosexual subject becomes the figure around which Reed's narrative art rethinks the relationship between history, society, and masculinity. In historical fiction: "History is other, and the present is familiar. The historian's job is often to explain transition from other to familiar. The historical novel similarly explores the dissonance between then and now, making the past both recognizable but simultaneously unfamiliar" (de Groot, *Consuming* 217). *The Grid*, however, stylises the past as a familiar place and erases the dissonance between then and now, becoming an anti-historical novel. This kind of novel rejects the idea of the future as "fatal repetition" (Davis and Funke 13) of the past, presenting a future in which the significance of time to transform the perception of sexual expression from the past is evident in how time has transformed both history and sexual identity. The protagonists, Billy (previously William Shakespeare) and Kit (previously Christopher Marlowe) are transposed from Elizabethan to futuristic London. In his rediscovery of the past, Reed's writing presents us with a fictionalised history in which past repression resurfaces in a radical present.[1] "In English studies," Jonathan Dollimore maintains, "there has always been an association of the Renaissance and the modern" (*Sexual* 23). That association is the subject of this chapter. Yet the purpose is neither to argue that the Renaissance is the "origin of the present" nor that the Renaissance is something "from which the present has declined" (Dollimore, *Sexual* 23), but to suggest that the Renaissance and the modern share similar forms of sexual dissent which allows us to look at each period from a new but shared angle, as one erotic time.

The Grid is a novel of shared time.[2] It is both a fictional account of Elizabethan London and a revisionary biography of some of its most prominent citizens. It juxtaposes post-AIDS Britain with England before the notion of sexuality was formed in the culture, in the way in which we understand it today. Thus Joseph Bristow reminds us that "the contemporary perspectives from which we view sexuality have for the most part arisen in the past century" (3). The narrative of *The Grid* looks both backward, towards the sexual subculture of sixteenth-century London, and forward, towards a futuristic dystopia of gay sex and identity, and of nation and politics. The London of Reed's novel is a metropolis about to implode. For Kit, London "was a city he felt certain would disappear in his lifetime from massive terrorist reprisals" (196). *The Grid* reacts not only against "objective" history but also against both biography and the historical novel as literary genres which gain in popularity every day. Reed rejects the historical versions of Marlowe's murder by Ingram Frazer on the 30th of May 1593 and makes the historical Shakespeare an accomplice in it. He creates two aliases for the two Elizabethan dramatists. In Reed's London, Billy has sex with Kit. Although the union of these two figures appears incongruous even to the narrator himself, the conviction that Kit and Christopher Marlowe were one person and that deep inside himself Kit carried the "psychic scar of Marlowe's death" (107) remains a central point of identification in the novel.

Yet the story of this identification is neither simple nor direct. In reconfiguring Marlowe's life as Kit's, Reed is also reconstructing, in Kit's mind, the last days of Marlowe's life before his assassination. Reed turns the two rivals of the Elizabethan stage world into erotic partners within the homosexual subculture of futuristic London. He also has Kit imagine that Shakespeare killed Marlowe over a small matter although this is ultimately not confirmed in the novel—or in history. In a moment of fictional brilliance, Reed becomes Kit too: just as Kit himself is reworking the history for his play about Shakespeare's role in the murder of Marlowe, so Reed's creative mind revisits the same history in the process of reworking it for his novel in which the death of a famous playwright is inextricable from the sexual charge that brought it on. Reed transforms the recorded historical rumours of "Marlowe's profligacy and reckless daring" (76), and a figure with "an interest in atrocity" (88), into a plot where literary rivalry turns into sexual partnership, plot in which Kit was ready to accept the idea that Marlowe, "far from being an alias for Shakespeare, may have been killed by his colleague out of jealousy" (76). The thin line that separates the sexual from the creative in this fiction is best illustrated in Kit's idea about the fatal murder in Deptford: "His theory was that all gay murders were essentially one murder, motivated by the killer seeing what he so disliked and feared in himself evident in another" (49). Specular abjection that so often defines relationships between gay men thus has a fictional equivalent in *The Grid* in the narrative in which the coming together of Billy and Kit is imagined as being inseparable from the competition in which they were embroiled as Shakespeare and Marlowe in the cut-throat world of Elizabethan theatre.

From the moment in the novel when Shakespeare features as Marlowe's double, the narrative of murder and sexual ecstasy intersects with the one of healing from AIDS and cruising. Whilst the actual sexual bond between Shakespeare and Marlowe has never been the subject of a mainstream biography of these two playwrights, the literary influence of Marlowe on Shakespeare has been well documented.[3] For example, the character of the Jewish usurer Barabas, from Marlowe's *The Jew of Malta* may have influenced its counterpart Shylock in *The Merchant of Venice*. The relationship of *Richard II* to *Edward II* is, Jonathan Bate argues, "so obvious that is it not very interesting" (113). It is possible, too, that Marlowe might have had a hand in Parts 2 and 3 of the early chronicle play *Henry VI*. And in the early comedy *As You Like It*, Shakespeare alludes to both the murder of Marlowe over a bill (reckoning) in a tavern in Deptford and to a verse in Barabas's opening monologue in *The Jew of Malta* ("Infinite riches in a little room" 1.1.37), in the jester Touchstone's line which reflects on Marlowe as "the dead shepherd": "it strikes a man more dead than a great reckoning in a little room" (3.2.13).[4]

One of the textual links between Part II of *Henry VI* and Marlowe's play *The Massacre at Paris* is of particular interest for the discussion in this chapter. In the second scene of Act 4 in Shakespeare's chronicle play, the rebel Jack Cade has Emmanuel, the Clerk of Chatham hung "with his pen and inkhorn about his neck" (2.4.109), only because he is literate ("I have been so well brought up that I can write my name" 4.2.105). For Bate, the murdered Clerk is "Shakespeare's first portrait of the artist as a young man" (123). The idea of the murdered poet may have come from Marlowe, Bate contends, where the Duke of Guise has the rhetorician Petrus Ramus stabbed because of his modernisation of logic and rhetoric, his attack on Aristotelian scholasticism (Scene 9, 40–9).[5] Bate considers the murdered Clerk "a Shakespearean self-portrait" (124), just as he sees a self-portrait of

Marlowe in the murdered rhetorician. At one point in this scene, Ramus's friend, Taleus, is described by Retes, as "Ramus's bedfellow" (scene 9, 12). The word "bedfellow" can in some early modern contexts be associated with same-sex eroticism. At this point Bate's argument sheds light on our debate about Reed's method of revising early modern history by homo-eroticising it. Bate makes his own version of fiction about his critical point about the deaths of self-portraits of Shakespeare and Marlowe as dead artists, and the exchange with Ramus and Taleus: "Imagine the character [Taleus] turning against Catholicism as a result of the assassination of his lover [Ramus]—he then becomes the homosexual who slips away from a near-encounter with death and lives on to witness in his drama against the barbarities of Catholicism (and in his life to assist in the suppression of Catholicism by means of his participation in Sir Thomas Walsingham's secret service)" (124). (Walsingham was Marlowe's patron.) No other pair of Elizabethan dramatists has given rise to so much critical speculation about the intertwining of the personal and the professional as the Marlowe-Shakespeare pair. By intertwining the inseparability of imagination of these two dramatists with the inseparability of one sexual body from another, Reed's novel casts a backward glance on the notions of literary influence and creativity as something that is erotically charged.

Reed's novel translates the "indeterminacy and mobility of the past" (Hackett 243) into a story about sexual acts, desires, and bodies in contact. By using sex and the erotic body to redefine a historical period, Reed makes homosexuality and temporality the primary elements in a futuristic anti-historical novel. The plot involving the sexual relationship between Shakespeare and Marlowe unfolds from within a narrative about the future of AIDS in a futuristic society. Within that futuristic society, Reed reanimates material traces of Elizabethan London as a place offering itself to seedy sexuality: "Marlowe's pink house was a rank urinal in Shoreditch, a constricted arena of sexual conflict, marble-slabbed like a mortuary" (77). The camp aesthetics of Marlowe's south London residence blends death and desire, as the spectre of the death of AIDS hovers over the scenes of gay sex in sordid places. Post-AIDS fiction imagines different ways of being in the body and in time, and Reed expands the limits of that fiction. The irony within Reed's futuristic dystopia is that London, a place where the annihilation of AIDS is imagined, is also the place that symbolises the annihilation of the culture that has produced the permanent cure for AIDS.

The Grid transforms the 1590s London of dramatic competition, zealous quest for patronage, political machinations, and ruthless politics at court into a place where multiculturalism, terrorism, AIDS, sex, urban cohesion, and political order, have exploded and acquired new meanings. Gone is the old world of new technology and democracy and a new London of terrorism and chaos has emerged. Reed also shatters the idea of the Bard as the iconic figure of English culture. The cultural capital embodied by Shakespeare is redefined when the Bard acquires a new life as a sexual being. Reed's

London is no longer a burgeoning city of courtiers and foreign merchants, but of outlaws brought to life from their Elizabethan obscurity. One of those is Nick, the Elizabethan Nicholas Skeres, who most of his life was drawn by the underworld and who "found it natural to be in the company of rent boys" (120–1). In Reed's London, he is undergoing hypnotherapy at The Grid, a minor role which has replaced the major and shady one he had in Elizabethan London where he was "an intelligencer" for Sir Francis Walsingham, the principal secretary to, and Spymaster for, Queen Elizabeth, turned into a "dodgy broker [. . .] a financier [. . .] whose criminal sexuality had taken him into yards, back rooms and cottages by the river," and a shady figure implicated in the murder of Christopher Marlowe. (120). The leap from the historical Walsingham, who was an ambiguous political figure associated with espionage and who used the methods of dubious morality to engineer the downfall of Mary Queen of Scots, to the Walsingham of *The Grid*, is small, as the system of his operation remains the same as in the historical past from where he comes into Reed's fiction.[6]

In addition to reacting against academic biographies of Shakespeare, *The Grid* also counters the kind of fiction in which gay lives are normalised within middle-class culture. In particular, Reed's novel is a reaction against the elision of sexuality, and especially queerness, in biographies of Shakespeare. Modern biographers of Shakespeare, from Samuel Schoenbaum's best modern biography of Shakespeare onwards, have avoided tackling the subject of Shakespeare's sexual life, let alone identity. The absence of evidence and the general disinterest of most biographers, writing from within the mainstream academic field of biographical writing which is often ruled by middle-class morality, in matters of intimacy are some of the reasons for this lack of interest in sexuality. Occasionally, biographers turn to Shakespeare's works for clues about their subject's erotic life, but they only end up exposing the unreliability of fiction as evidence for the argument about Shakespeare's sexuality. At best, measured speculation is as far as a biographer will go, as Stephen Greenblatt does in his version of the life of Shakespeare, in which he speculates about Shakespeare's sexual proclivities by reading his erotic poetry as an index of it. Yet, as one of the best Elizabethan scholars of the second half of the twentieth century, F. P. Wilson remarked (in a footnote) when writing about Shakespeare, "some kinds of indirect evidence are stronger than direct" (54). There is, of course, a difference between indirect (and historical) evidence and literary evidence, but Wilson's comment leaves the door open for a flexible and imaginative use of evidence from the larger historical context of the world which Shakespeare inhabited and for a creative re-envisaging of the silences in the life of the national literary icon. Wilson's remark indirectly creates an opening through which Reed's novel arrives on the scene of biographical writing with the force of conviction available to fiction only.

Reed rewrites the biographies of Marlowe and Shakespeare by reimagining the historical milieu of artistic patronage and the power it exercised upon those who sought patronage. The two playwrights, like their contemporaries, depended on patronage for their success and livelihood. Rather than disavowing the "homosexual" past of these two literary figures, Reed takes up the unspoken from historiography, Elizabethan homosexuality, and turns it into the defining dimension of the future. The meeting of the temporal and the sexual acquires power in Reed's fiction in "the queer ability to bond affectively with the past" (Castiglia and C. Reed 23). Reed's novel rediscovers the Elizabethan era of viscous politics by turning its alleged homosexual underground into the daily lives and nocturnal perversions of Elizabethan men of power and of letters.

In Reed's avant-garde novel, the erotic meaning of the past is sustained, transmitted, and transformed into a homosexual future. *The Grid* fictionalises what Elizabeth Freeman has postulated theoretically about the point where queer and temporality "touch one another," in launching the project of queer temporality. "If we reimagine," Freeman writes, "'queer' as a set of possibilities produced out of temporal and historical difference, or see the manipulation of time as a way to produce bodies and relationalities . . . we encounter a more productive porous queer studies." The result of these possibilities, Freeman continues, will be a "reshaping" of "various disciplines" ("Introduction" 159). Reed's novel offers an opportunity to reconceptualise and revive queer theory, while intervening in other kinds of writings about the past and homosexuality: history, biography, and gay fiction. Eroticism provides access to the past and it defines the future. Rewriting both sex and the body within a historical time represents in *The Grid* a radical reconfiguration of tradition. Tradition, Theodor Adorno argues, "claims that temporal succession sustains and transmits meaning" (81). Yet the kind of tradition represented in the culture and politics of Elizabethan England fictionalised in Reed's novel breaks away from an understanding of the early modern period described in academic criticism and historiography. Reed's storytelling, however, follows within its postmodern terms the narrative principle which his early modern predecessors were also accustomed to, that is, to mingle historical and contemporary references in their works of imagination. *The Grid*, therefore, presents us with the coexistence, not clash, of temporalities.

Post-AIDS fiction has also been made possible by the historiographic research and scholarship about the history of AIDS. Soon after the retrovirus HIV was identified, a French historian of medicine and the author of one of the first books about the history of AIDS, Mirko Grmek has asked whether AIDS is a new disease or not. His answer is both yes and no. By drawing on the latest discoveries in virology, microbiology, and immunology, Grmek presents the AIDS epidemic not as an isolated incident but as a part of a long and far from peaceful coexistence of humans and viruses. Not isolating AIDS from the history of other viruses, Grmek has given AIDS a history that is much longer than hitherto known. In Grmek's formulation, the retrovirus HIV represents an extreme and new manifestation produced in the manifold fight between the human body and viruses. I am making this short detour into the history of medicine to suggest that before AIDS research advanced in medical science, the meaning of AIDS was first extensively (and scientifically) written about within a historical paradigm and as a kind of temporality where the retrovirus HIV has its past and its present. Temporality and virus have thus been made two uneasy cohabitants very early in the history of research and writing about AIDS. Yet the virus has not only a history, it also tells a story about the human body in time. In Reed's novel, AIDS is about to be obliterated, and has become the idea of an incomplete past. Once a hindrance to pleasure it has now unlocked pleasure both as a practice and has facilitated the liberation of homosexuality from the writing about the past where it was routinely occluded.

Looking into Tudor history and zooming especially on the coterie of writers, patrons and their clients, who left a deep imprint on the literary scene in 1590s London, Reed stylises the relationship between Shakespeare and Marlowe in a series of sexual encounters. Reed opens up for debate temporal and spatial relationships between bodies and history, and sex and disease, in relation to time by reconceptualising the biographies of Marlowe and Shakespeare and by rethinking the Elizabethan patronage system upon which both playwrights would have depended for their future, a system now imagined as a network of lovers in futuristic London.

Reed's London is a city documenting its own apocalypse while also brimming with an excessive sexual energy. The city is now populated with a mixed Anglo-Japanese race created by the centuries of racial intermingling. To enter the central Anglo-Japanese zone, concentrated in the area between Soho and Bloomsbury, the Londoners have to show ID cards and give iris scans as a security measure. In Reed's London, Starbucks and Sainsbury's have survived the storm of technological progress, but not the Royal Family, recently killed by a terrorist cell that blows up one city landmark after another. The symbolical climax of their activity is evident in the devastation to Buckingham Palace caused by a bomb. Once fashionable parts of the city like Mayfair and Kensington are now partially ruined by rogue gangs that terrorise the city. When night falls, the armed units of cyborgs—part human and part machine, referred to as "robocops"—police the streets and skyline of the city. In Reed's London, terrorist have defeated the city. After the Prime Minister had been assassinated early in the novel and the city placed in the hands of the Commissar, "robosoldiers and robopolice" patrol London and are engaged in a "pathologically dehumanized programme aimed at cleaning up the city through fear politics" (83). London has become a no place, one of those "other places" which Michel Foucault describes as existing "outside of all other places" (24). Foucault calls these locations heterotopian places, and considers them the obverse of the "real" locations in history. Heterotopias do not tell a story of a place but reveal something that history has suppressed to a lesser or a larger degree.

Occasionally, the novel moves between nostalgia for the lost world of "cottaging," that is, of random sex in the city, and discovery of the new places for seduction which mushroom in the city. Transformation of the sexual history attached to a place is nowhere as pronounced as in the example of Piccadilly. The once fashionable pick-up place in the heart of London, Piccadilly has become a nexus of contemporary office blocks. Framed by the urban disaster that London has become in Reed's futuristic dystopia, *The Grid* dissolves the boundaries between time and place and between sex and gender, as one after another Elizabethan courtier and writer "still around" (85) reemerges as an HIV-positive vagabond of London's homosexual underground. Some of these resurfaced Elizabethans have developed AIDS, others have not, yet. But they are all undergoing a hypnotherapeutic procedure at The Grid, a facility on Coptic Street opposite the British Museum, a kind of facility in which humans are reconfigured through the processes of implanting "DNA-improved destinies" (47) of people one chooses to become, and by using the most recent methods of reproductive microbiology through genetic manipulation. Yet The Grid symbolises both the scientific progress in our science-obsessed age and exposes the limitations of that progress. The success of treatment in The Grid is achieved by empirical and technological procedures which are aided by mysterious hypnotherapy. The advancement in medical technology and DNA manipulation has thus become yet another mythography of our time which places so much emphasis and resources on DNA research. The combined effect of hypnotherapy and DNA-based procedure represents yet another instance of temporality in this novel, where the limitations of a new medical technology are overcome by the use of an alternative therapy from the past in the service of a dystopian future. The history of futuristic London is grafted on the history of Elizabethan sexual subculture. Reed says that the Elizabethan homosexual world "was a complex one, closeted, paranoid, ambiguous . . . layered in its documentation with rhetorical *double entendres* aimed at concealing the truth" (48). This observation is not too far from what queer early modern historiography has concluded about homosexuality in Elizabethan England.[7] The sexual underground of Elizabethan London has been brought out to light in Reed's dystopian metropolis.

This fictionalising of Elizabethan history opens up the possibility for a contemporary novelist to reimagine the pastness of the past as a new political present. In reconstructing the history of the homosexual underworld of Elizabethan London, "Facts," Reed speaks through Kit, "didn't help, largely because they were substitutes for the emotional content of what had really happened" (76). But even when facts are available, we never fully know what has really happened in the history of feeling and the history of sexual acts involving individuals of the past. Because the history of feeling and sex comes to us in the form of incomplete narratives and select knowledge, fictional reimaginings take the place of empirical referencing. Thus a reference to a postmodern reimagining of the Renaissance against the background of 1980s Thatcher-style politics becomes the closest artistic correlative to the kind of fiction Reed writes. *The Grid* contains numerous sign-postings intended as guides for the interpretation of the storytelling strategy which is unfolding in the pages of Reed's novel. So, Reed says: "Derek Jarman's film adaptation of Marlowe's Edward II [*Edward*] was precisely the sort of imaginative re-creation of history that excited" Kit (77). Or, the cultural icons from different eras of European gay past serve as signifiers of the kind of heroes Reed is celebrating: Joe Orton, Ossie Clark, Pier Paolo Pasolini, Jean Genet, Oscar Wilde, Michel Foucault, Derek Jarman, and Jean Cocteau. This catalogue of gay icons draws attention to a long history of creative and intellectual contribution made by gay men who identified themselves with sexual subculture and discursive dissent, the same modes of writing and being to which Reed's own fiction belongs.

The past is a reenactment and a metamorphosis in *The Grid*. Kit's thoughts reveal that the novel treats history as subjective narrative which, in the case of the early modern period, has left out homosexuality. Kit's play seems to want to redress this as much as Reed himself does in the novel: "Kit's personal belief was that the past was largely a media rewrite that factored events according to the ideological spin of the times. . . . invariably aimed at vindicating the oppressor" (109). Consisting of political violence and masculine aggression, the past intersects with a new history of homosexuality. Because history is a kind of narrative, it shares with fiction an interest in selecting and arranging the evidence of events and people: "That both Marlowe and Shakespeare were undoubtedly gay to his [Kit's] mind meant that whole chunks of their civil rights had disappeared as individuals and been rewritten to fit with a predominantly straight view of history" (109). This belief on Kit's part is also confirmed by the research he has conducted into the lives of such gay icons like Oscar Wilde, Jean Genet, and Jean Cocteau, lives distorted by the history which largely manipulated evidence of their sexuality. The juxtaposition of two historical moments marked by gay Elizabethan and modern gay icons erases the difference between past and present. The persecution of gay men throughout history, this juxtaposition further suggests, has been the result of rumours and innuendoes, and truth has always been compromised and elusive. The adverb "undoubtedly" implies certainty, yet Kit sounds as assured as any old-fashioned history book.

Rewriting history as fiction is a way out of the trap known to Kit both from the life of his Elizabethan alter ego and from the lives of the gay icons on his list because "in each of their cases biographically invented lives had often been substituted for truth" (109). Throughout the novel, the reader is reminded that Kit considers history an unreliable truth and source of evidence. Reed intervenes with a radically deconstructionist (his term, 111) view of the personal and erotic histories of Shakespeare and Marlowe in the "straight view of history" which dismisses the homoerotic as marginal and socially disturbing. Reed's deconstruction of the lives of Marlowe and

Shakespeare is a way of imitating Marlowe's own rebellious and sometimes anarchic stance on established views. In his fictional version of what went on between Marlowe and Shakespeare in London in the 1590s, Kit has no doubt that "Shakespeare was the dark outrider in Marlowe's life" (110).

When Kit and Billy meet, their meeting fuses two moments in queer time, the past and the future, in a new temporal model. During their sexual encounter in Billy's car, during which Billy performs oral sex on Kit, Kit wonders why their lives (Shakespeare and Marlowe's) have been reanimated in The Grid. Billy answers: "I suppose, partly, because you and I shone like no others. We were imagination at a time when there was none" and continues "some misguided academics claim you wrote my books, that your death was faked so that you could elude charges from the Privy Council and disappear in Europe for a time, and so our identities are somehow linked for even in the public mind and interchangeable. In a very real sense we're cloned" (180; 181). This episode of seduction is interrupted with details of the history of drama and the theorising about the goal of poetry. Literariness and literary history make an appearance in the references to Shakespeare and Marlowe's posthumous fame which Billy is proud of and Kit does not care about in keeping with their historical equivalents' eagerness to succeed and indifference to public opinion. Marlowe's influence on Shakespeare's drama in the early 1590s is implicit in this encounter and made explicit later on in the novel: "Kit was aware, too, how much Billy had stolen from him as a role model" (203). Despite this creative intertwining, Billy and Kit were not the only imagination in an imaginative age. But they shaped the language of drama, especially romantic tragedy in the early 1590s, and Shakespeare emulated Marlowe's "mighty line," unrhymed iambic pentameter (blank verse), in his history plays.

Yet the literary influence of Marlowe on Shakespeare can also figure as erotic, which resonates through Reed's fiction of their lives. It could be, for example, that Sonnet 73 ("That time of year when thou mayst in me behold") is a commemorative poem, in which Marlowe is remembered as a source of both poetic and erotic impression left on Shakespeare. The line "Consumed with that which it was nourished by" (line 12) is an almost verbatim quotation of the motto which appears in the putative portrait of Christopher Marlowe in Corpus Christi College in Cambridge, where it reads in Latin "Quod me nutrit me destruit" (Destroyed by that which nourishes me). The history of poetic language and of the politics of patronage is thus juxtaposed with the sexual politics within this influence.

In Billy and Kit's sexual encounter, Reed reverses the power agency between Marlowe and Shakespeare, by making Shakespeare-Billy the assertive lover to Marlowe-Kit's as a reticent partner: "Billy came down on him [Kit] relentlessly, and Kit let it happen. Billy took him in deep and resurfaced for air, tooling his cock against his cheek in the pause" (181). Reed's fiction of the new post-HIV sex as unbridled sexual consummation between Kit and Billy figures in the novel as the expected culmination of the intertwining of drama and poetry which has already occurred in cultural history. In this meeting between the source and the recipient, revenge comes in the form of sex and a reversal of power between the model and the imitator, Kit-Marlowe and Billy-Shakespeare. Past competition mutates into sexual intimacy in the future, but also in a fictional revelation of Shakespeare as the historical accomplice in the murder of Marlowe. The narrative creates this erotic-as-creative surrender as a kind of Shakespeare's revenge on Marlowe, where the creative power of one agent is reversed as the sexual power of the other.

Reed eroticises the history of literary contacts between writers whose lives and writings are full of the traces of erotic past. In the process, he brings together the premodern and modern times into one time. One could say that we live in the contemporary version of early modernity; that early modernity is not over yet, as illustrated in the post-Elizabethan dystopian London. Yet for us, the past is a repository of unfinished stories waiting to be retold. The enduring temporality of homoeroticism reveals competing tendencies of representation: the future is both the goal of homosexual sex and desire, but the future also wishes to straighten that desire. *The Grid* explodes the first tendency and crashes the other. Post-AIDS fiction as a mode of writing tends to imagine sex in the future as liberating from all the constraints and anxieties which surrounded homosexual encounters during the AIDS epidemic. But along the way to that imagined future, post-AIDS fiction encounters present-day conceptualisation of homosexuality that increasingly tends to blend homosexuality in the heterosexual culture and its privileges, including, for example, gay marriage. So Reed's novel extends the sex of the past beyond the moment of AIDS panic and beyond contemporary normalisation of homosexuality.

"People's pasts stay around [. . .] some people never really die" (85), says Kit at one point. Reed breathes life in the past that lingers until today by fictionalising social, cultural and, most importantly, literary history in one fictional narrative. Reed's novel is the fictional obverse of queer theory which has performed a similar task of shaking up the orthodoxy of the heterosexist and de-eroticised writing about the past. By privileging desire over gender, queer theory expanded ways of explaining and conceptualising different kinds of sexual practices that cannot be categorised within the clear-cut dichotomy of gay and straight, but that resist and often subvert the heterosexual way of ordering and thinking about sex. From the perspective of literary history and criticism, queer theory, especially queer early modern criticism, broke the silence that shrouded so much writing about past literature, by demonstrating the richness and variety of representations of both male and female same-sex eroticism present in literature of the past. Thus Reed's novel plays an important role as cultural critique because it is a work that disavows the slowness of modern writing to free itself from the chains of historical context which often determines and limits, rather than challenges and liberates, our thinking about the past. In addition to post-AIDS writing, queer liberation and social activism have been the frame within which Reed's innovative and liberating imagination has flourished for some time. In *The Grid* the power of refusal of traditional history is more powerful than in any previous novel.

Reed's novel performs the kind of cultural work that Jonathan Dollimore identifies as a challenge to the impediment of narrow approaches to historicisation. "The injunction 'always historicize' has become a truly worthy one," says Dollimore, "so much so that the urge to disobey it is now irresistible, not least because of its a priori assumption that explanation via historical context is always possible. The idea that anything can be explained if a full enough complete historical context for it can be recovered, may become, paradoxically, a way of disengaging from the past" (Dollimore, *Sex* 125). The search for context as a route to explanation and justification of the past, Dollimore implies, often closes down rather than opens up possibilities for criticism. But Reed rewrites the context, an always already speculative category, in order to give it a new posthistorical significance. Much work has been done to make intelligible to the modern reader the hidden and rhetorically opaque expressions of homoerotic desire in early modern England. Yet not even queer early modern criticism has demystified the kind of interaction between Marlowe and Shakespeare—two playwrights without whose body of work the field of queer early modern studies would not have come into being—despite the fact both playwrights created some of the most memorable "sexual types" (DiGangi 5) in early modern literature and that both lead unorthodox lives. The terms used to describe homosexual types in the early modern period were fluid and ambiguous, and they were adapted to situations in which the homosexual type might have found itself. Those terms were largely drawn from drama and the vernacular discourse of daily life; they were "composed of discursive strands" (DiGangi 7). When modern critics associate those types with specific agency, they still do not say much, if anything, about whether the agency of that person was or was not sexual in nature. It is fiction that enlivens the nature that always and already remains lost in the fog of history.

The Grid builds on this gap between naming and identification in the early modern homosexual culture. When Reed discards old scholarship as an impediment to fictional history of Elizabethan homosexuality, he is also starting a new chapter in the writing of that history. In a memorable moment of book burning, Kit relegates to fire a set of books on Christopher Marlowe, written by the eminent Oxford scholar of Elizabethan drama, Frederick Samuel Boas. Watching the fire consume the books "had given him the sort of catharsis he usually associated with random sexual encounters: brief, incandescent and self-annihilative" (250). Burning Boas's edition is "torching a little piece of history" (249), an act which in turn liberates Kit's creative energies. Kit is drawing knowledge not from dry-as-dust scholarship but is inspired by the music of the rock-music band "Velvet Underground" and the musician and singer Lou Reed, both known for the sensuous and queer content of their music. This act also liberates the readers of Reed's novel to explore that which does not exist in the academic version of Marlowe's life and work. The cultural signification of juxtaposing a scholarly edition with pop music is clear: the last word on the past does not belong to the academic establishment of the era before sexual liberation, but to a modern rock group and a singer that emerged from within the sexual liberation and queer movements of modern times.

The Grid is as much a fictional intervention into the genre of biography as it is a fictional response to queer theory, and just at the right time. For a while, queer theory has been coming to a halt. Yet the radical energy of Reed's fiction sheds light on the narrow perspective some queer theorists have written about the theoretical field they conceptualised over twenty years ago. Namely, the theoretical paradigm may be showing the signs of slowing down, but only if we assume that queer artistic production is no longer in need of theoretical elucidation; or, if we separate theoretical from creative queer discourses. This separation weakens the force queer people want literature and theory to have in order to resist the unstoppable stream of heterosexist tenor of culture and society. Literature continues to produce new queer fictions and contemporary culture continues to produce new queer discourses, and each new fiction, each new cultural object, will call for a new interpretation commensurate with the cultural conditions and the political moment that initiated it. The past is a queer place looked at from the modern (and postmodern) perspective, and thus the past will continue to offer material for new models of Renaissance time in fiction. Because queer temporality extends the work of theory across time, *The Grid* is a persuasive answer to the questions which have recently been explored in the collection of essays *After Sex?: On Writing Since Queer Theory*. As the last line of Reed's novel shows, the two national poets fixed in a sexual embrace against the apocalypse of London state symbolically that after sex, comes sex. That is, writing since queer theory has continued to produce powerful queer fictions showing that fiction has a more enduring life than even both the theory and "the activist energies that helped fuel academic work" (Halley and Parker 1). The idea behind *After Sex?* is also to encourage those who were once identified largely as queer critics to now work on something that is "*not* about sexuality" or that is not queer "at least in some significant way" (Halley and Parker 5). But does not this swerve into writing about something else but sex mean giving up on fighting for the important role, and presence, queer lives play in the composition of society? Reed's novel reminds us that there are other ways of writing about sexuality, and that sexuality, like desire, is the charge that is at the heart of aesthetic life and production. *The Grid* draws our attention to the productive connection between the novel as a literary form and gender—and sexuality—as its constituent elements.

The Grid is also a challenge to established biographies of Shakespeare. Not only do biographers of Shakespeare rehearse the same body of familiar information, but that there does not seem to be an end to these, often uncreative, speculations. Nevertheless, publishers continue to capitalise on our hunger for yet another Life of Shakespeare. As Russ McDonald has astutely observed in a recent essay reviewing two most recent biographies of Shakespeare, "For 300 years, Shakespeare has remained an irresistible subject, the attraction owing something to his unparalleled status and something to the relative paucity of fact, which challenges biographers to make more of the evidence than their predecessors have done" (11). Reed's fictional biography of Shakespeare, however, acquires the force of freshness and originality by using available evidence to bridge the gap between life and sex, a gap particularly deep in the established biographies of Shakespeare. In that sense, his is the historical novel for our times, revisionary in its handling of historical evidence and bold in putting sexual, literary, technological, and state politics in close relations with each other.

That fiction is a necessary mode in the writing of biography (and certainly in biographies of Shakespeare) has been taken for granted by many a biographer. One of the most popular recent biographies, Stephen Greenblatt's *Will in the World*, for example, blurs the line between historiography and fiction more than any other critical biography until his was published. Yet most biographies, including Greenblatt's, reaffirm the aesthetic uniqueness and cultural greatness of the Bard both as Britain's national poet and an important cultural icon with an international appeal. As Catherine Belsey remarks, even Greenblatt's version of life writing "irons out everything that makes the practice of interpretation itself surprising, invigorating, or satisfying" (Belsey 53). Written outside erotic time, most of these biographies of Shakespeare, like the one by Greenblatt (or the excellent new one by Lois Potter), de-eroticise Shakespeare's life even when they relate personal details of his life to his work. Even the most erotic of his non-dramatic poetry and the plays seem not to inspire our biographers to speculate about the matters of sexual life, although they are eager to make other kinds of speculations for which evidence is both limited and sometimes unstable. It is as if the literary text itself is not original evidence of life in its own right, especially if that life is framed, as biographers often do, by the social, artistic, and political circumstances of the age in which Shakespeare lived and, specifically, of the London in which he worked and came into contact with his contemporaries.

Yet when biographies take into account erotic elements in the making of the life of a writer, the results can be different. Among the penumbra of recent biographies, Graham Holderness's *Nine Lives of William Shakespeare* stands out precisely because it collapses the separation between the fictional and the factual and turns controlled speculation into a provocative and revisionary reconfiguration of Shakespeare's life as also an erotic life. His is the biography energised by queer temporality. Holderness's is indeed "a critical biography for our times" (Belsey 53). It pushes the fiction of Shakespeare's life further than Greenblatt does, but makes that fiction explain imaginatively the silences which surround the facts of Shakespeare's life. When in the chapter called "Shakespeare in Love: 'Fair Friend'," Holderness says that "We do not know . . . whether or not Shakespeare loved his wife. We do know, on the other hand, that he did make a written declaration of "love" to a beautiful and bisexual male aristocrat, Henry Wriothesley, the Earl of Southampton" (111), he is writing with the voice of a radically new biographer of Shakespeare. His biography of Shakespeare restores the fiction of an erotic relationship between the poet and his patron as a potential substitute for the rejection of such biographical readings by modern critics. In conclusion, Holderness pauses to think about other possibilities for reconstructing the life of Shakespeare: "the Shakespeare life-story has left enough traces, questions and tantalising possibilities for biographers to construct imaginary scenarios of the Shakespeare-Southampton relationship. The novelists have only extrapolated the same speculations to a further remove, imaginatively penetrating deep into the most private of places" (120). Reed's novel penetrates beyond the most private places and writes a fiction of Shakespeare's sexuality, as well as turning into fiction the popular old-chestnut of a question about whether Shakespeare was gay. Holderness's incisive observation reminds us why we need less, not more, "standard" biographies of Shakespeare. Reed's novel reminds us why we need less, not more, historical novels which fictionalise the Renaissance as either a lavish or gory background to historical strangeness.

The fiction of queer futurity in *The Grid* is attentive to the past as much as it is a critique of queer present.[8] *The Grid* resists the homophobia still prevalent in our times of progressive legislation and the freedom for homosexuals. While the history of London is coming to its cataclysmic end in a moment reminiscent of 9/11 New York, as Kit is running away from the fire created by the impact of the jet plane as it crashed into an office tower, the sexual histories of Kit and Billy are approaching a joint closure. They reach the climax of the sexual act performed on top of a building about to be destroyed by a rogue passenger jet plane over the London sky. Watching the uncertain trajectory of the plane above him, Kit "knew that whatever configuration their bodies took was to be a form of death rite" (277). At this point, homosexuality figures as a radical version of freedom. With London ablaze and disappearing in poisonous smoke, Kit rejoiced in the sexual union with Billy: "They were one body, the first and the last poets, and he intended to keep it this way" (278). Kit and Billy forge a new identity in the fire of burning London. They die ritualistically as queer lovers, but they continue to live as queer poets. The ending reminds us that in Reed's dystopian London, as in the Renaissance, desire is inseparable from sexuality, but not limited to it. The novel's finale confirms that chaos and social destruction are not brought about by homosexuality but by radical politics and a history of violence, as well as the separation of the ruling elite from the society it is supposed to govern and lead. As Joe Orton proclaimed in 1967, about using homosexuality to challenge different forms of repression and social ostracism—"It's the only way to smash the wretched civilization" (Lahr 135)—so Reed affirms homosexuality as a way to smash the heterosexual view of history across time.

Yet by forging a new queer identity which is also a poetic identity, whose vitality contrasts with the demise of London, Reed also privileges the sexual and the creative over the middle-brow and the commercial, symbolised by the upscale shops like Harrods, Liberty, Jaeger, Burberry, Pringle, and agnès b. Bringing to an end both the commercial and cyber eras of London's history, *The Grid* returns us to a pretechnological moment of sexual desire and poetic inspiration, each mysterious and complex in its own way. This ending thus illustrates the power of sex to transform the meaning of the past and time, and in the process of the subjects involved in that transformation, illustrates what Freeman has posited as the power of sex in relation to temporality: "sex may unbind selves and meanings, but these must be relatively quickly rebound into fantasies, or the sexual agents would perish after only one release of energy" (*Time* xxi). At the end of Reed's novel, the reader is made to believe that the fantasy Kit and Billy have created in the sexual act is not a perishable but eternal state.

By pushing the boundaries of the historical novel in a new direction of erotographic temporality, that is, the kind of erotic writing which is not bound by different moments of historical time, *The Grid* urges readers to think about tradition in writing differently. On the one hand, tradition is a form of representation and a repository of historical evidence and meaning. On the other, it is a historical and theoretical construct. *The Grid* also moves us to think about the past, not as tradition but as a phenomenon which emerges in the contact of bodies, desires, and time. Theodor Adorno says that "As soon as genuine traditional aspects of culture—significant art works of the past—are idolised as relics they degenerate into elements of an ideology which relishes the past so that the present will remain unaffected by it, at the cost of increasing narrowness and rigidity" (77). Reed's version of tradition imagines the past merged with the future, but a future in which tradition can never be fully overcome. Queer future after AIDS is no less rosy than the past decimated by the deadly virus; there are viruses that neither history nor future, and neither time nor imagination, can erase. Kit reminds us that the real, undefeatable virus is not HIV but homophobia: "Kit was still amazed that expressions of same-sex relations were still only sanitized within the ghetto [Soho] and that outside the village prejudice and brute hostility ruled." (211) Futuristic dystopia reminds us that the past shades into present time as a history of violence against homosexual dissent. One of the last lines in Reed's novel is therefore a call for new action: "It's time we looked seriously at why none of us can escape the past." (261). Nothing like the reminder of the resilience of homophobia to survive time brings Reed's novel close to the experience of the modern reader. In bringing to a fictional life the queer lives of the past precursors of futuristic queer men, Reed's novel represents a major (and much needed) step beyond the state of historical fiction at present, fiction "which might be said to be deferred in its workings, as its subject materials are distanced and othered from the experience of the reader" (de Groot, *The Historical* 115). Reed's fiction is othered in its futuristic projection from the experience of the reader, but it shares with the modern reader the extremes of sexual gratification and the hopes, and maybe illusions, about the future of homosexuality after HIV/AIDS, if not after homophobia.

ACKNOWLEDGMENTS

My research for this chapter was assisted with a grant from the Social Sciences and Humanities Research Council of Canada and from a Marie Curie Research Fellowship. I thank Ana María Sánchez-Arce and Jason Hartford for their incisive and detailed comments on this chapter, and I am grateful to Jane Grogan and Sharae Deckard for their generous discussion of my paper delivered at University College Dublin (UCD) in March 2012, on which this chapter is based. I am indebted to Anne Mulhall for inviting me to speak at UCD.

NOTES

1. Here I follow the basic line of argument developed by André Green.
2. The term is coined by Mieke Bal (7).
3. Robert A. Logan's assessment of Marlowe's influence on Shakespeare is the most recent detailed exploration of this topic.
4. Jonathan Bate discusses a range of these influences (101–132).
5. The classical analogue to the examples in Marlowe and Shakespeare is the exiled poet in Plato's *Republic*. I thank Ana María Sánchez-Arce for this suggestion.
6. Walsingham's life and career are brilliantly explored by John Cooper.
7. Alan Bray offers an insightful and concise view of the homosexual underworld of Elizabethan England.
8. I adapt the argument about queer futurity posited by José Esteban Muñoz (18).

REFERENCES

Adorno, Theodor. "On Tradition." Collaborative translation. *Telos* (21 December 1992): 75–82. Print.
Bal, Mieke. *Quoting Caravaggio: Contemporary Art, Preposterous History*. Chicago: University of Chicago Press, 1999. Print.
Bate, Jonathan. *The Genius of Shakespeare*. London: Picador, 1997. Print.
Belsey, Catherine. *A Future for Criticism*. Oxford: Wiley-Blackwell, 2001. Print.
Bray, Alan. *Homosexuality in Renaissance England*. New York: Columbia University Press, 1996. Print.
Bristow, Joseph. *Sexuality*. London: Routledge, 1997. Print.

Castiglia, Christopher, and Christopher Reed. *If Memory Serves: Gay Men, AIDS, and the Promise of Queer Future*. Minneapolis, MN: University of Minnesota Press, 2012. Print.

Cooper, John. *The Queen's Agent: Francis Walsingham and the Court of Elizabeth I*. London: Faber and Faber, 2012. Print.

Davis, Ben, and Jana Funke, eds. *Sex, Gender and Time in Fiction and Culture*. New York: Palgrave-Macmillan, 2011. Print.

de Groot, Jerome. *Consuming History: Historians and Heritage in Contemporary Popular Culture*. London: Routledge, 2008. Print.

———. *The Historical Novel*. London: Routledge, 2010. Print.

DiGangi, Mario. *Sexual Types: Embodiment, Agency and Dramatic Character from Shakespeare to Shirley*. Philadelphia: University of Pennsylvania Press, 2001. Print.

Dollimore, Jonathan. *Sex, Literature and Censorship*. Cambridge: Polity, 2001. Print.

———. *Sexual Dissidence: Augustine to Wilde/Freud to Foucault*. Oxford: Clarendon, 1991. Print.

Foucault, Michel. "Of Other Places." Trans. Jay Miskowiec. *Diacritic* 16.1 (Spring 1986): 22–7. Print.

Freeman, Elizabeth. "Introduction." *GLQ: A Journal of Lesbian and Gay Studies* 13.2–3 (2007): 159–76. Print.

———. *Time Binds: Queer Temporalities, Queer Histories*. Durham, NC: Duke University Press, 2010. Print.

Green, André. *The Chains of Eros: The Sexual in Psychoanalysis*. Trans. Luke Thurston. London: Karnac, 2001. Print.

Greenblatt, Stephen. *Will in the World: How Shakespeare Became Shakespeare*. New York: W. W. Norton, 2004. Print.

Grmek, D. Mirko. *Histoire du sida: debut et origine d'une pandemie actuelle*. Paris : Payot, 1990. Print. *History of AIDS: Emergence and Origin of a Modern Pandemic*. Trans. Russell Maulitz and Jacalyn Duffin. Princeton, NJ: Princeton University Press, 1993. Print.

Hackett, Helen. *Shakespeare and Elizabeth: The Meeting of Two Myths*. Princeton, NJ: Princeton University Press, 2009. Print.

Halley, Janet, and Andrew Parker, eds. *After Sex? On Writing Since Queer Theory*. Durham, NC: Duke University Press, 2011. Print.

Holderness, Graham. *New Lives of William Shakespeare*. London: Continuum, 2011. Print.

Lahr, John. *Prick Up Your Ears*. Harmondsworth: Penguin, 1980. Print.

Logan, Robert A. *Shakespeare's Marlowe: The Influence of Christopher Marlowe on Shakespeare's Artistry*. Aldershot: Ashgate, 2007. Print.

Marlowe, Christopher. *The Complete Plays*. Eds. Frank Romany and Robert Lindsey. London: Penguin, 2003. Print.

McDonald, Russ. "A re-fitted stage." *Times Literary Supplement* (10 August 2012): 11. Print.

Muñoz, José Esteban. *Cruising Utopia: The Then and There of Queer Theory*. New York: New York University Press, 2009. Print.

Potter, Lois. *The Life of William Shakespeare: A Critical Biography*. Oxford: Wiley-Blackwell, 2012. Print.

Reed, Jeremy. *Boy Caesar*. London: Peter Owen, 2004. Print.

———. *Dorian: A Sequel to The Picture of Dorian Gray*. London: Peter Owen, 1997. Print.

———. *Engaging Form*. London: Jonathan Cape, 1988. Print.

———. *The Grid*. London: Peter Owen, 2008. Print.

Schoenbaum, Samuel. *Shakespeare's Lives*. Oxford: Clarendon, 1979. Print.

Shakespeare, William. *The Complete Works*. The Oxford Shakespeare. Eds. John Jowett, William Montgomery, Gary Taylor, and Stanley Wells. Second edition. Oxford: Clarendon, 2005. Print.

Wilson, F. P. "Shakespeare's Comedies." *Shakespearean and Other Studies*. Ed. Helen Gardner. Oxford: Clarendon, 1969. 54–99. Print.

14 From Virginia's Sister to Friday's Silence*

Presence, Metaphor, and the Persistence of Disability in Contemporary Writing

Stuart Murray

VIRGINIA'S SISTER

This article aims to produce new thinking about the representation of disability in contemporary literature, especially understood with reference to uses of metaphor and the question of a material disabled presence. It also wishes to make a claim for what I term the "persistence" of disability in contemporary writing, an idea that connects writing over the last twenty-five years back to the modes of disability representation established early in the twentieth century. Such persistence can be read in a number of ways: in multiple texts it speaks of the continuous and highly problematic recourse made by fiction to characters with disabilities in order to emphasize values that negate the presence and meaning of disability; but in other writing it generates a sense of the productive presence of disability and characters with disabilities. As I hope to show, in this productive space, metaphor need not be something that has, at all times, to be policed for fear of the damage it does to disabled communities. Rather, disability metaphors can be subtle and meaningful in the ways that they speak of disability experiences and lives.

Before moving to a specific concentration on the contemporary, I want to start with an extended example from modernist writing that arcs around the article and ties into the later commentary on more recent literature. The sister in the title here is, in fact, a half sister—Laura Stephen, born prematurely in 1870 to Leslie Stephen and his first wife Minny Thackeray and so some twelve years older than her famous sibling, Virginia Woolf. In Leslie's letters, written during his eldest daughter's childhood, Laura emerges as a figure whose behaviour makes her seemingly beyond control—she has "fiendish" bursts of temper and "dreadful fits of passion," while her talk is described as "a queer squeaking or semi-stammering or spasmodic uttering" (Lee 101). Leslie finds her "intensely provoking" and in one letter declares, "I long to shake the little wretch" (Lee 102). As his ability to control his daughter increasingly failed, Leslie Stephen resorted to sedation and physical punishment, locking Laura up in her room in the

---

*Note to reader: please note that this chapter is referred to throughout as an article, as it was previously published in the *Journal of Literary & Cultural Disability Studies* 6.3, 2012.

family home before finally institutionalising her, probably in 1892. Virginia Woolf herself later wrote of her father's relationship with his oldest daughter that "the history of Laura is really the most tragic thing in his life I think [. . . His] letters are full of her" (Lee 100).

The information we have on Laura Stephen is almost entirely compiled from letters and journal entries from the Woolf family, and the perils of retrospective diagnosis notwithstanding, looking back it seems clear that she had some form of autism. Her repetitive communication and use of language, as well as her physical behaviour and emotional outbursts, point to this, and it is a suggestion put forward in Hermione Lee's 1996 biography of Woolf, where Laura is discussed in some detail (100–104). This in itself is interesting and unusual, as the majority of biographies (and virtually all criticism) of Woolf skip over Laura, who is usually presented as "mad" or "retarded" in some way, an "idiot" figure, with the specifics left unexplored. Yet Virginia lived in the same house as Laura for roughly the first ten years of her life, a fact that must have had consequences for her development during her childhood. If we choose to refuse such a dismissal, what might we say about Laura's disabled presence and its relation to her half sister, and the influence that presence had on the writer Woolf subsequently became? And, to continue with the extension of the example, how might any conclusions we reach in addressing that question help us think about the ways in which the "persistence" of disability, its inevitability and presence, threads through the questions of writing and identity from modern to contemporary literature? Seen productively, Laura herself becomes a guide to a necessary critical perspective.

One place to start answering these questions might come in a consideration of disability in Woolf's own writing, in which we might hazard some guesses as to the resonances of Laura's presence. Lee notes how Woolf went out of her way to distinguish her own mental health issues from what she termed "idiocy," and points to a famous diary observation from January 1915 in which she describes meeting a group of disabled adults while out on a walk:

> On the tow path we met & had to pass a long line of imbeciles [. . .] everyone in that long line was a miserable shuffling idiotic creature, with no forehead, or no chin, & an imbecile grin, or a wild suspicious stare. It was perfectly horrible. They should certainly be killed. (Lee 104)

Wool's fear and sense of repulsion here seem palpable. Possibly she was reminded too much of Laura at this moment, the thought that her sister too was a "shuffling idiotic creature," and that she herself must not and cannot be thought of in anything approaching the same terms.

Woolf understood and wrote about cognitive difference. Writing in the April 1919 issues of *The Athenaeum*, in a piece entitled "The Eccentrics," Woolf praises those individuals who do not, as she puts it, "die a Dean or a Professor, a hero or a Prime Minister," but rather do "stealthily and as if by the back door momentarily creep in" to the events of the world (*Essays: Volume 3* 38–39). The half-forgotten Aunt who, as Woolf terms it, "knew for certain that the world is shaped like a star-fish" (*Essays: Volume 3* 39), is "eccentric" and celebrated here in what is a clear account of neurodiversity, but such a suggestion of difference had, it seems, a different relation to the autism embodied by Laura. In Woolf's essays she seems implicitly aware of this question of difference—we can see it again for example in her long essay "On Being Ill" (written in bed when Woolf was herself ill), published in T. S. Eliot's *New Criterion*, January 1926, in which she talks of the "undiscovered countries that are then disclosed" following the onset of illness, and how though "literature does its best to maintain that its concern is with the mind; that the body is a sheet of plain glass through which the soul looks straight and clear," in fact "All day, all night, the body intervenes" (Woolf, *Essays: Volume 4* 317–18). Subjectivity, experience, and even reading, she suggests in this essay, are always subject to the difference that illness might bring.

Keeping our framing questions about Laura Stephen in mind, we can note the examples of disabled presence in Woolf 's fiction. Here, we might consider Septimus Warren Smith, the shell-shocked war veteran from her 1925 novel *Mrs Dalloway* (a character that, as readers, we first meet on the street, just as Woolf herself met that "long line of imbeciles" in 1915), where his "look of apprehension" and inability to judge the everyday marks the start of his own disabled experience (Woolf, *Dalloway* 12). Woolf herself, in her introduction to the 1928 Modern Library edition of the novel, noted that Septimus "is intended to be [Clarissa Dalloway's] double" (Woolf, *Dalloway*, xxi), and as a consequence all the many narrative threads that surround the novel's titular character need to be seen through the lens of Septimus's suicidal tendencies, or his visual, verbal, and aural distinctiveness (hallucinations, stuttering, hearing voices, etc.). In pursuing such a critical angle, it is not my point to stress, or even necessarily subscribe to, any psychoanalytic reading of Woolf herself, but it is surely worth noting that all the behavioural elements in this last list were experienced by her in her breakdowns of 1913 and 1921–22, the latter of these significant in its position immediately prior to the writing of *Mrs Dalloway*.

Following on from this, and with similar parallels in play, we might think of Rhoda's various obsessions and compulsions in *The Waves*. The vulnerable Rhoda, who "has no body as the others have" (Woolf, *Waves* 15) as one of the other characters in the novel puts it, has continually to touch the rail at the end of her bed, and always keep her chest of drawers within sight, if she is to avoid multiple panic attacks. Rhoda's OCD predates any clinical formulation of the disorder but, as Lennard Davis has shown in his cultural history of obsession, the "continuing interest" in "obsessive behaviors has a complex set of instantiations and rebirths through the period from the eighteenth century to the present moment" (21), and Woolf 's representation of

Rhoda should be seen precisely as one example of this. Following Septimus's Post-Traumatic Stress Disorder, this second reference to neurobehavioural difference underscores Woolf's interest in such conditions, a feature borne out by a letter she wrote in October 1931, shortly after the publication of *The Waves*, discussing the six central characters in terms that indicate a desire to include a range of cognitive states:

> The six characters were supposed to be one. I'm getting old myself—I shall be fifty next year; and I come to feel more and more how difficult it is to collect oneself into one Virginia; even though the special Virginia in whose body I live in for the moment is violently susceptible to all sorts of separate feelings. (Lee 621–22)

In light of such a comment, Rhoda's various obsessions in the novel are not only part of the tapestry that is her character; they also point to the centrality of a neurobehavioural spectrum in the text as a whole.

All of these examples offer convincing and coherent evidence of the benefits of thinking about Woolf's work within a framework of disability. The silence that surrounds disability when it comes to literary criticism is *still* profound, despite the prevalence of characters with disabilities in modern and contemporary writing and the emergence of a body of literary and cultural criticism over the last fifteen years. To engage with the topic, as opposed to neglecting it, allows for new readings of Woolf's representation of a wide range of issues—from the workings of culture to the patterning of the individual subject. It also allows us to chart new patterns of writing, and new trajectories of narrative, as the twentieth century transforms into the twenty-first.

Staying with Woolf, however, most obviously we might think of Laura, Woolf's own sister, in conjunction with Judith, the imagined sister of Shakespeare discussed in the third chapter of *A Room of One's Own*. It is worth looking at this parallel quite carefully, because it licenses a critical approach that helps in any understanding of how disability works in literature from the contemporary period. Woolf outlines the impossibility of Judith's life: the girl made to stay at home and not receive schooling; the talented teenager who finally leaves for London only to be told that "no woman [. . .] could possibly be an actress" (*Room* 83); the pregnant young woman who ultimately "killed herself one winter's night and lies buried at some crossroads where the omnibuses now stop outside the Elephant and Castle" (*Room* 83–84). Here, we surely can see the shape of other kinds of difference for which the culture makes little or no space. When Woolf is more explicit about the consequences of the prejudice Judith would have received in her attempt to become a successful writer, her own language becomes suffused with pejorative images and ideas associated with disability:

> When, however, one reads of a witch being ducked, of a woman possessed by devils, of a wise woman selling herbs, or even of a very

remarkable man who had a mother, then I think we are on the track of a lost novelist, a suppressed poet, of some mute and inglorious Jane Austen, some Emily Bronte who dashed her brains out on the moor or mopped and mowed about the highways crazed with the torture that her gifts had put her to [. . .]

This may be true or it may be false—who can say?—but what is true in it, so it seemed to me, reviewing the story of Shakespeare's sister as I had made it, is that any woman born with a great gift in the sixteenth century would certainly have gone crazed, shot herself, or ended her days in some lonely cottage outside the village, half witch, half wizard, feared and mocked at [. . .] To have lived a free life in London in the sixteenth century would have meant for a woman who was poet and playwright a nervous stress and dilemma which might well have killed her. Had she survived, whatever she had written would have been twisted and deformed, issuing from a strained and morbid imagination. (Woolf, *Room* 84–87)

The "mute," "crazed," and "deformed" life of Judith would, it seems clear from this, have been all but impossible. She would, like so many of those with disabilities, have become marginalised and the subject of prejudice and ridicule.

ON THE MARGINS

Woolf needed to invent Judith Shakespeare to make her point about patriarchy, whereas we have the reality of Laura Stephen to make a parallel observation about the persistence of disability. In Woolf's formation, that which is ignored, avoided, or suppressed is turned into its twisted other. And, following her logic, we might say that the normalcy of culture, whether in terms of gender or ideas about "acceptable" humanity, bodily integrity or mental health, erases the space in which its opposite yet parallel form might exist. As Clarissa Dalloway has Septimus as her double, so possibly Woolf is attached to the shadow that Laura became for her, the "feared and mocked" crazed girl who shared the childhood home.

Where does this leave us as we try to use this example to bring ideas of disability to bear on contemporary writing? First, we might think about the idea of Laura at the margins of someone else's story. Conceived in such a way, her story becomes the archetypal disability narrative, in which an impairment or disability condition figures as an indicator of absence, lack, or loss, and does so in relation to non-disabled characterisation in order to affirm the ableism of the text. In what is probably the most influential critical idea to have emerged in humanities disability studies, David Mitchell and Sharon Snyder call this formation "narrative prosthesis," a process by which disability works, in their terms, as a "stock feature of characterisation" or "an opportunistic metaphorical device" (47) in the stories in which it features. So, from the character of Stevie in Joseph Conrad's *The Secret Agent* to that of Sufiya Zinobia in Salman Rushdie's *Shame*, or from Clifford Chatterley in D. H. Lawrence's *Lady Chatterley's Lover* to Desmond Bates in David Lodge's *Deaf Sentence*, disability is always used to signal something other than itself, usually some idea of non-disabled human worth. Associated with this is the second major point we might note, and one contained in the latter of the two Mitchell and Snyder quotes given earlier, namely that it is metaphor that dominates in such workings of prosthesis. Mitchell and Snyder point out that, from Sophocles' *Oedipus the King* (in which Oedipus's lameness and blindness use an idea of a "working" body to augment the play's analysis of hubris) onwards, disability is continually used, through metaphor, to shore up ideas of the able human or tangible body. They note that "disability supplies a multiple utility to literary characterisations, even while literature abandons a serious contemplation of the difference that disability makes as a socially negotiated identity" (Mitchell and Snyder 10). Specifically continuing with the focus on blindness, it is possible to conceive of the often bitter debates about disability representation that surrounded Fernando Meirelles's 2008 film *Blindness* as only the latest cultural text in a line that includes—amongst others—*King Lear* and *Madame Bovary* to showcase such ideas. And as Davis has observed, this "abandonment" of any serious contemplation of disability includes metaphors that portray those with disabilities "as 'noble,' 'heroic' and 'special'"—the so-called "supercrip," the representation of which is, according to Davis, "a form of patronizing" (Normalcy 106). In a similar vein but different mode, we can see Paul de Man's 1971 book *Blindness and Insight* with its critical use of metaphor in its account of what he termed, in the text's subtitle, "contemporary criticism," as part of this prejudice. Indeed, Rosemarie Garland-Thomson, who along with Mitchell and Snyder, and Davis, is one of the foundational critics of disability studies in the humanities, has also noted the critical trend toward such a use of metaphor. When literary critics "look at disabled characters," she writes in *Extraordinary Bodies*, her 1997 study of physical disability in American literature and culture, "they often interpret them metaphorically or aesthetically, reading them without political awareness as conventional elements of the sentimental, romantic, Gothic, or grotesque tradition" (10–11).

Garland-Thomson's reference to a lack of "political awareness" in the preceding quotation serves to remind us that the misrepresentation of disability in cultural texts has been part of a wider political absence, the challenge to which formed part of the rights-based agenda that has risen to dominate contemporary disability studies. Nearly all criticism currently undertaken beneath the banner of humanities disability studies works within this frame, promoting the idea that—following on from the work of such figures as Mitchell and Snyder, Davis, and Garland-Thomson—a thoroughgoing critique of the workings of disability in culture and society has, as its baseline, a commitment to the fit and proper expression of the complexities of disabled lives and experiences. Whatever the successes of this rights movement and this criticism, however, we might note that the majority of representations of disability—as with *Blindness*—still work in these terms of absence and lack, still are shaped through metaphor, and still misrepresent those with disabilities in ways that simply would not be tolerated were they modes depicting ethnicity or gender, for example.

So, we can find endless lines through the twentieth century in which disability animates literary texts to produce wider narrative effects, whether it be the physical and cognitive differences of American Southern Gothic writing or the associations between children, "backwardness," and class in British and Irish literatures; and such representations still proliferate in contemporary fiction. One example is the depiction of autism in Roopa Farooki's 2009 novel *The Way Things Look to Me*, which is full of the worst kind of stereotypes of the condition and in which Yasmin, the teenage girl with autism, seems only to have a narrative existence to inform and better the lives of her brother and sister (and, arguably, the reader). Farooki's novel, in which the "very, very clever" Yasmin, who has "an Extraordinary Mind," nearly commits suicide because it appears to be a rational act once she has finished school (and so lost her sense of progress and the ordered structure of an average day), continues that long tradition of disability novels in which a genocidal impulse toward those with disabilities is all too clear (Farooki 48).

Similarly, Julian Barnes's 2011 novel *The Sense of an Ending*, which won the Man Booker prize for that year, has an explicit use of disability that, rather than contribute in any way to the complexity of those characters with disabilities that (briefly) appear in the text, works to both resolve a crucial plot line and to underscore the failings of central protagonist Tony Webster. Webster, mired in late middle-aged emotional failure, seeks to understand his past and especially his relationship with Veronica, an old girlfriend. In a crucial scene toward the end of the novel, Veronica takes Webster to see something that she hopes will explain her history. As they both sit in a parked car, Webster sees an approaching group of people in what is a strange echo of Woolf's street encounter from nearly a century before:

> A small group of people were coming along the pavement towards my side of the car. I counted five of them. In front was a man who, despite the heat, was wearing layers of heavy tweed, including a waistcoat and a kind of deerstalker helmet. His jacket and hat were covered with metal badges, thirty or forty of them at a guess, some glinting in the sun; there was a watch-chain slung between his waistcoat pockets. His expression was jolly: he looked like someone with an obscure function at a circus or fairground. Behind him came two men: the first had a black moustache and a kind of rolling gait; the second was small and malformed, with one shoulder much higher than the other—he paused

to spit briefly into a front garden. And behind them was a tall, goofy fellow with glasses, holding the hand of a plump, Indianish, woman. (Barnes 124–25)

"What's wrong with them?," Webster asks crassly. "Are they care-in-the-community or something?" (Barnes 125–26). He makes a crucial mistake in assuming that one of the group, Adrian, is Veronica's son when he is, in fact, her brother, and his misunderstanding is a pivotal part of the novel's evidence that Webster is a deluded and prejudiced figure; but it is vital to understand that the complexity this event gives to his character is founded upon a reading of disability as nothing other than absence and lack. "I thought of that poor, damaged man turning away from me in the shop and pressing his face into rolls of kitchen towel and jumbo packs of quilted toilet tissue so as to avoid my presence," Webster notes of a subsequent meeting with Adrian, while he also conjectures on how difficult Veronica's life must have been: "how long had she sacrificed her life for him, perhaps taking some crappy part-time job while he was at a special-needs school? [. . .] Imagine what that must have felt like; imagine the loss, the sense of failure, the guilt" (Barnes 139). Even while it has to be understood that the prejudice expressed here is part of Barnes's emphasis on the failings of Webster's character, it is nevertheless the case that Adrian, yet another character with disabilities at the margin of a text, only exists to make the plot turn in a certain direction and to underscore an ableist narrative in which a non-disabled character comes to know himself better through an interaction with disability.

There is, it appears, nothing exceptional about Farooki or Barnes's novels. There was no particular reaction to the representation of disability in either text when they were published: Farooki was rather welcomed as a promising newcomer and Barnes lauded as a master who had produced a serious literary exploration of memory and ageing. Yet, once again, the logic of such representation is entirely consistent with that which pushes Laura Stephen to the back of Woolf's story, and ignores the consequences. Seen within this frame, it seems not much has changed.

DOING MORE WITH METAPHORS

And yet there is a real way in which the idea of narrative prosthesis, for all that it seems obvious and for all that it has been useful, is itself in danger of limiting the ways in which disability in literature is discussed. It possesses the capacity to be reductive, allowing for a kind of critical spotting, in which the identities of disabled characters are located in texts and the power of their misrepresentation then discussed. Even given the frequency of such kinds of representation (which, to repeat what I have outlined previously, is still argu-ably the most common form of disability representation), is there not a need to acknowledge that there are instances in which disability representation not only resists the kinds of metaphorisation central to the prosthetic method, but actually uses disabled difference as the centrepiece for new readings of culture and society? In a recent article, Amy Vidali has asked again "what to do about disability metaphors," noting that a "re-evaluation" of such metaphors offers the opportunity of "creative and historic reinterpretations" (33–34). It is within such thinking that we can rework the idea of disability and writing, especially the use of metaphor. It is also here, as a consequence of such "reinterpretations," that the idea of the "persistence" of disability pertains. If, for example and as I hope I have already hinted, we decide that Laura Stephen is not at the edge of Virginia Woolf's story, we can claim a space for her that is both more central to Woolf's work and, as a result, produces a method of critical reading in which disability is not only, as Mitchell and Snyder term it, somehow "parasitic" (2), but is foundational.

So, it is possible to revise one of the trajectories noted earlier, and instead of going from the character of Stevie in Conrad's *The Secret Agent* to that of Desmond Bates in Lodge's *Deaf Sentence*, rather go from Stevie to Christopher Boone, in Mark Haddon's *The Curious Incident of the Dog in the Night-Time*. Christopher, subtly characterised by Haddon within an idea of autistic "literalism" that resonates with a majority idea of how the condition functions, makes it very clear that he does not want to be seen as a metaphor. Discussing his own name, he explicitly notes its metaphoric associations: "My name is a metaphor," he observes: "It means *carrying Christ* and [. . .] it was the name given to St Christopher because he carried Jesus Christ across a river" (italics in original). However, he goes on: "Mother used to say that it meant Christopher was a nice name because it was a story about being kind and helpful, but I do not want my name to mean a story about being kind and helpful. I want my name to mean me" (Haddon 20). The force of the assertion is meaningful and understandable in an age of disability rights, but even as we recognize this, maybe we might draw more critical profit from taking this logic *back* to look at Conrad, and instead of seeing Stevie as the isolated, peripheral figure in *The Secret Agent*'s exploration of terrorism, rather locate him at the centre of that text—the figure who detonates the bomb, the man whose disabled difference provides a sense of morality missing from just about everyone else in the novel. Famously, Stevie sits at a table in the family home and draws circles on a piece of paper—"circles; innumerable circles, concentric, eccentric; a coruscating whirl of circles that by their tangled multitude of repeated curves, uniformity of form, and confusion of intersecting lines suggested a rendering of cosmic chaos, the symbolism of a mad art attempting the inconceivable" (Conrad 45). I have suggested elsewhere that, for all that Conrad here implies how the circles should be read—the "mad art"—and for all that the scene has invited so much critical commentary because of the desire to interpret the drawings, it could be that we should read Stevie's geometry in terms of the pleasure that he gains from producing them; a disabled, here autistic, pleasure (Murray 78). Seen in these terms, terms of disabled presence, characters like Stevie do not simply reflect the values of others in a prosthetic manner; rather their embodied and material subjectivities make the texts in which they feature *cohere*. They help their narratives, as Christopher Boone might put it, "mean me."

Certainly this is a trend we can see in contemporary writing. In Jonathan Lethem's 1999 crime novel *Motherless Brooklyn* the narrator, Lionel Essrog, has Tourette's. When his friend and mentor Frank Minna is killed, Lionel (nicknamed "freakshow" throughout because of his tics and verbal outbursts) becomes the main agent in tracking down the murderer. In the following scene, approximately halfway through the novel, Lionel's Tourette's is conflated with his new, central role as detective:

> There are days when I get up in the morning and stagger into the bathroom and begin running water and then I look up and I don't even recognize my own toothbrush in the mirror. I mean, the object looks strange, oddly particular in its design, strange tapered handle and slotted miter-cut bristles, and I wonder if I've ever looked at it closely before or whether someone snuck in overnight and substituted this new toothbrush for my old one. I have this relationship to objects in general—they will sometimes become uncontrollably new and vivid to me, and I don't know whether this is a symptom of Tourette's or not. I've never seen it described in the literature. Here's the strangeness of having a Tourette's brain then: no control in my personal experiment of self. What might be only strangeness must always be auditioned to the domain of symptom, just as symptoms always push into other domains, demanding the chance to audition for their moment of acuity or relevance, their brief shot—coulda been a contender!—at centrality. Personalityness. There's a lot of traffic in my head, and it's two-way.
>
> This morning's strangeness was refreshing though. More than refreshing—revelatory. I woke early, having failed to draw my curtains. The wall above my bed and the table with melted candle, tumbler quarter full of melted ice, and sandwich crumbs from my ritual snack now caught in a blaze of white sunlight, like the glare of a projector's bulb before the film is threaded. It seemed possible I was the first awake in the world, possible the world was new. I dressed in my best suit, donned Minna's watch instead of my own, and clipped his beeper to my hip. Then I made myself coffee and toast, scooped the long-shadowed crumbs off the table, sat and savored breakfast, marveling at the richness of existence with each step. The radiator whined and sneezed and I imitated its sounds out of sheer joy, rather than helplessness. Perhaps I'd been expecting that Minna's absence would snuff the world, or at least Brooklyn, out of existence. That a sympathetic dimming would occur. Instead I'd woken into the realization that I was Minna's successor and avenger, that the city shone with clues.
>
> It seemed possible I was a detective on a case. (Lethem 131–32)

So, as Lionel literally takes up Minna's position as central investigator, his "Tourettic brain" produces his daily "strangeness" as "refreshing" and "revelatory," and has him imitating the noises from his radiator as an act of stress-free pleasure—an echo of Stevie's circles possibly. What is indisputable is that, with half the novel remaining, Lethem visibly moves Lionel centre stage; the freak becomes the hero, and in doing so his Tourette's is anything but peripheral. It is, rather, seminal to the methods by which he will solve the crime. The protagonist with "special powers" is nothing new to the detective genre, having a long history, but the particular incarnation of the disabled subject gains a contemporary edge here. In addition, the novel makes a series of *productive* metaphorical associations between disability and place—New York is, Lethem asserts, a Tourettic city: its lights, sounds, and activities all mirror the kind of "bubbling" of language that Lionel feels within himself. As he says about Court St, in Brooklyn: "my verbal Tourette's [was] flowering at last. Like Court Street, I seethed behind the scenes with languages and conspiracies, inversions of logic, sudden jerks and jabs of insults" (Lethem 57).

Similarly, the following description of the Papaya Czar restaurant, in Manhattan's Upper East Side, emphasizes its sense of place *through* the logic of Tourettic association:

> The Papaya Czar on Eighty-sixth street and Third Avenue is my kind of place—bright orange and yellow signs pasted on every available surface screaming, PAPAYA IS GOD'S GREATEST GIFT TO MAN'S HEALTH! OUR FRANKFURTERS ARE THE WORKING MAN'S FILET MIGNON! WE'RE POLITE NEW YORKERS, WE SUPPORT MAYOR GIULIANI! And so on. Papaya Czar's walls are so layered with language that I find myself immediately calmed inside their doors, as though I've stepped into a model interior of my own skull. (Lethem 160)

Here, the fabric of the city mirrors the *normality* of Tourettic difference. The associations tell us what New York is like from *within* a disability perspective, the inside of Lionel's skull. There is nothing prosthetic about such a method.

Lethem's novel is only one of a number of contemporary narratives that, in their concentration on neurobehavioural conditions or syndromes, offer what we might term a move from an interest in *psychology* to one in *neurology* when discussing individual agency and social context in particular. As Marco Roth has observed, such "neuronovels" explore ideas of the brain, as opposed to the mind, in their depiction of individuals often at the moment of crisis or stress. Recent examples of such fictions include Ian McEwan's *Enduring Love* (discussing de Clérambault's syndrome, or Erotomania) and *Saturday* (Huntington's Disease, as well having a neurologist as its central character), Benjamin Kunkel's *Indecision* (Abulia—sometimes known as Blocq's Disease—a diminished motivation disorder), Richard Powers' *The Echo Maker* (Capgras Syndrome, in which an individual believes that a loved one has been replaced by a double), Rivka Galchen's *Atmospheric Disturbances* (again centred around Capgras Syndrome), and Joshua Ferris's *The Unnamed* (which invents the condition of "benign idiopathic perambulation" in its representation of a central character forced, against his will, to walk without stopping). It is possible to extend this further and see a range of post-9/11 novels from America—including Don DeLillo's *Falling Man* and Jonathan Safran Foer's *Extremely Loud and Incredibly Close*—as being texts dominated by forms of Post-Traumatic Stress Disorder, narratives in which the use of a neurobehavioural syndrome offers ways into the analysis of contemporary trauma.

These neuronovels obviously can be read in terms of metaphor; Ferris's text invites thoughts on obsessive or addictive behaviour, for example. But in the majority of the earlier mentioned titles, the condition in question functions, as in the Lethem examples, not simply to create a parallel or marginal narrative that works to underscore ableist concerns, but rather as a more central phenomenon that invariably stresses cognitive difference. Neurology in *Saturday*, for example, is not simply a narrative topic that links an idea of individual consciousness to that novel's exploration of public sensibilities surrounding the Iraq war; rather the violence that takes place between Perowne and Baxter in the former's home is both a *material* consequence of the latter's Huntington's disease and manifestation of the condition's literal centrality (in terms of an invasion of the family home) to the concerns of the novel.

SPACE, SPEECH, AND SILENCE

In concluding, and in emphasising this article's core concerns surrounding the presence and persistence of disability, I want to focus on two novels that orchestrate a set of thoughts around disability and postcolonial concerns, especially ideas of the status of society and public culture.[1] In postcolonial writing, disabled characters frequently work to underscore notions of public and communal space, conceived of in terms of nationalism or cultural community, for example. We might think of characters like the mute and deafened Simon in Keri Hulme's novel *The Bone People*, Azaro, the abiku spirit-child of Ben Okri's *The Famished Road*, Michael K, in J. M. Coetzee's *Life & Times of Michael K*, or indeed the barbarian girl in his *Waiting for the Barbarians* in such terms. Despite the large amount of critical literature that has sought to read these characters' various disabilities or differences in terms of metaphors of postcolonial subjectivity or society (the complexities of bicultural relations in New Zealand for Hulme, the disordered nature of Nigerian civil society for Okri, or ideas of apartheid in South Africa with Coetzee, for example), I would argue that the specific

qualities of these characters' embodiment—what we can call the materiality of their presence—and in particular their engagement with the details of
communal life in each context, alert us to the fact that critical metaphorical
readings often simply *reinforce* the classic prosthetic use of texts, only here
in a manner that fetishizes disability in seeking to "explain" postcolonial
cultures. A specific example of this takes place in the opening scene of Bapsi
Sidhwa's 1991 Partition novel *Cracking India*, in which part of the reader's
initial introduction to the young Lenny, our narrator who has polio, comes
through her encounter with an Englishman:

> Lordly, lounging in my briskly rolling pram, immersed in dreams, my
> private world is rudely popped by the sudden appearance of an English
> gnome wagging a leathery finger in my ayah's face [. . .] "Let her walk.
> Shame. Shame! Such a big girl in a pram! She's at least four!"
>   He smiles down at me, his brown eyes twinkling intolerance [. . .]
>   "She not walk much [. . .] she get tired," drawls Ayah. And simul-
> taneously I raise my trouser cuff to reveal the leather straps and wicked
> steel callipers harnessing my right boot.
>   Confronted by Ayah's liquid eyes and prim gloating, and the trium-
> phant revelation of my callipers, the Englishman withers [. . .]
>   Ayah and I hold our eyes away, effectively dampening his good-Sa-
> maritan exuberance [. . .] and wagging his head and turning about,
> the Englishman quietly dissolves up the driveway from which he had so
> enthusiastically sprung. (Sidhwa 12)

The invitation here to read the scene in terms of postcolonial independence,
with Lenny's potential walking signalling Pakistan's disassociation from
colonial rule, is clear. But it is rather Lenny's "triumphant revelation" of
her straps and callipers, and her combative response to the "twinkling
intolerance" of the Englishman, in other words her material response to
his demands, which actually come to dominate the event. Ultimately, it is
Lenny's *disabled* presence here that underscores her status as a postcolonial
subject. In the narrative that follows, it is her embodied subjectivity that
acts as a continual marker of how we *should* read the relationship between
character and history. Sidhwa's exploration of the trauma of Partition, and
of the creation of a new nation, offers endless metaphorical possibilities to
think of the "cracking" of the subcontinent through the allegorical associations that come with a consideration of Lenny's disability. But, as with the
preceding example, the novel's detailing of history, and the violence and
social change that comes with it, actually demands that the material presence of Lenny's body is understood to be at its core. The allegory is invited,
but is shown to be a dead end—violence is material and real, as are the
novel's considerations of health and the body. Lenny is not reduced to being
a cipher in her own narrative; rather her viewpoint takes its source in the
nature of her condition, with the difference this entails.

Indeed, *Cracking India* negotiates an intelligent move from individual subject to collective in the scene that follows the one just quoted. As Lenny continues her journey down Jail Road in Lahore with her Ayah, they enter into the wider space of the community where "Holy men [. . .] hawkers, cart-drivers, cooks, coolies and cyclists" form part of the throng that surrounds them. But, crucially, that throng also includes "stub-handed twisted beggars and dusty old beggars on crutches" (Sidhwa 12), characters with disabilities who are part of the normality of the everyday street scene. In the same way that Lenny's disability is declared seminal to her narrative, this second scene points to the material reality of disability as part of the social and cultural world that surrounds her. And, even though the contexts may seem vastly different, it is possible to align this kind of writing *method*, this approach to the persistence of disability, with that which we find in Lethem or Haddon, where disability is integral, rather than peripheral, to the world described.

These points are not simply about the "reversal" of an idea of metaphor or of character identification. Crucially, they are also about the ethical dimensions of representing disability. Such an idea of ethics offers the possibility to conclude with reference to J. M. Coetzee's 1986 novel *Foe*, a text that foregrounds ethical concerns surrounding the representation of the other within a notoriously ambiguous ending. As part of its narrative project in being a postcolonial rewriting of Defoe's *Robinson Crusoe*, Coetzee's narrative prevents the slave figure Friday from speaking the language of the colonizer by making him a mute character whose tongue has been removed. Friday's muteness has many metaphorical meanings: it can represent the silence of the subaltern subject; the unspeakability of the experience of slavery; the uncertainty of interpreting cultural differences; or an ethical refusal to speak on behalf of an other—to represent the unrepresentable (Parry 47–48). As the narrator tells us, "The story of Friday's tongue is a story unable to be told [. . .] the true story is buried within Friday, who is mute" (Coetzee, *Foe* 118). As a postcolonial narrative, Coetzee's refusal to speak for the silenced victims of slavery has a profound integrity, and Friday's muteness facilitates this mode of ethical engagement with the atrocities of the past. But the question of such an ending as a *disability* narrative prompts a different set of concerns.

The end of *Foe* allows the reader to look 300 years into the past, to witness a slave ship buried at the bottom of the sea—a place of violent death and of silent testimony. Here, we encounter Friday one last time, removed from the realist mode of earlier sections, and the text ends not with his death, or with any cure for his muteness, but rather with a representation of his wordless and soundless utterance:

> His mouth opens. From inside him comes a slow stream, without breath, without interruption. It flows up through his body and out upon me; it passes through the cabin, through the wreck; washing the cliffs and shores of the island, it runs northward and southward to the

> ends of the earth. Soft and cold, dark and unending, it beats against my eyelids, against the skin of my face. (Coetzee, *Foe* 157)

The ending offers no simplistic resolution. Instead, while the powerful metaphorical resonances of Friday's disability are not undermined in any way, we are, crucially, left with a sense of his presence, both as a disabled character and as a victim of slavery. And this assertion of presence serves to remind us, in its status as an ethical move, of Friday's humanity and of his human dignity. This, in its own way, is a narrative of (to use a much-abused word in disability circles) care: care about the history of slavery, and care for the acts of disablement experienced by colonial subjects. It is only by reading with a holistic sense of care, that is, with an alertness to the narrative possibilities offered by metaphor as well as to the materiality of disability's social presence, that we can get past a simple notion of the disposability of disabled characters and toward a more complex engagement with the nuances of contemporary disability narratives. *Foe*, like other contemporary fictions, pushes the boundaries of current literary disability theory as it demonstrates how disability might be represented not as something deviant, abnormal, or exclusively prosthetic, but as a "normal," unremarkable (and yet exceptional), or inevitable part of everyday life in any cultural location. It is not necessarily the case that *representations* of disability are unsophisticated, inadequate, or one-dimensionally metaphorical. Rather, it is more the case that our reading strategies need updating to account for the great variety of disability representations with which contemporary literature presents us.

Virginia Woolf died in 1941. Laura Stephen outlived her by four years, dying in 1945. One way or another, one sister's life was entirely contained by the other. We might say more interesting things about disability, identity, and contemporary literature if we take time to dwell on the consequences of what this could mean.

NOTES

1. My ideas on disability and postcolonial writing come from my joint work on this topic with Clare Barker, and I am grateful to her for allowing me to use here material on which we have worked together.

REFERENCES

Barker, Clare. "Interdisciplinary Dialogues: Disability and Postcolonial Studies." *Review of Disability Studies* 6.3 (2010): 15–24. Print.
———. *Postcolonial Fiction and Disability: Exceptional Children, Metaphor and Materiality*. Basingstoke: Palgrave Macmillan, 2011. Print.
———, and Stuart Murray. "Disabling Postcolonialism: Global Disability Cultures and Democratic Criticism." *Journal of Literary & Cultural Disability Studies* 4.3 (2010): 219–36. Print.
Barnes, Julian. *The Sense of an Ending*. London: Jonathan Cape, 2011. Print.

Blindness. Screenplay by Don McKellar. Dir. Fernando Meirelles. Perf. Julianne Moore, Mark Ruffalo, and Gael Garcia Bernal. Rhombus Media, 2008. DVD.

Coetzee, J. M. *Waiting for the Barbarians*. 1980. London: Vintage, 2000. Print.

———. *Life & Times of Michael K*. 1983. London: Vintage, 1998. Print.

———. *Foe*. 1986. London: Penguin, 1987. Print.

Conrad, Joseph. *The Secret Agent*. 1907. Penguin: London, 1994. Print.

Davis, Lennard J. *Enforcing Normalcy: Disability, Deafness and the Body*. London: Verso, 1995. Print.

———. *Obsession: A History*. *Chicago*: University of Chicago Press, 2008. Print.

de Man, Paul. *Blindness and Insight: Essays in the Rhetoric of Contemporary Criticism*. London: Routledge, 1993. Print.

Farooki, Roopa. *The Way Things Look to Me*. London: Pan Books, 2009. Print.

Ferris, Joshua. *The Unnamed*. London: Viking, 2010. Print.

Foer, Jonathan Safran. *Extremely Loud and Incredibly Close*. London: Penguin, 2006. Print.

Galchen, Rivka. *Atmospheric Disturbances*. London: HarperPerennial, 2009. Print.

Garland-Thomson, Rosemarie. *Extraordinary Bodies: Figuring Physical Disability in American Culture and Literature*. New York: Columbia University Press, 1997. Print.

Haddon, Mark. *The Curious Incident of the Dog in the Night-Time*. London: Jonathan Cape, 2003. Print.

Hulme, Keri. *The Bone People*. 1983. London: Picador, 2001. Print.

Kunkel, Benjamin. *Indecision*. London: Picador, 2006. Print.

Lawrence, D. H. *Lady Chatterley's Lover*. 1928. London: Penguin, 1999. Print.

Lee, Hermione. *Virginia Woolf: A Biography*. London: Bloomsbury, 1996. Print.

Lethem, Jonathan. *Motherless Brooklyn*. London: Faber & Faber, 1999. Print.

Lodge, David. *Deaf Sentence*. London: Penguin, 2009. Print.

McEwan, Ian. *Enduring Love*. London: Vintage, 1998. Print.

———. *Saturday*. London: Jonathan Cape, 2005. Print.

Mitchell, David T., and Sharon L. Snyder. *Narrative Prosthesis: Disability and the Dependencies of Discourse*. Ann Arbor, MI: University of Michigan Press, 2000. Print.

Murray, Stuart. *Representing Autism: Culture, Narrative, Fascination*. Liverpool: Liverpool University Press, 2008. Print.

Okri, Ben. *The Famished Road*. London: Vintage, 1991. Print.

Parry, Benita. "Speech and Silence in the Fictions of J. M. Coetzee." *Critical Perspectives on J. M. Coetzee*. Eds. Graham Huggan and Stephen Watson. Basingstoke: Palgrave Macmillan, 1996. 37–65. Print.

Powers, Richard. *The Echo Maker*. London: Vintage, 2008. Print.

Roth, Marco. "The Rise of the Neuronovel," *n+1*, 8. n+1 Foundation. 14 September 2009. Web. 28 October 2009.

Rushdie, Salman. *Shame*. 1983. London: Vintage, 1995. Print.

Sidhwa, Bapsi. *Cracking India: A Novel*. Minneapolis, MN: Milkweed Editions, 1991. Print.

Vidali, Amy. "Seeing What We Know: Disability and Theories of Metaphor." *Journal of Literary & Cultural Disability Studies* 4.1 (2010): 33–54. Print.

Woolf, Virginia. *Mrs Dalloway*. 1925. Oxford: Oxford University Press, 2000. Print.

———. *A Room of One's Own*. London: Hogarth, 1929. Print

———. *The Waves*. 1931. Harmondsworth: Penguin, 1992. Print.

———. *The Essays of Virginia Woolf: Volume 3, 1919–1924*. Ed. Andrew McNeillie. London: Hogarth, 1989. Print.

———. *The Essays of Virginia Woolf: Volume 4, 1925–1928*. Ed. Andrew McNeillie. London: Hogarth, 1994. Print.

Contributors

Marsha Bryant, Professor of English at the University of Florida, teaches courses in modern and contemporary poetry, women's literature, and literature and visual culture. She held a fellowship from the National Endowment for the Humanities to complete her latest book, *Women's Poetry and Popular Culture* (2011). Her earlier books are *Auden and Documentary in the 1930s* (1997) and the edited collection *Photo-Textualities: Reading Photographs and Literature* (1996). Bryant's recent essays have appeared in the journals *American Literature, Modernism/Modernity, Mosaic, Pedagogy,* and *Tulsa Studies in Women's Literature,* as well as the edited collections *Approaches to Teaching H.D.'s Poetry and Prose* (2011) and *The Unraveling Archive: Essays on Sylvia Plath* (2007). She has also published in collaboration with Classical archaeologist Mary Ann Eaverly.

Thomas Docherty studied in Glasgow, Paris, and Oxford. He has taught in Oxford, Dublin (both UCD and TCD, where he was Chair of English), before returning to the UK as Director of Research in Kent, and then his current position as Professor of English and Comparative Literature in Warwick. He has published eleven books in most areas of English and comparative literature from the Renaissance to the present day. Among his recent publications are *After Theory* (1996), *Alterities* (1996), *Criticism and Modernity* (1999), *Aesthetic Democracy* (2006), *The English Question* (2008), and *Confessions: The Philosophy of Transparency* (2012). He is working on two new books, one on the University and Globalisation, and a second on Memory. In addition, he has also started to write fiction.

Zita Farkas has recently completed a PhD on the reception of Jeanette Winteson's work at The University of York and currently works at Umeå University, Sweden. She has contributed to the *Encyclopedia of Contemporary Writers and Their Work* (2010) and *The Multimedia Encyclopedia of Women in Today's World* (2011) and has several articles under consideration such as "History in the Making: the Romanian Revolution on Screen" (in *Studies in Eastern European Cinema*), "Mainstreaming Alternative Sexualities: Ryna and Lovesick" (in *Dilemmas of Visibility: Post-Socialist Sexualities*) and "The Lesbian Narrative of Universal Love and Sexuality in Jeanette Winterson's Fiction" (in *Sexualities and Contemporary Literature*). Her research interests include contemporary British/women's fiction, contemporary Romanian cinema, lesbian-feminist and queer literary theory, reception theory and conceptualising the "author."

Huw Marsh teaches at Queen Mary, University of London, where he gained his doctorate with an AHRC funded PhD thesis on Beryl Bainbridge. His research interests lie mainly in the fields of postwar and contemporary anglophone fiction, and he has previously published articles and book chapters on authors including Nicola Barker, Penelope Lively, and Angela Carter. His book on Beryl Bainbridge is forthcoming in the Northcote House series Writers and Their Work.

Kym Martindale is a Senior Lecturer in English with Media Studies/Creative Writing at University College Falmouth. She is currently investigating ideas of faith and place in the work of Frances Bellerby and Jack Clemo, two twentieth-century poets who lived and wrote in Cornwall, but has also published previously on Alice Oswald, in a collection titled *Process, Landscape, Text* (Rodopi Press, 2010). She is herself a poet, and in 2000 won the Redbrook Poetry Prize with her collection *Jujubes and Aspirins*.

Stuart Murray is Professor of Contemporary Literatures and Film in the School of English at the University of Leeds, where he teaches Medical Humanities, and modern, contemporary, and postcolonial cultures and narratives. He is the author or editor of six books, the most recent being *Representing Autism: Culture, Narrative, Fascination* (2008) and *Images of Dignity: Barry Barclay and Fourth Cinema* (2008), and *Autism* (2011).

Lucy Prodgers completed her MPhil at the Centre of Research in English (CoRE) at Manchester Metropolitan University in 2011. Her thesis is titled: Deleuzian Textual Dynamics in Contemporary British Fiction: A. L. Kennedy and Toby Litt.

Amy Prodromou has recently completed her Ph.D. at Lancaster University (UK), researching the writing of grief in women's contemporary memoir. She has received MAs in English and Creative Writing from Southern Connecticut State University (USA) and the University of Sydney. Her fiction has been published in journals including *EAPSU: An Online Journal of Critical and Creative Writing, Cadences: A Journal* *of Literature and the Arts in Cyprus, R.K.V.R.Y Literary Journal, Blood Lotus: An Online Literary Journal*, and most recently in *Flax*, the publishing imprint of Lancaster's Litfest. Amy currently runs the Women's Life Writing Network (WLN), a research forum for and researchers and practitioners of women's life writing (www.womenslifewriting.net), and is working on a book proposal for her research on memoirs of textured recovery. Her article, "'That Weeping Constellation': Navigating Loss in 'Memoirs of Textured Recovery'", has appeared recently in the journal *Life Writing* (2012). She currently teaches at the Language Centre, University of Cyprus.

Michelle Ryan-Sautour is Associate Professor at the Université d'Angers, France (PRES UNAM) where she is director of the short story section of the CRILA research group and associate editor of *Journal of the Short Story* in English. Her research focus is the speculative fiction and short stories of Angela Carter and Rikki Ducornet with a special emphasis on authorship, reading pragmatics, game theory, and gender. She has published in *Marvels and Tales. Journal of the Short Story in English, Etudes Britanniques Contemporaines*, and in several edited collections.

Ranu Samantrai is Associate Professor of English at Indiana University. She is the author of *AlterNatives: Black Feminism in the Postimperial Nation* (Stanford UP, 2002) and coeditor of *Interdisciplinarity and Social Justice* (SUNY Press, 2010).

Ana María Sánchez-Arce is Senior Lecturer in twentieth and twenty-first century literature and critical theory at Sheffield Hallam University. She's coeditor of *European Intertexts: Women's Writing in English in a European Context* (2005). She is currently finishing a monograph, *Pedro Almodóvar*, for Manchester University Press and working on a study of authenticity in contemporary literature.

Goran Stanivukovic is Professor of English at Saint Mary's University, Halifax, Canada, where he teaches English non-dramatic and dramatic literature, queer theory, and cultural studies. He has edited *Ovid and the Renaissance Body* (Toronto, 2001), *Prose Fiction and Early Modern Sexualities in Early Modern England, 1570–1640* (with Constance Relihan, Palgrave 2003), *The Most Pleasant History of Ornatus and Artesia* (Dovehouse, 2003), and *Remapping the Mediterranean World in Early Modern English Writings* (Palgrave, 2007), and has published articles on Shakespeare, Marlowe, queer early modern England, and contemporary appropriations of the Renaissance.

Ulrike Tancke has taught at Johannes Gutenberg-Universität Mainz (Germany), Lancaster University (UK), and Universität Trier (Germany). She has published on early modern literature and contemporary British fiction. During 2010–2011 she held a Research Fellowship at the Centre for Contemporary Writing, Brunel University, UK, to pursue her current research project, which focuses on violence and trauma in British novels around the Millennium.

Karen Zouaoui is an English lecturer (agrégée) at the University of Paris Descartes (Paris 5). Her research on the British experimental fiction of the 1960s has led her to co-found the B.S. Johnson Society. She is about to complete her PhD on the British avant-garde of the 1960s and radicalism at the University of Paris Diderot (Paris 7).

Index